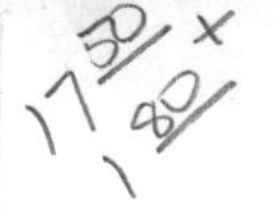

THE INHUMAN RACE

THE INHUMAN RACE

The Racial Grotesque in American Literature and Culture

LEONARD CASSUTO

Columbia University Press NEW YORK

Columbia University Press
Publishers Since 1893
New York   Chichester, West Sussex

Library of Congress Cataloging-in-Publication Data

Cassuto, Leonard

The inhuman race : the racial grotesque in American literature and culture / Leonard Cassuto.

p. cm.

Includes bibliographical references (p.) and index.

ISBN 0-231-10336-0 (cloth : alk. paper). — ISBN 0-231-10337-9 (paper : alk. paper)

1. American literature—History and criticism. 2. Racism—United States—History. 3. Stereotype (Psychology) in literature.

4. Difference (Psychology) in literature. 5. Afro-Americans in literature. 6. Grotesque in literature. 7. Monsters in literature. 8. Indians in literature. 9. Slaves in literature. 10. Race in literature. I. Title.

PS217.R28C37 1996

810.9'355—dc20   96-16785

Casebound editions of Columbia University Press books are printed on permanent and durable acid-free paper.

Printed in the United States of America

c 10 9 8 7 6 5 4 3 2 1

p 10 9 8 7 6 5 4 3 2 1

To my parents,
Isadore and Thalia Cassuto

CONTENTS

ACKNOWLEDGMENTS

When a book has been with an author for as long as this one has been with me, the acknowledgments can read like an autobiography. In this case, it's a life story of ongoing education. This book began many transformations ago as a dissertation advised by Joel Porte and Alan Heimert that had nothing to do with race when I completed it in 1989. Ann and Gene Feldman probably don't remember the 1990 conversation that kindled my thinking about what I started calling "the moral grotesque," but turning that notion over in mind helped me remember a question that Alan Heimert had asked me a couple of years earlier about the "racial grotesque." Once I put those two together, this book began to coalesce in mind. Andrew Delbanco recognized its final shape before I did, and his advice was crucial in the planning, as it has been since we met.

Stacks of annotated typescript have long cluttered my apartment and office, but the mess has given my argument a firmer foundation. For careful reading and valuable commentary, I am grateful to Noëlle Arrangoíz, Lawrence Buell, Alan Filreis, Joseph Finder, Jim Hartman, Pat Jones, Kate Levin, Jeanne Campbell Reesman, Thomas Riggio, Bruce

Robbins, Frank Shuffelton, Rosemarie Garland Thomson, and my Fordham colleagues Joanne Dobson, Lawrence Kramer, Fawzia Mustafa, Wayne Storey, and Fred Wertz. I'd also like to recognize the anonymous press readers whose helpful comments improved the book.

Thanks also to Alan Trachtenberg for pushing me to be more historical; to Jerry Doolittle for his Tabasco clarity; to Jane Hogan for help with the research; to Laura Greeney for negotiating the permissions, editing the notes and list of works cited, and for guiding the manuscript through the early stages of production while I was out of the country; to Elizabeth Amrhein, Robert Bogdan, and Peter Ford for help locating the illustrations; to Linda Ainsworth for preparing the index; to Christine Merser and Lisa Pedicini for suggestions and support; and to Lenore Skenazy for the title. I'm grateful to Fordham University for a summer faculty fellowship granted in 1992.

Frank Boyle, Clare Eby, and Robert S. Levine read the whole manuscript—some parts of it more than once—with insight and meticulous attention. They have been terrific colleagues and terrific friends. The staff at Columbia University Press have been a pleasure to work with; I am especially grateful to Jennifer Crewe for her consistent commitment to this book, to Roy Thomas for careful and sensitive editing, to Anne McCoy for attentive management, and to all for their skilled and patient professionalism throughout the publication process, meeting deadlines even when parts of the manuscript had to travel back and forth to Africa.

Finally, the dedication is to my two earliest teachers, who have also been helpful readers of this book. And I wouldn't be sitting here writing this final list without the love and support I've received from Debra Osofsky, my generous partner who made the tenure track a less onerous path.

The following are gratefully acknowledged for permission to reprint material:

Chapter 1: Excerpt from *Pilgrim at Tinker Creek* by Annie Dillard, copyright © 1974 by Annie Dillard, reprinted by permission of Harper Collins Publishers, Inc.

"The Lynching" by Claude McKay, reprinted by permission of the Archives of Claude McKay, Carl Cowl, Administrator.

A shortened version of chapter 3 was published as "Frederick Douglass and the Work of Freedom: Hegel's Master/Slave Dialectic in the Fugitive Slave Narrative," in *Prospects: An Annual of American Cultural*

Studies 21 (New York: Cambridge University Press, 1996); reprinted with the permission of Cambridge University Press.

Parts of chapter 5 were published in slightly different form as "'What an object he would have made of me!': Tattooing and the Racial Freak in Melville's *Typee*," in Rosemarie Garland Thomson, ed., *Freakery: Cultural Displays of the Extraordinary Body* (New York: New York University Press, 1996), pp. 234–47.

early America, whites tried hard to imagine nonwhites as non-people as part of the justification for slavery and Indian removal. Though fraught with uncertainty, that imagined nonhumanity nevertheless became the basis for an entire social understanding. It became the source of ideologies of whiteness and institutions to protect them—increasingly elaborate designs to guard a construction of the imagination, a construction which in turn supported the designs and actions that flowed from it. The image of person as thing also sparked resistance from below, stimulating the creation of a culture of the oppressed that reacted to and continues to oppose it. Toni Morrison has called for more studies of the way that blackness participates in the creation of difference and the self-definition of whiteness.[1] This book is, among other things, an answer to that call, a close look at some of the strange topography of the national imaginative landscape.

My approach is naturally informed by history, but it might be more accurate to say that I bring anthropological methodology to bear on points within a historical period. Structural anthropology has provided a model for understanding culture through the scrutiny of fundamental categories and oppositions, a model that has proved usefully malleable in the critical forge. I draw on structural anthropologists like Claude Lévi-Strauss and Mary Douglas, and also on their critics, who have refined and built on aspects of their work from within and without, such as Clifford Geertz, Renato Rosaldo, and Edward Said. Essentially, anthropologists (followed by historians and literary and cultural critics) have shown that people divide themselves into categories and hierarchies, structures which then need constant maintenance, and which sometimes fail to hold up even with such ministrations. Cultures define an "us" and a "them." The stronger group defines what is human and embodies that definition, while the weaker one falls short by design and is exiled to a category of indeterminate otherness. Speaking of this tendency, Sartre says that "the European has only been able to become a man through creating slaves and monsters."[2] The consequences of this human desire to divide and rank—in effect, to exclude—are at the conceptual core of more theorizing about race and difference than I can summarize here. But this exclusiveness becomes an issue only because it is opposed.

This opposition takes place from within and without, but I focus on one particular countervailing tendency, one of *in*clusion. I am referring not to *humanism*—a loaded term and a complicated value—but to the largely mysterious mechanics of human perception that draw us to other people wherever and whenever possible. Theorists from a variety of different disciplines have argued (for different reasons) that people perceive the world anthropomorphically. In other words, humans are perceptually wired to see and respond to the presence of other humans wherever we can possibly find them. The persistence of the human image is on one level simply biological: children, for example, recognize faces very early in their development, while adults can see human faces and bodies in the simplest stick figures and schematic drawings, or in ambiguous designs like Rorschach blots. Like all human biological traits, this one is also intertwined with culture. We need other people because we are social, and therefore it benefits us to seek them out. But we also need to make categories to define our own specialness. Simply put, we are exclusive and inclusive at the same time.

On its most basic level, this book is about the collision of these two human behaviors: the tendency to form groups which then try to deny the humanity of others, and our competing tendency to see humanity wherever we can find it. The result is a persistent, almost unbearable tension and anxiety, felt in the form of the grotesque (which I define in terms of liminality in chapter 1). Roughly speaking, one group tries to objectify the other, but even as they do so, they admit that they see these "objects" as human all the time. Tugged in the competing directions of "human" and "not-human," the victims of this objectifying treatment are not completely transformed in the dominator's eyes. Instead, they find themselves in-between, in flux. Neither one thing nor the other, they become grotesque. This conflict, accompanying contradiction, and consequent experience of the grotesque is, I think, an important structural dynamic underlying race relations in this country. I will be arguing in the following chapters that the American encounter with racial difference may be usefully understood in terms of the grotesque.

Any discussion of objectification must position itself in relation to the dominant paradigm, the complicated analysis of self and other that draws its inspiration from Frantz Fanon's writings on the highly charged confrontation between the colonizer and the colonized. Fanon's focus on the potential for action by the colonized other has given impetus and direction to much current postcolonial theorizing. This book reflects my belief that the past action of the colonizer—that is, the attempt to deny the humanity of other people—has immediate and long-lasting implications that have not received enough attention. The tangled consequences for the colonizer of the endemic weakness attached to the attempt to objectify humans has, I think, been underestimated by current theorists whose main focus has been on the experience of the objectified other.

Fanon's legacy is a much-contested rhetorical space. His description of the colonized native's coming-to-consciousness and consequent rebellion is highly indeterminate, and this has resulted in divergent readings of his texts. A major question centers on how much power the colonized group actually has, and by extension, how much the colonizer retains. Which leads to another crucial question: on what basis can resistance take place? As they confront these questions, Fanon's critics oscillate between giving the possibility of power to the oppressed, thereby slighting the power of the oppressor; or alternatively, seeing the oppressor in total control, effectively denying the "subjectivity and agency" of the oppressed.[3]

In this book I offer the grotesque as a new way of looking at these problems, one that is by its very nature respectful of their dynamic instability. Viewing the colonial relation in terms of the encounter with the grotesque enables an escape from rigid distinctions and polarized choices. Because the grotesque is a floating variable in the perceptual field, shifting with the boundaries of what is known and categorized, the objectifying self and the objectified (and thus grotesque) other occupy a relation that is always changing. As the various dramatizations of the story of John Merrick ("the Elephant Man") show, for example, the otherness of the grotesque is differently perceived over time, a relation affected by knowledge, context (for example, those who saw Merrick in the freak show where he was originally being displayed were apt to view him differently than those who met him at tea with the Queen), familiarity (based, among other things, on personal contact and communication with him), and—perhaps most crucially—by Merrick's own necessarily human behavior as he interacted with the society that had earlier attempted to deny his humanity. Merrick's example shows that the experience of the grotesque is active and highly volatile.

The essence of Merrick's story is readily recognizable within the larger context of the American cultural attempts to objectify groups of people, be they Indians, slaves, immigrants, freaks, or any of many others. A study of the relation between dominant and dominated groups will show that many of the opposing positions taken by some of Fanon's best-known interpreters are not mutually exclusive, that the dynamic nature of the grotesque—a response-governed structure that is constantly shifting in perception and value in the beholder's eyes—means that otherness does not ever hold a given position for long enough to be discussed as a fixed relation between two groups (or objectifier and objectified). Such analysis should instead be compared to studying the movement of water in a tidal pool: the waves wash back and forth within the same space, holding a given position for only an instant. So with the experience of otherness: I treat it here as a constantly shifting value, floating within a given range governed by the boundaries of the pool—which correspond to the cultural categories whose violation results in the grotesque.

The grotesque is a threat to the system of knowledge by virtue of its liminal position within that system. This liminality demands resolution; for a human being caught between the categories of human and thing, the pressure will be exerted toward a return to the human category, for that is the only choice that offers the possibility of resolution. The pages that follow will elaborate this conclusion and explore the different forms of the racial grotesque in a variety of American narrative contexts.

In this vein, I argue that the literature of race in America is the story of the attempt to force the grotesque, which is defined in terms of the shifting cultural margins, to occupy a fixed place in a category system of shared belief. This is ultimately a tilt at a cultural windmill: the grotesque can't be captured in this way, else it would cease to be grotesque and would instead become a known value. Though this study draws on many of Fanon's insights into the multifaceted and equivocal relation between the dominant self and the oppressed other, my broad conclusion takes a less extreme view of the necessities than Fanon does. The need for action by the objectified other is finally less determinant than the basic unsoundness of the past action of the objectifier, an action that creates an inherent weakness and instability in the relationship between the two parties.

The anxiety that accompanies the attempt to turn a human being into something nonhuman produces tension and contradiction throughout a culture's belief system. These equivocal feelings are marked by a need to create what are in effect fictions of difference—in the master's belief, for instance, that his slaves love him. But these fictions are paradoxically coupled with the capacity, often unwanted, to see through them. Literature gives free rein to these conflicted expressions of the imagination, and it is for that reason that human objectification can be deeply studied when writers try to work through it in narratives. Not surprisingly, the antebellum period highlights the American literature of objectification best; the uneasy racial and ethnic mixture that characterized and defined America from the beginning contains a rich variety of revealing conflicts that highlight the benighted human tendency to try to deny the humanity of other people. From the Puritans on through the age of slavery, American literary and cultural institutions provide a cauldron of fascinating examples of how white American racial perceptions have worked during a time when they were institutionalized and codified into law. Puritan theocratic and later American democratic societies viewed these problems from different angles, from the clumsy attempts of the Puritans to create indestructible categories that would set the world right, to the prescient questioning of Herman Melville, who wondered in his fiction whether too-rigid adherence to such categories would destroy the country.

Many of the examples I cite (especially in the first chapter) come from outside the antebellum period, and occasionally from other countries as well. There are two reasons for this. First, chronological and cross-cultural contrasts throw the peculiarities of a particular time into high relief, as Andrew Delbanco demonstrated, for example, when he compared the Puritan experience to other American immigrant accounts, particularly those of Jews coming to the United States early in the twentieth century. Such juxtapositions are unusual in literary and cultural study, but I think they enrich our pursuit. Second, I want to emphasize that my focus, the tense and ultimately incomplete attempt to turn a human into something not-human, is not isolated in one particular moment in time. Indeed, it appears almost everywhere we look. Antebellum America is my *locus classicus* because it offers some particularly revealing examples of these complications at work, but the social structures that I analyze cut across history. I focus on several specific American historical sites in order to illustrate the tensions embodied by a set of attitudes, tensions that contribute to the ongoing course of history.

Because my goal is to link different literary and historical effects stemming from the same root cultural causes, I focus on illuminating literary and historical moments—one might call them cultural snapshots. But I am finally aiming beyond the borders of these snapshots to encompass the larger panorama of a dynamic that has threatened and preoccupied the American nation since before its founding. By this method I hope to clarify what I see as the essential relevance of my thesis, which describes a tendency whose significance extends—as a look at almost any day's front page will show—beyond a particular place or time. We've never stopped doing these things to one another. We have only stopped codifying the practice. But how revealing it was when such behavior was the law of the land.

THE INHUMAN RACE

CHAPTER ONE

HUMAN OBJECTIFICATION AND THE RACIAL GROTESQUE

All that is not race in this world is trash.
—Adolf Hitler

Racism is a blight on the human conscience. The idea that any people can be inferior to another, to the point where those who consider themselves superior define and treat the rest as subhuman, denies the humanity even of those who elevate themselves to the status of gods.
—Nelson Mandela, address to the British Parliament, July 1996

This book begins with a frog. Early in *Pilgrim at Tinker Creek*, Annie Dillard sees one at an unusual climacteric:

> At the end of the island I noticed a small green frog. He was exactly half in and half out of the water, looking like a schematic diagram of an amphibian, and he didn't jump.
>
> He didn't jump; I crept closer. . . . And just as I looked at him, he slowly crumpled and began to sag. The spirit vanished from his eyes as if snuffed. His skin emptied and drooped; his very skull seemed to collapse and settle like a kicked tent. He was shrinking before my eyes like a deflated football. I watched the taut, glistening skin on his shoulders ruck, rumple, and fall. Soon, part of his skin, formless as a pricked balloon, lay in floating folds like bright scum on top of the water: it was a monstrous and terrifying thing. I gaped bewildered, appalled. An oval

> shadow hung in the water behind the drained frog; then the shadow glided away. The frog skin bag started to sink.[1]

The frog, Dillard explains, has been killed and eaten by a common giant waterbug, which injects a digestive enzyme into its prey that liquefies its bones and viscera, which the predator then sucks out, as if through a straw.

The compelling power of transformation gives this spectacle a peculiar magnetism. A change from animate to inanimate takes place: the frog's innards are turned into soup and sucked dry. The animal is thereby transformed into a frog skin bag, a thing. The conversion also disturbs. (It leaves Dillard breathless.) It disturbs despite the fact that we are quite used to seeing animals as things. We buy and sell them as livestock, food, and pets, and when they get sick we frankly and often dispassionately measure the pecuniary cost of curing them. Even so, Dillard's account has a horrific aspect to it. The key to the horror lies in the transformation. The frog is objectified. Its life is literally sucked out of it, and a change of status consequently takes place: a living frog becomes a frog skin sac. Animated life becomes an inanimate thing.

Dillard uses a lot of similes throughout the passage to compare the frog to inanimate objects as it dies. It is "like a kicked tent," "like a deflated football," "as a pricked balloon," "like bright scum." At the end of the process, though, the change is real. After the waterbug finishes its meal, the frog isn't "like" a frog skin bag; it *is* one. Dillard finds this bag "a monstrous and terrifying thing." Her reaction is consistent with those of millions of viewers of other dramatic metamorphoses. Such transformations are horrifying because they violate the understood assumption that fundamental category divisions are permanent. Transformations create anxiety by undermining the knowledge and belief that is built upon those divisions. Not surprisingly, transformations are the staple of memorable horror movies that exploit these anxieties, like *Dracula* (1931), *Invasion of the Body Snatchers* (1956), and *Night of the Living Dead* (1968). What viewer of *Frankenstein* (1931) forgets the moment when the creation, an amalgamation of inanimate parts, gains the vital spark and moves? Who watches *Dracula* without imagining what it would be like to have one's blood slowly sucked out—or what it would be like to do the sucking? Dillard's fascination with her frog grows from the same root that draws people to these horror fictions. Her experience at the edge of the creek is a brief instant of grotesque terror in everyday life.

This book is about what happens when this change is effected upon a person. I want to look at what happens when a person is seen as a not-person, a thing, an "it." With people, the transformation is much more complicated than with frogs. Often the shift involves a figurative rather than a literal and permanent physical transformation; in the case of slavery, for example, person becomes property without undergoing corporeal change. Whether literal or figurative, the results of human objectification are much more equivocal than the transformation of a frog into a bag. Even when the change is physical and permanent (as, say, with cremation), it resonates with problematic liminality.

The complications attached to the objectification of human beings hinge mainly on one crucial point: that people look at people in a unique and special way. We human beings accord a special position to ourselves. We place ourselves at the top of our own taxonomies of living things, and we attach special value to human life as distinct from other life. Because of the unique status that people give to people, turning a human being into a thing isn't so easy. The effort is fraught with deep ambivalence and anxiety. And its implications color a wide and important band of the American literary spectrum.

Human objectification can result from all kinds of perceived differences, but in American culture it happens most readily to people with dark skin. Such "racial objectification" is the subject of this book. Racial objectification was institutionalized in the United States in the form of slavery—my main focus—but (as the colonial experience demonstrates) it has never been limited to that practice. How did articulators of slave-owning consciousness perceive their "possessions," and how did these human chattel view themselves? Answering this question in general terms would take many volumes; I am specifically interested in how literature pictures the divided consciousness of racial difference in America before the Civil War. I will examine how early American writing renders an imaginative portrait of racial perception, and how this portrait contains the mingled psychological and historical contradiction that accompanied colonization and slavery. William R. Taylor has demonstrated that the antebellum Southern literary imagination participated in the creation of real-life social contradictions, "and hence in producing the tinderbox of 1861."[2] Extending some of Taylor's methods and insights to other literature of the time (and in the case of chapter 2, the colonial period), I will show how literature became a crucible for conflicting, objectification-related pressures during the years leading up to the Civil War. Unlike Taylor, I do not foreground the specific interactions of literature with social life. My primary goal is to show the complex ways that imaginative writing about race (both fiction and factually based accounts) embodies and enacts a set of fundamental contradictions centering on the attempt to see a human being as something nonhuman, and how these contradictions have plagued American writers from the very beginning of the national experience.

The unclear conceptual reality of race (hotly debated in recent years) is only tangentially relevant to my argument here. Whatever "race" is—fact, metaphor, or both—it has had a historically measurable (and varying) effect on all classes of American society since the settling of the continent. I am interested in this historical reality of race, the fact that people have believed in it, and continue to believe in it, as empirical truth. Perception is the issue, in other words, not philosophical or even biological reality, for objectification is in the eye of the beholder.[3] As such, racial objectification is the last step in a process of differentiation. People first perceive difference among themselves, and then they perceive race on the basis of that difference. I take that initial perception of difference as a historical fact and work outward from it. When the differences polarize, as they have tended to in American experience, human objectification follows.[4]

The difference that leads to objectification can result from a simple difference in complexion, or it can result from physical action motivated by perception of such difference, as in the following sonnet by Claude McKay:

THE LYNCHING
His Spirit in smoke ascended to high heaven.
His father, by the cruelest way of pain,
Had bidden him to his bosom once again;
The awful sin remained still unforgiven.
All night a bright and solitary star
(Perchance the one that ever guided him,
Yet gave him up at last to Fate's wild whim)
Hung pitifully o'er the swinging char.

Day dawned, and soon the mixed crowds came to
view
The ghastly body swaying in the sun.
The women thronged to look, but never a one
Showed sorrow in her eyes of steely blue.

And little lads, lynchers that were to be,
Danced round the dreadful thing in fiendish glee.[5]

There are important differences between Dillard's frog skin bag and the "dreadful thing" at the end of the hanging rope. Like Dillard, McKay puts forward an image of literal grotesque transformation, but McKay's image is more volatile. The objectification of Dillard's frog is complete and irrevocable. The frog has been transformed into something, and won't change back. Not so with McKay's lynching victim, who changes constantly before the reader's eyes.

McKay's poem shows that the objectification of people is far more complicated than the objectification of frogs. Turning a person into a thing (or trying to) makes for a prolonged and uneasy tension between those two states. McKay points to this tension in his sonnet. The victim's body is in figurative flux throughout the poem; it changes status several times before the chilling final couplet. By isolating the word "view" at the end of the ninth line of the poem, McKay indirectly emphasizes the way that perception creates this shifting in category. We stand at the speaker's side and watch with him as the lynching victim changes from one state to another. The poet focuses first on the victim's ascending spirit (ll. 1–3). This ethereal beginning gives way to a jarring earthbound contrast with the "swinging char" which the victim becomes in the second quatrain (l. 8). The third quatrain continues in this vein—though restoring "the ghastly body" of the man (l. 10)—before the poem ends with the final description of the corpse as a "dreadful thing" (l. 14). The "thing" is—as we well know—a person. Its status as "thing" is unstable and resonant with personhood. In other words, this "thing" is always threatening to change back into a person as we look at it. The victim's body may be mutilated, but his human image maintains a unique staying power in the eyes of the human observer. In contrast to the transformed frog, the tension surrounding a transformed human never goes away.

I

The Cultural Grotesque

This tension is the unique and specific tension of the grotesque, the anomalous embodiment of cultural anxiety. The grotesque is born of the violation of basic categories. It occurs when an image cannot be easily classified even on the most fundamental level: when it is both one thing and another, and thus neither one. McKay's lynching victim is grotesque because of his liminality. Both human and thing, the body occupies two basic categories at once, creating overlap where we expect none to exist. McKay's sonnet also creates a grotesque tension of this sort around the lynchers. The callousness of the steely-eyed women and the dancing children—which also extends to the unseen men who actually murdered the victim—speaks for a coldness that we commonly call "inhuman" and "monstrous." The process of racial objectification thus reverberates back to the white subjects, calling their humanity into question in a different way, and thereby making them grotesque also. This rebound effect carries with it fascinating complications and enormous rhetorical potential that, as I will show in chapter 3, is exploited most productively by American fugitive slave narrators.

Because I define the grotesque in terms of cultural categories, my argument takes as its starting point that the grotesque be understood as a social construction rather than an absolute value. Curiously, it has rarely been analyzed this way.[6] Clifford Geertz argues that human beings simply cannot be understood apart from their culture; I suggest that the same is true of the grotesque. A Balinese example cited by Geertz makes clear the cultural specificity of the effect:

> Consider Balinese trance. The Balinese fall into extreme associated states in which they perform all sorts of spectacular activities—biting off the heads of living chickens, stabbing themselves with daggers, throwing themselves wildly about, speaking with tongues, performing miraculous feats of equilibration, mimicking sexual intercourse, eating feces, and so on—rather more easily and much more suddenly than most of us fall asleep. Trance states are a crucial part of every ceremony. In some, fifty or sixty people may fall, one after the other ("like a string of firecrackers going off," as one observer puts it), emerg-

> ing anywhere from five minutes to several hours later, totally unaware of what they have been doing and convinced, despite the amnesia, that they have had the most extraordinary and deeply satisfying experience a man can have.[7]

It is safe to say that this behavior would strike most Western observers as grotesque. Indeed, non-Westerners from locales similar to Bali were staples of the American freak show from its beginnings in the 1830s. Promoters like P. T. Barnum would arrange for the natives (who were almost always nonwhite) to be shipped to the United States, where they would be displayed in full native dress and regalia before a delighted populace who would pay a few cents to gawk at them. The perception would have been reciprocal, however, if it had been granted equally. Geertz tells us that "the Balinese definition of a madman [is] someone who, like an American, smiles when there is nothing to laugh at."[8] Given the opportunity then, the Balinese would be apt to look at us and judge some of our behaviors to be grotesque as well. Anthropologist Renato Rosaldo had an epiphanic moment of this sort during his fieldwork among the Ilongot tribe of the Philippines when their questions about the Vietnam War penetrated his assumptions and made his American cultural world "suddenly appear[] grotesque" to him.[9] Such examples suggest that cultural boundaries are among the most important governing the formation and perception of the grotesque.[10]

Every culture has its grotesque. As cultures differ across time and place, so does the grotesque. (This variability is one reason the term is so difficult to define.) For the American Puritans, the Indians were grotesque. For nineteenth-century Americans, the objectified African slave and his descendants came to occupy a similar shifting space in the system of meaning and value. Neither the Indian nor the slave was seen consistently as a person in the Western worldview, but on the other hand—as I will show in the succeeding chapters—neither could be seen consistently as a thing, either. Each occupied a liminal state between human and thing, bearing elements of both. In both cases, the grotesque emerges from this conflict on the edges of the category system.

The grotesque is that which is in constant motion on the edges of fundamental boundaries within this shared system. Before anything else, divisions are responsible for the grotesque. This is clear from the social usage of the grotesque in American culture: it is commonly viewed opposite the normal, shunted off into a corner. Grotesque humor (such as dead baby jokes) is relegated to the disparaged, often banned, realm of "bad taste."[11] Disabled or disfigured people rarely appear on the sanitized medium of television. Instead, there is a long history of displaying them in freak shows, which are specially designated liminal spaces that construct their human exhibits as different—even as they implicitly acknowledge the element of sameness ("There but for the grace of God go I") that draws onlookers to the spectacle.[12] Both off-color humor and anomalous human bodies somehow threaten, in varying degrees and different ways, the beliefs we share about what constitutes the "human."

The grotesque has a peculiar disruptive power—it is a conflicting mixture of signals that intrudes upon the desired order of the world. This idea of disorder is central to the working of the grotesque; tension is the common element to virtually every definition of the term.[13] This tension results from anomalousness. That is, the grotesque is hard to apprehend because it doesn't fit neatly into a category. This makes it a threat to the entire system. Dracula, for example, is "undead," a word that is virtually impossible to define, except as "alive"—which the vampire most assuredly is not. Dracula's undefinable state of being bridges fundamental categories. His (its?) embodiment of anomalousness and taboo—that is, its grotesqueness—has made it the subject of many affecting fictions. The freak show has fascinated tens of millions of American spectators over the years for similar reasons.

This grotesque disturbs particularly because categorization is the way in which human beings know the world and organize it. Categories define individual human cultures as all humans recognize them. The organization that they provide lies at the heart of order, for without categories the essential distinctions (e.g., good and evil, us and them)—the ones that give rise to further divisions—would not be possible. The grotesque is an unusually persistent violation of that order, which explains the disturbance that it can cause.

Claude Lévi-Strauss says that all human category systems begin with the division between us and it, between culture ("our" social creation) and whatever lies outside of it. Lévi-Strauss studies the internal mechanics of classification, and how it is a response to the natural and social needs of human beings. He begins with our antipathy for chaos and corresponding desire for order. Order is not just useful then, but preferable. We *like* it. Freud theorized that "there is an intellectual function in us that demands unity, connection and intelligibility from any material, whether of perception or thought, that comes within its grasp."[14]

The desire described in this statement finds many different forms of expression across the intellectual spectrum of cultural analysis. Geertz, for example, says that "the drive to make sense out of experience, to give it form and order, is evidently as real and as pressing as the more familiar biological needs."[15] Categories satisfy this demand for form and order. They are created because they are both needed (for understanding) and *wanted*, to assure the habitual and thus emphasize the image—or illusion—of control. Separation and division of knowledge, in this view, is more than the goal—it is the motive.[16]

In viewing cultural categories as representing an effort to order the world, I want especially to stress the distinction between the strong human desire for cultural order and the actual complexities and limitations of real life. In critiquing Manichaean conceptions of culture as the thin line separating order from chaos, Renato Rosaldo points to the historical embeddedness of such anthropological views in Enlightenment thought, especially that of Hobbes. Reality, he says, is less clear; the collapse of norms need not necessarily lead to total social breakdown.[17] But the failure of lived experience to uphold polar oppositions between civilized order and uncivilized chaos is less important for my purposes than the continuing human desire for such oppositions. Rosaldo's untidy (if accurate) description of an unpredictable world should, I want to emphasize, be viewed separately from the unequivocal and powerful efforts exerted by the individual and collective imagination to summon forth a world of absolutes and clear oppositions. The failure of that summons, and the consequent collision of the desire for perfect order with less than perfect surroundings, forms the broad basis for much of what follows.

My analysis of the grotesque is accordingly founded upon the *desire* for order and its persistent violation by the grotesque, and not on any assumption that this order is actually possible. Individuals seek order in their own lives, and so repress disturbing childhood fears with varying degrees of partial success. Cultures do the same, banning threats to their own order via taboo. The grotesque always manages to evade these thought police. It is a constant intrusion on order, an anomalous agent of chaos. It is therefore significant to note that to the Puritans, the Indians represented actual chaos. Orderly division was so important to the New

England colonists that one of their reasons for not wanting to go into the woods was because doing so meant entering the unordered darkness.

The desire for order is so strong that it borders on the sacred, and it finds expression in that realm. Categories thus have an important role to play not just in organizing knowledge but also in the cultural value system. The sacred occupies its own category, defined by reference to the others, as a part of the system. But as might be expected, its position is an especially important one. Geertz describes religion as "in part an [implicit] attempt . . . to conserve the fund of general meanings."[18] Religious symbols, he says, "must formulate a world in which [social] values, as well as the forces opposing their realization, are fundamental ingredients." The enduring problem of the grotesque, it seems to me, is that it combines elements of both of these forces—and so defies categorization. In doing so, it throws the viability of the system into doubt. Again, the Puritan antipathy for the Indians can be clearly understood in this context. The Puritans articulated their purpose in explicitly sacred terms; they then placed Indians in opposition to it. The grotesque—in the unstable, objectified form of the Indians—amounts to a visceral attack on their grand plan.

This is not to say that the grotesque does not provoke desire as well as fear. Despite the strictures of category, the grotesque remains a frequent intruder upon the order of everyday experience. People seek it out because they are drawn to the borders even as they fear what lies beyond them. Why else would horror movies be so popular? As Captain Ahab says in a quiet moment as his obsessive quest for Moby Dick nears its fatal conclusion, "What is best let alone, that accursed thing is not always what least allures."[19] The attraction of the grotesque is a more involved topic than I can fully address here; as the succeeding chapters will show, it encompasses not only cultural boundaries but also the frequently self-destructive forces of individual unconscious desire that draw people to the edges. But as succeeding chapters will also show, those edges are where the action is.

A system of cultural categories is a collection of similarities and differences which both stores meaning and provides the basis for it. Wholly self-referential, the system unifies the world according to its own guidelines and provides the basis for the rules by which a group of people choose to live. Categories form the ontological foundation for society itself. They are the defining frame for all knowledge.

Violating accepted boundaries is a serious business, then. It represents an attack on the entire cultural enterprise. Likewise, it becomes a threat to the entire learning endeavor, for it questions the context of knowledge. As Freud points out, "Our concepts owe their existence to comparisons."[20] A threat to established categories is an attack on the basis of comparison. The grotesque does precisely this, which makes it a phenomenon of great cultural consequence. The grotesque is felt in the form of anomalies that bridge categories and resist integration. It consequently questions the basis on which knowledge rests.

The soundness of the human cultural endeavor always lurks in the background to this questioning, but when the human being is the literal subject of the grotesque—as when one questions whether slaves are human—the threat to order becomes very serious.[21] To view people as nonhuman is an open invitation to the most fundamental and enduring category problems. The mulatto, a black-white mixture, was one such problem for the slaveholding American South. Slaveholders had to find a place for the mulatto, or else this piece of "cultural baggage" would unbalance and topple the entire conceptual structure supporting the peculiar institution. American slaveholders gradually resolved this embarrassing category problem by classifying mulattoes as "black." This division was practiced from the beginning of English colonial slavery; it became a matter of law for the first time in the eighteenth century, having been taken up in different colonies during that period. Court cases centering on fine definitional distinctions (e.g., how much "black blood" constituted a mulatto/Negro) were argued well into the nineteenth century. The American slaveholders' "solution" to their mulatto problem reflects the encompassing effort made in the South to link blackness with the nonhuman. It also masks white fear of black sexuality, for as Winthrop Jordan points out, this exclusive approach also serves to "deny[] that intermixture had occurred at all"—notwithstanding the fact that the mixed-race offspring of such unions provided walking, talking evidence that white-black sexual unions had indeed taken place.[22] Fear of blacks sleeping with whites is easily inverted as a fear of whites sleeping with—and being attracted to—blacks. This attraction, which put slaves on a human level with their masters, had to be denied.

From the Southern perspective, mulattoes "had" to be black to erase the interracial attraction that brought them into being, and to "prove" that it had never occurred. As a result of this show of forced resolution, the Southern category system was protected for a while. But the human image cannot be foreclosed so simply, and the persistence of the grotesque in the literature of slavery stands as evidence of this dynamic instability.

II

The "Grotesquification" of the Human

Dillard's frog becomes grotesque for an instant, the actual moment when it falls in between categories, during the time of the transformation itself. Before that instant, it's a frog. Afterwards, it's a frog skin sac. The corpse in the tree in McKay's sonnet has a more persistent anomalous status; it shimmers between the categories of human and thing. Stuck in an unending state of transformation, its grotesqueness continues over time. Human objectification liberates the grotesque here, and with it a realm of ontological and epistemological complications. Once allowed to emerge from its taboo-barred crypt, the grotesque inherent within the objectification process refuses to be recaged. Unlike Dillard's frog skin bag, the "dreadful thing" of McKay's poem maintains an identity as a human being, even though its spirit has, according to the poet, departed to meet its maker. What I am suggesting is that the frog skin bag isn't a frog in the way that a dead human being is still a person, even if the body has been charred beyond visual recognition.

A different example may make this point more strongly. When most people wear leather jackets, they don't generally think about the fact that they are (in a sense) wearing cows. That's because the cow has been completely transformed—it's a cow no longer. The process of making cows into things has a grotesque aspect—as Upton Sinclair amply demonstrated in his 1906 exposé of the meat-packing industry in *The Jungle*—but few would see a leather jacket as "grotesque." Though the existence of such mechanized animal-killing angers some people, not even its detractors treat the product as a corpse. (Animal rights activists spray indelible paint on fur coats, for example, an act of protest which hardly shows respect for the "bodies" of the animals involved. Some members of the same group of people bury their pets in special cemeteries.) Like the frog skin sac, the leather jacket is a fully objectified article.

As a corollary to the leather jacket, consider the difficulties faced by the administrators of the United States Holocaust Memorial Museum as they debated how best to handle the twenty pounds of human hair (shorn from Auschwitz arrivees before and after death) received among the artifacts for display:

> "When we first received the hair, we regarded it as just another artifact for the museum," Jacek Nowakowski, who was in charge of acquiring objects for the exhibition, says, "but then, when the Content Committee met to discuss the best way to display it, it became clear that the members viewed human hair differently from the other objects."[23]

The hair was eventually displayed, but the equivocation continues. According to museum conservator Witold Smrek, "Some people are telling us that the exhibition is offensive, that it is in poor taste to have human hair on display like this." Among such detractors, Adam Zak of the Jesuit College in Cracow argues that the hair should be buried because it "is part of the victim's body and, as such, should be accorded the dignity due to it."[24]

Now imagine a lampshade made of human skin or a bar of soap rendered from human fat. (The Nazis manufactured these articles from the bodies of their concentration camp victims.) In this case, I hold that no one who knew where these products came from would be able to use them without perceiving their humanity. When one is aware of human origins, in other words, one automatically acknowledges them. The point is not that everyone would be horrified at such monstrous industry (if everyone were, it wouldn't happen), but rather that everyone who knew of it would perceive the human aspect of the objects produced. Essentially, informed users would experience the constant awareness that their products are also "bodies." Just as we treat a pile of ashes as a person if we know where those ashes originally came from, so can we give reverent burial to a lampshade or a bar of soap.

This ability to see the person through the thing-making process is not limited to those with warm hearts and good consciences. It's involuntary. Nazi sympathizers might use these lamps and soap even if they knew their origins, but my point is that this knowledge would make a permanent difference in how they viewed them. As evidence, I turn to an analogous incident, also from this period in history, as recalled by a middle-aged woman in an interview by Studs Terkel:

> A white girl invited us to her home in Maine . . . .
> Her brother came home unexpectedly and for some reason he had a thing about race. He had been in the army, and I wondered if that had something to do with it. He pulled out a cigarette case and said the skin on it "was from some nigger we lynched overseas." The young woman was very embarrassed. We left the next day.[25]

The woman and her brother both treat his cigarette case in a special way precisely because of its human origins; the man's pride in his possession is of course abhorrent, but the very specialness he sees in his cigarette case comes from his own perception of the human within the thing. So too with the Nazi lamps and soap. A person retains his humanity even when turned into a trophy or a household object—even if the user supports the violence that created it.[26]

This special perception of the human operates also in the figurative sphere. The first male and the first female taken aboard slave ships, for example, were usually named Adam and Eve by the slavers.[27] If the institution of slavery necessarily involved turning a blind eye to the humanity of the slaves, this naming ritual suggests that it was impossible to blind *both* eyes to it. Naming slaves would appear to be highly counterproductive for the enslaver, for naming calls attention to the human identity of the cargo. Indeed, this paradoxical practice shows that despite whatever desensitization they might have acquired from years in the business, slave traders were hardly exempt from the difficulties that accompany human objectification. The continuation of this mock-biblical naming ritual from ship to ship reflects the widespread anxiety that lies behind the attempt to remove actual human beings from the category of "human."

This anxiety usually makes its appearance unbeknownst to the would-be objectifier. In his autobiography, *I Had a Hammer*, baseball star Henry Aaron (who is black) quotes from one of the thousands of pieces of hate-mail he received as he neared the all-time home run record set by

Fig. 1.1 Engraving from Richard Drake's *Revelations of a Slave Smuggler* (1860). Especially striking here are the grotesque renderings of the slaves. (Given the confessional nature of the book, in which Drake repents his sins, these portrayals are highly ironic.) (Reproduced by permission of the Photographs and Prints Division, Schomburg Center for Research in Black Culture, the New York Public Library; Astor, Lenox, and Tilden Foundations)

Babe Ruth (who was white, and who played at a time when baseball was segregated):

> Dear Nigger,
> You black animal. I hope you never live long enough to hit more home runs than the great Babe Ruth. Niggers are like animals and have a short life span. Martin Luther King was a trouble-maker, and he had a short life span.[28]

This writer badly wants to see Aaron as an animal and tries to turn him into one. But even as he writes the words, he can't complete the transformation in his own mind. He starts by calling Aaron a "black animal," but a moment later he backpedals, saying that Negroes are only "like animals." The difference between "animal" and "like an animal" is at the heart of this book. Aaron's hate-mongering correspondent was certainly not calibrating the nuances of meaning in his letter, but the declension between his first and third sentences nevertheless illustrates the ontological dilemma created by human objectification. The letter writer wants to deny Aaron's humanity, *but he can't do it*. He can easily compare black people to animals, but as much as he wants to, he is unable actually to turn them into animals, even in his own bigoted mind.

Successful (that is, complete) human objectification is fantasy, and thus becomes the stuff of horror stories. Thomas Harris's novel, *The Silence of the Lambs* (1988), is a good example of the genre. Hannibal "the Cannibal" Lecter, the charismatic rogue psychiatrist who eats his patients, sees no humanity in most of his fellow beings, thus allowing him to treat them as potential entrées. The novel is a horror story, and Lecter a monster, because people don't behave that way. There has never been a serial killer like the completely self-contained Lecter.[29] People identify with other people, and that is why objectification can never be a casual act. Even when the would-be objectifier is enthusiastic, the acknowledgment that human life is at stake is what gives the act its import—and its complications. Thus, the attempt to objectify is always fraught with unarticulated ambivalence, and this ambivalence guarantees that it cannot be completed.

Because of this incompleteness, the objectification of people is the most complex kind of objectification there is. Human objectification never fully succeeds; that is, a person never actually becomes a thing. Instead, the attempt to objectify a person places him into an ontological netherworld, part human and part thing. When I refer to "human objectification" in the pages that follow, therefore, I am pointing not to simple and complete transformation (as with Dillard's frog) but to this complicated and equivocal phenomenon, in which the categories of "human" and "thing" are conflated, with neither being erased. It might be more precise to call this "attempted objectification," a process in which a person is made to enter into the liminal space between human and thing, a grotesque space where the person's essential humanness is questioned but not altogether denied. A frog can be turned into a thing, but a person can never be pushed all the way into that category. The enduring complexity of the human image is at the center of this book.

This endurance brings some needed emphasis to the problems of the objectifier, which, thanks to the long historical reach of Frantz Fanon, have been overshadowed by the difficulties faced by the objectified, oppressed other. According to Fanon, only the colonized native can enable his own mobility and effect his own personhood.[30] While this may indeed offer the quickest path to personhood, I suggest that because of the problems of the objectifier, all roads end at the same place. The position of the objectified other is inherently unstable in the objectifier's eyes simply by virtue of its shaky place in the objectifier's unsound category system, a system that is bound to collapse under its own weight. Humans just can't see other people as nonpersons for long; the effort goes against our wiring for anthropomorphic perception (which I will discuss more fully later in this chapter). If desire pushes a group away from the human category, perception will always prevent their being seen fully as nonhuman. Artificially pushed in between the two categories, the objectified other will, once the strength behind the effort gives out, be seen as human once more.[31]

This rubber-band effect arises from the built-in instability of the grotesque. The grotesque is inherently difficult to manage—as illustrated by the narratives I will examine throughout this book—but this difficulty arises not so much because of the risk of uprising by the resentful other, but rather from the essential unsoundness of human objectification itself. The enslaved is not necessarily dangerous to the enslaver (though he may be, and often is), but a structure based on objectification is always a dangerous foundation for the enslaver's cultural belief: it's built on shifting sands, and requires constant, perpetual bolstering.

This conclusion raises a comparison with Homi K. Bhabha's useful concept of "hybridity," but it is based on a different metaphor: the objectified (and thus grotesque) human being is not both human and thing but neither; not double—like Bhabha's hybrid—but in between. Bhabha says that hybridity of the object makes the basis of the colonizer's authority "problematic" and thus causes him to become "tongue-tied."[32] This book explores the "mutation" of the other, but it ultimately focuses on the objectifier's dilemma and his complicated struggles to write his way out of it.

Close analysis of human objectification up to now has centered almost exclusively on the dehumanizing effects of industrialization.[33] This emphasis has its origin in Marxist theory, but current work on the subject grows a certain distance from these roots. Marx describes a condition similar to what I have been calling "objectification," but he calls it "alienation" and locates it at the end of a series of transformations. In Marx's terminology, "objectification" refers to an early point in the capitalist production process. I have some differences with Marx's model; a brief summary will help to clarify matters of concept and vocabulary.

Ideally, in Marx's view, the worker should be projected through his labor into an economically organized world whose image is understood in terms of the humans who inhabit it. The worker and his work then become identified with each other. In Marx's ideal version of this scenario, the worker would maintain a continuously self-creating connection to the world through the process of making. As Elaine Scarry shows in her reading of *Capital*, this would be a process of creative exchange between laborer and labor. Marx would like to see the worker (seen through the work) as possessing "the character of living matter," while the object of labor (the product) would come to pick up a certain "aliveness" from the worker and the vitalizing activity of labor.[34] The made object, in other words, would be a projection of the worker's body, and the existence of this object in turn confers meaning back upon its creator. The worker and the product would thus confer meaning on each other through the creativity of the work. But in the capitalist system this dynamic reciprocity is lost between the worker-creator and the thing created. Marx sees alienation as the inevitable result. Alienation is a social crisis marked by stasis and loss: the worker ceases to be defined in terms of his creative work and is thus turned into a cog in the system by the production process that separates him from it. This is objectification—as I have been using the term.[35]

Though Marx bases his model of objectification and alienation on a dynamic tension between the body and the economic system, there has been a frequent tendency to oversimplify its complexities by assuming that the process leading to alienation is always a prosaic effect. Recent critics of postbellum American literature have returned the tension to the process, in effect suggesting that alienation is neither simple nor always complete. In their analyses of "commodification" in a newly technological America, these new historical critics have revised our understanding of the equivocal nature of human objectification. In light of this reemphasized tension between human and thing, it is clear that "economic objectification" possesses many of the complexities that I have generally ascribed to racially motivated objectification.[36]

Moving from the Marxian version of the concept, I argue that human objectification can exist independently of economic issues, or it can precede them. Marx argues that all theories of history, art, and consciousness itself are determined by material (that is, economic) considerations. One might argue on this basis that all objectification has an economic basis, but I am skeptical of such an all-encompassing economic worldview. For example, the Puritan view of the Indians (the subject of the next chapter) was based on religious considerations that may have preceded economic ones. Slavery is certainly a form of economic objectification, but in this case it is worth pointing out that racial objectification (viewing blacks as nonhuman on the hierarchical chain of being) actually precedes their degradation within the economic system.[37] The slave may of course be productively viewed as a kind of man-machine, a victim of Marxian-type alienation. Without denying the existence of the economic motive for human objectification, I want to privilege other possible original causes. Following Albert Memmi, and contrary to Marx, I will argue that the motivation to dominate another person has its roots in a desire for superiority, something deeper than money.[38] I will have more to say about this in chapters 3 and 4, when my treatment of objectification within slavery will center on the master-slave dialectic of Hegel, Marx's most influential source.

The continuing critical preoccupation with the dehumanizing effects of "the machine" may have decentered the idea of objectification from our understanding of the pretechnological American experience before the Civil War. More than twenty years ago, in *The Black Image in the White Mind*, George Fredrickson traced the history of the degraded perceptions of blacks in the religion, science, and politics of nineteenth- and early twentieth-century white culture. Fredrickson's important work explores the purpose of the rhetoric of race; I analyze the tensions inherent within much of this rhetoric, tensions which ultimately help to undermine that very purpose. Specifically, these rhetorical tensions arise from the hidden reality of objectification: its complicated failure.

Historians have long concerned themselves with the documentation of the central contradictions of slavery and the fluctuating conception of the slave, but the ways that these contradictions find their expression in literature—the ways that creative writers *struggle*, and often flounder, with them—deserve much more attention. Accordingly, my method is literary before it is historical; that is, it centers on the close reading of selected texts. In this respect, my project is perhaps most similar to Tzevetan Todorov's *The Conquest of America*, an analysis of the Spanish encounter with the New World through the careful study of the explorers' writings. Like Todorov, I am concerned with attempts by the physically dominant group to make textual sense out of the encounter with the other; but unlike Todorov, I am also interested in the voice of resistance, for I want to emphasize that the sustained efforts to articulate the shape and meaning of racial difference take place in the form of a dialogue between the subjugator and the subjugated. This dialogue most clearly illustrates the struggle with contradiction that is my focus.[39] By looking closely at certain textual "objectification sites" (some within Fredrickson's chronology, and some—like the Puritan encounter with the Indians—outside of it), I will show how the "black image" (as well as that of the Native American) depends on various attempts at objectification that fail in complicated and interesting ways. This failure can always be traced back to one enduring reality: the person can never be banished from within the object.

But what causes the human image to persist when others do not? How can McKay and his readers look at a "swinging char" hanging from a tree and see a human being? The answer lies in our anthropomorphic perception. We *need* to look for people wherever we are capable of finding them. This need is based on the human tendency to see the world in terms of ourselves. As James Baldwin puts it, "The human imagination is perpetually required to examine, control and redefine reality, of which we must assume ourselves to be the center and the key."[40]

Arguments for anthropomorphism in human perception proliferate, following from both biological and cultural premises. They cross the disciplines, ranging from cognitive science (where Piaget's *The Child's Conception of the World* remains a touchstone) to philosophy (where Hume and Nietzsche are among those who have identified and argued for it), anthropology (Lévi-Strauss and Robin Horton are two prominent thinkers), psychoanalysis (Freud's *The Future of an Illusion* stands out from among his works), art (where Ernest Gombrich's work is very valuable), and of course religious studies, where the issue proves especially vexing because of its potential to undercut the claim for the spiritual origin of religious ideas. Stewart Guthrie summarizes the long history of this idea in his excellent book, *Faces In the Clouds*. He argues persuasively that the human tendency to anthropomorphize stems from a strategy that is both rational and practical. According to Guthrie, "We anthropomorphize because it is a good bet to guess that the world is humanlike. It is a bet, because the world is uncertain, ambiguous, and in need of interpretation. It is a good bet, because the most valuable interpretations are those which disclose the presence of whatever is most important to us. That usually is other humans."[41]

The need for people to see human faces in the world is partly biological. Only people with damage to a specific part of the brain will fail to see this figure as a face:

The human desire to see the world in human terms is dramatized in strikingly grotesque fashion by H. G. Wells in *The Island of Dr. Moreau* (1896). Moreau, a mad vivisectionist, creates humanlike creatures out of amalgamations of various animals. When the narrator asks him "why he had taken the human form as a model," Moreau confesses that "there is something in the human form that appeals to the artistic turn of mind more powerfully than any animal shape can."[42] This unarticulated "something" that attracts Moreau is also what makes humanity persist even in the face of objectification. Moreau creates grotesques by forcing animals toward the borders of "human"—as opposed to McKay's sonnet, for example, which depicts the human being pushed toward the nonhuman. Wells's novel further shows that the anthropomorphic world that we build gives full expressive range to the grotesque whenever humanity is questioned or threatened within it.

One need not resort to Moreau-like surgery—or to the tar, feathers, and burning brands of lynchers—to imagine a human as a thing. A person can be physically whole and still be seen that way. Human objectification on the basis of race was of course institutionalized in the antebellum United States in the form of legal slavery. When Harriet Beecher Stowe serialized *Uncle Tom's Cabin* in 1852, she subtitled it "The Man That Was a Thing." Stowe's subtitle implies a question that captures the essence of the rhetorical battle over slavery: is a slave a person or a piece of property (that is, a thing)? Martin Luther King makes the same distinction a century later in his "Letter from the Birmingham Jail": "Segregation, to use the terminology of the Jewish philosopher Martin Buber, substitutes an 'I-it' relationship for an 'I-thou' relationship and ends up relegating persons to the status of things."[43]

But this central issue antedates slavery and continues extralegally long after abolition. Before Negro slavery became an issue in the American republic, before there *was* an American republic, the English settlers in North America sought to objectify the Indians. Even before legislation following the Civil War removed the legal postulates supporting slavery, Stowe's implied question had taken a slightly different form: are blacks equal to whites, or are they a lower life form on the Chain of Being and therefore not truly human? This question was debated both before and after the changes wrought by the Civil War and the appearance of Darwin's *Origin of Species* in 1859.[44] I will argue in the following chapters that this racial grotesque has never been free of the diverse complications that arise from the persistence of the human image. The pervasive tension of the racial grotesque highlights what it really is: an effort to categorize that only partially succeeds. This tension, which runs beneath and constantly informs the rhetorical strategy of objectification, is what makes the process worth examining. Human objectification creates not a discretely bounded thing but a grotesque anomaly. And that anomaly doesn't go away.

In this book I explore the workings of the grotesque in the American rhetoric of racially motivated objectification. By "rhetoric of objectification," I mean a hierarchical ordering of concepts that separates people, semantically transforming a segment of the population into objects. The grotesque plays an important role at the end of the process, separating the anomaly from what is "normal." I focus not only on the objectification of people but also on its opposite process of transforming ostensible objects back into humans.

Throughout American history, racial difference has repeatedly generated such threats to humanity—at least as "humanity" has been defined by the stronger group.[45] For example, the Indians of New England cre-

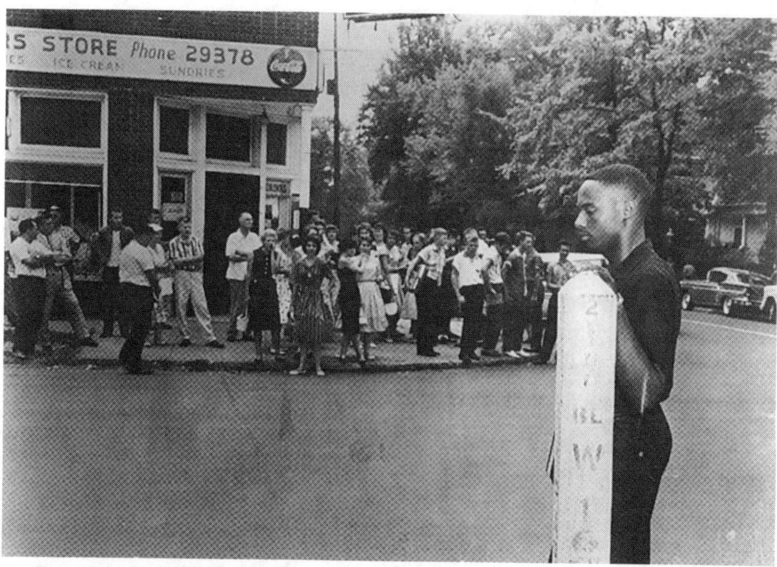

Fig. 1.2 Jefferson Thomas was one of nine black students who integrated Central High School in Little Rock, Arkansas, in September 1957. In this picture, Thomas waits for the school bus while being jeered by an angry white crowd. (Reproduced by permission of the Photographs and Prints Division, Schomburg Center for Research in Black Culture, the New York Public Library; Astor, Lenox, and Tilden Foundations)

ated a crisis for the Puritans because the settlers defined "human" in narrow European terms. The Native Americans perceived the English as human, on the other hand, because the boundaries of the "human" category happened to be more permeable in their own cultural system. If whites joined them, survived their initiation rituals, and learned their ways, the new arrivals then gained full membership in the tribe and the "human" category that it described. Such examples show that objectification is not an inevitable recourse for all peoples in all circumstances, but it is likewise the case that the possibility of it always exists for a group, whether as a first or last resort.

This contrast between Puritan and Native American cultural practice illustrates particularly sharply my goal of studying the racial grotesque as a deep structure embedded within a cultural subject position, as a part functioning within a self-conscious whole. My position is essentially this: I see human objectification as a human tendency that is shaped by cultural forces (which are themselves variable), making the urge to objectify other human beings more or less likely under a given set of circumstances. I am arguing not for reflexes then, but for inclinations—inclinations that are subject to human agency, but which are not by themselves a deterministic guarantee of action or result. Orientation is crucial: we can expect that a ball balanced at the top of a hill is more likely to roll downward than one that lies at a distance from the edge of the decline. Similarly, societies with imperialistic designs may be more likely to objectify those in their paths—more likely, that is, than other groups whose goals are (for whatever accident or reason) more pluralistic. Robert Bogdan says that "'Freak' is a way of thinking, a set of practices"; some groups are more prone to it than others. Because dominant (white) American category systems have generally been extremely rigid, the very presence of the designated "other" race has amounted to a challenge to the white definition of what is human. If, as Geertz suggests, "Every man has a right to create his own savage for his own purposes," then it is a right that Americans have exercised—and abundantly abused—over the years.[46] Historically, objectification has been the chosen American strategy to uphold the Western category system—and myriad social, legal, philosophical, ideological, and imaginative complications have been the result, building upon one another over the years.

I will be exploring some of these complications in the pages that follow, with a special focus on the literary imagination. Following Renato Rosaldo's conception of ritual as "a busy intersection" filled with "positioned subjects who have a distinctive mix of insight and blindness," I will be paying special attention to the social and historical context surrounding the effort at racial objectification in New England and the antebellum United States.[47] Among my focal points will be Puritan religious motives and territorial imperatives; early American expansion and the rise of abolitionism; and the popularity of adventure stories, slave narratives, plantation fiction, and freak shows. All of these were both causes and effects of human objectification and the racial grotesque, and the awareness possessed by their practitioners of their own different, frequently opposing roles in the process makes the study of their interplay both rich and complex.

The Inhuman Race separates a strand of American cultural history and scrutinizes it through its literary markers. Beginning with the next chapter, the book moves back and forth between the voices of the objectifier

Fig. 1.3 The white marcher doesn't need a sign. (Reproduced by permission of the Photographs and Prints Division, Schomburg Center for Research in Black Culture, the New York Public Library; Astor, Lenox, and Tilden Foundations)

and the objectified. The idea is to show how the two sides talk to each other. Recent work by Eric Sundquist, Edward Said, and others has demonstrated that the exchange between the voice of domination and the voice of resistance is an important creative force in the literature of the United States and elsewhere. The structure of this book represents an attempt to organize the conversation by alternating sides. Moving from captivity narratives (by Puritans and slaves) to fiction (by both proslavery and abolitionist authors), I end with Melville, who somehow manages to analyze the conflict from different positions at the same time. The transition from colonial New England to the nineteenth-century South is chronologically abrupt but thematically consistent; Werner Sollors, for example, traces the American preoccupation with racial and ethnic differences back to the Puritans, arguing for "the importance of New England's typological vision for the emergence of different peoplehoods in America." The link between the Native American and the African-American slave goes back to Tocqueville, who saw the extermination of Indians and the enslavement of blacks as two sides of the same American coin. In this book their pairing corresponds to the historical continuum between a colonial ideology of inequality and domination and a later American society built on this foundation and, by the mid-nineteenth century, deeply conflicted over the enslavement that it produced.[48]

Chapter 2, "The Puritans and Their Indians," reaches back to the colonial roots of racial objectification in America, examining the problems faced by the Puritans in their self-appointed task of objectifying the Indians. The Puritan settlers in New England consistently seek to objectify the Indians and cast them as monsters in their typologically oriented world. But the Indians just as consistently fail to fit the role: they periodically revert to humanity in the Puritans' eyes. For the Puritans, the result is a blurring of ontological boundaries. Their struggle, which I analyze in terms introduced in Mary Douglas's *Purity and Danger*, is to devise a strategy to cope with the presence of a dangerous threat to their Christian-centered definition of "human" and thus save the cultural system. This attempt cannot succeed, because Indians are people. The result of the effort is that the Indians lose their fixed place in the Puritan system of knowledge and belief. Now human, now monster, the Indian becomes a tense, unstable anomaly. This dynamic flux across fundamental categories creates the grotesque, an effect most evident in the writings of those who actually spent time with the Indians. Accordingly, I establish this destabilizing presence of the grotesque primarily through the analysis of Puritan narratives of Indian captivity. Puritan accounts of such experience have a kind of reflexive honesty about them which exposes the writers' ambivalence about their captors, and about their colonial experience generally—which can be traced in part to the attack on their views by the New Science of the Enlightenment and the politics of post-Puritan England.

The third chapter, "A Different Power of Blackness," turns the viewfinder around to the vantage point of American slaves, as I focus on the genre that they created, the scores of narratives telling of their treatment as things. Here I apply this concept of "grotesquification" to the experience of the American slave. Slave narratives serve here as a prism through which I look at the complicated relationship between master and slave. If the rhetoric of racial difference relies at its extremes on the grotesque to attempt the key transformation from person to thing, then slave narratives show that there also exists a corresponding opposite paradigm, exemplified by Frederick Douglass's account in his *Narrative* of his change from a "brute" (one whose personhood is compromised because he sees himself as a thing) back to a human being. Both kinds of transformations are at work in the slave narratives, and in related writings by and about slaves. Despite the apparently simple equation posited by the peculiar institution (person becomes property), narratives on both sides of the slavery question vibrate with an equivocal tension which surrounds the central transformation. This ontological equivocation is explained in significant part by the workings of Hegel's dialectic of master and slave. The slave is deemed property but, like the Indians, he doesn't fit the role and cannot play it consistently, neither in his own eyes nor in those of the slaveowner. Hegel describes an instability that lies at the core of the slavery issue; the grotesque expresses this instability in a swaying, unstable dance along the edges of the system of knowledge and belief. Through a flexible rereading of Hegel, I show how the slave narrator draws on the conventions of the popular American adventure story to exploit his own grotesqueness by spotlighting his passage from objectification back into the realm of unchallenged humanity.

Chapter 4, "Sambo Agonistes," is an objectification-oriented analysis of the famous Sambo stereotype as it appears in antebellum fiction. I argue first that the literary propagation of Sambo, the happy and childlike slave, represents a proslavery strategy to mask the objectification of slaves. I then trace the different roles of the Sambo character in both pro- and antislavery novels and measure the general efficacy of the Southern rhetorical strategy of portraying slaves overtly as permanent children in need of guidance, and only covertly as things. The results of this literary survey suggest that Sambo had a certain appeal on both sides of the Mason-Dixon line; even an ostensibly antislavery book like Sarah Hale's *Northwood*, for example, infantilizes slaves in a way that would appear to do as much harm as good. The use of Sambo by proslavery writers may have avoided the harsh immediacy of crude objectification, but the motive behind the character's creation does not usually stay hidden for long. Carefully targeted abolitionist attack exposes the stereotype; I read Stowe's *Uncle Tom's Cabin* and William Wells Brown's *Clotel* as multilayered critiques of the Sambo figure, critiques that prepare for a concluding Hegelian analysis of Sambo as the symbol of the master's frustrated quest for recognition from the slave.

This investigation of antebellum fiction finishes with a chapter on Melville, whose problematic texts often center pointedly on racial objectification. Toni Morrison says that Melville was fascinated with the "successful assertion of whiteness as ideology" in society.[49] His fiction shows a multilayered preoccupation with not just the social effects of categories of whiteness and blackness (including slavery), but also of the grotesque tension that lies at the heart of such racial distinctions. "The Racial Freak, the Happy Slave, and the Problem of Melville's Universal Men" centers on a reading of *Typee*, a highly self-conscious exploration of the role of the racial grotesque in an individual's futile attempt to resist the urge to objectify, matched by his wild fear of being objectified himself. His panic at the prospect of being tattooed betrays his fear of being seen as a living exhibit in an emerging nineteenth-century freak show culture, an experience that would figure him as "black." This reading of the individual's struggle is paired with an analysis of *Benito Cereno*, which symbolically represents the tangled social ramifications of the racial objectification in a murky, topical treatment of slavery. The "Siamese ligature" binding these two analyses is a brief look at the relationship between Ishmael and Queequeg in *Moby-Dick*.

The idea for this book germinated in my mind partly because it received continual nourishment from current events. In America and elsewhere, racial objectification shifts with the times, seeking new life in different social, economic, and literary forms. The persistence of this cultural symptom alone makes it important, but its significance is also historical: racial objectification continues to affect and inform the way people see each other in this country. I argue here that the American literature of race is, on the most basic and fundamental level, a continuing story of the encounter with the grotesque. The value of such literary and cultural history should lie not only in the light that it shines on the past but also in how that light is reflected back onto the present. This book looks at old texts, but their subject remains very much with us. From Bensonhurst to Los Angeles, from Mary Rowlandson's captivity narrative to Charles Johnson's 1990 *Middle Passage* and beyond, racially motivated objectification clearly continues to simmer beneath the structure and expression of race relations in this country. The result, as these examples show, is that people still see other people through the distorting lens of the grotesque. Regrettable though it is, much remains to be said about the destabilizing role of the racial grotesque in determining the way that Americans look at one another. The continuing long life of racial objectification gives new meaning to something Richard Wright said in 1940, that "if Poe were alive he would not have to invent horror; horror would invent him."[50]

CHAPTER TWO

THE PURITANS AND THEIR INDIANS: MAKING A HUMAN MONSTER, AND VICE VERSA

> To Humanize these Miserable Animals, and in any measure to *Cicurate* [i.e., tame] them & Civilize them, were a work of no little Difficulty; and a Performance little short of what One of our most famous *Physicians* esteemed the *Greatest Cure* that ever himself had wrought in all his Practice; *To bring an Idiot unto the Use of Reason*.
>
> —Cotton Mather, *India Christiana*

The Puritans tried hard to settle the American "wilderness" in their own way. A large portion of their struggle centered on the Native American inhabitants of New England. The colonists fought two bloody wars and numerous smaller engagements with the land's original tenants, but their greatest Indian battle may have been the one inside themselves, as they struggled for generations with the humanity of their neighbors. Puritan views of Indians fluctuated wildly; Indians were alternately portrayed as potential but misguided converts, or as wilderness creatures to be exterminated. Swinging back and forth between human and thing before the Puritans' eyes, the Indians took associations from both sides, winding up somewhere in the grotesque middle of Puritan perception.

The unresolved status of the Indians was the source of considerable ontological discomfort for the Puritans. Nowhere is this more apparent than in Indian captivity narratives, a genre the Puritans developed, and one that puts their tension and ambivalence on display. The Puritan authors want badly to deny the humanity of their Indian captors, but for all their efforts, they cannot help acknowledging the Indians as people.

Even so, the Puritans were never able to admit Indians as full members of their community; their continuing discomfort may have reflected their need to scapegoat the Indians for the perceived failure of their own enterprise. At the same time, the captivity narratives provided a necessary outlet for Puritan thinking about prodigies and other wonders, beliefs that were being attacked as superstition by the late seventeenth century. Because of the rise of the New Science in England and France, the later Puritan generations couldn't openly advocate prodigies without looking like fanatics in the eyes of those in England whom they could—at a time when their political capital was diminishing—ill afford to impress that way. By deflecting the vocabulary of prodigies onto Indians, the American Puritans sought to preserve their world of signs and wonders, a key intellectual rescue because this view of the world was linked to their understanding of their covenant with God.

In Java, says Clifford Geertz, "To be human is to be Javanese." Anyone who does not fit the Javanese definition of humanity—which naturally depends on knowledge of Javanese customs—is said to be *ndurung djawa*, or "not yet Javanese." This separation between "Javanese" and "human" reflects the human tendency to address any void in terms of one's own space. The subheading of an early section of Werner Sollors's *Beyond Ethnicity*, "We Are Not Like Them," bluntly describes how people apply categories to other people in this way. When a person inside the boundary (a member of a culture) opposes another person outside of it, the alien is pushed toward the human-but-not-human: the grotesque. In other words, Sollors's "us-them" distinction easily moves in practice toward the more drastic "us-it" separation. Cultural difference thus results in an attempt to make a person into a thing, creating a grotesque transformation of a person into an entity whose humanity is uncertain and under threat.[1]

The American Puritans have something in common with Geertz's Javanese: just as the Javanese saw outsiders as "not yet Javanese," so the Puritans saw Native Americans as "not yet" English, and therefore not yet human. Still, it might be more accurate to say that there was no room in the Puritan worldview for the Indians to move from "not yet human" to "human," and that—as with certain arguments in favor of Negro slavery that I will examine later on—"not yet" really meant "not ever." Keeping the Indians lodged in the "nonhuman" category was an ongoing and difficult epistemological task for the New England settlers, requiring constant vigilance and emotional energy. It was also a strikingly audacious one to attempt, for the collective Puritan effort to construct themselves as insiders and the Indians as outsiders amounted to an overwriting of many empirical facts, including the simple one that the Indians were already living in North America when the Puritans arrived. The Puritans' configuration of themselves as residents and the natives as aliens was a crucial first step in a process of conquest whose eventual success was fraught with ideological tension and unexpected psychological and social consequences.

As for the Indians, theirs was an impossible category to occupy successfully. (My use of the now-controversial term *Indian* is consistent with my emphasis on the Puritan view of the world. It also invokes Columbus's original act of naming—related to his quest for a passage to India—and the way that his imposed perspective placed the Native Americans into his own structure of meaning.) Besides being at a technological disadvantage in warfare, the Indians faced an extreme rhetorical deficit in any peaceful scenarios, as the English view of things prevented Indian and New Englander from ever facing each other as equals. The Indians could never be unalloyed "English," not only because they had less practice at European ways but also because their "savage" ethnicity marked them as permanently different.

This difference rests partly on the foundation of shared national identity, where "nation" is a representation of social life that is part of a larger cultural system.[2] Nationality involves, among other things, a sense of present and past—of communal belonging and a collection of shared, constructed memories. For the Puritans these would center on England, as both place and idea. The Indians could never share these memories, making them ineligible on this basis for inclusion in the Puritans' "human" group. But since being human is a matter of experiencing the human situation—that is, of sharing social needs and desires common to all people—the Puritans surely recognized the human experience of the Indians. This contradiction becomes the major basis for the Puritans' experience of the Indians as shifting, unmanageable grotesque figures.

Among current theorists of the colonial situation, Homi K. Bhabha's representation of the colonizer (or enslaver) comes closest to what I'm trying to describe in terms of the objectifier's encounter with the self-created grotesque. Bhabha sees the voice of power as dialogic, multiple, ambivalent, and contradictory—"a repertoire of conflictual positions" which he understands in poststructuralist psychoanalytic terms.[3]

Bhabha sees these divisions and disunities as a result of an implicit interrogation of the dominant account by the weaker group (which itself is limited to reactive response, of which the best example is the complex act of mimicry, which I will examine later on). My model is broadly consistent with Bhabha's in these respects—hence his periodic appearance in these pages—but it is based on a different model of perception and thus centers on a different metaphor, the grotesque, which extends beyond the colonial relation. I argue throughout this book that the conflicted and divided mind of the dominant group—in this case, the Puritans—primarily arises from the very nature of the objectification project that they are attempting, as opposed to any specific action by the objectified other. My focus in this chapter is on the way the Puritans' imaginative construction of the Indians interacted with the realities of actual contact between the two groups. By trying to imagine people as nonhuman, the objectifier opens a Pandora's box and releases the grotesque. The problems that result are such that the simple presence of the objectified (and therefore grotesque) other will unbalance the edifice of asserted difference.

The Puritans place the Indians into an epistemological setup that creates tangled and unsolvable problems for both groups. For the Puritans, the attempt to objectify the Indians leads to unending cultural labor, shoring up a category system whose unsoundness continually erodes it, eating away at the foundation for their theocratic mission—even as it serves as a necessary support for that mission as they see it. As for the Indians, they face grave problems in the Puritan setup, for it essentially dooms them. They can't be themselves because that's not being human. But they can't be English either. A selective survey of Puritan writings will show that, to the English colonists, Indians are finally neither human nor inhuman. Seen alternately as one or the other, they come to occupy a halfway, anomalous status that has glimmers of humanity, but without the full attributes of that condition. These glimmerings create the liminal basis for the grotesque and provide myriad complications for both sides. Seen through Puritan eyes, the Indians become grotesque in-between figures, man-beasts whose descriptions recall the creatures of Greek mythology, or the fictional creations of H. G. Wells's Dr. Moreau.[4]

Puritan writings on Indians sometimes center on the capacity of the natives to convert to Christianity and so redeem their heathen souls. Though the Indians possess certain attributes of humanity in Puritan eyes that justified this effort, the colonists still try hard to see them as not completely human. Even so, I will argue that the grotesqueness of the Indians in the Puritans' eyes—resulting from the effort to see them as nonhuman—lands them in an anomalous area between categories in the Puritan scheme, and that the occupation of this liminal space effectively prevents the Puritans from seeing the Indians as unequivocally Christian. Betwixt and between the categories of human and beast, they are sentenced to a grotesque space. In other words, the potential Christianity of the Indians becomes a rhetorical smokescreen that obscures what is really happening at the same time behind it: an effort at objectification. But the objectification of human beings proves to be a most complicated business, for it involves the management of the unpredictable grotesque, which compromises the whole missionary effort.

Puritan rhetoric describing their own perception thus causes the Indians' humanity to become unstable within the New England system of values. Nowhere is their liminality more evident than in the captivity narrative, a genre the Puritans developed from biblical sources into a distinctive narrative genre that continues to thrive today. New England captivity narratives represent a historical showcase for growing tensions and ambivalence surrounding the Puritan views of Indians, and of the rest of their world. Through their ambivalent, liminal portrayals of Indians, captivity narratives offer a capsule view of the problem faced by later Puritan generations of maintaining the austere integrity of their original typological view of the world and the society that they built on it. These portrayals provided an outlet through which to describe a providential world, the religious society that the Puritans organized in it, and God's role in both. At the same time, as I will show, the genre appears at a critical moment, to help prop up that world at a time when Puritan political capital was diminishing at home and abroad, and their cosmology had come under intellectual attack.

Puritan perception of the Indians (and there was a wide range of it) consistently engages the idea of their grotesqueness, with judgment of them accordingly tempered by it, but the captivity narrative reveals exceptionally clearly the intense emotional effort behind the Puritan attempt at rigid categorization of Indians, and the ultimate failure of their effort to objectify their fellow humans. This failure to maintain the Indians in their category may be broadly transposed against the larger-scale disintegration of Puritan authority; the rhetorical failure to manage the Indians and keep them separate is thus representative in its way of the general breakdown of the Puritan political and ideological enterprise in America.

The Puritans' Indian experience obviously varied over time. It began before the two groups came into contact and ranged from long-distance constructions of Indian identity in terms favorable to Puritan motives, to anxiety-filled descriptions of first encounters with the "savages," to diverse accounts of the concerted Puritan effort to live alongside the Indians, trade with them, convert them, and at different times, to make war upon them. From the wondering and fearful early descriptions of Indians (often made from a distance) to the frustrations Cotton Mather expressed as he wrote much later of the activity of tribes both sympathetic and hostile, the Puritan culture's view of Indians is marked by an ambitious continuing attempt to order the world by objectifying the Indians who inhabit it. These efforts are repeatedly frustrated by the simple fact that the Indians are human, and their mere presence requires that the Puritans see them that way.

This conflicted view of the Indians is common to the diverse views of the natives over Puritan history. Cotton Mather's enormous historical efforts at retrospective unity notwithstanding, Puritan Indian policy was never monolithic. It oscillated within and across time, affected not only by the two Indian wars (the Pequot War of the mid-1630s and King Philip's campaign of 1675–76), but also by differences of opinion within the community at any given time.[5] My argument about Puritan Indian policy has three prongs: first, that all of these Puritan views of Indians—even the more humane ones—can be brought together and understood within the context of the encounter with the grotesque; and second, that the Puritan narrative of Indian captivity, a product of later generations, is the best place to do this. Third, I will suggest that the captivity narrative both expresses and tries to defend against the larger social anxiety over the intellectual decline in both America and England of the Puritan view of a world filled with divine signs and wonders, which were marked by "prodigies," the legitimacy of which came under increasing intellectual attack during the seventeenth century from the New Science. New England writing is thick with denial of the humanity of the Indians, but this rhetorical armor is not impenetrable; captivity narratives offer a particularly well-placed crack through which it is possible to see the

Fig. 2.1 The technological difference between the Puritans and the Indians is emphasized in this 1810 illustration of the two sides in King Philip's War. Engraving in Henry Trumbull, *History of the Discovery of America* (1810). (From the Rare Book Division, Library of Congress)

racial grotesque at its varied work. In this early American genre, captives open a window through which we can see the contorted workings of a classification process—and a society based on it—under stress.

I

Early Views: Neoclassical Heathen Monsters

The Puritan dehumanization of the Indians originated with the classification of them as lower beings. This view had its basis in the classical philosophy that mind should rule over body, and intellect over appetite. Those who fail to adhere to this dictum become savages by definition. To the Puritans, Indians lacked self-control and therefore occupied a lower category in the hierarchy of being from those who displayed this higher virtue. As a result, such "savages" were "potential human beings" only—that is, humans who did not live to the extent of their potential.

Aristotle says in his *Politics* that beings who fail to subordinate body to soul deserve to be enslaved. It is, he says, part of the natural order of things that such people *should* be reduced in status to the equivalent of property so that their will becomes subject to one with the proper balance of faculties. Even so, Aristotle explicitly maintains the human status of slaves. "A slave," he says, "is another's man who, being a human being, is also a possession."[6] The implicit tension in this view arises from the difficulty in fitting human beings into the latter category. It requires an argument to place them there.

Applying Aristotle's dictum within the Puritan world complicated and increased the tension contained within it. The individualistic worldview of Puritan theology held that each person has a unique and special relationship with God. Savages who live for body rather than soul, cannot—in the Puritan application of the classical schema—ever be good Christians without reversing that ordering. But for the Puritans, being a Christian essentially equals being a human being, for Christians use the human gift of reason to harness appetite and reach for the divine light. Thus, a declension in which savages lose their humanity in the Puritans' eyes becomes understandable.[7] (Though they saw the Indians as "being of the cursed race of Ham," the Puritans did not try to enslave them, choosing instead to make them and their ways taboo. Aristotle's reasoning provides a logical basis for the New Englanders' classification of the natives.)[8] Despite their status as possible Christians, the Indians are seen most often as others: creatures, animals, and as I will presently argue in more detail, monsters. William Bradford, in an early example, sees them as "savage barbarians . . . readier to fill [the colonists'] sides full of arrows than otherwise." Bradford's perception of Indian nature as violent clearly derives from the lack of self-control that makes them "savage" in his eyes; he describes them as "wild men" who are of a piece with the wild beasts that roam the "hideous and desolate wilderness" they inhabit.[9]

Less inflammatory rhetoric betrays similar assumptions. In "Reasons and Considerations Touching the Lawfulness of Removing Out of England into the Parts of America" (1622), Robert Cushman portrays the Indians as potential converts:

> And first, seeing we daily pray for the conversion of the heathens, we must consider whether there be not some ordinary means and course for us to take to convert them, or whether prayer for them be only referred to God's extraordinary work from heaven. Now it seemeth unto me that we ought also to

> endeavor and use the means to convert them, and the means cannot be used unless we go to them or they come to us; to us they cannot come, our land is full; to them we may go, their land is empty.[10]

This mandate is less charitable than its author might have supposed. Writing from England, Cushman cites the "emptiness" of the Indian lands, thereby ignoring the very presence of the Indians. The territory is "spacious and void," he tells us, traversed only by Indians and "wild beasts." Cushman's lumping together of the Indians and animals is worthy of notice. This metaphor participates centrally in the Puritans' concerted rhetorical and physical conquest of the land and its inhabitants, centering on the English process of designing and constructing a new and unfamiliar place as "New England." Cushman builds from this point to reasons for appropriating the land:

> [The Indians] are not industrious, neither have art, science, skill or faculty to use either the land or the commodities of it, but all spoils, rots, and is marred for want of manuring, gathering, ordering, etc. As the ancient patriarchs therefore removed from straiter places into more roomy, where the land lay idle and waste, and none used it, though there dwelt inhabitants by them (as Genesis 13:6, 11, 12, and 34:21, and 41:20), so it is lawful now to take a land which none useth, and make use of it.[11]

Cushman's argument (which John Winthrop, longtime governor of the Massachusetts Bay Colony, made in similar terms in 1629) assumes that those who do not use the land in European fashion must not possess human faculties of reason and industry, and (as we see from their equation with the beasts) such wild types must not be truly human at all.[12] Why, we might ask, does Cushman advocate conversion of such creatures? His land-grabbing wish does not easily accord with his wish to bring the heathen to salvation. There exists an uneasy tension in his argument between the desire to treat the Indians as persons and convert them and the countervailing desire to treat them as animals, sweep them out of the way, and occupy the land. In practice, the Indians' predictable unwillingness to part with their land helped the Puritans portray them as enemies of God rather than wayward would-be Christians.

Puritan typology significantly informs their treatment of the Indians. The typological search for symbolic meaning in all experience encourages categorization of everything and everybody in terms of the Puritans' millennial scheme of predestined history. Mitchell Breitwieser has observed the power of this kind of thinking to "subdu[e] fact with category"; its implied sense of divine right demands primacy, dominating other systems of interpretation.[13] Aided by the rhetorical dehumanization inflicted upon them, the Indians take a place in this scheme as selfish creatures of a wilderness that exists in order to be bent to God's will. Roy Harvey Pearce sums it up succinctly: "Convinced . . . of his divine right to Indian lands, the Puritan discovered in the Indians themselves evidence of a Satanic opposition to the very principle of divinity."[14] In such a calculus, it is at least as moral to kill such creatures as it would be to save them. As the heathen embodiments of sin from Bradford and Winthrop through later generations of Puritan writing, the Indians thereby become symbolic obstacles to the Puritans' North American experiment.

Seeing the Indians as constitutionally different has disturbing consequences for all Puritan discussion of them, even when the reference is intended as benign. Because the Indians fall under a different set of expectations, the Puritans generally see them as governed by a different set of norms. (The New Englanders actually passed laws forbidding the imitation or praise of Indian life.)[15] This difference tends to crowd out the companion notion that Indians are human beings, capable of a relationship with God. Given both similarities and differences between themselves and the Indians, the Puritans generally focused on the latter.

II

Later Difficulties: The Case of Cotton Mather

The early views of Bradford, Cushman, and Winthrop set the stage for conflict with the Indians. The writings of the first generation patriarchs, in some cases penned before the author ever set eyes on the Indians, are fueled by the felt necessity to organize the land—and its inhabitants—in clear and unambiguous fashion and prepare it for settlement. The Indians are thus assigned their space: below Puritan, and thus below human.

Two generations and two Indian wars later, Puritan patriarchs were still trying to enclose the Indians within a rigid semantic space set aside for them, but they were now doing so from the perspective of familiarity, usually leavened generously with contempt. Cotton Mather, the prolific historian and later-generation religious leader of an increasingly secular community, epitomizes this attempt to draw these harsh boundaries. I use Mather as the later generations' representative man here partly because he saw himself that way (and many historians have followed his lead), and also because his extraordinary output of public and private writing gives an unusually well-articulated picture of his mind at work.

Mather's Massachusetts had a permanent Indian presence within and without; a number of converted Indians lived within the Puritan community, and different tribes lived in territories adjacent to the colony. Mather himself drew a sharp distinction between these two groups. Judging from his diary accounts, he appears to have devoted a fair amount of time to the concerns of Christian Indians. (He even served as a Commissioner of Indian Affairs for the New England Company for a time, helping to "civilize" the Indians.) Besides writing various religious primers for translation into Indian languages, he lamented their drinking and "debauchery" (reproaching his fellow Christians publicly as well as privately for encouraging this), and provided regular reports on the progress of the Indians' religious education. He writes at one point of a gift of clothing to "a poor Mohegin Indian, and his wife, sojourning at *Braintree*," but with an instruction to the minister there to give it along with "the best instruction in Christianity."[16]

Mather's sympathy for Christian Indians is matched by a hostility for their "wild" counterparts unsurpassed in early American literature for its unremitting anger and harshness. Mather saw all unconverted Indians as enemies and subjected them to a withering rhetorical attack that was designed to push them as far from humanity as possible. For example, he uses his 1702 account of John Eliot's life as an opportunity to view the Indians from a degrading perspective of difference. Eliot (1604–1690) ministered to the Indians more vigorously than any other Puritan. He even learned their language, the lexicon of which Mather mocks.[17] Mather views Indian living conditions thus:

> They live in a Country, where *we* now have all the Conveniencies of human Life: But as for *them*, their *housing* is nothing but a few

Fig. 2.2 An 1856 rendering of the Puritan missionary John Eliot preaching to the Indians. Wood engraving in *Ballou's Pictorial Drawing-Room Companion* (April 12, 1856). (From the Library of Congress)

> *Mats* tied about *Poles* fastened in the *Earth*, where a good *Fire* is their *Bed Clothes* in the coldest Seasons; their *Clothing* is but a Skin of a Beast, covering their *Hind-parts*, their *Fore-parts* having but a little Apron, where Nature calls for Secrecy. (*Magnalia* 1:558; Mather's emphasis)

The details of this pointed rhetoric deserve close examination. Mather implies that the Puritan people live a "human life," while the Indians do not. The names given to the Indians' body parts, along with the contemptuous description of their clothes, emphasize bestiality. Mather even offers the suggestion that the very nature of the Indians is something other than human, an impression enforced by his account of the tribal medicine as conducted by "a *Priest* [note the echo of hated Papism], who has more Familiarity with Satan than his Neighbors; this Conjurer comes and Roars, and Howls, and uses Magical Ceremonies over the Sick Man" (*Magnalia* 1:505). Mather praises Eliot for "raising a Number of these Hideous Creatures, unto the *Elevations* of our Holy Religion" (*Magnalia* 1:505), but from the tone of his account one might assume that he was wondering why Eliot bothered. Mather's description of the Indians as "hideous creatures" is only the most explicit signal of a transformation accomplished by means of an unrelenting series of rhetorical blows. This pummeling drives the Indians from the human realm and reduces them to monster status.[18]

Mather certainly projected onto the Indians some of his anger and frustration at the steady decline in religious faith he was living through and witnessing in the Massachusetts Bay Colony, a declension that has been much studied since. In *The Puritan Ordeal*, Andrew Delbanco tracks the changing Puritan views of evil and sin, a back-and-forth movement from an emphasis on privation (lack of grace) to the opposite view relying on an outside agent (Satan). Mather's view of the "heathen" Indians typifies the latter tendency—increasingly relied upon in later Puritan generations—to view evil in reified form, as the ultimate threat from the outside.

This view would help to explain Mather's fascination with Indian "evil." In September 1715, Mather wrote a letter describing the atrocities accompanying an Indian uprising in North Carolina as "*Barbarities* . . . too hideous to be related." But then he gives some juicy details anyway, of the torture of a woman slowly burned to death and forced to cannibalize her child, after which her husband was also "Barbiku[ed]."[19] Though he admits the Indians were provoked, he sees their deeds as having independent significance. This passage is fairly typical of Mather's frequent and explicit descriptions of Indian torture. He takes the time to describe it in order to fan the flames of his own anger.

Mather's bifurcation of the Native American population into "wild" and "civilized" Indians is a crucial part of his rhetorical strategy. By dividing the Indians he knows (and whose humanity he would have trouble denying) from the undifferentiated group he does not know, he creates "inside" and "outside" categories, a structure that provides support for the attempt to objectify the latter group.[20] Because of their different customs in war and peace, the Indians become a suitable repository for Mather's rage at the evil forces that he saw in the way of a Puritan society which had long been declining in theological vigor.

There is great general importance to Mather's rhetorical example. Put simply, objectification makes monsters. The Puritans wrote no fiction, but they clearly anticipated one of the essential requirements of the Gothic: if you're going to make an entity truly menacing, it helps to create it as something not-human. Mather's efforts notwithstanding, the problem is that the Indians usually don't stay where they are placed. They continually complicate the equation by reasserting their humanity in Puritan eyes, which makes their monstrosity highly problematic.

Noel Carroll defines monsters in his study of the horror genre as entities both physically threatening and ontologically impure. The first characteristic is simple. The Indians obviously threaten the Puritans; they often kill the settlers and stand as a perceived (and real) threat to Puritan plans to establish a God-fearing community in New England. Following Mary Douglas, Carroll describes impurity as the breach of ontological categories. To Carroll, a monster must fall outside the categories that classify the natural world. The pod-people of *Invasion of the Body Snatchers*, for example, bridge the categories of animal, vegetable, and human. Their anomalousness makes them "impure," and this impurity, coupled with the threat they represent, makes them monsters.[21] This modern analysis is generally consistent with the definition of monstrosity in Puritan times, but for the Puritans and their contemporaries, "unnatural" monstrosity had a strong divine component.

Monsters played an important role in Puritan thought from its English beginnings onward. The Puritan view of monsters grew from common European religious roots. Following from beliefs that were widespread in England and France during the early modern period, monsters were seen as divine portents. Monstrous births and people with odd bodies (the "freaks" of later generations)—as well as anomalous animals—were grouped with disruptive and difficult-to-explain natural occurrences like earthquakes, floods, comets, apparitions, and the like as "prodigies." In the fifteenth century, prodigies had apocalyptic connotations; they were seen to herald the day of doom and the ascent of the elect, associations that would obviously have been particularly hospitable to the Calvinist theology of the Puritans. By the early sixteenth century, the general lesson conveyed by prodigies, drawn from

Augustine, came to be that all of nature is "a cipher" that reflects the will of God. Preternatural and supernatural phenomena were thus seen as actions taken by God in the human world.[22]

The American Puritans, whose need to see the hand of God at work was an integral part of their theology, adopted this general interpretation of prodigies with deep conviction. They used accounts of prodigies and other wonders for evangelical ends. In *Wonder-Working Providence*, for example, Edward Johnson interpreted a plague of ravenous caterpillars as a divine judgment against Puritan overreaching into the wilderness.[23] In another well-documented instance, John Winthrop reported on the stillborn "monster" born to Anne Hutchinson in 1638. Hutchinson, whose unconventional religious views—which Winthrop calls "errors" —provoked the Antinomian Crisis in Massachusetts and resulted in her eventual exile to Rhode Island, gave birth to a "woman child" whose spectacular deformity Winthrop records literally from head to toe:

> It had a face, but no head, and the ears stood upon the shoulders and were like an ape's; it had no forehead but over the eyes four horns, hard and sharp; two of them were above one inch long, the other two shorter; the eyes standing out, and the mouth also; the nose hooked upward; all over the breast and back full of sharp pricks and scales, like a thornback; the navel and all the belly, with the distinction of the sex, were where the back should be, and the back and hips before, where the belly should have been; behind, between the shoulders, it had two mouths, and in each of them a piece of red flesh sticking out; it had arms and legs as other children; but instead of toes, it had on each foot three claws, like a young fowl, with sharp talons.[24]

Thomas Laqueur links the grotesque body of the child to the "perverted" beliefs that the Puritan elders attributed to her mother, but the significance of the birth in Winthrop's eyes went further than that. The governor drew the child's death in the womb together with a shaking of the bed and a "noisome savor" in the room, and he used its appearance to account for the "extreme vomiting and purging" of the women on the scene, as well as with the convulsions suffered by the children ("which they never had before nor after"). In all, he saw "a providence of God" in the birth that was consistent with similar prodigious events in the past, by which "God might intend only the instruction of the parents, and such other to whom it was known."[25] This view was fully consistent with the treatment of prodigies at the time.

Interpretations like Winthrop's were common in the early years of the Reformation, when monsters were seen exclusively as prodigies and thus as signs of God's angry or benevolent will. Led by the New Science of the Enlightenment (which pulled popular culture behind it) these portentous interpretations gave way in the sixteenth and seventeenth centuries to a more rational view of monstrosities and other surprising events as natural occurrences, not the products of specific divine interventions. Though the Puritans were generally friendly to new scientific developments, they were less than welcoming of the scientific shift away from the religious interpretation of prodigies.[26] As I will suggest later in this chapter, this shift caused ideological pressure that affected the rise of Indian captivity narratives and the use of the vocabulary of prodigies to describe Indians.

Perhaps Cotton Mather could objectify the Indians easily and unequivocally because he was at a physical and historical distance from the "wild" Indians he writes so angrily about. Mather was drawn early to the captivity narrative because of its didactic possibilities, but the captivity narratives he wrote on the basis of interviews he conducted with the freed prisoners (and there were many of these) display little of the ambiguity surrounding the Indians that I will highlight presently in non-ghost-written narratives. His descriptions of New England captivity experiences among the Indians (many of which were later collected in the *Magnalia*) read chiefly as tendentious propaganda whose main goal is to describe the unnatural murders and tortures committed by monsters. Unsurprisingly, Mather does not shrink from the use of that epithet to describe the Indians, and makes a continuing rhetorical effort to cast the Indians as monstrous, threatening, and separate.

The total picture of Puritan-Indian relations was of course quite different. The two societies did not live such separate lives (as Mather would have it in his rhetorical construction). They traded and negotiated with each other. Puritans and Indians even lived in one another's communities to a limited extent. The Puritans had a problem with defection in this regard. Many New Englanders taken captive by the Indians simply chose to stay with them, often escaping back to the wilderness after their "redemption."[27] Mather's orotund descriptions mask the activity that was always taking place on the Puritan-Indian boundary, activity that makes it difficult to separate the Indians from their human identity. Such difficulty breeds the lingering tension characteristic of the grotesque, a tension clearly visible in Puritan narratives of Indian captivity.

III

Captivity Narratives: The Grotesque Tension of a Human Monster

Captivity narratives became popular during the late seventeenth century, a time when Puritan society was becoming increasingly secular. Mary Rowlandson's famous narrative of her time among the Wampanoags during King Philip's War (1675–76) was the first Puritan captivity narrative to be published as a single book, inaugurating a long and successful genre whose popularity continued well beyond the end of the Indian wars, and of Puritan culture itself.

The Puritan authors of firsthand captivity narratives, a small group who experienced prolonged close contact with Indians, have considerable trouble keeping the Indians in the narrow rhetorical space marked "inhuman." Captivity narrators seem almost confused about how to classify their captors and, by implication, themselves. Their perceptions of Indians flash back and forth from monster to human and back again. Indeed, the captivity narrative turns out to be the site where this tense ambivalence can be best viewed. It serves as a microcosm of the Puritans' tortured and conflicted struggle with the objectification of the Indians at a time when their own ideology—and the society that was built on it—was threatened by increasing secularization at home and religious and intellectual hostility in England after the Restoration.[28]

Because Mather separates the Indians he knows (the converted ones) from those he does not, he succeeds in keeping his human sympathies largely separate from his epistemological views, which in turn allows him to subject the Indians to a sustained verbal thrashing. Captivity narrators simply cannot do this. They live amongst the Indians, albeit involuntarily, and this proximity affords irresistible evidence of Indian humanity. In *The Redeemed Captive Returning to Zion* (1707), John Williams initially sees from the perspective of difference. He refers to the Indians as "an evil," and "the Enemy"—as opposed to "the Soldiers" on his own side. The lack of a plural in the former instance signifies an undifferentiated Indian mass, a horde of creatures. His impression of the Indians is limited to their "Painted Faces, and hideous Acclamations."[29] Nor does Williams stint from describing the fate of those in his party, including his wife, who is tomahawked to death by "a cruel and bloodthirsty savage" when she loses her strength to travel (176). In this first part of Williams's narrative, the Indians personify the worst kind of menace.

But Williams's tone changes, and his focus shifts. Though he continues to cite instances of Indian brutality as captors and captives march toward Montreal, Williams dwells at greater length upon the kindnesses extended to him by his captors. He notes that his young daughter was "looked after with a great deal of tenderness," and that the Indians carry his son even when they themselves are obviously fatigued (179). (The daughter, Eunice, would remain with the Indians and eventually join them despite her father's later negotiations and entreaties.)[30] For his own part, Williams observes that his own master "would always give me the best he had to eat" (180). His captor also gives him a fragment of the Bible and permits him to pray. When Williams is too tired to keep up the pace of the march, his master allows him an unsupervised head start rather than kill him. This succession of humane references by Williams builds considerable sympathy for the Indians after his astringent beginning.

Williams first encourages the reader to see the Indians as fiends, and then as human beings capable of kindness. What causes this discrepancy? The answer lies in the broad conflict that fuels this book, the collision between the human inclination to divide and rank, and the competing human tendency to perceive the world anthropomorphically. The first behavior leads to "us-them" divisions that quickly slide toward "us-it" polarizations—an attempt to deny humanity. But anthropomorphic perception does the opposite; when people look at the world in terms of the human, they affirm humanity as they seek it.[31]

This conflict leads to the dynamic instability of the grotesque, simultaneously the source of the Indians' monstrosity and humanity. The grotesque emerges from a category system that strives unsuccessfully for clearly defined categories and absolute values. It is the undefinable anomaly that refuses to stay within the margins of the most important categories: life/death, human/nonhuman, and other crucial divisions. The grotesque is capable of generating monsters because it is a product of the human category system. The effect results from play with the boundaries of this system, arising when fundamental categories are threatened by unclassifiable anomalies.

Consider how the Indians become grotesque to the Puritans. The New Englanders define themselves as the chosen people, a distinct and special group. The Indians live outside that group, both literally and (especially) figuratively. The Puritans define their own ways as normal and human. Indian ways thus become associated with the abnormal, even the inhuman, and become taboo threats to New England culture. But the example of John Williams illustrates how difficult it is *not* to see the Indians as people, all their perceived (and often actual) cruelty notwithstanding. The idea that the Indians are closer to them than they outwardly acknowledge constantly threatens the Puritan system of meaning and belief. The figurative component of the Indians' outsiderness accordingly receives special cultural support and maintenance. As threats to English culture and tradition, the Indians are deemed monstrous; even so, the Puritans can never completely deny their humanity. It soon becomes clear that the Indians don't fit any mold: and that is precisely what makes them grotesque.[32]

This argument follows from Edward Said's analysis in *Orientalism* of how a dominant culture constructs a version of the subjugated group that is designed to meet its own ideological needs, but there is a difference here: Said's opposing groups are geographically far apart, while the Indians and the Puritans live right next to, even among, one another. Said specifically points out that the physical distance of the Orient from Europe makes it easier to maintain the Western idea of the exoticism of the place. The experience of the American Puritans illustrates how important that distance is. Inversely, the physical presence (and evident humanity) of the Indians in America discombobulates the Puritans' attempts to objectify them, thereby showing how much easier it is dehumanize (or demonize) people when you don't actually have to spend time with them. (The later success of the freak show depends on this.) In light of the Puritans' difficulties (and those of American slaveholders later on), it is clear that proximity creates complications that will turn the cultural other into a grotesque.

For the Puritans, with their extremely rigid category system, the grotesque (which sits astride categories) would be especially distressing. The sobriquet "Puritan" (which the group did not use themselves) suggests how much the community valued order. The American Puritans journeyed to the New World in part because they assumed that it could be set up as they wished, according to their typological organizing plan. Even that which could not be understood could still be given its role in the divine plan (perhaps to be interpreted by later savants), but that which could not even be categorized presented a more serious problem. Typology offered the Puritans more than a method; it gave them a peculiar and special reason for categorizing the Indians the way that they did, and a special need to do so. The grotesque, with its tense bridging of basic categories, created great cultural anxiety for the Puritans, as is clear from the rhetorical and emotional extremes they reach in their writings about Indians.

IV

Strategies for Managing the Monster

Mary Rowlandson's well-known 1682 captivity narrative is a significant example of a Puritan struggling to manage the grotesque in a difficult practical situation.[33] Rowlandson's captivity (which lasted around two months) places her into prolonged and direct contact with hated and feared Indians. She cannot banish them from her presence, so what else can she do? Her response reflects a divided consciousness. Like John Williams, she first objectifies the Indians, and then sees them escape their category. Faced with their anomalous status and her growing similarity to them, Rowlandson comes to recognize qualities in herself that she would have denied before her captivity. Though she apparently regains her equilibrium by the end of her narrative when she is "restored," it is clear that her experience with the grotesque seriously destabilizes her world.

At first, the Indians are intruders in Rowlandson's world. Then she becomes part of theirs, bending and blurring her own categories to justify what she must do out of necessity. The first response to a stimulus that does not fit existing categories—a potential threat—is to create a new slot for it. Such contradictions must be expected, and any classificatory system must be flexible enough to accommodate them, at least until it is decided what to do with them. Claude Lévi-Strauss suggests that this procedure is normal and expected, for "it would be a remarkable coincidence if a harmonious synthesis of the social and natural order

Fig. 2.3 Frontispiece from Frederic Manheim's 1794 captivity narrative, *Affecting History of the Dreadful Distresses of Frederic Manheim's Family . . . with an Account of the Destruction of the Settlements at Wyoming*. Manheim's family was captured in the Indian attack in Pennsylvania's Wyoming Valley. The graphic depiction of Indian torture reflects the increasing emphasis on the sensational as the captivity narrative gradually became a secular genre. (From the collection of the American Antiquarian Society; reproduced courtesy of the American Antiquarian Society)

were to be achieved at once."[34] Rowlandson's behavior throughout her narrative suggests an ongoing unconscious attempt to reclassify the Indians, to find a space into which they will fit.

Rowlandson's account of her kidnapping and captivity points to her clear awareness of the rhetorical power of objectification. Her first paragraphs feature a forceful flurry of objectifying rhetoric so intense that it allows the Indians no hope for full membership in her category of humanity. She starts by describing her attackers as cannibals ("gaping before us . . . to devour us" [34]). She then fires off a rapid salvo of animal comparisons, in which the Indians are described as "wolves," "ravenous beasts," "black creatures," and "hellhounds, roaring, singing, ranting, and insulting, as if they would have torn our very hearts out" (35–36). She calls their dancing hell-inspired, and their behavior "inhumane," savage, and brutish. This unrelenting hail of epithets comes down on the Indian "pagans" within about two pages. Rowlandson's tongue-lashing is an attack delivered in compensation for the one she receives at the Indians' hands. Its intensity recalls the flammable extremes of Cotton Mather's anti-Indian rhetoric.

Rowlandson turns the Indians into monsters, but the transformation doesn't take. Instead, it is followed by a peculiar ambiguity: once she objectifies the Indians, she proceeds to interact with them as human beings. She never resolves the tension between her early rhetoric and her later behavior and descriptions; indeed, how could she? This tension follows human objectification everywhere. Humans, it seems, do not easily conform to nonhuman categories.

What if an anomaly-inspired contradiction cannot be resolved? What if the tension it forms with the system will not go away? Rowlandson's dealings with the Indians raise these questions. When classified, a thing is defined through its relation to other things. The threat to the organization of people and things is ameliorated. Ambiguity is averted, and order is saved. When the system cannot accomplish this rescue, the tension between system and anomaly remains—and the threat is renewed with force all the greater for its continuing resistance. The grotesque, with its unresolved tension and its tenuous perch on the fence dividing the acceptable and the forbidden, thus constitutes an attack on the fundaments of culture itself. Rowlandson reacts to this assault on her beliefs by reconceiving her relationship with the Indians. This movement toward a new perspective has two related vectors: the Indians approach her human status, and she moves toward their monstrous one.

Perhaps the most important human attributes Rowlandson gives to the Indians are names. In addition to King Philip, the chief of the tribe, Rowlandson refers by name to Quanopin, her master, and his squaw, Weetamoo. Such references are uncommon in Puritan writings about Indians, and with good reason: more than any other gesture, naming confers individuality, a prerequisite for humanity. Rather than representing the typologically inspired agents of sin, the Indians gain the individuality of personality. Rowlandson's narrative in fact draws several of them quite distinctly.

These portraits include details of kindness and respect. Like John Williams, Rowlandson cannot help noticing when her captors are nice to her. During the Nineteenth Remove (i.e., movement) of her party, for example, King Philip buoys Rowlandson's sagging confidence with reassuring words and actions. "He fetched me some water himself and bid me wash and gave me the glass to see how I looked and bid his squaw give me something to eat" (60–61). Jane Tompkins finds significance in Rowlandson's informal mien when she earlier meets King Philip for the first time,[35] but in this second instance she seems fully aware that the chief himself is ministering to her needs. She is honestly grateful for "this favor showed me." Weetamoo, who appears to treat Rowlandson well, receives likewise dignified treatment in the narrative. Rowlandson describes her toilette in elegant terms, and calls her "a severe and proud dame"(61).

Much of the generosity shown Rowlandson centers on exchange with the Indians, and much of this exchange centers on food. Breitwieser has analyzed in detail Rowlandson's entry into the Indian economy. He says that such exchange "pries her loose" from her typological ways of looking at the Indians.[36] It is certainly true that in exchanging with the Indians, Rowlandson must de-objectify them to a considerable extent, but it is possible that the process was going on before that. Guthrie argues that when people look at the world, we *want* to see other people. "Removed" and separated from her family and everything that is familiar to her, Rowlandson would surely have wanted to feel that she was conducting her dealings with fellow humans, but she might simply have wanted human company. Perceiving the Indians as human gives her a certain kind of companionship.

The result of Rowlandson's exchanges is very important: she does what the Indians do, eats what they eat, and even enjoys it, as she frankly acknowledges. Through this participation in Indian culture, she edges toward the Indian category in her own mind. Rowlandson's bartering (and also her treatment as a captive) lead her to eat barely cooked, bloody horse liver in Indian fashion (45), horse's feet (60), and bear meat (47, 49). Furthermore, she *likes* this food. To the surprise of the Indian who gives her the liver off the coals ("'What,' says he, 'can you eat horse liver?' " [45]), she finds it "a savory bit." Despite earlier misgivings about eating bear, Rowlandson says that she "never tasted pleasanter meat in my life" (47, 49). Rowlandson uses biblical typology to account for many of her actions in captivity, but not for her "wolfish appetite" (57), a simile that rhetorically places her in Indian company.

But not even typology prevents the commingling of English and Indian worlds in Rowlandson's life. When she uses a biblical verse to compare the taste of offal to honey (59), for example, her textual justification repays close attention. On the one hand, Rowlandson is using the Bible to place the offal into a scheme that is comprehensible to her. But the conversion is not just metaphoric: she really does like the taste, suggesting that biblical defenses notwithstanding, her experience breaks down the boundaries between her "civilized" world and the Indian way of life. Her encounter with the grotesque thus leads to an intimate relationship with it.

In *Purity and Danger*, Mary Douglas describes how cultures protect themselves against anomalies. Her book can be read as a handbook of the ways that groups confront the grotesque. Following Lévi-Strauss, Douglas sees a basic cultural need for order through categories, postulating that "it is part of our human condition to long for hard lines and clear concepts."[37] Her focus on the exceptions rather than the rules of the system makes her work especially valuable to understanding the grotesque. Douglas suggests that progressively more stringent lines of defense are thrown up against such exceptions. The first attempt is to try to create a new category. If this strategy does not resolve the conflict, the possible solutions become more drastic. Another possibility is to resolve the ambiguity through brute strength, forcing the issue in favor of one interpretation of the anomaly. This tactic can take extreme forms in some cases, such as the strategy of the Nuer tribe for dealing with deformed births. They "treat monstrous births as baby hippopotamuses, accidentally born to humans, and with this labelling, the appropriate action is clear. They gently lay them in the river where they belong."[38] Besides skirting ambiguity, such responses have the additional virtue of strengthening the original system of definition through successful confrontation of a difficult epistemological challenge.

The Nuer practice of selective infanticide recalls Winthrop's classification of Anne Hutchinson's stillbirth as a prodigy. The comparison reveals some of the important cultural work done by prodigies in Puritan society. Hutchinson's deformed baby, a "monster" in Winthrop's eyes, is assigned a place in the divine plan that gives the anomaly a purpose in the New England millennial scheme. Similarly, when Cotton Mather spotted a cabbage shaped like a cutlass shortly before King Philip's War, he retrospectively characterized this prodigy as a divine portent of the conflict.[39] Such examples demonstrate the American Puritans' strong collective need to bring anomalies into the service of their self-identified goals. The rhetoric of prodigies was notably useful for their evangelical purposes—so useful, in fact, that the Puritans also used it to describe the Indians, whose depiction as "monsters" has been in evidence throughout this chapter. Winthrop, for example, compares Hutchinson's child to an ape, while he describes the Indians as "beastlike men."[40] In this important respect, monstrous births and monstrous humans were of a piece. But they were also breeds apart at the same time. Though the Indians were obviously anomalous for the Puritans, they were *not* prodigies, not wondrous phenomena reflecting specific divine intervention in the natural world. It is thus highly significant that the Puritans described the Indians in the same vocabulary that they used for certain kinds of prodigies. This rhetorical extension shows the importance of clarity and resolution of category problems in the Puritan worldview, and the value of the discourse of prodigies as a kind of template to resolve the anomalies that interfered with these goals.

Rowlandson's captivity narrative offers a striking example of the Puritan effort to employ the vocabulary of prodigies to manage anomalies, and also of the practical limitations of this effort. These limitations expose an unusual tension in the operation of these defensive strategies. Rowlandson is obviously in a position of weakness when she is among the Indians. She can't impose her beliefs on them, so she joins them, if only for a while. Her view of them as monsters is only temporary, then, preceding her own entry into their group. This flexible strategy allows her to accommodate, but at the price of the powerfully resonant contradictions within her descriptions of the Indians.

This flexibility is displayed even more prominently—and with many fewer contradictions—in John Gyles's 1736 captivity narrative, *Memoirs of Odd Adventures, Strange Deliverances, etc.*[41] Gyles maintains an anthropologist's tone of tolerant involvement even when he is describing Indian practices horrific to Puritan sensibilities, such as eating dog brains raw as a preparation for battle (120). He respects Indian practices ranging from the practical (such as food preservation) to the mythic (he recounts Indian fables [115–16]) and the ritual (the marriage ceremony, for example [121]). Even his own cruel early treatment receives a calm explanation of its regulation: "A captive among the Indians is exposed to all manners of abuse and to the utmost tortures unless his master . . . lay down a ransom such as a bag of corn . . . by which they may redeem them from their cruelties" (100). Most important is what makes this respect possible for Gyles: a rare ability among Puritans to view the Indians in their own context. For a time, Gyles actually becomes a "White Indian"—the label given by colonists to those who joined Native American tribes—but his shifting social memberships show his remarkable cultural flexibility, a flexibility that allows him to maintain real empathy for both Indians and whites.[42] Perhaps Gyles found this balancing act possible because he was taken captive at the impressionable age of ten and held for a long time (six years, plus three more among the French). Remarkably, he remains friends with his Indian master after his redemption and welcomes him to his home over two decades later (125).[43]

The example of Gyles shows that Puritan objectification of Indians is not necessarily inevitable. But Gyles, who went on to make a career in between cultures as an interpreter and negotiator for more than fifty years after rejoining New England society, had a rare comfort on the cultural margins. The exceptional qualities of his personality and experience contrast sharply with those of the equally exceptional but more orthodox Cotton Mather, who wrote and edited many captivity narratives in his Manichaean style. Comparing Gyles and Mather pits the exception against the rule and underscores the fact that Indian objectification was a matter of normal course in New England. It follows that the Puritan way of looking at the world must have encouraged the practice. Cultural formation is of course not rational—there need be no logical reason for a given social practice—but it is guided by imperatives. In the case of the Puritans, the religious ideology that underlaid their statecraft and the territorial demands that emerged from it made human objectification into an attractive alternative, a seemingly efficient way of banishing anomalies from a belief structure that could ill tolerate their presence.

The foregoing examples show that not every threat to order can be overcome by the means at hand. Puritan captives of Indians had to forge a new relationship with the grotesque to replace the socially mediated one they had when they were at home. The polarized view of Indians as monstrous heathen (against their own civilized example) generates plenty of contradiction even within the safe confines of Puritan society, but it is clearly inadequate to handle the experience of captivity within the Indian community. The captives find that the former edges of their existence (the wilderness and its inhabitants) move to the center of their lives and perceptions. For them, Indians must be reckoned with not just as monsters but also as humans, not just as typological concepts of sin but as part of real life, with all of its uncertainties.

These examples show that the grotesque qualifies as an anomaly of the most fundamental sort, threatening always to disrupt the consistency of our expectations. As long as categories exist, so must the grotesque. The condition of its definition is that it cannot be resolved, which brings us back to the original problem of how to deal with anomalies that resist assimilation. According to Douglas, such phenomena are labeled "dangerous" and assume a forbidden status within the culture. They are thus rendered separate and placed outside the whole: unable to be exterminated according to the rules of the system, they are instead exiled from it.

Like Geertz, Douglas finds religious implications in these divisions. She defines religion as an expression of the human urge to create a common unity of experience—as the classificatory urge does. In Douglas's model, religion safeguards the cultural apprehension of the universe defined by a culture's system of classification. Thus, clean is sacred, and dirt, born of disorder, is unholy and dangerous.

Even with this separation, there remains a necessity for contact between the two realms. According to Douglas, the crucial rules governing the transgression of the boundary between the two form the genesis of taboo. Where the forbidden exists there must also be a mechanism in place for contact with it, even if that contact is only to keep it away.

Therefore, even exile cannot drive anomalies out completely, especially with new ones always on the horizon. The boundaries separating the clean from the unclean require constant policing. Taboos provide the guide to staying within bounds.

Puritan treatment of the Indians conforms to Douglas's theories of division nicely, and in the process illustrates the persistence of the grotesque on the boundaries. The Indians were obviously "dangerous" to the Puritans, and were kept on the literal and figurative edges of New England. But the Indians could not be banished so easily. The Puritan and Indian communities meshed at their borders; trade brought them into contact, as did war. Very often the Puritans brought Indians under the jurisdiction of their legal system. Furthermore, a few members of each group were always living among the other, sometimes voluntarily and sometimes not, and this overlap created further problems.[44] Were Puritan members of the Indian community treated as heathen monsters? Were the few Indian converts living with the settlers viewed as full members of the New England polity? The answer is "no" in both cases, but granting the very presence of such exceptions blurred the boundary between English ("human") self and Indian monster.

"Cultures," says Edward Said, "have always been inclined to impose complete transformations on other cultures, receiving these other cultures not as they are but as, for the benefit of the receiver, they ought to be." This accurately describes the Puritans' Indian agenda, but not the historical result. The Puritan attempt to define the Indians broke down because of proximity. The Puritans could not maintain the idea that "'we' are this" and "'they' are that" because the two cultures lived in the same place and did so in many of the same ways. Ironically, many of the similarities were, as James Axtell shows, due to Indian tutelage of the colonists. The polar divisions sought by the Puritans (we are people, the Indians are not) were too extreme in the face of the reality of their cohabitation.[45]

Managing the meaning of "Indian" thus became a constant epistemological chore for the Puritans. The monsterhood of the Indians needed always to be reinforced against the reality of human contact with them. The grotesque tension of the Indians' otherness became like a spring that keeps bouncing back and forth between monstrosity and humanity, a motion driven by what Michael Zuckerman calls the "moral centrifuge of [the settlers'] own making."[46] The result is that the Indians never fit anywhere in the Puritan worldview. They were tabooed others who generated a lot of attention because they were also potential civilized beings—and try as they might, the Puritans could never completely distance themselves from this fact. These two views of the Indians (as irredeemably savage and potentially Christian like everyone else) coexisted with extreme difficulty, but even so, the two ultimately were never separated.

One might argue that I have exaggerated Puritan enmity for the Indians by focusing primarily on their view of them as savage monsters, and not enough on the New Englanders' actual efforts to convert them and so bring them under the Christian (i.e., human) heading. To be sure, the Puritans sometimes spoke benignly about the Indians. They did put together a missionary movement to convert them, though it never gained any real momentum. The missionary cause also gave the Indians some good press. Prominent ministers like John Cotton and Thomas Shepard went on record as viewing the Indians as dwelling just a step outside the human fold, ready to be brought into its confines. Thomas Morton, though not a Puritan, described New World Indians in the Old World terms of the noble savage. The Indians were even analogized to the Jews; a theory of their Jewish origins was offered as a justification for the attempt to convert them. (Conversion of the Jews was considered a prerequisite for Christ's appearance on earth at the Last Judgment.) This theory was popular for a time during the mid-seventeenth century, even leading a New England authority on Indians like John Eliot to include the natives in the covenant promise of God to Abraham. William Wood described the Indians in a 1634 advertisement for New England as "affable, courteous, and well disposed," though as Robert Berkhofer argues, such early portrayals were colored by the self-interested desire to encourage English immigration to America.[47]

With high-level encouragement such as this, why was the Puritan missionary movement weak? Part of the problem may center in language. The Puritan emphasis on understanding the Word meant that the Indians essentially had to master English in order to be converted.[48] But a greater problem, I think, was the cross-cutting, conflicted set of motives that plagued the Puritan missionary project from the beginning. Cushman, for example, speaks of converting the Indians in almost the same breath as he advocates taking their lands; similarly, John Cotton cautions in "God's Promise to His Plantations" (1630) that the New

Englanders "offend not the poor natives, but as you partake in their land, so make them partakers in your precious faith." Conversion is invoked as a pious motive then, but it is clearly and uneasily implicated with a self-interested desire to erase the Indians from the land. Berkhofer says that the Virginia settlers painted the Indians as the devil's servants even as they tried to bring the natives over to their own ways; extending his observation to the Puritans reinforces my point that the New Englanders were engaged in doublethink—that they attempted to view the Indians simultaneously as monsters *and* potential Christians. Their approach, as I have said, transforms the Indians into an anomalous group that resonates with unstable, uncertain, grotesque difference. Even those Puritans with liberal notions about the Indians had to grapple with the cultural presumption that the Indians were less than human, a belief that surely hindered missionary efforts. Possessing qualities of both humanity and objectified monstrosity, the Indians finally don't fit into either category.[49]

Analyzing Columbus's encounter with the Indians in 1492, Tzevetan Todorov argues that Columbus saw the Indians alternately as fully human (that is, potentially Spanish) or fundamentally inferior. For Todorov, the key point is that both of these views have their basis in Columbus himself, in the outward projection of his "I." This opposition is not stable, however. Todorov observes that Columbus ultimately "shift[s] from assimilationism . . . to an ideology of enslavement," which assures the Indians' inferiority.[50]

The Puritans follow the same basic pattern. I have argued throughout that this shift takes place because the idea of "thing-ness" pervades Puritan perceptions of Indians and infects the corresponding view of "potential" humanity. The imbalance thus generated explains why the Indians' "potential Christianity" did little to prevent their consequent liminality. It would have been enormously difficult for a Puritan to regard a dangerous monster as a possible Christian whose potential for piety equaled her own. How easy could it be to expect a nonhuman to be able to experience a conversion that would make him human? The Reverend Charles Ingles suggested how large this task might have looked when he wrote of the Indians in 1770 that "in order to make them Christians, they must first be made Men."[51]

It follows that an Indian who became "civilized" would nevertheless be viewed with suspicion by the Puritans. This was in fact the case.

Rowlandson uses the categories of "Friend-Indian" and "Praying-Indian" to describe such characters. The nomenclature, which was common Puritan usage, is most revealing: despite their Christianity, these Indians cannot escape their "Indian" category. Their separateness from the English was further emphasized by the Puritans' physical segregation of them in "Praying Towns," in which they were taught "civilized" ways under special laws. Such towns (of which Natick, Massachusetts, was the first) were designed for the Indians "to live in an orderly way *amongst us*" (emphasis added).[52] Again, the phrasing says a great deal: the Indians couldn't be members of the Puritan "us," even when they chose to live within its geographic and ideological boundaries. Even reclassified, the implication is that such Indians were still unbelieving savages. They remained anomalies.[53]

Rowlandson regards these converts with extreme distrust, in part, it should be said, because some of them really were spies. Converted Indians received Christian names from the English, and Rowlandson uses these names to address them. Even so, their Christian status is permanently tainted in her eyes. She details the iniquities of supposedly pious Praying Indians at some length in her narrative (Vaughan and Clark, eds., *Puritans Among the Indians*, 62–63). The few she trusts, she does so "though they were Indians" (61). Rowlandson's reaction is the inevitable product of what Bhabha calls "flawed colonial mimesis, in which to be Anglicized is *emphatically* not to be English." Though the colonial program called for the Indians to act English, Rowlandson's reaction shows that even when they do this, they become dangerous, not assimilated. Her fear of Praying Indians is a powerful illustration of the way that for the colonizer, acts of mimicry by the colonized ("a difference that is almost the same, but not quite") easily slide toward menace. Bhabha ties the effectiveness of mimicry to a certain intentionality on the part of the colonized, but this example suggests that mimicry's subversive potential may instead be tied more closely to the colonizer.[54] Rowlandson's Praying Indians may truly be on her side, but whether they are or not, there is nothing they can do that would convince her of their allegiance. She sees their English-looking actions as dangerous.

Breitwieser suggests that Praying Indians served a synechdochic function in Puritan society, as a designated (and readily available) object of fear and loathing.[55] "Little do many think what is the savageness and brutishness of this barbarous enemy," writes Rowlandson (36). She suspects that the converted Indians are only acting a role, that their true savage nature remains unchanged underneath the religious veneer. Her passionate stance conforms with my argument that the rigid Puritan classification system prevents the Indians from ever attaining full human status within it.

Ironically, the Indians harbored no such hostility toward the New Englanders. James Axtell details the ways that Indians assimilated their captives, bringing them into their society as equals. The strength of the attachment of these Puritan initiates to their adopted society can be measured by the colonists' justified fears of their escape back into it, even after being ransomed.[56] The difference in the treatment of assimilated Indians and Puritans results from the different rules governing Indian and Puritan classificatory systems. Contrasting the flexibility of Indian treatment of captive Puritans to the Puritan missionary work with the Indians on their side opposes two divergent strategies for coping with the threat of the alien other. The differences arise from two different ways of defining the "human" category, differences that proceed from different cultural demands and different evolved practices to meet them. The inclusive Indian definition of "human" readily admitted newcomers who adopted their ways; the Puritans were less accommodating of Indians who tried to enter their community, refusing to grant them full status or privileges. The European settlers called their defectors "White Indians," but to the Indians themselves such people were family members or friends, with no qualification on the basis of color or national origin.[57] Notwithstanding the Puritan effort to convert the heathen, the Indians were, Axtell says, "conceded to be the best cultural missionaries and educators on the continent." Correspondingly, the Puritans had more trouble facing Indian otherness than their North American colonial contemporaries did.[58]

Despite periodically lamenting that the failure of their own missionary work was corrupting their society, the Puritans warred on the Indians more often than they prayed with them. Delbanco sees some significance in the relationships the Puritans forged with different Indian tribes, but this does not, he says, halt the gradual rhetorical bankruptcy of the Indian conversion idea. He suggests that converting Indians was harder than the Puritans thought it would be, and their failure at it spurred them to look for other ways of dealing with their neighbors. Puritan support for the conversion and education of even friendly

Indians never gained equal priority with keeping them at a safe distance, both physically and rhetorically. But this distancing always proves difficult to achieve, and it comes at a price: Captain John Mason burned down a Pequot village in 1637 during the first great Indian war, for example, killing hundreds of men, women, and children. The "self-doubt" in his account of the massacre presages more explicit questions during the next generation of whether the English colonists were not edging closer to savage Indian ways and away from their own.[59] Mason's experience parallels Rowlandson's during her captivity years later, during which she also saw herself changing, and similarly questioned the categories governing her perception of herself. For Rowlandson the change is permanent. At the end of her narrative she praises her deliverance, but admits that she doesn't sleep so well anymore (74). This edgy discomfort reflects ongoing Puritan difficulties in managing the *idea* of Indian-ness.[60]

This insecurity (exacerbated by the strict Puritan approach to classification) caused the Puritans to want—and need—a lot of room between themselves and the Indians. The attempt to objectify the Indians dates back to the first Puritan encounter with them (as do the difficulties accompanying the effort) but the ontological problems faced by the Puritans become particularly onerous in the later generations, when the Indians were increasingly linked to Satanic designs to overthrow the community.

Given that the objectifying effort demanded all this work, why did the Puritans do it? Why did they target the Indians as reified evil, as the designated enemies of New England, when the Native Americans were so hard to maintain in that role? Part of the reason was economic, of course: the Puritans wanted Indian lands and needed a reason to take them. But another important motivation intertwined the religious, political, and ideological. The Puritans cast the Indians as villains because they were looking indirectly inward for a solution to a complex of weaknesses that surrounded their enterprise after the first generation of the settlement. As a result, the Indians and their ostensible misdeeds became not only a cause assigned by Puritan writers for the declension of their religious society, but the rhetoric of these writers also stands as a symptom of that decline which can be detected after the fact, with the Indians serving as a key rhetorical outlet for the New Englanders' threatened beliefs in signs and wonders. These beliefs were rapidly becoming unacceptable in European intellectual circles during the later seventeenth century—but they were nonetheless vital to the intellectual integrity of the Puritan religious worldview, and so needed to be preserved. These twin political and ideological crises, marked by Indians as assigned cause of Puritan troubles and Indian rhetoric as noticeable effect of them, will be the subject of the concluding section of this chapter.

V

Exit the Puritans, Pursued by the Grotesque

Broadly speaking, the Puritans turned the Indians into scapegoats for the decline of their own society. As the conservative elders looked increasingly for outside forces of evil to blame for the increasing secularism of their society, the Indians, with their wild and un-Christian ways, were conveniently positioned to take on the burden. Samuel Nowell complained in 1678 that the Indians "will not joyn or mix with us to make one body," but it seems more likely that the Puritans actually wanted them to be "a thorn in our sides."[61] James Schramer and Timothy Sweet argue that violence against the Indian body results from the Puritans' felt need to protect the body politic. Indeed, Indian war, as an inherently unifying social effort, would have served this nationalistic purpose by helping to image the shared ideal against an enemy whose purposes could be constructed as antithetical to the New England mission.[62]

It would be extreme, of course, to suggest that Indians represented either the major cause or crucial effect of the vitiation of Puritanism, but as John Canup has shown, the Puritan view of Indians is easily connected to Puritan views of other social and political issues. I think that it is more than coincidence that the increasing Puritan difficulty in maintaining a consistent view of the Indians—exemplified by the captivity narratives—coincides with the increasing difficulty in maintaining the basis for their governmental authority itself. It thus seems likely that some of the anger directed at the Indians had a different cause. The Indians became evil at least partly because the Puritans needed someone to see that way.

This identification effectively denies the Indians any chance for permanent entry into the Puritans' human circle. Because any similarity between the two groups was to be feared and denied by the Puritans, an Indian could not be a Puritan. According to Pearce, this unbridgeable gap (unbridgeable in the minds of the Puritans, anyway) ensured the failure of the missionary enterprise.[63] Further, the ease with which a Christian could become an Indian (as captivity experiences proved) surely increased the settlers' anxiety. The need for space between the two meant that Indians could be absorbed into the Puritan classificatory system, but not into the Puritan category. Puritan references to "the converted heathen" suggest that a Christian Indian was to the Puritans just that: still and always a former savage, still and always a breed apart.[64]

The captivity narrative reflected this tension and a good many others that were implicated with it. Puritan beliefs about prodigies—paralleled with their views of Indians—offer a means of explicating these tensions and drawing them together, thereby uncovering the increasing conceptual and rhetorical burden that the New Englanders assigned to the Indians as their own authority lessened. The captivity narrative both supports and reveals this multifaceted cultural work.

The genre emerged toward the end of the seventeenth century, when the integrity of the Puritan state faced political, social, and ideological trouble that was fueled by outside events at home and in England. New England society was secularizing as it prospered economically, so much so that the halfway covenant (which extended the privilege of baptism to the children of "halfway" church members who had not stepped forward to publicly proclaim their faith) was approved in 1662 to remedy dropping church membership. The society was also losing cohesion because of the outward diffusion of a growing population; territorial expansion accelerated during the last quarter of the century, after the end of King Philip's War.[65] This domestic growth took place at a time when Puritan political influence was shrinking abroad. Puritan rule in England had ended with the Restoration, and King Charles II, a Catholic, proved decidedly less inclined toward New England's interests than the mainly indifferent former regimes. Long-festering disputes over legal and economic governance led the Massachusetts colonial charter to be revoked in 1684 by a Crown that had become increasingly interested in colonial affairs. The charter was renegotiated to the

Puritans' overall disadvantage in 1691, following a period of protracted political maneuvering by New England's lead negotiator Increase Mather to save even a fraction of the Puritans' former authority over the colony. The new charter mandated a colonial governor to be appointed by the Crown.

Meanwhile, the Puritan belief in divine signs and wonders that underlaid their theology was in at least as much trouble as the New England polity itself. The rise in England and France of natural philosophy, including the New Science, led to a sustained intellectual attack on the idea of prodigies—which were now deemed natural occurrences—and a more exclusive definition of the category of "miracle." Mechanistic views of God's workings replaced the spiritism that infused the Puritan view, as Enlightenment philosophy largely moved away from theological positions long maintained by the Puritans. The result was that the new scientific establishment branded Puritan beliefs about prodigies as superstitions and Puritans as "enthusiasts" rather than reasoning intellectuals.[66]

Within this context, my focus here will be on the way that the authors of captivity narratives use the same objectifying vocabulary for Indians as their fellow Puritans had formerly used to describe prodigies. Captivity narratives also come to the same providential conclusions that accounts of prodigies do. Rowlandson's summing-up of her experience is typical:

> O the wonderful power of God that I have seen and the experience that I have had! I have been in the midst of these roaring lions and savage bears that feared neither God nor man nor the devil, by night and day, alone and in company, sleeping all sorts together, and yet not one of them ever offered me the least abuse of unchastity to me in word or action. Though some are ready to say that I speak it for my own credit, I speak it in the presence of God and to his glory. (70)

Rowlandson emphasizes the bestial monstrosity of the Indians in her analysis of her providential deliverance—as she does elsewhere in her narrative—but as I have said, the Indians were not prodigies. The bundling of Indian captivity narratives with providence tales in Puritan publications like Mather's *Magnalia* suggests an important association between Indians and prodigies, but Puritan thinkers did not consider Indian behavior to be one of God's mysteries. Unlike earthquakes, monstrous births, or other unusual events, the Native Americans could not be considered divine wonders. This distinction is crucial to what follows.

Both the rise of the captivity narrative and its ambivalent representation of Indians are, I want to suggest, cultural symptoms of the weakening of Puritan religious authority in the intellectual and political arena. They are also key components of a rhetorical strategy to save as much of the contested ground as possible. As a providential narrative of sorts, the captivity narrative expresses an old-fashioned but consistently Puritan view of divine intervention in the world through the use of wonders, a view formerly conveyed by the prodigy.[67] By highlighting the wondrous actions of God as they are manifest in New England, the genre supports the American Calvinist worldview by example, even as the authors explicitly affirm that view. At the same time, by generally abandoning traditional evangelical accounts of prodigies from their public writing and essentially substituting captivity narratives—with their equivocally monstrous descriptions of Indians—in their place, Puritan authors also reflect the growing inability of American Puritan thought to sustain itself in the larger Enlightenment marketplace of modern ideas.

To illustrate this difficulty, it is worth returning to the representative example of Cotton Mather. Michael Winship persuasively argues that Mather never resolved his relationship with Enlightenment science and its mechanistic rationalism, and his anxiety over the scientific repudiation of spiritism was never quieted. Mather's evocation of prodigies went into public retreat after the 1680s, but his writings show that his private belief in them remained vital to the end of his life.[68] Mather's attempt to preserve the prodigy paralleled the attempt by the Puritans (in which he was also a key participant) to preserve their theocratic state against the encroachments of the Crown during the Restoration period, and their theocratic beliefs against the demands of a rapidly secularizing society. His public-private division represents a personal and political compromise between his long-held traditional religious convictions and the need he understood for the Puritans to remain intellectually respectable in England. As Lorraine Daston has shown, the scientific establishment—which was still entwined with religion, exerting pressure toward Deism—targeted the fanatic rather than the devil as the main public enemy as the seventeenth century neared its end.[69] Prodigies and miracles became "the marker of the boundary between genuine knowledge and superstition."[70] The fight over how to interpret prodigies, as Winship says, was therefore about power as much as about science. The American Puritans couldn't afford to be considered fanatics at a time when their political resources were diminishing, so Mather—himself a member of the Royal Society—backed away from his public belief in prodigies.

The religious ground lost was crucial for the Puritans, and had to be recouped for two important reasons. First, signs and wonders were necessary in order to preserve New England's new covenant—their communal version of Calvinism's starkly individualistic relationship between man and God. Calvinists were not alone in working prodigies and miracles into their account of the world's workings, of course, but the American Puritans had a particular doctrinal need for them because divine wonders were a vital ingredient in their conception of God's relationship with the community. Puritan covenant theology regularized the ways of God, as Perry Miller has famously shown, but it did not mechanize them or do away with "the sense of something mysterious and terrible, of something that leaped when least expected, something that upset all regularizations and defied all logic."[71] Indeed, such unexpected, nonrational occurrences could be read as signals that God was noticing his chosen people—and the need to be noticed in this way became particularly pronounced in the late seventeenth century, when the luster of New England idealism had dimmed somewhat. In New England theology, God's adherence to his side of the covenant with the community was marked in significant part by preternatural and supernatural interventions, including prodigies and miracles. These divine wonders formed a foundation stone of the American Puritans' theological and communal edifice, offering limited but crucial insights into the ways of an inscrutable God—insights that were vital to the rationale for their society. Prodigies were divine signs for the Puritans, one of the ways that God reached out and showed himself. Admitting this belief to be a form of ignorant superstition—as the New Science held it to be—would be to knock a prop out of the overall support of the entire New England conception of the world.

Second, the rationalizing and secularizing of prodigies diffused knowledge horizontally, which was not the Puritan way. Reason (which could be exercised by anyone) and cheap entertainment (available to all) were becoming the ways to approach prodigies by the second half of the seventeenth century; this inherently democratic spread of knowledge and entertainment was in perpendicular opposition to the vertical model of Puritan religion and education, where ministers were the primary authorities. Though Protestantism was predicated on Luther's "priesthood of all believers," Puritan religious and social organization dictated that the clergy serve as primary interpreters of the Word for the congregation, and that all entertainment be explicitly and avowedly didactic. The migration of prodigies to the jurisdictions of science and entertainment therefore threatened to undermine authority and educational order as well as doctrine. (Puritan concerns in this area seem to have been justified: the shift of prodigies into the scientific and secular worlds anticipated teratology, the "science of monsters," and the freak show it was used to justify later on.)

Because the American Puritans needed to preserve a world where signs and wonders operated, they transferred that need—along with the objectifying vocabulary and rhetoric of prodigies—onto the Indians. Thus, while Mather had to excuse himself for "Livian superstition in reporting prodigies" in his account of the sounds of invisible armies in the sky as heralding the coming of King Philip's War, he could describe the Indians who fought in that war in familiar terms of prodigious monstrosity.[72] The Indians were safe rhetorical ground for Mather because they lay literally within his own province. Though the displacing link with prodigies naturally associated the Indians with the Puritan scientific enterprise, the study of Indians was not co-opted by science (and would not be until the ascent of ethnology during the next century). This distinction meant that descriptions of Indians in prodigious terms didn't have to be defended before the English scientific establishment. Though Mather had to carefully insist on his interpretation of monstrous births as "omens" in his communications with the Royal Society, he and his fellow New Englanders could claim full authoritative expertise on Indians—whom the American Puritans knew better than anyone in England did.[73]

Indian captivity narratives thus offered an escape hatch for Puritan providential thinking in the form of the prodigious description of the Indians. Despite the grotesque tension that accompanied their efforts to objectify the Indians in these narratives, the Puritans seized a valuable opportunity in the new genre to talk about the Indians in a way that they could no longer talk about prodigies. The colonists deflected their need for portentous monsters onto the Indians in order to preserve their providential worldview in a different rhetorical sphere.

Cotton Mather was instrumental both in the American Puritan reception of the New Science and the dissemination of the captivity narratives throughout New England and England. His public retreat from prodigies coincided with the rise of captivity narratives, many of which he wrote. The link in both of these pairings is causal. Mather's example therefore makes it especially clear how captivity narratives became the new home for the discourse of prodigies: the genre diverted onto the Indians the Puritan need to interpret wonder-working providence in the world. The discourse of prodigies that was pushed from New England science thus reappears in the literature of the New England frontier, the ancestor of the American adventure story (which I will discuss in more detail in chapter 3). This movement displaces the prodigious tale onto unscientific ground, with the captivity narrative becoming a new version of the narrative of wonder, one that didn't conflict with the larger scientific developments that were driving the idea of the prodigy underground. Rather than directly contest the battle over prodigies as evidence of God's presence in the world—a battle that Mather and the rest of the outnumbered New England Puritan intellectuals were increasingly ill-equipped to win on the opponent's turf—the American Puritans sidestepped the conflict, ceding the control of prodigies to the New Scientists, and instead appropriating uncontested rhetorical "Indian space" (following Cushman, they might have called it "empty space") for their accounts of divine wonders.

As a result, the allegedly malignant actions of the Native Americans could be held up as instruments of God's will on earth, an assignment made with the same rhetoric and vocabulary as had been reserved for prodigies. But now, instead of *arguing* over what prodigies meant, the Puritans could use the same ideas to *assert* what the Indians meant. And there could be no scientific rejoinder, because Indians weren't yet a matter of science. When New Englander Daniel Gookin dedicated his study of Christian Indians to the influential English scientist Robert Boyle, for example, his gesture held up the Indians as a matter over which the Puritans believed they had control and authority, which Gookin would have wanted to demonstrate to the renowned Boyle and his fellow natural philosophers.[74] By avoiding attacks from English natural philosophers by staking out their own intellectual ground in this way, the American Puritans maintained the structure of their covenant theology and the social organization built on it.

In addition to allowing the later New England generations to celebrate miracles without having to debate their scientific validity, captivity narratives offered stories of individual religious success at a time when collective success was getting harder to argue for. The displacing connection between monstrous births (prodigies) and monstrous humans (Indians) offered a way to meet a political and philosophical crisis of widening proportions; not only was the actual Puritan government weakening, but its very way of organizing and thinking about the world was also under stress. The Indians provided a convenient and useful psychological receptacle for the anxiety accompanying these developments in much the same way that the freak show would contain displaced racial anxiety in the nineteenth-century United States (a development I discuss in chapter 5). The Indians, already scapegoats for the general decline of Puritan authority, became displaced burden-bearers for a religious philosophy under intellectual attack.

The objectification of the Indians thus emerges as a crucial strategy not only to uphold the Puritans' "human" category but also to support their religious ideas against forces from within and without. Saddled with so much cultural baggage, the Native Americans experienced considerable stress themselves—and they didn't last long under it. In the end, war and disease all but wiped out the Indians, but before these scourges came the objectification that allowed the settlers to look on impassively as their enemies were felled or fell away. The Puritan objectification of the Indians is a landmark cultural event that began a long tradition of similar activity.

Liminality makes this objectification grotesque at the core, and fear keeps this core white-hot. It is reductive to say simply that the Indians are fully transfigured human beings who become permanently objectified creatures in Puritan eyes. The Puritan transformation of the Indians into monsters is highly unstable by virtue of the empirical truth beneath it: that the subjects retain a link to their earlier humanity. The Puritans seek to transform the Indians irrevocably from one state to another, but the Indians wind up grotesque instead: astraddle basic categories, occupying neither one nor the other. Historians have recently argued for the importance of Puritan-Indian relations as an emblem of the Puritans' central struggle with self-definition.[75] The powerful, uncertain grotesqueness of the Indians in their eyes underscores this connection. In this state of ambiguity proximate to Puritan existence, the Indians become more threatening, more monstrous, as they come to represent a possible Puritan self, a dark reminder of what awaits the failure of their authority—even as their status as rhetorical receptacle helps to bolster what's left of it.

This fear infiltrates their narratives. Nation and narration go together, says Edward Said, with narrative as a historicizing force, capturing national preoccupations within a story.[76] The Puritan captivity narrative epitomizes the tension and conflict of the society in its later generations; the genre's ambiguous view of the Indians says more than, say, Cotton Mather's one-sided attempts to ram the "wild" and "civilized" Indians into their respective categories. Like Mather, Puritan former captives are also keen to keep their epistemological house in order. But unlike Mather—who brought no experience as a captive to his prolific literary efforts as captivity narrative writer, editor, and amanuensis—the former captives themselves find that the nature of their experience, which erases seemingly clear boundaries, makes this rational order difficult to construct even in the retelling. Confusion about whether to view the Indians as people or monsters is evident throughout many of the most popular and influential captivity narratives. Their authors are struggling to manage the grotesque according to the demands of their own cultural surroundings; they are trying to use their stories to prop up a world whose supports are cracking. Standing out from polarized descriptions of Indians dating from every Puritan generation, the captivity narrative embodies the Puritans' Indian tensions within the story itself. These tensions in turn correspond to the social, political, and ideological crises of the later New England generations. The captivity narrative offers the best of many literary sites from which to see that the Indians, being people, made less than ideal demons. But they were all that the Puritans had.

Because human objectification creates the grotesque, it makes the objectified other into a liminal variable that can never be fixed. Frantz Fanon is obviously aware of the instability of the relation between Imperial Self and Colonial Other, but he sees the key to liberation as lying in the other's potential for violent, subversive action. It is the responsibility of the colonized, in other words, to exploit his position and destroy the system that culturally enslaves him. In chapter 3 I will show how American slaves conceive and carry out that task. But the experience of the American Puritans reflects the greater emphasis I give throughout this book to the weakness and instability of the act of objectification itself, based as it is on the eventually unsupportable central postulate that certain human beings are not human. The struggles of the Puritans—and those of slaveowners I will spotlight later on—suggest that such a system is doomed even if the subordinate group doesn't overturn it. It is destined to crack because of the perpetual difficulty in managing the grotesque, the impossibility of fixing a value that lies between categories, and the consequent impossibility to deny humanity indefinitely. The objectifier can't domesticate the grotesque permanently, no more than human beings can stay awake indefinitely, or keep an "eternal flame" lit forever. The fiction of objectification always gives way eventually—the only question is when—and the human reasserts itself.

The tangled Puritan view of Indians anticipates the similarly conflicted and equivocal portrayals of Native Americans in United States fiction later on. In early American novels, the familiar contradictions become infused with what Renato Rosaldo calls "imperialist nostalgia," where the monstrous savage becomes noble in retrospect.[77] When constructed objectification meets constructed virtue, the results—not surprisingly—range to extremes. In Charles Brockden Brown's *Edgar Huntly* (1799), for example, the Indians are mute save for screams, grunts, and yells; Edgar attributes death-dealing designs to them in place of words, and he spends much of the novel hunting them down on the Pennsylvania frontier. Standing over the bodies of three of his victims, however, Edgar unexpectedly describes them as "beings full of energy and heroism, endowed with minds strenuous and lofty." Then scarcely thirty pages later, he reverts to seeing them as "adepts in killing, with appetites that longed to feast upon my bowels and quaff my heart's blood." Edgar's trouble sorting out his impressions of Indians turns out to be a major source of his insomniac discontents.[78]

Edgar's oscillations become reified in early American fiction in the form of the polarized character types of "good Indian" and "bad Indian." This division forms the basis for Lydia Maria Child's *Hobomok* (1823), James Fenimore Cooper's Leatherstocking tales, and scores of other Indian stories from last century to the American present. The popular movie *Dances with Wolves* (1990)—where the nameless, speechless, murderous Pawnees contrast with the verbal and virtuous Lakotas—stands as a good contemporary example of this crucial dichotomy, a tangible portion of the Puritan legacy.

The Puritans tried by rhetorical, typological, and even physical force to make the Indians into unalterably alien others innately opposed to their own way of life. The effort never fully succeeded. René Girard says that demonizing and scapegoating the other is the fundamental way that a community achieves solidarity. For the Puritans, this designation of what Girard calls a "surrogate victim" yielded complications without end. Schramer and Sweet emphasize the instability of a social structure based on difference, for it "requires continual violence against the outside, against the other." For the Puritans, this violence found many outlets, but it never gave them the security they sought.[79]

When King Philip was finally killed in 1676 (by a Christian Indian!), essentially ending the bloody Indian war that bears his name, historical irony surrounded the event. Not only was Philip killed by a Praying Indian, but Benjamin Church, the white leader of the band that tracked him down, was a marginal figure of the sort feared and despised by the Puritan establishment. As Richard Slotkin observes, Church was a wilderness man who preferred secular pursuits to the gospel, and who liked and trusted unconverted Indians as he fought beside them in Indian fashion. After successfully hunting down King Philip, Church willingly submitted to a ritual in which one of Philip's lieutenants crowned him the new king of the wilderness. This gesture, which would have horrified any orthodox Puritan, made Church very proud.[80]

The Puritans had King Philip decapitated and kept his head as a public trophy—an act not far removed from the abhorred Indian practice of scalping. This mutilation (which foreshadows the rebel slave Babo's fate in Melville's *Benito Cereno*) represents a telling attempt to objectify the Indian enemy by literal brute force. The victorious Puritans try to remove Philip from the human category in the most direct way, by turning him into a hunting prize.[81]

But Philip's head is still Philip's head. It may be a thing, but it is also

CHAPTER THREE

A DIFFERENT POWER OF BLACKNESS: *The Work of Freedom in the Fugitive Slave Narrative*

> This man born in degradation, this stranger brought by slavery into our midst, is hardly recognized as sharing the common features of humanity. His face appears to us hideous, his intelligence limited, and his tastes low; we almost take him for some being intermediate between beast and man.
>
> —Alexis de Tocqueville, *Democracy in America*

> I regard all the upright demeanour, gentlemanly bearing, Christian character, social progress, and material prosperity, of every coloured man, especially if he be a native of the United States, as, in its kind, anti-slavery labour.
>
> —Samuel Ringgold Ward, *Autobiography of a Fugitive Negro*

> Do your work and I shall know you. Do your work, and you shall reinforce yourself.
>
> —Ralph Waldo Emerson, *"Self Reliance"*

This chapter examines the theory and practice of objectification from the perspective of the objectified person—in this case, the African-American slave. Just as the Puritan narrative of Indian captivity offers exceptional insight into the complications that accompany human objectification, so does the fugitive slave narrative (also a story of captivity) provide a fertile site of a corresponding "de-objectification," or humanization. Slave narratives recount a key moment of transformation from human/thing to person, a transition accomplished during the movement—in thought and act—from slavery to freedom. Hegel's dialectic of master and slave helps to explain the psychological difficulty of maintaining the state of objectification for both parties, and how the slave gains a kind of freedom through work. The humanization of the slave exemplifies how the rhetorical objectification process can be reversed. But the American fugitive slave performs a different kind of labor than Hegel prescribes, this one centering on direct resistance to the master's control. The various narrative strategies devised by American slaves to get and keep their humanity, many of them fashioned after the popular nineteenth-century adventure story, show the flexibility and versatility of this "rhetoric of humanization," and the centrality to their experience of the racial grotesque.

When Frederick L. Olmstead came face to face with slavery in his travels through the South, he wrote that it was "difficult" to treat a human as property, but "embarrass[ing]" to treat property as human.[1] Olmstead's dilemma encapsulates the difficulties that white slaveholders had in objectifying their slaves. American slaveholders tried to treat the slave as property, but couldn't consistently maintain that stance because they understood all along that the slave was human. Furthermore, the owners had to exploit that humanity in daily practice in order to manage the slave as property.[2] Alexis de Tocqueville saw this conflict in action when he visited the South and witnessed the treatment of slaves: "Not wishing to raise them to their own level, [the owners] keep them *as close to the beasts as possible*" (emphasis added).[3] Tocqueville's qualification is important. The masters do not succeed in turning the slaves into beasts; they can only approximate doing so. (The "almost" that Tocqueville inserts into the epigraph quotation above further suggests this key gap.) Tocqueville's phrasing shows that he sees slaves as people who are being degraded to the status of objects—but who are nonetheless not objects. Moreover, Tocqueville's use of the plural "we" suggests that he is not the only one who sees them as people. For Tocqueville and others unnamed, the slaves retain their human connection. They are not things but people who are being uneasily forced into the category of "thing."

Not surprisingly, the antebellum American legal system was confused and divided on this much-discussed "core contradiction" of slavery.[4] The legal swamp for slaveholders in a democratic system of government started out deep and kept getting deeper as slave codes swelled with laws delineating the slave's few "human" rights.[5] In the Alabama Slave Code of 1852, for example, whipping a slave to death with malice aforethought carried the charge of first degree murder. Dropping the intent to kill would reduce the charge to second degree murder. And the Louisiana Slave Code of 1824 stated that any manumission agreement between slave and master would be "*inter vivos*"—between living people. Even antebellum intellectuals were aware that Southern law treated slaves as things and people at the same time. Proslavery legal scholar Thomas R. R. Cobb argued for the humanization of the slave code, challenging a complicated rationale for the lack of a rape charge for sexual violation of a slave, which itself argued that "carnal forcible knowledge of a slave" did not threaten the slave's existence—the latter being all that she had a right to.[6]

The law forbidding slaves to testify against white persons surely limited the courtroom testing of these laws. Within this limitation, the laws were actually enforced, though with an inconsistency that befitted their framing. The courts would in one case treat slaves as human, and in the next uphold laws treating them as property, with the 1857 Dred Scott decision being only the most infamous of many such tortured opinions. Particularly interesting are the cases that took masters and overseers before the bench on grounds of cruelty. Helen T. Catterall cites a case where the court declined to rule on a master's near-fatal beating of a slave on the grounds that what a man does with his property is his own business. But in another case, a master tortured a slave to death with medieval creativity and was sentenced to five years in prison for second degree murder.[7] The inconsistency in the legal argument is obvious. How can you murder a piece of property?

Frederick Douglass saw the special import of this contradiction. In his famous speech, "What to a Slave Is the Fourth of July?" he declares that the owners always know that their slaves are people, because they wouldn't punish disobedience so severely if they believed otherwise. "What is this," asks Douglass of such cruelty, "but the acknowledgement that the slave is a moral, intellectual and responsible being? The slave's manhood is conceded."[8] The precise eloquence of Douglass and Tocqueville articulates the epistemological dilemma of the slaveholder, whose effort to objectify requires constant vigilance, and even so, only partially succeeds. Instead of becoming simple objects, the slaves gain a much more complex status, resulting, among other things, in the convoluted courtroom contradictions I just described. Left suspended between the categories of person and object, slaves enter a liminal space. As partially transformed human/things, they become grotesque.

It is the slave's view of his own grotesqueness that I will examine in the following pages. For African-American slaves as well as the colonial Puritans, the captivity narrative provides a unique vantage point. The slave narrator essentially wants to reclaim his humanity from those who

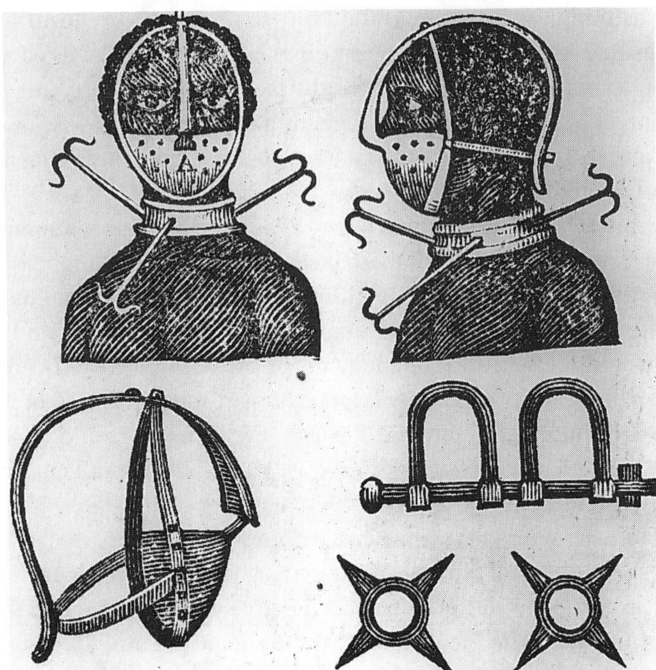

Fig. 3.1 Instruments of slave torture. A slave wearing this contraption (which includes the leg shackles and spurs pictured here) could neither eat nor rest, as the protruding spikes prevented one from lying down. Reproduced by permission of the Photographs and Prints Division, Schomburg Center for Research in Black Culture; the New York Public Library; Astor, Lenox, and Tilden Foundations)

are trying to take it away. The fugitive slave narrative—a genre whose conventions borrowed not only from captivity narrative and spiritual autobiography but also from the popular adventure tale—evolved during the age of abolitionism as the narrative vehicle to carry the slave to the human state. The slave's central experience as an objectified person is the discovery that, for human beings, the objectification process is both incomplete and reversible. Slave narratives show that if a person can be equated with a thing, this human/thing can become a full-fledged person again. Douglass's *Narrative* stands out as perhaps the paradigmatic example of this two-stage transformation, and Hegel's dialectic of master and slave—largely de-centered in African-American literary and cultural criticism—offers crucial insight to illuminate its workings.

Fig. 3.2 This Northern attack on slavery anticipates Frederick Douglass's speech, "What to a Slave Is the Fourth of July?" The caption on the scroll reads:

Fourth of July Celebration, or, Southern ideas of Liberty—July 4, '40. Behold! the degraded son of Africa, reading the Declaration of Independence, handcuffed as he is; and stared at with astonishment by the *Husband* and *Wife*, in front of him, who are also chained; and whose appearance seems to say, "are these things so." The *Musicians*, no doubt, could perform better, at least with more care to themselves, if they had the use of both hands. On the back ground is to be seen, the notorious Judge Lynch, with whip in hand, and his foot on the Constitution—bolstered up with bales of Cotton and hog-heads of Tobacco—surrounded by his *Mob Court*, condemning the friends of humanity, and executing them upon the spot, merely for supporting that clause of the Declaration, viz. *"All men are created free and equal,"* and acting in conformity with 192 pages of Holy writ, which are either directly or indirectly, against the system of SLAVERY.

(Reproduced by permission of the Photographs and Prints Division, Schomburg Center for Research in Black Culture, the New York Public Library; Astor, Lenox, and Tilden Foundations)

The force behind the proslavery position was the force of difference. But precisely *how* did slaves differ from the free population? It is easier to justify involuntary servitude when people's rights are not at issue—or better still, when they are not truly people at all. Orlando Patterson calls slavery a condition of "social death," in which the master deprives the slave of all independent connection to society. Though physically

Fig. 3.3 Scene aboard a slave ship. A female slave is being branded at the left. Engraving by Andrew and Filmer in Drake, *Revelations of a Slave Smuggler; Being the Autobiography of Capt. Rich'd Drake, an African Trader for Fifty Years, from 1807–1857; during which he was concerned in the transportation of half a million blacks from African coasts to America* (1860). (From the Rare Book Division, the Library of Congress)

inside the community, the slave has no social existence within it. Because the master limits the slave's social coordinates to those emanating from the master's own position, he cuts the slave off from any independent existence.

As "non-beings," slaves were consequently deprived of their social personhood. Patterson's emphasis on this marginality of the slave makes it natural to carry his findings over to the theme of grotesque objectification. Whether portrayed as a child who never grows up, an inferior race of human being, or simply as a piece of property to be used, the slave stands out as an anomaly of human existence: at once outwardly normal yet inwardly abnormal, a living thing that has human form, but without the full complement of qualities that make someone into a person.[9]

Using the typology outlined by Mary Douglas in *Purity and Danger*, Patterson argues that "it is the very dirtiness, *grotesqueness*, and ineradicable defilement of the slave eunuch that explain his ritual necessity" (emphasis added).[10] Though Patterson is speaking of a specific historical case of Chinese slavery (the eunuch servants to the emperor) which results in a physical anomaly, I think that his basic point can be extended: the social purpose of slavery is served by the grotesqueness of the slave. The slave's living death enhances the authority of his owner, and the social system to which they both belong. Patterson and others supply historical evidence of how American slaves were physically and institutionally marginalized, citing such practices as renaming, and even branding.[11]

Hegel's famous dialectic of master and slave accords with Patterson's argument up to a point, but with an important difference: in Hegel's model, human objectification through slavery is a dynamic and unstable process that does not objectify the slave for long. In light of the demonstrated volatility of the slave's status in the master's eyes, Hegel's depiction of unstable human objectification deserves a closer look.[12]

I

Objectification in the Master-Slave Dialectic: Hegel on the African-American Literary Stage

To Hegel, self-consciousness comes about as a result of desire. The ego divides into self and other as part of a strategy "so that one half is observed and desired by the other; for desire is awakened by objects that the mind places before itself." The self, says Hegel, seeks an-Other to broaden the base upon which knowledge must rest. What the self wants from the Other is recognition, an act "of knowing the self again in an other."[13]

This desire for recognition is central to Hegel's description of identity formation. According to Hegel, all human beings desire to be treated with decency and respect. The catch is that each person wants this without having to recognize another in exchange. People will therefore fight each other and risk their lives for this nonreciprocal recognition. The battle results in a victor and a vanquished. The vanquished chooses self-preservation over recognition, and therefore submits to slavery under the domain of the opponent (the "master"). Because the slave fails to get the desired recognition as an individual, the master becomes the "I" of the slave.[14] Two people thus become one. The slave is objectified as a thing, a possession with no human individuality.

Dialectical paradoxes now assert themselves; enslavement of the opponent backfires on the master and unexpectedly benefits the slave. Because the slave is not a fully human being but rather a piece of property (a thing), the recognition he confers on the master (by working for him) paradoxically fails to satisfy the master's own original desire for recognition *from another person*. (For Hegel, "recognition" means acknowledgment as an independent and autonomous being.) So the master's conquest of the slave fails to bring about the desired outcome. In fact, it brings about the opposite result: the master ironically finds himself in a position of dependence on the slave for whatever recognition he can get from him. "Without slaves [the master] is no master. . . . He has defined himself in terms of the 'thing' he owns."[15] Thus the master, not the slave, finds himself in a state of what Hegel calls "being for another."[16]

The slave, by contrast, achieves a kind of spiritual independence, an inner discipline gained by fear and work. He acknowledges his fear of the master and gains self-worth through the work he does for him. He thereby gains a sense of himself as a human being and not a thing: "through work. . . the bondsman becomes conscious of what he truly is." The slave's productive work humanizes nature, and more importantly, it rehumanizes himself: "Through this rediscovery of himself by himself, the bondsman realizes that it is precisely in his work wherein he seemed to have only an alienated existence that he acquires a mind of his own."[17] Master and slave thus come to resemble each other in their own humanity. For Hegel, "Labor is primarily a means of self-realization, whereby things with no point or purpose come to take on the purposes of their creators."[18] Recognition, freedom, work, and discipline are all parts of the process of achieving self-consciousness. Because both sides achieve self-consciousness, the master-slave state remains very unstable. The master and actualized slave now fight for recognition. And they retreat into worlds of thought, a condition of "Unhappy Consciousness."[19]

Aristotle's thoughts on slavery provide a good contrast. According to Aristotle, objectification of the slave is possible—even necessary—because inequality is a natural law. In his calculus, slaves are human beings who are also possessions. Aristotle says that slaves should be counted as members of a household's population, but he also says they should be listed in the inventory of household possessions. The slave, in other words, is a separate human being but also a part of the master.[20] These might appear to be difficult oppositions to maintain, but they aren't for Aristotle. For him, slavery is simply part of duality-oriented order in which people as well as things can be divided into high and low.

Hegel isn't as sanguine. He sees slavery as an inherently (re-)humanizing process, a revision that helps to destroy the Aristotelian stability of the objectifier-objectified relationship. It follows from Hegel's dialectic that the objectification process also goes the other way, reversing the grotesque conversion of person into thing. Just as slavery can transform a person into a thing, so can a slave effect her own transformation back into a person. The Hegelian dialectic helps to explain the characteristic instability of human objectification. Hegel postulates generally what the Puritans found to be true in their own experience: that human beings can be objectified, but they can't be kept that way.

Just as Puritan narratives of captivity and redemption offer insight into the objectifier's state of mind, so do fugitive slave narratives of captivity and escape provide a glimpse of the mind of the objectified person. Like narratives of Indian captivity, fugitive slave narratives describe the author's thought and action during a stressful challenge to his definition of humanity (in this case, his own human status). Hegel's dialectic helps to understand the nature and meaning of this challenge. Though I will have cause to expand certain of Hegel's definitions, the basic structure of his argument provides a fundamental understanding of the slave's predicament.[21]

That Hegel's master-slave relation has rarely been brought to bear on the modern literary study of slavery has much to do, I think, with his longtime status as intellectual pariah within the African-American literary critical establishment. Hegel has received scant attention from writers about the literature of American slavery up to now, mainly because of his dismissive writings about the African tradition, an interpretation that has, for good reason, aged very poorly. In *The Philosophy of History*, Hegel accused Africans of living without self-control in a "completely wild and untamed state," lacking a collective historical, political, or literary tradition, or indeed, a culture at all. Not surprisingly, this argument—glowingly praised in at least one American proslavery novel—has since attracted a lot of (deserved) criticism. An unfortunate side effect of Hegel's wrongheaded assessment of African culture has been the widespread neglect of the rest of his work—including the

Phenomenology—by most literary critics of the African and African-American tradition. David Brion Davis has called Hegel's master-slave dialectic "the most profound analysis of slavery ever written." Its recovery in African-American literary analysis has begun only recently, most notably in the work of Eric Sundquist and Paul Gilroy. I continue the project here.[22]

Hegel's outline of the master-slave relation offers a useful angle from which to see and understand the workings of the objectification process in fugitive slave narratives because the genre itself spotlights human objectification. Fugitive slave authors share a broad agenda: first, to articulate the profound cruelty, the very grotesqueness of slavery, and to project themselves into it. Second, they recount the acts which free them from that state. The writer retrospectively questions his own humanity as a prelude to grabbing it back triumphantly. Broadly speaking, the history of the slave narrative is the history of the development of literary strategies for representing objectification and the slaves' corresponding strategies for fighting it.

The fugitive slave narrative was the last stage in the evolution of this literary formula before abolition made it an early antique. John G. Cawelti says that story formulas "affirm existing interests and attitudes" and that as attitudes change, the formulas evolve. Maximizing a balance between escapism and reality, such formulas articulate a fantasy that readers accept or want, and one that they can share.[23] The structure of the fugitive slave narrative emerged from two other formulaic genres—spiritual autobiography and Indian captivity narratives—with the new form taking on different contours to meet the needs of a new and different time: the heyday of abolitionism.

In eighteenth- and early nineteenth-century slave narratives, religious conversion became the first dominant rhetorical strategy to assert and maintain the slave's personhood. Early slave narrators like Olaudah Equiano point to their Christianity as a way of asserting their humanity within the state of slavery. Such spiritual autobiographies execute a non-confrontational strategy of humanization: the slave becomes a person by becoming a Christian.[24] As the slave narrative genre entered its period of peak popularity around the 1840s, its emphasis shifted from spiritual autobiography to what William L. Andrews calls the "quasi-scientific" fugitive slave narrative, which aimed foremost at exposing and authenticating the inhumanity of the peculiar institution in rationally detached fashion. In adopting a tone of clinical distance that evoked the newly authoritative and rapidly legitimized discourse of science, fugitive slave narrators positioned their stories to respond to the work of scientists of the time, much of which was devoted to the empirical "proof" of non-white inferiority through the examination of black (and Native American) heads, skulls, bones, and—in the case of ethnologists—behavior.[25]

The African-American literary rejoinder to proslavery racial science was part of a widespread and rising tide of Northern outrage over slavery that carried abolitionism from the church meeting to the public hall, and from there to the ballot box. From modest beginnings in the 1830s, the American Antislavery Society gained more than two thousand local auxiliaries in less than ten years. These increasing numbers of abolitionists engaged in widespread agitation. One popular tactic was the antislavery petition submitted to Congress. Petition drives produced thousands of petitions containing millions of signatures each year, and were so effective that they resulted in the famous Southern-sponsored "gag rule" legislation of 1836, which automatically tabled them.[26] This controversial tactic didn't afford long respite, however; fueled by abolitionist sentiment, the law was overturned in 1844. Abolitionists carried this newfound clout into national elections. In the 1848 presidential contest the Free Soil Party garnered nearly 300,000 votes (10 percent of the popular tally), won twelve congressional seats, and effectively decided the outcome of the presidential election by decisively affecting the vote in two key swing states.[27] With their focus on the specific and general cruelties of slavery, fugitive slave narratives were important to the abolitionist cause and an integral part of the movement's overall success from the 1840s onward.

Fugitive slave narratives focus more explicitly on racial objectification than do slave autobiographies of any other period. This change in the formula reflects a similar shift in emphasis in American society at the time: Northern and Southern intellectuals certainly did not agree about the human status of the slave, but the fugitive slave narrative appeared during a time when the debate over slavery was a major preoccupation of both sides. Cawelti argues that formula art exploits a "network of assumptions" held by members of a culture.[28] Building on the gains made by the abolitionist movement during the 1830s and 1840s, the slave narrative establishes a number of key assumptions among its Northern readers. To begin with, the narrator stresses the cruelty and injustice of the slave's world in order to assert the necessity of escape from it. Slaves are invariably mistreated in this world, and masters emerge as the villains of the story. Like all formula stories, the fugitive slave narrative is structured around ritual tension and release; it is clear from the beginning that the protagonist is going to escape and show up the institution—the only question is how and when. Most important, the slave narrative formula assumes that the reader recognizes the slave (in the Hegelian sense) as a fellow human.

The collective value of these assumptions was to bind together a Northern society whose opinions of blacks varied. Work by David Roediger, Eric Lott, and others has spotlighted the anxiety that attached itself to Northern conceptions of whiteness that were implicitly (and often explicitly) based on ideologies of black inferiority.[29] Indeed, opposing slavery in antebellum America did not necessarily mean favoring black equality, and many Northern workers were decidedly concerned about their own prospects in a postslavery society where free blacks might take their jobs. (In the South, slaveowners actively encouraged and exploited this fear among poor Southern whites.) For abolitionism to grow as it did, members of the movement—which was fundamentally a middle-class, grass-roots effort—had to put aside their differences and work for the common goal of ending slavery.[30] Fugitive slave narratives helped to maintain this clear focus, even as they also served an important purpose as propaganda, whereby they pulled their readers into the web of abolitionist ideology by acquainting them with the horrors of slavery and the heroism (and humanity) of the slaves who endured and escaped it.

All these assumptions rested on the perceived need for specific cultural work—in other words, the formula existed because it was desired by those who consumed it. In the age of abolitionism that fostered the growth of the fugitive slave narrative (and which was nourished by it in turn), the emphasis was on the slave's human agency. Accordingly, the ingredient that the fugitive slave narrative adds to the spiritual autobiography and the captivity narrative is a sense of individual empowerment compared to the redeemed captive or the converted slave, both of whom give the major credit to Providence for their salvation. Fugitive slave narrators don't deny the power of God, but they emphasize the importance of individual action as a means of effecting one's own deliverance in a way that the earlier forms do not. This focus on individual action—vital to Hegel's dialectic—thus helps construct the slave as a willful *human* agent in the narrative.

In what follows, I will offer not a Procrustean application of Hegel by way of proving that he was right, but rather the use of the master-slave dialectic as a prism, using the opposition and instabilities that Hegel outlines as a flexible basis for uncovering and interpreting the active and subversive presence of objectification in American fugitive slave narratives. As with Puritan captives, the slave's confrontation with basic category divisions exposes the objectification process, making visible its grotesque inner workings.

II

Frederick Douglass and the Rhetoric of Humanization

Frederick Douglass distills and crystallizes the most important paradoxes of Hegel's master-slave dialectic in his first autobiography, developing them further in his rewriting of his life story a decade later. Analysis of Douglass's famous *Narrative of the Life of Frederick Douglass, An American Slave* has generally centered on the way the slave gains humanity through the use of language, especially his largely self-taught literacy. The importance of this issue is of course undeniable, but the intensity and centrality of Douglass's thoughts and feelings about human objectification in his *Narrative* have not received enough attention from past critics of this book. In particular, the violence of Douglass's figurative rebirth during his confrontation with Edward Covey repays close attention.[31] This episode, which Douglass himself marks as formative in his life, gives him the attitude and perspective that make all his later triumphs possible. By risking his life for recognition, Douglass de-objectifies himself in Hegelian fashion and redefines Hegel's idea of slave labor.

The *Narrative* tells Douglass's story of his self-discovery, attainment of dignity, and final escape to freedom, a process that Houston Baker summarizes as a "quest for being."[32] Douglass's account opposes and ultimately reverses the grotesque transformation wrought by slavery. The narrative is a story of how the slave as grotesque (a liminal human/beast) becomes wholly human. The argument that drives Douglass's book is that a slave is in fact a human being and is therefore entitled to human rights. Indeed, Douglass wrote the narrative partly to convince doubters that he, a former slave, was capable of such a transformation (from laboring chattel into literate abolitionist) on his own. He lays out the distance between the states of anonymous slavery and individual humanity in the dense opening paragraph of his book, when, in the first of many such comparisons, he explicitly sets himself on a par with animals:

> I was born in Tuckahoe, near Hillsborough, and about twelve miles from Easton, in Talbot County, Maryland. I have no accurate knowledge of my age, never having seen any authentic record containing it. By far the larger part of the slaves know as little of their age as horses know of theirs, and it is the wish of most masters within my knowledge to keep their slaves thus ignorant.[33]

The ignorance Douglass describes effectively removes the slave from the current of human history, even as it equates him with the rest of the owner's property. Henry Louis Gates says that this deprivation of temporal space creates the gap between slave and master that makes objectification possible.[34] Douglass's simple message is not just that he wasn't like other kids. He is saying that he was never a kid at all. Slavery wipes out his childhood, destroying, among other things, his bond with his mother (24–25). One of the striking features of Douglass's entire opening chapter is its remarkably economical description of the alienation of objectification, the basis for Patterson's description of slavery as "social death."[35]

Literacy vitalizes the young Douglass, giving him his earliest sense of his own humanity. Sparked by the innocent efforts of his mistress to teach him to read, he labors to educate himself. His subsequent account of his slavery remains a description of a state of social death, but now he makes clear that his objectification lies only in the view of others; he refuses to acknowledge it in himself. This distinction highlights the importance of Douglass's own perspective on the process. Although he knows that he has been objectified before others, Douglass does not see himself as (socially) dead—and so the reader does not see him that way either. He is enslaved, yes, and is consequently viewed by his owners as less than human. (His second owner, Hugh Auld, acts on this belief and calls a halt—though too late—to his wife's tutoring of the young

Douglass.) Despite his objectification in the eyes of society, Douglass retains a strong sense of himself as a human being. His awakened consciousness makes him resent his enslaved state.[36]

The Puritans' experience with the Indians shows that the perspective of the objectifier makes it hard to see the objectified subject as a fully human being. The perspective of the objectified, here exemplified by Douglass, has the opposite effect: his emphasis on his own humanity makes it hard to see him as *not*-human. Marked as nonhuman, the Indians cannot be made to stay in that category in the Puritans' eyes; they instead come to occupy a grotesque in-between space. The slave is similarly marked in his master's eyes, but that doesn't mean that he must see things the same way. Once Douglass learns to read, he asserts his human identity—and this means that he escapes this liminal space. How does Douglass manage to distance himself from the grotesque? The difference between him and the Indians lies in nature and perspective. Put simply, it is as natural for the reader to see Douglass as human as it is unnatural for the Puritans to see the Indians as monsters. Stewart Guthrie says that the human strategy is, in the presence of any doubt, to assume that something is alive and to test to see if it is human, a perceptual strategy designed to allow us to detect other people wherever possible.[37] Because Douglass *is* a person, and because he is telling his own story from his own vantage point, the rhetorical power given by his own perspective makes the decisive difference in his fight to be perceived as human. (Of course the sympathies of his Northern reading audience would provide no resistance to Douglass's assertion of full humanity, making this effort at recognition easier.) This battle for the first human right forms the basis for numerous literacy-centered readings of Douglass's book.

But Douglass's crucial change under the brutal reign of Edward Covey affects everything. He is sent to the slavebreaker Covey by his master Auld because of the resentful, "unmanageable" behavior which arises from his consciousness of his unfair lot. Covey is good at what he does, and when he beats Douglass down, the slave's whole perspective shifts. The inner liberation he gained through reading ends abruptly, and he loses his assertive spirit. As a result, Douglass says that he accepts his own objectification.[38] He sinks back down to where he was at the book's opening—and because he falls from heights previously unattained, the impact is all the greater.

Covey is literally tasked with breaking Douglass's rebellious spirit. This he does by stripping the slave of his dignity:

> Mr. Covey succeeded in breaking me. I was broken in body, soul, and spirit. My natural elasticity was crushed, my intellect languished, the disposition to read departed, the cheerful spark that lingered about my eye died; the dark night of slavery closed in upon me; and behold a man transformed into a brute! (95)

In this well-known passage Douglass once again dies a social death. The significant difference from his earlier belligerence—when his enslavement made him angry—is that now he is dead to himself as well as to others. Beaten down by his master and defeated in a struggle for recognition, he becomes the slave that Hegel describes in his dialectic. Douglass's description of his inert state exposes the kernel of grotesque objectification at the center of slavery. Though he retains human form, Douglass describes himself as taking on the inner qualities of an animal. The man/brute that he describes is a Caliban-like grotesque. Douglass's inner humanity, communicated through his own defiance in the face of his bondage, is compromised. He is objectified in his own eyes.

Douglass follows himself through this transformation and then heralds his coming liberation from his grotesque state in another famous passage: "You have seen how a man was made a slave; you shall see how a slave was made a man" (97). His transformation back into a human being results from his spontaneous rebellion against Covey. The change is sudden: Covey tries to whip Douglass one day, and the slave abruptly fights back. He successfully resists his master's assault, an act that "rekindled the few expiring embers of freedom, and revived within me a sense of my own manhood" (104). At this self-described "turning point" of his life as a slave, Douglass consciously throws off the animal comparisons. He becomes a fully human being again, grotesque no more.

Douglass thus returns to his former state of inner freedom, where he views himself as a person, in contradiction with his objectification in the eyes of others. He himself points to this inside/outside distinction:

> I now resolved that however long I might remain a slave in form, the day had passed forever when I could be a slave in fact.

> I did not hesitate to let it be known of me, that the white man who expected to succeed in whipping, must also succeed in killing me. (105)

This, I think, is the moment that Douglass declares his true and permanent liberation. Annotating this incident again in his second autobiography, *My Bondage and My Freedom* (1855), Douglass says that "a man, without force, is without the essential dignity of humanity."[39] One might argue that his literacy gets Douglass to this point of resistance, but once there, Douglass himself makes no special connection between his literacy and his decision to resist. He admits that he doesn't know the source of his sudden resolve to fight back (103).[40] Violence, not reading, is what sets him free.

Douglass's willingness to die has great significance in the Hegelian scheme of things, as Paul Gilroy has shown.[41] In *My Bondage and My Freedom*, Douglass describes himself after the Covey episode in telling terms: "I was a changed being after that fight. I was *nothing* before; I *was a man now*. . . . I had reached the point, at which I was *not afraid to die*. This spirit made me a freeman in *fact*, while I remained a slave in *form*" (246–47; Douglass's emphasis).

For Hegel, this defiance of mortality confers the upper hand in the original battle for recognition; it is this quality that enables the master to win the early fight and enslave his vanquished opponent. The loser's fear for self-preservation makes him into an objectified slave. By privileging recognition over his own life in the fight with Covey, Douglass humanizes himself for the second and final time in the *Narrative*.

With this self-creating movement across the boundaries, Douglass effectively reverses Hegel's narrative. Though he is already Covey's slave when they clash, he succeeds in turning the conflict back into a fight for recognition between two people, a struggle that—according to Hegel—actually precedes the creation of the master-slave relationship. A sign of Douglass's success at turning back the clock is that Covey meets Hegel's standard and recognizes Douglass's humanity after their fight. Though Douglass remains in his employ, the slavebreaker never tries to whip him again.[42] Covey does not turn Douglass in to the law, either. Though the slave would certainly have been whipped then, his punishment would, as Douglass says, have come at a price to Covey's reputation as a slavebreaker (*My Bondage*, 248). Covey's willingness to let the matter pass illustrates the master's dependence on the slave as outlined in Hegel's dialectic.

By resisting Covey, Douglass re-creates himself as a human being, this time as an adult. Recall the beginning of the narrative, when Douglass describes how his birth as a slave has deprived him of a child's chronological markers and has thus kept him out of human history. Originally born as a slave child without history into what Frances Smith Foster calls "a drama already begun,"[43] Douglass's victory over Covey thrusts him back into history, at a point selected by himself. He denies his own enslavement, denies his own objectification, and wakes from the "beast-like stupor" he describes in the *Narrative* (95) into human historical consciousness.

III

The Work of Freedom

Douglass's rebellious efforts do not exactly correspond to "work" as Hegel defines it. Hegel says that forced labor (working for the master's interests) humanizes the slave by allowing him to see how his consciousness can shape the process of creation. To Hegel, the slave's act of making something for the master shows the bondsman that he is a person. In Douglass's case, though, working for Covey has the opposite result, as he describes in his *Narrative*:

> If at any one time of my life more than another, I was made to drink the bitterest dregs of slavery, that time was during the first six months of my stay with Mr. Covey. We were worked in all weathers. . . . Work, work, work, was scarcely more the order of the day than of the night. . . . I was somewhat unmanageable when I first went there, but a few months of this discipline tamed me. (94)

Speaking in *My Bondage and My Freedom* of his master's effectiveness as a slavebreaker, Douglass says that for Covey, "hard and long continued labor" was even more effective than the lash as a means of breaking the spirits of rebellious slaves like himself (215). The point is crucial: doing Covey's work makes Douglass feel more like a slave, not less. Rather than bringing indirect consciousness of freedom, the slave's labor makes him into a "brute" in his own eyes. On the other hand, Douglass's battle against the slavebreaker results in the kind of freedom that Hegel says work will provide: Douglass uses his conscious resistance to create and define himself as a person independent of his master.[44] There is no question that this exertion of the slave's creative force takes considerable effort and energy. For the purposes of the American slave experience, particularly the final generation before the Civil War, I think that Hegel's "work" needs to be redefined in terms of conscious, pointed resistance against the master's control.[45] In Hegel's dialectic, labor indirectly causes the slave to realize his humanity; in the life of Douglass and other fugitive American slaves, active resistance accomplishes this directly.

Hegel's dialectic depends on the slave's identification with his forced labor, but in Douglass's case this identification is compromised. In Hegel's dialectic the slave comes to see his work as his own, even if the master appropriates the product. Douglass's description of his work for Covey contradicts this expectation. Why? I think that the answer lies in the explicit racist ideology of American slavery. Unlike Hegel's bondsman, the American slave was held captive by a doctrine of black inferiority that encompassed his entire existence. The law held that whites could never be enslaved. On the other hand, blacks were, as Thomas R. R. Cobb pointed out, fairly presumed to be slaves solely on the basis of their color.[46] During the time that Douglass was writing his first two autobiographies, proslavery intellectuals were working harder than ever before to strengthen their arguments for black inferiority and slavery. Their efforts (which I will consider in more detail in the next chapter) were made in response to rising slave resistance at home and growing abolitionism in the North, and they resulted in increasingly virulent racism in theory and practice, a pervasive racism that restricted the American slave in many ways. Orlando Patterson's point, made in criticism of Hegel, that "there is nothing in the nature of slavery which requires that the slave be a worker,"[47] has particular relevance to the American system, which held a slave a slave regardless of the work he did—or did not do—for his master.

Frantz Fanon's reading of Hegel's master-slave dialectic gives some support to this argument. Fanon follows Hegel's description of the master-slave relation up to a point. Hegel says that the slave's action becomes the source of his own liberation, but unlike Hegel, Fanon envisions a violent confrontation between the slave and the master. Hegel's faith that work can break up the master-slave relationship is based on his insight into the fundamental weakness of the master's objectification of the slave. The system is weak at its perceptive core, and its weakness comes from the attempt to deny and domesticate the grotesque. Moreover, this weakness is a sign—seen by Hegel—that the attempt to enslave (or colonize, perhaps) is doomed to fail over time.

While Hegel sees work as the key to freedom, Fanon relies on violent uprising. Fanon says that the Negro must fight for freedom in order to know and understand it. He uses the example of America as a constant racial battleground to argue that conflict is the only way for the slave to achieve the mental state of freedom. In his preface to Fanon, Sartre says that the violence of the colonized against the colonizer "is man re-creating himself. . . . [H]e comes to know himself in that he himself creates his self." Fanon himself says that "it is the intuition of the colonized masses that their liberation must, and can only, be achieved by force." For Fanon, violence is the only force that can destroy an unsound category system. For blacks to do whites' bidding solves nothing.[48]

If white racist belief effectively disempowers the work the slave does for the master, then the problem for Douglass—and for other American slaves living under such a slavery system—was to find a way for the slave to reappropriate the idea of work for himself. In Hegel's model, the slave requires a connection between work and freedom. If forced labor doesn't provide that connection, the slave must find another kind of work. If the slave is cut off in this way, as Douglass was, he has to seize the definition of work and remake it for himself. Only thus can labor gain the possibility of freeing the slave in mind, body, and eventually, in word.

The American fugitive slave narrator links the idea of work directly to resistance. This resistance need not be violent (as Douglass's was); it is a matter of working directly counter to the master's wishes rather than obeying them. Eugene D. Genovese has proposed a Hegel-inspired model of slave existence in which blacks avoid dehumanization by taking whatever their masters allow and using it for their own cultural purposes. The slave narrative, a story of direct resistance, goes beyond this give-and-take; it describes a special case of great importance. When the slave steps over the line to oppose the master directly, he redefines the nature of their struggle for recognition. Slave narrators like Douglass follow Hegel's paradigm when they connect work to freedom, but they do so in a strikingly different way than Hegel predicts.

My epigraph quotation from Samuel Ringgold Ward's 1855 *Autobiography* points to the American variation on the Hegelian model. Ward's book turns on the motif of "anti-slavery labour," which he defines as any work that will help refute the "nonsense and heresy" of slavery.[49] Ward, a prolific lecturer, devoted his own labor to such fervent denunciations of slavery. The examples of Douglass, Ward, and others in the following pages show that Hegel's link between work and self-value does not necessarily take place under the slavemaster's yoke. In the world of the American slave, physical resistance is work. And escape is work. Describing his service as a conductor on the underground railroad during the years following his own escape, Douglass wrote in his third and final autobiography that he "never did more congenial, attractive, fascinating, and satisfactory work."[50] Douglass was free when he worked on the underground railroad, but his contact with and labor on behalf of other slaves surely made him recall his own time in bondage.

In the American reworking of Hegel, the best work is the kind that opposes the master and thus points directly to freedom. It is no accident that slave narrators, in detailing their various forms of resistance, praise hard work in the highest terms. Responding to a racist ideology that renders forced labor meaningless as a source of self-consciousness, American slave narrators throw their effort against the master, a gesture that unites labor, resistance, and freedom.

In the following pages I will trace this adaptation of Hegel's master-slave dialectic in American fugitive slave narratives. There are two intertwined forms of "work" for the American fugitive slave narrator: the resistance, and the writing of that resistance. The "work" of resistance covers direct rebellion against the master, escape, and other less common ways of reaching for freedom.[51] The "work" of writing follows a rhetorical pattern of self-objectification and then liberation, a movement that points directly back to Hegel's dialectic. The telling completes the slave's act of resistance.

This telling follows a predictable formula of escape and rescue. Fugitive slave narrators escape both physically and taxonomically, rescuing themselves and sometimes their loved ones. This standard progression toward liberation borrows liberally from that of another successful formula story, the adventure tale. This debt to a more established, less overtly propagandistic genre is central to the workings of the slave narrators' achievement in their own time, as well as afterward.

The peak popularity of fugitive slave narratives corresponds to the rise of abolitionism, which, beginning in the late 1830s, transformed itself from a small group of agitators into a national social and political movement of transformative power in about a decade's time. Fugitive slave narratives rode the tide of abolitionism even as they helped to fuel that tide. Sales figures stayed high until the Civil War, and the genre persisted even afterwards in a different form: memoirs of slavery, some of them of high literary quality, continued to appear for many years after the war was over. Fugitive slave narratives transferred the conventions of popular formula stories of adventure into a specifically abolitionist mold.

"Adventure" is a somewhat nebulous genre, but most readers would agree, I think, on a set of conventions that center on courageous behavior expressed in a time of trial. Martin Green, for example, defines "adventure" as a virtuous response to the challenges of experience in a place far from home, or even from civilization itself, while Cawelti identifies the central fantasy of the adventure as the "hero overcoming obstacles and dangers and accomplishing some important and moral mission."[52] Adventure stories became popular in the United States during the early nineteenth century, shortly before fugitive slave narratives did. The roots of the genre were English, and spread easily to the United States; the historical novels of Sir Walter Scott were bestsellers in early America and exerted an admitted influence on the young nation's writers; *Robinson Crusoe* (1719) was also quite popular. American adventure stories varied in form and setting. They took place abroad—Royall Tyler's *The Algerine Captive* (1797) was one of many adventures set in "the Orient"—or on the frontier (as with James Fenimore Cooper's popular Leatherstocking tales). They could also be based in actual experience rather than imagination, witnessed by the success of autobiographical frontier narrative (for example, Washington Irving's *A Tour on the Prairies* [1835] or Richard Henry Dana's *Two Years Before the Mast* [1840], both of which sold well during the first half of the nineteenth century).

The most obvious link between slave narratives and adventure stories is the devotion of both genres to escape and rescue. In escaping from both slavery and the in-betweenness of the grotesque, the fugitive slave narrator exploits the grotesqueness of slavery as a narrative device. As I will show, fugitive slave narrators successfully appropriate the conventions of the adventure story for their own propagandistic ends. Moreover, they do so in order to avoid being appropriated themselves by these very conventions, to keep themselves from being co-opted by the (white) tale of exploration and conquest. The adventure story conveys a set of ideas and associations which I will explore—including national identity and heroic virtue—that are highly beneficial to slave narrators, who seek above all to establish their deliverance from liminality to full human status. Wrapping themselves in these associations of virtuous American freedom enables slave narrators to forcefully declare their own humanity and thereby avoid another set of associations that were widely applied to blacks: the discourses of scientific racism (which supported black inferiority and therefore slavery) and teratology (literally, the study of monsters, an early discipline that underwrote the freak show and served as the basis for a subgenre of proto-adventure stories of its own).

Telling their stories, fugitive slaves invariably objectify themselves—usually by cataloguing masters' atrocities against them—and then humanize themselves by tracing their own paths to freedom. What often follows this self-liberation is a rhetorical attempt by the former slaves to objectify their masters. These rhetorical movements are best understood in terms of the racial grotesque. Having escaped the grotesque state of slavery visited upon them by their masters, the liberated slave narrators manipulate the grotesqueness of slavery to their own advantage. Hegel speaks of objectification as a definite, if unstable, state of being. Exploring the complications attached to objectification in slavery—especially its incompleteness—allows the richness of Hegel's dynamic conception to deepen the understanding of the experience of the American slave in the age of abolitionism.

Humanizing the Slave

The slave's resistance should be understood in terms of the grotesqueness of slavery itself and the desire of the slave to escape that state. As the example of Douglass most clearly shows, slaves could humanize themselves by direct resistance. They had many ways to resist that varied in risk and danger, ranging from malingering to stealing, arson, and even to self-mutilation and suicide.[53] I will focus on overt acts of resistance here—for these are the ones that become the stuff of narrative—but these actions (which are mainly recounted by male slave narrators) describe a generalized power of resistance that was exploited by both sexes.

These acts of direct resistance to an existing order are also crucial to adventure stories. Green holds three elements to be basic to an adventure story: a frontier locale (which can be interpreted loosely as a place where civilization does not exist), the presence of romance (i.e., treachery, revenge, injustice, and the like), and what he calls "anthropological reflection"—where the hero compares "civilized people" with other groups who don't meet this set standard.[54] These typologies fit the slave narrative comfortably. The plantation, filled with barbaric slave owners, is an "uncivilized" place, and once the slave actually escapes it, the South becomes a kind of frontier filled with armed marauders seeking to capture the fugitive. The fugitive relies on people of goodwill and tries to outwit the forces of evil, who often masquerade in white hats in order to fool him. Cawelti links the adventure fantasy to a victory over death, which in the case of slave narratives applies to social as well as corporeal extinction. The adventure hero, he says, "confirm[s] an idealized self-image" that enhances the ego.[55] This is obviously a very good thing for slave narrators to promote, laboring as they are in a state of compromised humanity.

Having an adventure also meant being an American. It meant being willing to explore dangerous places and pioneer American values there, and it especially meant being willing to fight. William C. Spengemann argues that the American adventure story had its own national purpose, which he sees as "fundamentally antithetical to the Domestic Romance." American adventure stories accordingly point away from home and toward unfamiliar places, with personal liberation taking place at a remove from familiar surroundings. (This model would also help to account for the great popularity of *Robinson Crusoe* in the United States; though an English story, Crusoe's adventure touched American pressure points and could be read in the service of American national aims.)[56] Similarly, Green reads American adventure stories as relentlessly expansionist, masculinist, and nationalist—as a body of work directing and describing the growth of the United States. All fugitive slave narrators have a dangerous adventure in the "uncivilized" South and assert their democratic, freedom-based values by fighting their way to Northern "civilization." In doing so, they construct themselves away from their Southern homes as authentic "Americans." Their geographic mobility translates directly into social and economic mobility, as the slave's sheer force of will results in a change of status from "slave" to "free." Cawelti says that formula stories involve the reader in something larger than the story itself; for Green this larger entity is "the national myth."[57] The form of the fugitive slave narrative confirms this link between the particular and the general. By spotlighting the slave's ascent to "human," the fugitive slave narrative implicates itself with the familiar American story of rags to riches. This is an important piece of cultural work, not only because of the Southern denial of the slave's humanity but also because of the ongoing antebellum Northern colonization debate over the "problem" of what to do with free blacks and the ostensible virtues of shipping them to Africa.

For the fugitive slave narrator, the most important convention of the adventure tale may be that it legitimizes violence. According to Green, adventure stories make violence acceptable by linking "the culture of reflection" (as manifest in universities and other seats of rational thought) to that of "action" or violence, as exemplified by institutional authorities like the army and the police.[58] For the fugitive slave narrator, conventions borrowed from the adventure tale help to justify violence directed against the master (including direct conflict and escape) by wrapping these actions in the mantle of considered, rational justice. When fugitive slave narrators adopted this air of implicit authority, it must have helped to assuage some of the doubts and anxieties of Northerners who feared that immediate abolition would lead to a violent overturning of their own social and economic order.

By analogizing their own activities to socially accepted forms of white violence, fugitive slave narrators positioned their work to accomplish what militant and caustic protests like David Walker's 1830 *Appeal to the Coloured Citizens of the World* . . . could not.[59] Though Walker's *Appeal* also endorsed violence, it was written directly for blacks, and for the sole benefit of the enslaved population. Moreover, the controversy immediately incited by Walker's admittedly subversive work would have kept most moderate whites from accepting slave violence as a rational solution to the slaves' treatment. Though Walker's influence should not be underestimated—Sterling Stuckey calls him "one of the greatest ideologists of African liberation of the nineteenth century"—his message was obviously not aimed at white moderates.[60] The fugitive slave narrative, on the other hand, was directed at precisely that crucial Northern group, and the genre helped to make violence palatable for them. The links with adventure stories gave institutional associations and intellectual foundation to what was, by official Southern standards, an act of anarchic lawlessness. The slave narrator also uses these borrowed conventions to weave violent action into his larger work of self-liberation.

Violent rebellion like Douglass's is an attempt by the slave to free himself from a grotesque state of being, a life as a human thing. The use of violence to grasp one's own humanity is perhaps best illustrated by a small but memorable incident narrated by Bruno Bettelheim from a German history of the Nazi concentration camps:

> Once, a group of naked prisoners about to enter the gas chamber stood lined up in front of it. In some way the commanding SS officer learned that one of the women prisoners had been a dancer. So he ordered her to dance for him. She did, and as she danced, she approached him, seized his gun, and shot him down. She too was immediately shot to death.

Bettelheim's analysis of this "example of supreme self assertion" supports the expanded definition of "work" in the Hegelian scheme. Asks Bettelheim: "Isn't it probable that despite the grotesque setting in which she danced, dancing made her once again a person? Dancing, she was singled out as an individual, asked to perform in what had once been her chosen vocation."[61] As it did for Douglass, the doomed dancer's work mixes with violence; though part of a "grotesque" scene, her last labor is a self-actualizing dance of death.

Though it is impossible to tabulate, violent resistance was not uncommon among American slaves. Southern court records are filled with cases where slaves were prosecuted for rising up against their masters, while various historians have gathered an abundance of evidence documenting individual and collective slave uprisings.[62] When Douglass explicitly endorses individual resistance in *My Bondage and My Freedom*, he implies at the same time that it was far from rare. Describing the defiance of his fellow slave Nelly, he says that such resistance acts as a strong disincentive for the overseer in the future. The courageous slave, "although he may have many hard stripes at first, becomes, in the end, a freeman, even though he sustain the formal relation of slave" (95). The question, in the words of James Oakes, "is not whether the slaves resisted but what difference it made, whether resistance was effectively contained, whether slavery functioned, survived, and even flourished in spite of resistance, or whether it disturbed the balance of power between master and slave enough to weaken slavery itself."[63]

Slave narrators, not surprisingly, show a long memory for acts of direct physical resistance. John Thompson takes a page from Douglass's book and rebels violently against his hired master, choking him "until he was as black as I am." Solomon Northup also finds the opportunity to rise up against his overseer and whip him "until my right arm ached." In a factual aside to his novel, *Clotel*, William Wells Brown describes a slave who killed his master after the master attempted to "correct" him for objecting to the planned flogging of the slave's wife. Many slave narrators, including Thompson himself, recall hideous retaliation by slaveowners to such acts of resistance, and these must have had some deterrent effect. The slave in Brown's account, for example, was shortly shot to death in the swamp. A less violent but equally confrontational rebellion is Harriet Jacobs's refusal, recounted in *Incidents in the Life of a Slave Girl* (1861), to permit the sexual approaches of her master. She won't let him touch her because she already sees herself as a human being with a dignity worth spending seven years in a garret to preserve. Not all slaves had an attic to hide in, though; most were simply not in a position to retaliate. Their humanization had to take a different shape in the narrative.[64]

Escape was an important form of direct resistance, and one with an extensive literature. Many slaves' stories lacked a distinct moment of confrontational rebellion. In the absence of a face-off like the one between Douglass and Covey, the decision to escape itself becomes the rebellion. Escape was a specific instance of a more general liberation: the entry of the objectified slave into personhood. That moment takes place on an emotional and intellectual level before the escape itself does. Hegel says that "the essence of humanity is freedom"; given this postulate, it follows that the slave must see himself as both human and not-free before he can decide that escape is imperative.[65] This moment necessarily implies learning. It also implies rebellion, for the slave is casting off the definition of himself as "thing" assigned by the master, in favor of his own self-definition as "person." Douglass and other narrators dramatize

Fig. 3.4 A slave rising up against the overseer, as described by Austin Steward in *Twenty-two Years a Slave and Forty Years a Freeman* (1856). This beating, says Steward, "vanquished" the overseer, causing him to quit his job and move to another state. (Reproduced from Austin Steward, *Twenty-two Years a Slave*; reprint, Negro Universities Press, 1968)

the moment of rebellion as distinct from the escape; others collapse the two events together.

It thus made rhetorical sense for many fugitive slave narrators to spotlight the escape as the central symbol of their rebellion against objectification. The most memorable such narratives usually describe creative escapes, and these escapes usually comment in a pointed way on the state of human objectification. William and Ellen Craft took advantage of Ellen Craft's light complexion to disguise themselves as a white man and his slave. The two traveled thus to Philadelphia and freedom. William Craft's narrative of the deception, *Running a Thousand Miles for Freedom*

Fig. 3.5 A Suriname maroon. Maroons were bands of escaped slaves who lived in communities in forests or swamps. Note the skull on the ground. (Reproduced by permission of the Photographs and Prints Division, Schomburg Center for Research in Black Culture, the New York Public Library; Astor, Lenox, and Tilden Foundations)

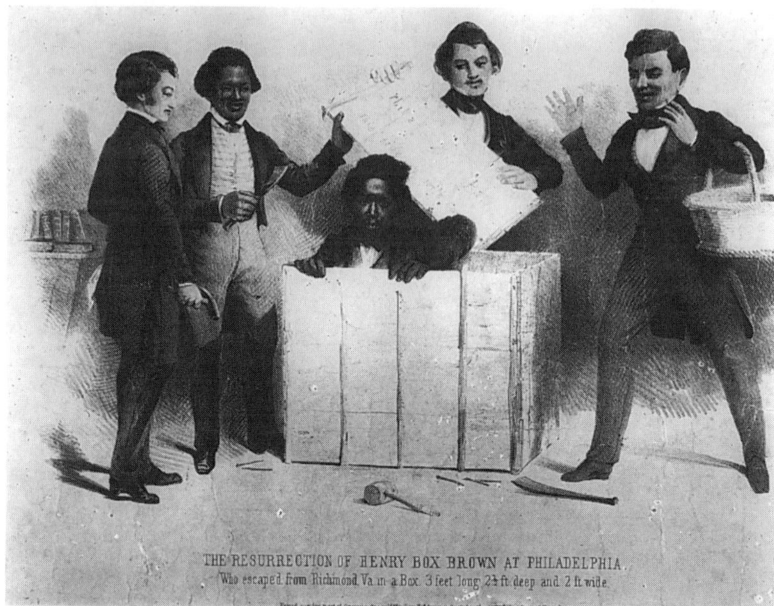

THE RESURRECTION OF HENRY BOX BROWN AT PHILADELPHIA.
Who escaped from Richmond Va. in a Box 3 feet long 2½ ft. deep and 2 ft wide.

Fig. 3.6 Henry Box Brown emerging as a free man from the box from which he took his name. Brown arranged to have the box shipped from Richmond, Virginia, to Philadelphia, a journey that took twenty-six hours. (Reproduced by permission of the Photographs and Prints Division, Schomburg Center for Research in Black Culture, the New York Public Library; Astor, Lenox, and Tilden Foundations)

(1860), plays pointedly with the idea of person as property. He refers to his disguised wife as "my master" even in the expository portion of the narrative, and when asked at one point if he belongs to her ("him"), he writes that his affirmative answer was no lie.[66] Many slavery sympathizers revile the attitudes of slaves and abolitionists in conversation with the disguised Crafts on the train; their successful escape is an indirect but deliberate slap at all of them.

The Crafts' widely celebrated escape was fictionalized in two novels before the firsthand factual account appeared in 1860.[67] The version in Brown's *Clotel*, in which the two fugitive slaves are not married, treats objectification issues even more trenchantly than William Craft does. In Brown's version, when the disguised woman is asked to show papers proving "his" ownership of the "slave," "he" pretends to grumble about a "strange law. . . that one can't take his property with him" (216). After the two make it to freedom, they split up. The man takes a train and finds himself a victim of early Jim Crow laws. Ordered out of first class into the baggage car, he insists on paying his fare based on his weight—making literal the analogy of himself to luggage. The conductor is startled, but has no rejoinder. Brown concludes by testifying that the incident is "no fiction," having actually taken place on that very railroad (219).

For Henry Box Brown, humanity literally bursts from out of slavery's closed box. The supreme irony of Brown's escape is that he accomplishes it by a kind of self-objectification. The slave actually turns himself into a mail parcel—even referring to himself as "mail"—and has himself "delivered" to freedom. (The box is pictured in the narrative.) Brown is transformed inside the box; he enters it a slave and emerges from it a human being. He then names himself after the method of his escape, a symbolic connection not only to his revolt against his own slavery but also to the thing that he disguised himself as in order to free himself.

Moses Roper's narrative is a more understated account of a similar revolt through escape. Roper details his repeated escapes in a flat tone which rarely varies, but his severe style indirectly points to his indomitable spirit. The bulk of Roper's narrative is taken up by a description of a series of unsuccessful escapes, each of which is followed by a bout of sadistic torture meant to break him. Roper never comments on his master's emotional agenda, except through his own rebellious actions, nor does he try to raise his hand against his torturers. Instead, once he recovers from whatever beating has been administered to him and is freed from whatever contraption intended to impair his movement, he immediately begins planning his next escape. Despite suffering perhaps the worst tortures of any slave narrator, he is never broken—and his escape stands out as his moment of triumphant revolt against the system.

William Wells Brown puts this rebellion neatly into words. Brown's escape is not great theater; he walks off a boat when it docks in a free state and disappears into a crowd. The drama comes from the author's annotations. Brown writes that he "wanted to see Captain Price [his former master], and let him know from my own lips that I was no more a chattel, but a man!"[68] For Brown, freedom means a physical sensation of change of status: "The fact that I was a freeman—could walk, talk, eat and sleep, as a man, and no one to stand over me with the blood-clotted cow-hide—all this made me feel that I was not myself" (66). In gaining

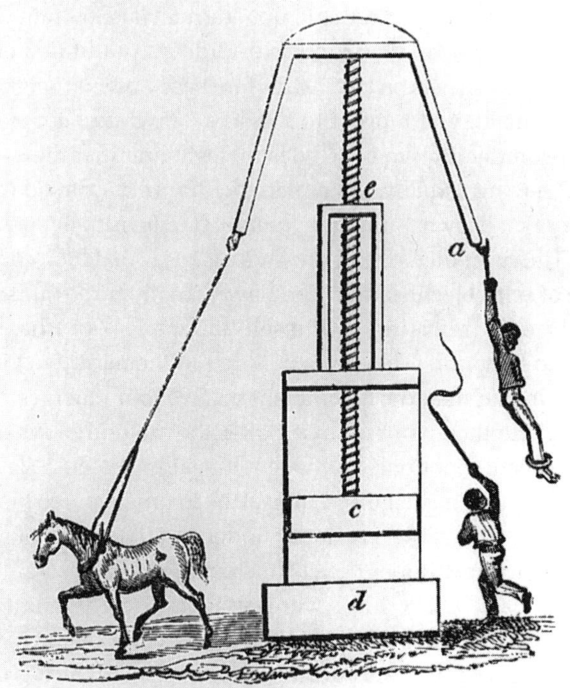

Fig. 3.7 This illustration from Moses Roper's *Narrative* diagrams one of the tortures inflicted upon him by his master, Mr. Gooch, as punishment for one of his many escape attempts. He describes how Gooch "hung me up by the hands at letter *a*, a horse moving round the screw *e*, and carrying it up and down, pressing the block *c* into the box *d*, into which the cotton is put." Gooch then put Roper into the box also. Especially striking is the way that Roper's description, including his caption, makes him part of the machine.

"After this torture," he writes, "I stayed with [Mr. Gooch] several months, and did my work very well." (From Moses Roper, *A Narrative of the Adventures and Escape of Moses Roper from American Slavery*, 1838; reprint, Negro Universities Press, 1970)

this new self, Brown takes back his life, as Hegel says the slave must do. Though he does not physically stand off his master, he lets his escape and his narrative stand as his rebellion.

The fugitive slave narrator's reappropriation of the idea of work clearly has its roots in violence. Even escape is a kind of physical confrontation; it carries with it the understanding that the slave risks an outbreak of violence and its uncertain outcome if exposed. In the context of Hegel's dialectic, the violent quality of slave resistance points back to the original battle for recognition, the conflict that determines the roles of master and slave.

This defining clash is reenacted in the life of every slave. Historical recollections suggest that it centers on the slave's first whipping. Jacob Stroyer's account of this event has been quoted and cited so often that it is practically archetypal. When the young Stroyer is beaten by Boney Young, a horse trainer employed by his master, he goes to his father for help and is astonished when his father counsels submission and says that he can do no more than pray for his son. His mother tries to intercede and is herself whipped, after which Stroyer is whipped again. Boney Young whips and otherwise tortures the child repeatedly and capriciously after that, with Stroyer having no choice but to submit. "This cruel treatment hardened me," Stroyer says, "so that I did not care for him at all."[69]

Willie Lee Rose describes the child's accommodation to slavery as "a social process" in which he learns from his parents "how to accommodate and when to resist," and to live with the hope of freedom.[70] Rose describes slave rebellion as resulting from a trauma in which the master crosses a line invisible to all at the time, including the slave himself. Confrontational rebellion leaves all effort at accommodation behind; the slave instead seeks to reenact and reverse the outcome of the original clash for recognition with the one who became his master. For his part, the master senses the danger involved in working with such psychic explosives and, as I will show next chapter, tries hard to stay within limits and so keep the master-slave relationship in place. The slave has the initiative, though, for as Hegel understands, the slave's struggle for self-consciousness and freedom doesn't depend on anyone else.

Objectifying the Slave

I have described how slave narrators make resistance into a form of work which the slaves humanize themselves by doing. Now I want to go back and look at what happens before that. Before they humanize themselves, slave narrators first objectify themselves: they make themselves into grotesques. Fugitive slave narrators degrade themselves as a rhetorical pose. Witness Douglass's witty defense in *My Bondage and My Freedom* of his own stealing during slavery: he defends taking meat from a tub as not stealing but "removal" of the meat from one tub to another; his master first "owned it in the tub, and last, he owned it in me" (189). This example highlights the raison d'être of the fugitive slave narrative genre—to present the slave as a thoughtful and sensitive human being who is being treated as a thing until his just and fortunate liberation. The formula demands that the slave must objectify himself before he can free himself. Objectification is not automatic for the fugitive slave narrator; in fact, the opposite is true, for the implied author of any autobiography is human. When the slave narrator does manage to objectify himself, he enters the same liminal state the Indians occupied in the Puritans' eyes. Placing himself between thing and human, the slave becomes a grotesque.

Douglass's *Narrative* may not strike certain readers as being about the grotesque, mostly because he omits most of the explicit details that would give it the kind of impact that we associate with the effect. It is true that the grotesque is more implied than actually present due to the author's restrained presentation, but the structure of the narrative is nevertheless exemplary of what I've been talking about throughout, for Douglass explicitly describes the role of the grotesque in objectification, and liberation from that status, as it is played out in numerous other narratives of slavery.

William Douglas O'Connor, for one, gives full reign to the grotesque implications of Douglass's work. The first part of *Harrington*, O'Connor's 1860 abolitionist novel, is a kind of fictional slave narrative, following the slave Antony's torturous escape from bondage (after which the novel shifts gears to romance). O'Connor's depiction of slavery is in the spirit of the grotesque paintings of Hieronymus Bosch:

> The reeking mules, panting and straining, with drooping heads, as they dragged the groaning ploughs through the soil of the cotton fields, or pulled the clanking harrows over the furrowed rows, had their monstrous jags of sooty shadow, like the malformed beasts of a devil's dream, jerking along with shapeless instruments beside them. The black drudges, men and women, plodding and tottering in the sweltering heat, behind the ploughs, beside the harrows, or dropping seed into the drills, had hunched and ugly goblin dwarfs of shadow, vigilantly dogging their footsteps, and bobbing and dodging with their more active movements. The burly overseer on horseback had his horsed demon of lubber shadow, which aped his every gesture

> and movement, ambling fantastically with him hither and thither among the rows, and grotesquely motioning into squirms of phantom glee the shadows of the writhing slaves on whom his frequent whip-lash fell.[71]

O'Connor renders the workers as weird, nonhuman creatures in a panoramic vision of slavery as hell.

To realize these grotesque implications of slavery, the fugitive slave narrator objectifies himself in two basic ways: internally and externally. In other words, the author can state that he believes that, inside himself, he is a thing (as Douglass does at the depth of his own despair), or he can describe slaves being used as things, a characterization that he implicitly or explicitly extends to himself. Internal self-objectification is rare, perhaps because it means giving up, and slave narrators generally avoid defeatism.[72] Moses Roper, for example, escapes and is caught again and again, with progressively more hideous tortures following each failed attempt. If his spirit flags, he never says so. Because a narrator's belief in his own objectification can only happen when he admits his own thingness, and because we know that the same author has come through the ordeal to write (or dictate) a book, such internal self-objectification is automatically understood to be temporary. Douglass exploits this implication beautifully when he prepares the reader for his victory over Covey even as he describes his own abasement at the slavebreaker's hands.[73]

Virtually all fugitive slave narrators objectify themselves from the outside. External objectification in their narratives takes place according to a fairly standard set of conventions, most of which simply extend the basic and frequent comparison of people to cattle. Accordingly, slave narratives often feature scenes involving the auction block, the pen (in which slaves are displayed in order to be sold), chains, collars, and coffles. Occasionally, as in the narratives of Moses Roper and others, these devices are modified and exaggerated in order to shock, but more often their prosaic quality is what enforces the equation of human to beast.

The slave narrator's most effective, flexible, and varied self-objectification strategies are emotional, not physical. Of these, the cleaving of the family becomes an especially fertile site of objectification in the slave narrative. All fugitive slave narratives highlight the way that slavery broke up families through the sale of their members. Even when their own families manage to survive the passage from slavery together (as William and Ellen Crafts do in their tale of escape), slave narrators never fail to enumerate instances of others less fortunate. This emotional torture extends the comparison of slave to cattle, and it does so more reliably than physical cruelty. Perhaps family breakups tug at the edges of human perception of the slaves because of the adaptability of the victims: their social groups are smashed, yet they go on and survive. Stowe recognized the power of this theme when she made the family into the central emblem of the slaves' humanity in *Uncle Tom's Cabin*.[74] Not all fugitive slave narratives are so pointed, but all exploit the dehumanizing effect surrounding the destruction of the family institution. To deny the slave's human connections is to deny the slave's humanity.

Connected to the denial of the slave family was the perversion of sex in their lives. Sexual exploitation of slaves enforced their objectification. First, slaveholders burlesqued the slaves' marital state by using it to serve their own interests and ignoring it when it did not. Henry Bibb notes that "there is no legal marriage among the slaves of the South," and of all slave narrators, perhaps he knew this best.[75] Bibb recounts his successful escape from slavery in his narrative, and then his return to the site of his captivity to try and liberate his wife. He is caught and sold back into slavery. Again he escapes, again he returns, and again he is apprehended and re-enslaved. Not to be denied, he escapes yet again and risks his liberty to return to Kentucky. This time he discovers his wife living as the concubine of her master. Only then does Bibb give her up. His futile efforts make his narrative a particularly good example of the way that slavery officially denied the social existence of its victims, and with it their humanity. Slaveholders exploited the marital state, making it into a seeming parody of the slaves' ostensibly human one.

Marriage was usually manipulated by slaveowners in this way for profit. In his *Narrative*, William Wells Brown tells of a master who sells a slave's husband and then orders her to marry another of his chattels immediately afterwards (60). Though Brown does not say so, the slaveholder surely did this because he wanted the woman to bear a child, thereby increasing the number and value of his possessions. As one minister put it, "By converting woman into a commodity, to be bought and sold, and used by her claimant as his avarice or lust may dictate, he totally annihilates the marriage institution; and transforms the wife into what he very significantly terms a 'BREEDER,' and her children into 'STOCK.' "[76]

Douglass mentions in his *Narrative* that Covey, the cruelest of his masters, was also in the habit of using his female slaves as breeders (93–94). Douglass sees this practice as forced adultery, but his view implies chosen sin, albeit chosen under duress. The description is certainly accurate, but I think that "breeding" slaves propagates something more disturbing: the idea that the slaves are incapable of choosing their "correct" mates because they lack the human judgment necessary to do so, and that their outrage at having their partners chosen for them necessarily recedes because—as slaveholding logic goes—only humans would find such control cruel, and slaves are not human at all.[77]

Sex outside of marriage also helps to objectify the slaves, both the female victims and the forced male bystanders. Many slave narrators write of masters' sexual abuse of female slaves. This activity is riddled with ironic contradiction, simply captured by Frances Harper in her 1892 novel, *Iola Leroy*, in which a slave remarks that "these white folks look down on colored people, an' then mix up with them."[78] Bibb compares slavery to a whorehouse in which "licentious" slaveholders "break up the bonds of affection in families [and] destroy all their domestic and social union for life" (38). This degrading treatment enforces internal objectification. Jacobs says that "some poor creatures have been so brutalized by the lash that they will sneak out of the way to give their masters free access to their wives and daughters."[79] In Hegel's terms, such slaves forfeit their human ties in favor of self-preservation, and so accept their own objectified state.

Of course such sex leads also to illegitimate children. Countless slave narrators were fathered by their masters, or by other whites. Such slaves sometimes know the identity of their fathers, but often they do not. Gates describes Frederick Douglass's relationship to his father, an unidentified white man who may have owned him, as "grotesque," a reference that speaks to the transgression of categories that results from the conflation of "father" and "master."[80] Such acts of unacknowledged paternity make kinship histories next to impossible for slaves to maintain. The consequent lack of genealogy weakens the slave's human definition, for people define themselves partly according to their kinship connections to other people. Animals have bloodlines, but people need to have relatives.

William Wells Brown's *Narrative* stands out among fugitive slave narratives for its artful rendering of external objectification. Brown's terse, economical prose depicts the systematic dehumanization of slaves (including himself) with supreme understatement. All fugitive slave narratives exploit the spectacle of humans as property, but Brown's is preoccupied with the process of objectification to a degree that few others are. The acuteness of this focus is aided by the fact that Brown's most interesting times as a slave were those he spent working for a slave trader. He devotes the largest part of his narrative to this period. This is a smart choice from a literary standpoint, as his horrific account of the slavery business takes some of the burden off his relatively undramatic escape (in which he persuades his master that if taken into a free state, he will not escape, and then does).

The bulk of Brown's narrative is devoted to a virtual catalogue of external objectification. Slavery in his telling is a state of almost unremitting physical and emotional violence, violence that always seeks to break and transform human into chattel. The narrative begins with an original spin on the standard form of self-objectification: "I was born in Lexington, Ky. The man who stole me as soon as I was born, recorded the births of all the infants which he claimed to be born his property, in a book which he kept for that purpose" (28).

Notwithstanding the convoluted syntax, this is one of the most effective beginnings in the history of a genre whose conventions for openings were most confining. Brown's prosaic statement of his "theft," along with his master's entry of his birth into his ledger, illustrates—as Douglass's beginning does—how the slave is forcibly removed ("stolen") from the current of human history at birth. The master's notation becomes a parody of what should happen when a child is born: a new birth is normally recorded in a genealogy, not a list of assets. Brown's own book (his narrative) essentially rewrites and replaces his master's "account" of his birth.[81]

The first specific incident that Brown recounts is of a whipping of his mother. Soon afterward, Brown's master sells the boy's whole family except for Brown himself. Brown then broadens his focus (as most slave narrators do) to include the objectifying treatment of other slaves. He describes the "taming" of a slave named John, a spirited man who is broken in body and soul (34). This incident prepares for the litany of similar atrocities that Brown witnesses as the slave of a slave trader, which he relates with a reporter's eye for detail and a writer's ear for understatement. For example, he follows a matter-of-fact description of the boathold in which the slaves are crowded and chained with a resonant one-sentence paragraph: "It was almost impossible to keep that part of the boat clean" (39). Literary restraint of this kind compares favorably with Douglass's emotionally taut phrasing.

Brown's mastery of his form grows out of the originality of his objectifying rhetoric. Comparing slaves to cattle was a common device in slave narratives, but Brown makes it new when he tells of how the slaves up for sale are "turned out into the yard during the day" (39). A boatload of slaves is a "cargo of human flesh" whose sale Brown observes with ironically tinged detachment: "As slaves were in good demand at that time, they were all soon disposed of" (40–41). The separation of child from mother is another commonly recounted horror of slavery. Brown recounts a particularly callous incident in which the trader, Mr. Walker, gives a young child away to an acquaintance because the child would not stop crying during a long march. Brown describes the scene thus:

> Walker stepped up to [the mother] and told her to give the child to him. The mother tremblingly obeyed. He took the child by one arm, as you would a cat by the leg, walked into the house, and said to the lady,
> "Madam, I will make you a present of this little nigger; it keeps such a noise that I can't bear it."
> "Thank you, sir," said the lady. (43)

Brown's impassive distance and masterful phrasing makes the reality of human objectification palpable—no mean feat in light of the desensitization brought on by the scores of slave narratives that preceded his own. Brown is rigorous about maintaining emotional detachment from what he sees. At one point, he watches a gang of white men murder a slave. The body is left overnight, thrown into a trash cart, covered with dirt, and taken summarily away (48). The entire passage, in which a human being is literally turned into garbage, receives no editorial comment. William L. Andrews says that this distancing technique generally provided the measure of truth in the slave narrative, and truth—that is,

Fig. 3.8 Northern depiction of a South Carolina slave auction (1861). (Reproduced by permission of the Photographs and Prints Division, Schomburg Center for Research in Black Culture, the New York Public Library; Astor, Lenox, and Tilden Foundations)

authenticity of the narrator's portrayal of slavery—was the author's dearest goal.[82]

According to Abdul JanMohamed, such realism provides the means by which the oppressed gains an emancipatory voice that reclaims the group's debased past on newly dignified terms.[83] JanMohamed focuses on the voice of the oppressed as something other than meaning-laden silence or a reflection of the voice of the dominant group. Instead, it becomes an act of signifying, fully liberating aggression, part of a Manichaean opposition whose basis stems from Fanon. But it seems to me that JanMohamed underestimates the persistence of the connection between self and other that characterizes Fanon's version of the colonial relationship, as well as those of his interpreters. For JanMohamed, the voice (and consciousness) gained by the other is definitive and self-constitutive, but I would suggest that the variability of the grotesque, including the definitional need for the "normal" that is the continuing basis of the connection between them, dictates against such polarizing oppositions.

Analysis of the slave narrative instead suggests that the master's attempt to objectify the slave forms the continuing basis for the relationship between the two. Homi K. Bhabha, for example, locates resistance between opposition and negation, as "the effect of an ambivalence produced within the rules of recognition of dominating discourses."[84] In this case, the slave's need for authenticity particularly and directly relates to the master's failed act of signification. The slave author must be reliable in order for him to objectify himself. And he must objectify himself in order to prepare for the next step, the reclamation of his humanity.

Objectifying the Master

After objectifying and then humanizing themselves, many slave narrators go after their masters, seeking rhetorical payback for past injuries suffered. Frantz Fanon says that the colonized native is "ready at a moment's notice to exchange the *role* of the quarry for that of the hunter."[85] It is in this spirit—one that reconceives rather than discards the connection to the master—that the slave narrator "repossess[es] the signifying function."[86] Unable to confront the slaveholders in person, former slaves use their narratives to subject their masters to the same kind of dehumanizing treatment that they themselves received. The objectification of the master is a common rhetorical occurrence in antislavery literature of the mid-nineteenth century, both fact and fiction.

As with so many conventions of the fugitive slave narrative, the roots of this practice lie partly in the adventure story. Green argues that the adventure story is inherently undemocratic in its tendency to separate the good, virtuous, and powerful from the rest. Autobiographical works like Dana's *Two Years Before the Mast* (1840) and Parkman's *The Oregon Trail* (1849), for example, stand as stories of how adventure shaped men of quality into men of action, of how elevated human potential is realized in practice.[87] Fugitive slave narratives turned their heroes into men (and women) of higher virtue, while their masters, as the villains, were exiled to the lower orders—toward the very borders of humanity that the slave-heroes had previously occupied. This narrative tendency to social division contributed further to the slave narrator's social mobility—and it also provided an ironic rejoinder to the slaveholding class that was trying to exert similar power against them.

William O'Connor's fiction again provides a good lead illustration of how the slave can make the master into a grotesque. When the slave

Antony rises up and attacks his master as Douglass did, he figuratively transforms the slaveholder into a monster:

> His whole being rose in a wild, red burst of lightning, and the throat of Lafitte was in his right hand. . . . He saw the devilish face beneath him begin to redden in his gripe, and deepen into horrible purple, and blacken into the visage of a fiend, with bloody, starting eyeballs, and protruding tongue. (30)

O'Connor supplies the explicit details that Douglass leaves out, bringing out the grotesque transformation inherent in the objectification of human beings.

Slave narrators don't usually write in such a lurid fashion, but their purpose is often similar. Solomon Northup rises up against his master and sees his opponent change as he overpowers him: "I felt as if I had a serpent by the neck, watching the slightest relaxation of my grip, to coil itself round my body, crushing and stinging it to death" (98). Douglass also sees Covey as a "snakish creature" during his second retelling of their struggle (*My Bondage and My Freedom*, 215, 242). In addition, he describes the slavebreaker as "wolfish," as a "monster," and—in a precise echo of his own earlier description of himself in extremis—as a "brute" (210, 225). (This later account adds a further detail of Covey's abasement: the fight ends with the slave dragging the master through cow manure.) Again, these reversals accord with Hegel's formulation that these victorious fighters gain from their victories the power to enslave—and thereby objectify—their masters. Of course certain practical realities (as well as their own inclinations) make enslaving their masters unfeasible for them; their self-discovery usually gives them the gumption to escape instead.

Lafitte's transformation recalls the hirsute monstrosity of Simon Legree in Harriet Beecher Stowe's *Uncle Tom's Cabin*. Former slave Austin Steward writes—with his own mistress in mind—that "slavery transforms more than one excellent woman into a feminine monster." When Madison Washington, the title character of Douglass's *The Heroic Slave*, liberates the slaves aboard the brig *Creole*, the defeated white sailors flee into the rigging, where Douglass has his narrator describe them as "like so many frightened monkeys." Mrs. Bellmont, the pathological mistress in Harriet Wilson's autobiographical novel, *Our Nig*, resembles Legree in many ways: her sadism opposes love and religion. Just as Uncle Tom invites his own death by refusing Legree's order and Douglass does the same by standing up to Covey, so does Wilson's Frado take a stand and resist her mistress. When she fights back, she "feels the stirring of free and independent thoughts." Having previously lost her personhood (as is clear from the appellation "Nig" and its derisive use), she regains it by asserting her individuality.[88]

Objectifying the master means turning him into a monster in the narrative. In this respect, fugitive slave narratives are inverted rewrites of freak show pamphlets, which are themselves hybrid adventure stories that turned people into grotesque trophy monsters to be displayed by their hunters. The pamphlets, which were sold in front of each individual freak show exhibit, were souvenir advertisements that told the stories behind particular freaks. Their popularity, along with that of the freak show, grew rapidly during the 1840s and 1850s. Pamphlet narratives followed a standard formula.[89] The human anomalies were explained teratologically, as scientific "monstrosities," with explanations of how they "got that way." The racial freaks (whom I will be discussing in detail in chapter 5) received different treatment. They were generally Africans and South Seas Islanders who had nothing anomalous about them except that they were from a different (and always nonwhite) culture. Promoters exploited this difference to depict them as dangerous cannibals, headhunters, and atavistic throwbacks to lower life forms and "primitive" ways of living.[90]

The racial freaks were the villainous monsters in lurid African and Polynesian adventure tales, the objects of the missions conducted by the "heroic" explorers who ostensibly risked life and limb to "capture" these "things" and "bring them back alive" to civilization.[91] Though racial freak pamphlets mined the conventions of the adventure story in this way, they focused not on the heroes but on the villains: the "monsters" that had been brought back as trophies to show the populace.[92] (It is notable that, as Robert Bogdan puts it, disability frequently wears "the black hat" in adventure stories.[93] Then and now, audiences readily identify with freaks as villains.) Racial freak pamphlets are search-and-capture stories of white achievement. They fit into an imperialistic framework which implies that whites are masters of the world. Similarly, Green describes the adventure story as an "energizing myth" of empire whose heroes are fundamentally frontiersmen doing the "national work."[94]

Fugitive slave narrators wrote stories that opposed the formula that governed the freak show pamphlet, and so turned this association with national mythic heroism to their own profit. While freak show pamphlets first describe the capture of the natives in the jungle, and then "capture" them again within the categories of teratology and ethnology, slave narratives reverse this movement. Instead, they reorder the conventions of the freak show pamphlet and oppose the dogma of the science that underwrote it—just as the slave inverts the master-slave relationship according to Hegel's paradigm. In fugitive slave narratives, the "thing" talks and escapes—and then declares his superiority to the master who enslaved him. The slave narrator thus substitutes a story of conquest for one of submission; the conquered becomes the conqueror and the master is renamed "monster."

Being able to rewrite the standard story of exploration in this way signals that the slave has become human, for only humans, beginning with Adam, have the power to name other creatures. Like Mary Rowlandson before them, slave narrators show a deep appreciation of the power of names and naming. Slave narrators pick up where Rowlandson leaves off in her captivity narrative, exploiting the capacity of names to confer humanity upon their holders. Wilson tells how "Nig" (which sounds like "thing") claims her humanity and becomes Frado. Frederick Douglass goes by four different surnames during the period covered by his *Narrative*; he finally allows his benefactor to name him "Douglass" as a ritual symbol of his freedom. Douglass at least keeps his first name throughout his life, but William Wells Brown has even this stripped from him during his captivity. At the end of his 1847 narrative, Brown reveals that for most of the period he has been describing, he has been called not William but Sandford. Brown had lost his name because William was the name of his master's ward, and his master would not permit his slave to carry the same one. This stricture shows Brown that his name was really "Slave."[95] Brown links his quest for freedom with a desire to repair this wrong: "I was not hunting for my liberty, but also hunting for my name" (64). Like Douglass, Brown allows a white samaritan, Wells Brown, to complete his name after he gains freedom. The Quaker tells the escaped slave that "since thee has got out of slavery, thee has become a man, and men always have two names" (66). Names, then, connect to the slave's resistance and act as humanity's badge. They grant both power and history, acting as part of a liberation in Hegelian terms: the slave risks his life, takes power, and enters into history. William L. Andrews compares the best slave narrators to Emerson's Poet, as "'namers' who realize that 'words are also actions, and actions are a kind of words.'"[96]

The power to name is an essential part of the movement to freedom in many slave narratives. Ann Kibbey says of the slaveholder that "the authority to command carried with it the authority to accuse—in effect, the authority to name." She sees the slave as a prisoner of the language of slavery, which "destroy[s] the meaning of all words except 'master' and 'slave.'"[97] When the slave can name himself, he can name others. He can make "master" into "monster," and frequently does. By assuming his own narrative perspective and grabbing the opportunity to tell his own human story, the slave breaks out of the prison-house of language. Once granted this freedom, the slave can execute the rhetoric of objectification in the same way that a slaveholder does. Objectifying the master thereby becomes a part of naming oneself.

And of course there is physical torture. All slave narrators describe whipping, and many recount much worse tortures than that. But who is finally objectified by this? The exceptionally sadistic torture of slaves—widely and variously recounted in their narratives—degrades the master perhaps more than the slave, transforming the torturer into something less than human: a monster lacking human sympathy, conscience, and morals. Recall Douglass's point that slaveholders would not torture their slaves unless they had already accepted the assumption that their victims had a human understanding of what was happening to them. The more bizarre the torture, then, the more it paradoxically serves to emphasize the slave's humanity; why, after all, would someone devise such exotic cruelties for a mere brute animal?

This striving for ever greater cruelty reflects the dilemma of the master in Hegel's dialectic: he is trying to get human recognition from someone whom he has already reduced to the status of thing. Fueled by frustration, the torture becomes a compulsive search for an unattainable goal. (Nor was it the only such doomed gesture for recognition. Next chapter I will examine some of the master's more subtle strategies for maintaining the slave in his grotesque state.) In recounting ordeals of torture, the slave uses the conventions of the narrative to help the master objectify himself. Thus, the account of torture in every slave narrative has a subversive effect. If the power to name helps to humanize the slave and allows him to objectify the master, then the ritual description of torture covertly accomplishes the same thing. It becomes part of an overall figurative strategy to reverse the places of slave and master in the objectifying equation.

Douglass argues that torture participates in the larger dehumanization of the master by slavery itself. Recalling his desperate, supplicating return home to Thomas Auld after a savage beating by Covey, Douglass says that his master was first "somewhat affected" by his story, "but he soon repressed his feelings and became cold as iron." This example of how human sympathy is forcibly banished from mind is, according to Douglass in *My Bondage and My Freedom*, living proof of how "humanity fell before the systematic tyranny of slavery" (229).

IV

"Resistance to Theory"

More than any other genre of American writing, fugitive slave narratives owe their existence to the complex, ambiguous, unstable grotesqueness of the objectified person. Slave authors exploited the former tenuousness of their own humanity with a persistence that grew over time. During the quarter century preceding the Civil War, fugitive slave narrators delved more and more deeply and explicitly into the category violation and grotesque monstrosity which lay at the ontological roots of the peculiar institution. By the time Douglass sat down to write his *Narrative* in 1845, the fugitive slave narrator had evolved a straightforward formula: he first placed himself into the liminal space of human-as-thing and then reversed the "grotesquification," liberating himself into full-fledged personhood. Each slave narrative enacts the transformation from person into grotesque and back again. Their authors ask two basic questions: How can a person be seen as a thing? And then, how does a human/thing become a person again? The books thus begin and end with the ideas of objectification and transformation.

As the writings of the American Puritans clearly show, human objectification becomes a constant struggle for the objectifier. Slave narratives manipulate the anxiety that accompanies this conflict. Like Puritan accounts of captivity, they highlight the troublesome issues that mark the objectification process—but the difference is that slave authors invoke these issues consciously and explicitly because, as they show, they have the advantage: they know that they are human, and that their readers know it. Further, slave narrators know that however they may gesture toward denying their own humanity, their masters also know it. The slaves' chosen literary genre during the age of abolitionism exposes a specific denial by the white objectifier, a denial marked by the strenuous assertion of the idea that Werner Sollors locates at the basis of ethnicity: "We are not like them." Objectification of other people takes this denial to its logical extreme: "they" are not human like "us." By working explicitly with the underlying idea of transformation, slave narrators expose the entire workings of the objectification mechanism, and with it the grotesqueness of slavery itself. Slave narrators willingly objectify themselves because they know—as does Hegel and a growing number of their Northern countrymen—that this mechanism is unsound, that people who assert their humanity can't be kept out of the human race for long.

It may be true that, as many critics have said, the slave narrator writes his way into humanity, but if this is so, he works his way there before taking that last step into the public eye. Hegel says that the slave realizes his humanity through work; the slave narrative is the story of that work, but it is also part of that work. The narrative effort begins with resistance in life and ends with resistance in words. The act of telling is only the last portion of the slave's task, the concluding gesture that brings his completed work into public being. With his narrative, the slave publicly declares the humanity that he has already displayed before his owner. This simple assertion flies in the face of the enormous amount of proslavery propaganda—both written and oral—that proliferated in the antebellum South. The peak of the fugitive slave narrative coincided with a boom in proslavery literature of all kinds, from pamphlets to fiction to special church services for slaves. The escalating slavery debate eventually had to be settled on the battlefield, but in the 1840s and 1850s the war was waged by printing press with growing intensity.

Because the slave narrative directly opposed proslavery doctrine, it served as a nineteenth-century version of "resistance to theory," the theory being the entire social structure of black inferiority, supported by its underlying racist rationale.[98] The slave narrator rejects prevailing arguments for black inferiority propagated by slaveholders, dismisses the economic system that underlies them, and asserts a clear alternative vision of society. The final act of telling is an important part of the slave's task, for the narration is what brings the slave's resistance to the master's theory into the arena of public discourse where the two could oppose each other directly. The rebellion and the telling together comprise a work of self-making, an act of creation that defines itself through its own opposition.

This opposition is complicated, implicated as it is with the dominating culture from which it springs. Edward Said has argued for a dialectical relationship between imperialism and resistance. He cites the slave narrative as part of what he calls "the culture of resistance," a literary movement among the oppressed whose purposes amount to nothing less than "an alternative way of conceiving human history."[99] By daring to imagine an America without racism or slavery, each fugitive slave narrative reaches far beyond the life of the individual slave.

But in inventing such an America, the slave author cannot—indeed, most likely would not—reinvent the history in which slavery *did* exist. Following Frantz Fanon, Said suggests that imperialism can be an animating force; this is certainly true for the slave narrator, who appropriates slavery—a kind of domestic imperialism—for his own use.[100] Given that Fanon's work has lately become the paradigmatic site for contesting the essential meaning of the colonial exchange, it is worth stating that my adoption of Said's reading underscores my contention in this book that the tension between the dominator and the dominated produces an ongoing dialogue between two groups whose identities as master and (former) slave have been forged out of the same event, creating a shared past that locks them together so that their discourses are—like the grotesque and the "normal"—unavoidably implicated with each other. Contra Gayatri Chakravorty Spivak and Homi K. Bhabha (among others), I propose that black and white in America form a kind of binary star, attracted by gravitation but repelled by magnetism, historically and eternally in motion, orbiting about each other.[101]

Bhabha's suspicion of any fixed opposition of the dominator and the dominated merits special attention, as he specifically rejects Hegel's master-slave dialectic as a viable way of describing the colonial relation.[102] Bhabha argues that Hegel effectively fixes the positions of master and slave, while the "ambivalence" of the colonizer dictates that both the colonizer and the colonized should be viewed within a psychically split, unconsciously conflicted field. But reading the fugitive slave narrative in terms of Hegel's master-slave dialectic requires approaching his terms—

which are, after all, abstract—in a flexible way. While I share Bhabha's special concern for preserving the movement and tension in a relationship that is meant to shift, I have done so by placing Hegel's model within the context of the culturally created, always shifting grotesque. This setting allows Hegel's basic values to float within a range of conflicted perception on the part of both master and slave, a perception shared and governed by the misguided and highly resonant attempt to objectify. Specifically, I've tried here to contextualize Hegel's basic oppositions—seen in terms of the grotesque—within the historical situation of the nineteenth-century American slave and, as will be seen in the next chapter, that of the master as well.

For the American slave, storytelling becomes a special kind of work, gaining its status in conjunction with the slave narrator's redefinition of labor. Forced labor doesn't awaken the slave's self-consciousness because American slaveholders divorce slave inferiority from labor and tie it to race—as backed up by biology, religion, law, and virtually every other field of antebellum intellectual inquiry. In redefining work for himself, the American slave makes the rebellion and the telling of it into labor against objectification.[103] In abolitionist America, the fugitive slave narrative thus becomes part of the discourse of resistance.

The slave's movement inside the dynamic, shifting mesh of the dialectic of master and slave (a saga of change from person to thing and then back to older and wiser person again) finds natural structural expression in fugitive slave narratives. The action is the action of creation: the master defines the slave as a thing. Slave narrators reverse the grammar; instead of the master creating the slave as a thing, the slave becomes the subject and defines the master, casting him as monstrous villain in a drama of human cruelty. The narrative enacts the slave's degradation as object and subsequent rise to power as subject. Only by telling the story can the slave narrator fully execute this reversal. Focusing on the slave's work at human self-creation thus dramatizes a variation on Hegel's dialectic: the slave works his way to a sense of humanity first in deed, then in word.

This way of reading fugitive slave narratives provides for the entry of Hegel's thought into the mainstream of African-American literary dialogue, where it offers a useful way of thinking about the difficulties accompanying the attempt to turn human beings into things. The example of Douglass shows particularly clearly how Hegel and the literature of slavery can be used to implicate each other in a rich vision of the literature of human bondage.

By questioning who (or what) is a human being, the slave narrator challenges the root division of cultural knowledge and belief. The slave narrative destroys and then reconstructs the definition of "human." This invariably means playing with the grotesque, which depends on the construction of an opposing other sitting on the edge of the human category. Slave narratives set this other in place and then transform it by having it make a defiant assertion: I am a human being. The widely followed custom of including photographic frontispieces in slave narratives can thus be seen as a way of allaying the uncertainty and fear brought on by the grotesque in the narrative. Before you begin, the author seems to be saying, here is a picture of me: you can see that I am human.[104]

Reflecting on his early agonizing days at the slavebreaker's, Frederick Douglass says in *My Bondage and My Freedom* that "I shall never be able to narrate the mental experience through which it was my lot to pass during my stay at Covey's" (221). This admission points to the black hole at the center of every slave narrative. William L. Andrews says that the slave narrative genre is united partly by "a search for language through which the unknown within the self and the unspeakable within slavery might be expressed."[105] But what is this ineffable quality of slavery? Not physical cruelty, certainly—that is discussed readily by most narrators, as is emotional torture. What cannot be spoken is the objectification. Slave narrators adopt a rhetorical pose in which they readily (and temporarily) objectify themselves because there is no other way for them to speak of their experience. Because things can't talk, people must do the next best thing and speak of what it was like to be seen as things. In other words, it might be possible to describe one's own objectification from memory, but the experience has to be retrospective, for to be objectified in one's own mind would necessarily mean losing one's own consciousness. By subjecting themselves to objectification within their narratives, slave narrators use rhetorical artifice to make their readers feel what they cannot say.

Within this unspeakable blank space lies the depth and complexity of the slave narrative, and of human objectification in literature generally. The opposition between the slave as person and the slave as thing is cited relatively frequently in the historical analysis of slavery, but it has been too quickly dismissed in literary studies of the institution. This central contradiction is much more complicated than it seems to be at first glance. Viewing it through the lens of the grotesque shows how the slave's existence on the epistemological edges creates continually shifting, agonizing complexities for both slave and master. My focus here has been on the rebellious slave, and how he views his own grotesque state of slavery. I have traced some of the ways the fugitive slave narrator manipulates his own grotesqueness in order to deny it dramatically, sometimes objectifying the master in the process. This drama of rebellion was never far from the master's consciousness. In the next chapter I will take up the master's side of the opposition and examine some of his doomed strategies for maintaining the slave in his grotesque state.

The reflexiveness with which we see the human image through the master's efforts and the slave narrator's trials shows the depth of the denial required in order to objectify a person. Slave narratives dramatize that denial; they deconstruct and reenact the entire experience of anxiety attached to the creation of the grotesque other. Moving across the human boundary from the outside in, slave narrators force the reading audience to face the reality of objectification: not just that the grotesque other is human, but also that we humans are the ones who made him out as different in the first place.

CHAPTER FOUR

SAMBO AGONISTES:
Racial Stereotyping and Fictional Strategies of Objectification

Speak not of my Maker to me. Under the lash, I believe my masters, and account myself a brute; but in my dreams, bethink myself an angel.

—Herman Melville, *Mardi*

A worse evil to the slave than the cruelty he sometimes endures, is the moral degradation that results from his condition. Falsehood, theft, licentiousness, are the natural consequence of his situation. He steals,—why should he not?—he cannot, except occasionally, earn money . . . . He lies,—it is the natural weapon of weakness against tyrant strength. He goes to excess in eating and drinking and animal pleasures—for he has no access to any higher pleasures. I do not mean that there are no exceptions. there are pure, honest, and virtuous slaves. . . . But there is one evil inherent in the system, that no care can obviate it. The slave's nature never *grows*. The slave is always a child. Slavery is the parent of vices . . . abject submission or deadly vindictiveness are now as they have always been the fruits of slavery.

—James Freeman Clarke, *Slavery in the United States: A Sermon Delivered in Armory Hall on Thanksgiving Day, November 24, 1842*

Anxiety over the slave's objectified status results in the dynamic instability of the figure of the slave in literature. Last chapter focused on how slave narrators exploit this instability to stage a Hegelian drama of regained humanity. This one spotlights the hostile dialogue between proslavery and abolitionist fictions, focusing on the proslavery effort to confine the slave within the category of "thing." Writers of plantation fiction tried to do this through indirection and ambiguity, centering on the clever use of the vaguely defined Sambo stereotype, a happy slave whose humanity was always questionable but never fully denied. Sambo became a unifying symbol of the proslavery movement, a mainstay of proslavery fiction, and a target of abolitionist writers—when they weren't being seduced by it themselves.

This rhetorical ploy failed to conceal Hegelian-type anxiety. As constructed by slaveholders, Sambo, with his love of comedy and performance, was an essentially imaginary figure, a slaveholder's fantasy representing the master's futile attempt to gain recognition from the slave and repress the nightmare possibility of rebellion.

In 1853 William Wells Brown wrote in the preface to *Clotel* that "the great aim of the true friends of the slave should be to lay bare the institution, so that the gaze of the world may be upon it" (74). *Clotel* was the first novel by an African-American, and in it Brown—himself a former slave—thoroughly practiced what he preached. From its beginning scene (of a slave auction) onward, *Clotel* places a heavy and repeated emphasis on the human face of chattel slavery.

Brown wanted to highlight the essential *peculiarity* of the peculiar institution. His rhetorical goal was simple and direct: to unmask slavery for what it was: a crude attempt to turn a person into a thing. Speaking against the illegality of slave marriage in the South, for example, Brown's narrative voice is trenchant and pointed:

> As the only asylum for true education, [marriage] is the first and last sanctuary of human culture. As husband and wife through each other become conscious of complete humanity, and every human feeling, and every human virtue,; so children . . . find an image of complete humanity leagued in free love. (117–18)

It's hard to miss the point here: the author uses the words "human" or "humanity" five times in two sentences. Such sermonic didacticism overwhelms the narrative of *Clotel* at times. Given that the abolitionist movement had been leading a strong and vocal existence for about twenty years by the time the novel came out, why did Brown feel the necessity to stress the slave's humanity so stridently? A look at the literary historical context of *Clotel* offers an answer. The novel was a salvo in an ongoing rhetorical war for control over the literary depiction of slavery—and fiction was one battlefield that the abolitionist side entered rather late. While the slave narrative was Northern territory in this war of words, fiction was the major rhetorical battleground for the South. Brown's novel was a challenge to the Southern literary plantation. In *Clotel*, Brown presented ringing rebuttals to stock portrayals common to Southern proslavery novels, books that made up a large propaganda movement which had been thriving for some two decades. Plantation fiction was a genre dedicated to papering over the human aspect of slavery; *Clotel* was the first black voice to enter the literary debate in a field that the South had dominated for decades. Though Harriet Beecher Stowe's *Uncle Tom's Cabin* turned out to be a heavy rejoinder to the proslavery writers, the book had not come out in full until mid-1852, only a year before Brown's novel (after Stowe had serialized it during the previous ten months). Moreover, the appearance of *Uncle Tom's Cabin* inspired a burst of novelistic rebuttal, which meant that *Clotel* entered a literary marketplace into which more proslavery fiction than ever was being produced.[1]

The slavery debate in fiction had begun in earnest in the early 1830s, with the first word going to the apologists for slavery. Plantation fiction by John Pendleton Kennedy (whose 1832 novel *Swallow Barn* had great influence on the development of the genre), William Gilmore Simms, Nathaniel Beverly Tucker, and many others had blanketed the field before antislavery forces made a concerted effort at fiction. Plantation fiction was highly didactic, and insidiously effective—hence the need Brown must have felt to write his own book in a tub-thumping style. In particular, the Southern genre manipulated the image of the slave in a canny way, making him a contented participant in a pastoral fantasy. Plantation fiction amounted to a sustained attempt to camouflage slavery by covering its ontological foundations and masking its cruelties. Walking the point in this rhetorical campaign was America's most famous racial stereotype: Sambo.

I

Overview

Sambo was an omnibus stereotype, the original and continuing basis for the myriad of black stock figures that arose during the nineteenth century. Though many of these—such as Jim Crow, Zip Coon, Jim Dandy, and Old Dan Tucker—developed within the Northern minstrel tradition, it's important to keep in mind that minstrelsy was itself inspired by plantation stereotype, a connection that remained in force even after the blackface show transcended its southwestern roots and gained a life of its own. A minstrel character like Zip Coon, for example, is typified in *Uncle Tom's Cabin* by Augustine St. Clare's slave valet Adolph, a portrayal by a Northern writer that nonetheless suggests the ways that the basic Sambo type could be tailored to custom-fit specific members of the slave community. As the root of all slave stereotype, Sambo represented a clear object (the happy slave) surrounded by blurry, but recognizably Southern, outlines.

Sambo was a peculiarly American institution. Orlando Patterson argues that the Sambo stereotype is "an ideological imperative of all systems of slavery," but even so, no other slave society in history tried as the American South did to portray its slaves as happy and contented.[2] Why should American slavery have needed constantly to justify its own existence? Because the basis for that existence, an ideology of black inferiority, was always shaky, supported as it was by the grotesque: the shifting, unstable idea of the person/thing.

Slaveholders used Sambo as the image of the person/thing in such a way as to elide the essential grotesqueness of the slave's role. Homi Bhabha, the postcolonial theorist whose model is most compatible with the one I have employed here, actually evokes the grotesque in his description of the stereotyping process. Bhabha sees derogatory stereotyping as a form of metonymic substitution arising from "strategies of desire" that turn an anomaly (the colonized) into a "production[] of contradictory and multiple belief." As a result, "Black skin splits under the racist gaze, displaced into signs of bestiality, genitalia, [and] grotesquerie."[3] It follows from Bhabha's argument that the Sambo stereotype could not have succeeded in assuaging the slaveowner's ambivalence. In fact, slaveowners felt the slave's liminality even as they denied it, and like people walking on ice, had to expend prodigious amounts of energy to keep their rhetorical balance. The concerted Southern defense of slavery thus stands as evidence of the tenuousness of human objectification—a tenuousness implicit, as I will demonstrate, on both sides of the debate.

The central requirement of the Sambo stereotype was to infantilize the slave. Sambo was the reification of this need. The infantilization rationale is crucial to the practice of slavery itself: turning someone into a permanent child makes it easier to justify his enslavement under the guise of parental care. Stanley Elkins, whose controversial 1959 analysis of Sambo provoked a firestorm of competing views that have kept the figure in the historical spotlight ever since, says that the Sambo stereotype depends on the absence of human dignity, or "manhood" in the slave.[4] Immaturity averts sexuality, and this lack of sexual threat is crucial to the stereotype. Indeed, the classic Sambo is thoroughly emasculated, a point that Joseph Boskin cites as explanation for why Sambo is almost always male. Brown indirectly attacks the emasculated image of Sambo in *Clotel* by having one of his male heroes—a virile and highly principled rebel slave—dress in women's clothes in order to escape from jail, days before he is to be hanged for rebellion. From the portrayal of the slave as a harmless child comes the notion that he is happy to serve his white parental figures, and eager to show it. Boskin describes Sambo as good-natured, immature, and needy of management—a figure "centered on working *and* entertaining, producing *and* laughing, servicing *and* grinning."[5]

This infantilization practice was fraught with complication for the slaveholders, and these complications are the focus of this chapter. I will be limiting myself here to the white invention of Sambo in antebellum fiction. I am less concerned with how Sambo existed (or whether he existed) than with the way that whites answered their own need to believe in his existence. In essence, I argue that the slaveowner constructs blacks as grotesque Sambos because he has no other choice but to see them that way. My central goal is to show how the Sambo stereotype marks an ultimately unsuccessful attempt by the master to solve his greatest problem: the impossibility of complete human objectification. By depicting the slave as a happy servant, eternal child, and perpetual dependent, slaveholders were able to largely efface the inherent grotesqueness of a human/thing. This deliberate ambiguity lent considerable versatility to the stereotype. Such versatility results from the essential purpose that Sambo served: to evade the central reality of slavery. Rather than face the question of the slave's humanity, Sambo throws a veil over it.

Proslavery writers deployed the Sambo stereotype in different situations, in a conscious and unconscious effort to efface the reality of human objectification. In the next section I show how the ambiguous humanity of Sambo allowed the stereotype simultaneously to symbolize two implicitly contradictory arguments for Negro inferiority—those based on biological and social causes. The vagueness of Sambo's attributes allowed the stereotype to interact flexibly with different proslavery arguments, thus representing an attempt to defend slavery that was both ingenious and thoroughly disingenuous. In the last section of this chapter I will return to Hegel's master-slave dialectic, showing how Sambo's long-standing associations with humor and performance take on special meaning within the context of the dynamic balance between master and slave. I argue that the comic slave performer stood as a doomed attempt by the master to extract human recognition from a figure whom he had already deemed nonhuman. At the same time, the figure of the performing Sambo masked the master's well-documented fear of slave rebellion.

Examining the Sambo stereotype in light of the literary debate over slavery highlights the multiple roles played by the stereotype in obscuring the naked reality of the practice—the attempted objectification of human beings. When Brown calls for writing that will "lay bare" the peculiar institution, he is calling for the unmasking of Sambo to reveal an unwilling captive of a system that tortures and dehumanizes him. *Clotel* was Brown's answer to his own call to rhetorical arms against the Sambo stereotype.[6] The single-mindedness with which he approached his task—and Stowe hers—suggests how entrenched was the proslavery opposition, and how familiar its reified symbol.

Sambo's American emergence can be traced to the eighteenth century, but Southern use of the stereotype increased markedly in response to rising abolitionist sentiment in the North, as a product of the increasingly heated arguments on both sides of the slavery question. The antebellum popularity of the stereotype peaked during the thirty years before the Civil War.[7] This period coincided with the rise of abolitionism, including the heyday of the fugitive slave narrative, Nat Turner's violent rebellion of 1831, the Compromise of 1850 that led to the Fugitive Slave Law, the Dred Scott case (which reached the Supreme Court in 1856), and John Brown's 1859 raid on Harper's Ferry. Increasing abolitionist activism required answers from the slaveholding side; Sambo's popularity therefore met a clear social need.

Sambo was a central figure in a Southern paternalist ideology which, says Carolyn Porter, "was generated not only by a slave economy, but also by Indian removal." Just as portraying the Indians as children provided a built-in justification for their forced relocation, so did the infantilization of slaves readily allow for their economic exploitation by their white "fathers." Paternalism evolved as a kind of overlay then, a rationalization that arose from the discomfort that accompanies objectification—whether of Indians or slaves—and which concealed what was really being done to them under a veneer of benevolent concern, coupled with Christian charity.[8]

This evasion was meant not only to oppose Northern abolitionists; it likewise helped the Southern slaveholders convince themselves of the benevolence and necessity of their institution by masking its most unpleasant reality. The infantilizing Sambo stereotype softened the harshness of objectification, thereby assuaging some of the guilt that many historians have offered as one motivation for slaveowners' behavior. Eugene Genovese, in one of the best-known discussions of this topic, says that such guilt would be impossible to measure, being part of "an extreme inner tension" that results from the vexing contradictions upon which the institution hinged. James Oakes, who rejects many of Genovese's conclusions about Southern slave-owning society, agrees with this one, arguing that the masters' guilt resulted from a clash between their humanistic religious values (which held the slave a person, if a limited one) and their profit-driven economic ones (which marked the slave as a thing). The slaveowners' guilt stands out as a symptom of their attempt to objectify their slaves. In addition to this guilt, the Sambo stereotype also masked the masters' fear of slave revolt, a fear that was very much in the public mind during the years following Nat Turner's slave uprising. These lurking fears and insoluble oppositions required psychological relief—which was gained by the imagined presence of an ambiguously portrayed, happy slave. Sambo, the smiling childlike slave, is essentially a trick of the mind's eye.[9]

Southern paternalism found its most involved expression in the fiction of the period, and this fiction was itself a major propaganda source for the way of life it represented. I want to suggest that the paternalistic stance of proslavery fiction writers, exemplified by the Sambo stereotype (either the docile, contented worker or the mischievous but essentially harmless scamp), carefully pretends to be conciliatory, but it is better described as obfuscatory.[10] Plantation novelists used Sambo as a kind of rhetorical smokescreen thrown up to obscure, and thus avoid, the grotesqueness of the slave's state of being, a condition caused by the crucial difficulty and central contradiction for slaveowners: the impossible-to-evade fact that the slave is human in spite of the myriad attempts to objectify him as property.

Proslavery fiction relies on bucolic settings full of wise and loving masters and matrons, and loyal but lazy, morally inert but happy slaves. One could say that the genre represents a collective attempt to picture a kind of Edenic Sambo's paradise.[11] But these careful efforts can be read differently, for it is perhaps easier to see the slave as a pet, not a child. David Brion Davis argues that the model for the slave's alienation was in fact the domesticated animal. He offers as evidence "the continuing practice of pricing slaves according to their equivalent in cows, horses, camels, pigs, and chickens."[12] Infantilization tries to sneak away from the grotesque aspect of slavery, embodied by the fact that a person is being viewed as property. Even so, it is not surprising that the contented "children" basking in the plantation sun in book after book often resemble animals more than humans. Frequently aided by atavistic descriptions of their bodies and facial characteristics, the slaves become domesticated wild things, savages tamed—and the objectification idea thus reasserts itself. But the treatment of Sambo also shows that the perception of humanity is impossible to suppress fully—the attempt alone requires constant effort and vigilance, and it is ultimately doomed because human beings can't help acknowledging the presence of their fellows. This assertion of humanity that rises amidst the continuing effort to deny that humanity results in a conceptual blending of person and thing. Sambo—often seen as grotesque—embodies that ambiguity.

By creating a black child whose difference from white children was that he would never grow up, proslavery fiction writers did their part for the anti-abolitionist propaganda movement. They used novels to enact a world where they had things both ways, in effect keeping the slave human and nonhuman at the same time. In the pages that follow I will be analyzing the persistence of this contradiction in antebellum and abolitionist fiction, showing how slaveowners used the Sambo stereotype as a way to dodge the objectification question through a psychologically fabricated escape hatch. Abolitionist fiction was slow to challenge the fictional incarnation of Sambo, and the delay allowed the stereotype to gain a stronghold in the literary imagination, even among Northerners. But as Stowe, Brown, and others ultimately showed through their withering scrutinies of Sambo, the attempt by slaveholders to duck their own

in heathen Africa, the race needed to be cared for by white Christian masters until the infinitely distant future point when its members would be able to take care of themselves. These arguments held different positions relative to the American revolutionary legacy. The biological side held that all people were created equal, but that slaves were not people; the social argument posited inequality among people, and was therefore inherently undemocratic at its core, with its adherents eventually calling for a society based on caste, with Negroes at the bottom.

The implied conflict between the biological and social views has not gone unnoticed by modern historians. William R. Taylor sees an uneasy link between the nineteenth-century South's sentimental values (the emphasis on family and "evangelical benevolence") and "the grave inconsistencies in the planter's social code." These inconsistencies, says Taylor, center on the conflicting assumptions behind the biological and social arguments: the "conflict between the Negro as child and the Negro as animal." George Fredrickson likewise sees an ambiguity embedded in the question of whether the slave is a domestic tool (and therefore subhuman), or childlike (and therefore human). As a result of this division, he says, "The South's fundamental conception of itself as a slaveholding society was unstable." This instability—with its resulting grotesque tension between human and thing—drives the slavery debate as it appears in literature.[16]

The biological and social arguments for black inferiority overlapped to a certain extent, but they had separate intellectual sources. The social argument centered on the paternalistic philosophy, defending slavery (and inequality generally) as a "positive good," a phrase popularized by John C. Calhoun's famous 1837 defense of slavery (made in a speech to the Senate) as a benefit to the slave. The "positive good" argument is at bottom an attempt to dodge slavery's cruelties, but this argument grew more and more complex over time, becoming intertwined with economics and politics, centering on an opposition to market capitalism (from which the slave was allegedly to be protected). The best-known spokesman for this view, George Fitzhugh, was essentially a socialist, but an eccentric one who called for institutionalized social inequality in the form of an enlightened caste system. The "positive good" faction relied on a stock opposition between the English laborer and the American slave; they argued that the slave, whose livelihood was assured by the benevolent planter, had a better deal than the starving British laborer.[17]

This comparison was common (and presumably effective) enough for Brown to attempt to refute it in one of *Clotel*'s many narrative asides (195). Such conceits might suggest that the "positive good" argument was free of racial assumptions, but this was not the case. Fitzhugh's views became more explicitly racial under abolitionist pressure, for example, a development that shows that the "positive good" argument could not be readily separated from its roots in black inferiority. The title of Fitzhugh's best-known proslavery argument, *Cannibals All! or, Slaves Without Masters,* reflects this craven essence of the agrarian fantasy and points to the racism that is clumsily hidden behind the supposedly benign view of slaves as dependent children. Though the book is far less inflammatory than its sensational title would suggest, the title goes a long way toward exposing the malignant underside of Fitzhugh's benevolent facade.[18]

The rise of the morally based "positive good" argument roughly coincided with a corresponding emphasis on the biological doctrine of permanent black inferiority. Biological arguments for black inferiority have a history that antedates the creation of the United States, but mid-nineteenth-century America saw a surge in such arguments, propagated by slaveholders who wanted to augment their relatively small numbers with the Southern white lower classes. The planter class made "democratic" overtures to Southern non-slaveholders to preserve the institution against the fear of the "unnatural" rise of blacks above poorer whites. This "*herrenvolk* egalitarianism" fanned the populist flames of proslavery and so served as insurance for the slaveowners against Northern attacks.[19] Biological inferiority was the key component of this ideology; spokesmen for this point of view contorted themselves in spectacular fashion to defend their position. For example, Samuel Cartwright wrote a medical essay describing slave "diseases" such as "drapetomia" (running away) and "rascality."[20] Underlying the existence of separate diseases, of course, is the assumption that the slave is a separate physical type.

The results of pre- (and later post-) Darwinian racial science, resulting from various intertwining scientific debates on the species and origin of nonwhites, served to buttress this broad conclusion. Together, these early studies amounted to a concerted scientific enterprise dedicated to demarcating immutable racial categories and demonstrating the innate inferiority of the colored races. Early scientists supported their racialist conclusions with evidence from fields like phrenology (which compared the skulls of "lower races" with those of "higher" ones), the related field of craniometry, and naturalism (which combined taxonomy with biblical study to produce the doctrine of "polygenesis," which held that there had been a separate creation of different Adams and Eves of different races, who had developed separately and at different rates). Evolutionary thought both before and after Darwin trafficked heavily in throwback imagery, with "inferior races" being put forward in both freak shows and scientific publications as unevolved humans or "missing links." Reginald Horsman documents the exhaustive and highly convoluted attempts to construct racial difference for social ends, efforts by an early scientific establishment that built its present reputation for empirical rigor on the early foundation of racialist analysis of freaks (both racial freaks and human oddities), blacks, and Native Americans.[21]

Straddling all these nature and nurture arguments is the Sambo stereotype, a comic figure whose vaguely childlike affability unified diverse viewpoints and masked a set of serious concerns, obscuring the untenable objectification problem and the differing Southern approaches to it. Sambo reflected and symbolized *both* the biological and social arguments for slavery—a neat feat, considering that they start out from fundamentally different assumptions. The stereotype bridged the areas where the biological and social factions agreed, at the same time obscuring their large areas of disagreement under the blurry outlines of a slave childhood that was designed never to end. For the social proslavery argument, the great problem was that the notion of a permanent child lay dangerously close to that of a whole different biological type. For the biological view, this proximity was itself the problem: the idea of the slave as a (human) child promoted an unwelcome link between white and black. By eliding the question of whether the slave is human, the Sambo stereotype provided a banner beneath which the proslavery rhetoricians of all stripes could fight side by side for their shared goal.

It is striking that a single stereotype could come to personify such diverse intellectual strands of the proslavery movement. It is a measure of the rhetorical work that was assigned to the Sambo stereotype that he had to carry the flag for the entire proslavery movement. And it is a measure of the endemic weakness of the ideology behind that movement that an inherently unstable grotesque should be the only one to fit the qualifications demanded of a standard-bearer. The ambiguity of Sambo's childlike quality is what allows this unlikely symbolic unity; the very grotesqueness of Sambo permits the character to mediate between the countervailing assumptions of two major proslavery ideologies. Sambo was an example of what Willie Lee Rose calls the "special and different kind of humanity" assigned to slaves.[22] This shaky concept (more than one kind of humanity?) could not be examined too closely without raising unanswerable questions, so the unity it provided was necessarily shallow. Sambo offered these groups a chance to unite by *not* raising these questions, instead projecting a deliberately vague image of undefined inferiority and contentment in bondage, an image whose ambiguity helped to unify the different proslavery arguments.

Brown points to this vagueness as part of his general campaign against the Sambo stereotype in *Clotel*. He describes Mr. Carlton, a once-dilettantish Northern white man now turned ardent abolitionist, reflecting on his former attitude toward blacks: "He had looked upon the negro as an ill-treated distant link of the human family" (231). Simultaneously pushing blacks away ("distant") and drawing them close (into the "human family" chain), this view is finally hard to categorize, except as a result of Carlton's uncritical acceptance of the Sambo stereotype. Brown uses the character's benign ignorance to show how the Sambo stereotype insinuated itself into the minds of unconcerned onlookers.

The existence of Sambo obviously rationalized slavery, but the stereotype did more than that—it obscured the entire conceptual structure underlying the peculiar institution. In addition, as Fredrickson says, the stereotype offered an efficient means of social communication, a public relations shorthand that enabled slave-owning ideology to reach those, like the fictional Mr. Carlton, who lived their lives outside the particular intellectual arena where the battle over representation was taking place.[23]

Sambo may have been able to mediate between proslavery factions, but part of this success may be a result of the blending of the two views at the edges. For example, Mrs. H. R. Schoolcraft says in her proslavery novel, *The Black Gauntlet*, that "Africans hate civilization, and are never happier . . . than when allowed to live in the abandonment, nakedness, and filth, that their instincts crave." This characterization takes its rationale from both sides of the biology-society divide. Indeed, Schoolcraft avails herself abundantly of both cultural and biological arguments for black inferiority throughout her heavily sourced novel.[24]

In essence, Sambo functioned as a sneaky way of relegating blacks to a different conceptual category, and this movement itself carries a subtle tilt toward biology. Nevertheless, by portraying slaves as "naturally" funny, "naturally" good-natured, and "naturally" happy to be in bondage, the slave-owning class was able to recast themselves in turn as benevolent parent-figures, doing charity by caring for a group of permanent children who, they claimed, did not want to be free.[25] Following this logic, the different natures of whites and blacks justified different treatment, different places in taxonomic hierarchy. Sambo is neither a cause of such hierarchical thinking nor a simple effect of it; the stereotype arose from a vertical conception of race, and once in place, it helped to support such hierarchical thinking. The power of a stereotype to determine a group's thinking about another group allowed Sambo to take an important place in an evolving rhetorical strategy to evade the question—and the reality—of Negro humanity.

Beginning in the 1830s, plantation fiction fixed the Sambo stereotype in place in Southern cultural lore. However, as Taylor shows, the popular fictional depictions of slavery as a pastoral idyll all shared an underlying tension, a "general uncertainty and uneasiness about slavery." Indeed, "Not far beneath the surface of these fleeting portrayals lurks the uneasy sense that slavery is a wretched, insupportable, human condition." It is the indefatigability of the "human" condition of the slave that causes this problem to recur. Taylor argues that the need to do something about the slave's humanity was what incited the growth of paternalism, an ideology that gave the slave a limited role in the planter's extended family. Treating the slave as a child proves an unstable support, both intellectually and emotionally. To Taylor, the slave's admission into the plantation "family"—an event central to the formation of the Sambo stereotype—amounted to a rhetorical risk. The conflict between the slave as child and as animal "set[ ] a trap for plantation novelists."[26] Granting family status to the slave meant an implicit move from the biological to the social justification for slavery—but this was a move that most Southern novelists didn't want to make without keeping their biological assumptions. How to reconcile the installation of the slave into the paternalistic setup with the need to keep the slave biologically different by nature? The novelist's solution was to do both at the same time.

John Pendleton Kennedy's *Swallow Barn*, the flagship novel of the plantation genre, illustrates the typical proslavery struggle with slave identity and status. Setting the tone for a tradition of similarly contorted fictional portrayals, Kennedy's narrator gives the slaves "grotesque natures."[27] Kennedy evokes the fundamental objectification conflict in the novel, giving the slaves both human and nonhuman qualities at the same time. This opposition results in strangely shifting portrayals of slaves and slavery in the novel, an instability most likely not intended by the author. On the surface, *Swallow Barn* appears ideologically consistent and politically benign. Kennedy depicts the usual gangs of happy Sambos, and on the white side he showcases a passionately wrought example of the "positive good" argument for their continued enslavement. But the figure of Sambo cannot be examined closely and critically without revealing its structural flaws; in this case, Kennedy undermines his own position by consistently depicting the slaves in animal terms. Their debased portraits give special meaning to the author's prefaced description of Southern life as "grotesque, peculiar, and amusing."[28]

Kennedy portrays slavery as a traditional paternalistic fantasy. His narrator, Mark Littleton, says that his "design . . . has been simply to paint in true colors the scenes of domestic life as I have found them in Virginia" (228). These "colors" mingle in absolute contentment, as Mistress Lucretia Meriwether presides over a "numerous family, both white and black" (39). The slaves themselves exude an "air of contentment and good humor and kind family attachment" (452). As Lucinda MacKethan observes in her introduction to *Swallow Barn*, even the drawn illustrations of blacks accompanying the novel fit right into the minstrel tradition of contented Sambos who sing while they work (xxv). This domestic bliss receives lengthy forensic defense in "The Quarter," a chapter Kennedy extensively reworked and expanded in his 1851 revision of the book. Reflecting on slavery near the end of his stay in Virginia, the narrator says that "all organized slavery is but a temporary phase of the human condition" (454). Though he claims no knowledge of the Negro's future, he says that the slaves' fortunes are moving upward. Frank Meriwether, the owner of the slaves at Swallow Barn, expounds on the responsibilities of the slaveowner and the dangers of freedom. He proposes modest reforms to ameliorate some of the glaring cruelties of the institution (vicious masters, divided families), while making it clear that slaveowners are the group best qualified to implement them. "The question of emancipation," he says, "is exclusively our own" (458).

Kennedy does all he can to depict the plantation as a slave's paradise. The slaves at Swallow Barn are all much too happy to contemplate escape, but Kennedy still manages an oblique comment on runaway slaves in the form of a two-part sketch about a trained hawk. All words and actions surrounding the hawk carry suggestive double meaning. In the first part of the sketch, the majestic bird escapes because of its mistress's inexperience in managing its flight. In the second part of the sketch, the hawk is recaptured weeks later (by a man, Ned Hazard). This change proves fortunate for the bird, for freedom has left it "bedraggled, travel-worn and soiled" (358). We see it headed back into "slavery" (the narrator actually uses the word), and better off for it. Ned Hazard later fights—and soundly defeats—a blustery man who challenges the value of keeping the hawk. An encounter with an abolitionist, perhaps? Ned's friend Harvey Riggs subsequently laments the lost time when hawks "were not flown like kites, with a string, but came at a whistle, and did as they were told" (380).[29]

The story of the hawk carries delicate implications, but more typical of *Swallow Barn*'s treatment of slavery are trenchant human/animal comparisons that uniformly degrade and objectify the slaves. In unspoken and apparently unnoticed contradiction with the extended family scenario, Kennedy renders the slaves in atavistic terms. Scipio, the first slave we meet, has a face "principally composed of a pair of protuberant lips" (21). Slave children have "wonderfully flat noses, and the most oddly disproportioned mouths" (309), while adults possess "that grave, momentous elongation peculiar to the African face" (327). As if this were not sufficient to convey the point, Kennedy's narrator repeatedly compares the slaves to monkeys.[30] Showing himself aware of the evolutionary debate that eventually produced Darwin's *Origin of Species*, the author has his narrator describe a group of domestic slaves as "a lively type of the progress of civilization, or the march of intellect . . . a gallery of caricatures, a sort of scenic satire upon man in his various stages" (327).

Kennedy shows a sure hand during much of the novel (which is really more of a collection of sketches of country life), but when he turns to slavery *Swallow Barn* becomes a conceptual mess, the kind that is bound to result from a desire to evade an issue rather than confront it. While it is true that Kennedy faces slavery squarely, the question he avoids is that of the slave's humanity. In a curious coda he devotes the last several chapters of the book to the story of Abe, a high-spirited slave (of West Indian descent, not African) who is sold to a sea captain in whose service he heroically sacrifices his life in a daring rescue mission that fails on the high seas. What is the character of Abe (who embodies "the full perfection of manhood" [477]) doing in a book whose black population is mainly composed of simian throwbacks? Perhaps Kennedy was indulging his own version of slaveholder's guilt, for his narrator says that he tells the story to call attention to the "agreeable peculiarities" of a "neglected race" (470). In any case, the many-voiced *Swallow Barn* makes for a striking contrast with, say, *Clotel*, which has a straightforward argument and uncomplicated didactic point of view. Kennedy's novel exemplifies the plight of plantation fiction: like a fragile political coalition trying to draw different views under one party umbrella, the novel is made up of a mass of contradictions subsumed under a vaguely defined proslavery mantle: the figure of Sambo.[31]

Swallow Barn and other novels of the plantation genre swing on a pendulum impelled by objectification: the slave comes across as human, swings to nonhuman, and back and forth again. After a few passes, the slave picks up traits from both sides. Just as the pendulum spends its time traveling between points, so does the slave end up in between categories. Drawing on Genovese's Marxist analysis, Carolyn Porter sums up the problem:

> The slave, in effect, embodied in a flesh-and-blood form the transformation of man into a thing. By implicitly acknowledging the slave's human status as a child and member of the human family, the South's paternalist ideal rendered palpable and visible . . . the exploitation of human labor required for the growth of capital. What added to the slaveholder's complex "agony," furthermore, was that he *did* often believe in his paternal role.

Porter distills the slaveowner's dilemma to that of having to "daily extract forced labor from those he thought of as his own children."[32]

Because confronting this problem was not an acceptable option (the master's doing so would have meant ending either the forced labor or the fiction of fatherhood), the slaveowner needed to avoid it. Sambo, the quasi-human grotesque, was the slaveowner's attempt to get around this emotional obstacle. The stereotype thus becomes the slaveowner's construction of deferral, muteness, and evasion. But the equivocation that accompanies Sambo's appearance in literature shows that the evasion finally doesn't work. Although it was devised as a way to avoid slavery's unsolvable problem, the stereotype ironically leads to a continual struggle with it anyway.

It is nevertheless an unusual measure of the social effectiveness of the Sambo stereotype that even antislavery fiction writers wound up buying into it. Such Northern use of the stereotype was enabled by the fact that many critics of slavery accepted (either consciously or unconsciously) the idea of innate racial difference. Believing blacks to be socially needy spurred Northern writers to find a special place for them in the social matrix. This resulted in what Fredrickson calls "romantic racialism," a less malignant but still recognizable argument for racial difference. In this scenario, the Negro's distinctive qualities were used as the basis for a flattering portrait of the black as good Christian and an accompanying argument for his freedom on human rights grounds. This argument—of which *Uncle Tom's Cabin* is perhaps the famous example—paradoxically owed much to the proslavery Sambo stereotype, linking the childlike quality of the happy slave to the idea that such emotionally driven innocents as blacks make the best Christians.[33]

As a result of these beliefs, antislavery fiction writers aim at liberating the slaves, but they don't always aim at granting them humanity. One might expect that abolitionist fiction would hammer away at the idea of man as property, and try to expose its grotesque underpinnings. It obviously benefited abolitionist authors to portray slavery at its most horrible, and the objectifying aspect of slavery is the most fundamental horror of the institution. Indeed, the spectacle of a human being turned into a thing—even if only partially—provided the kernel of the opposition to slavery.[34] Many fictions did take a militant stance explicitly against objectification—not only Brown's *Clotel*, and O'Connor's *Harrington* (among those books I have already noted), but also Richard Hildreth's *The Slave* (1836), Frederick Douglass's novella, *The Heroic Slave* (1853), and Martin Delany's *Blake* (1859–1862), the last two being well-known depictions of slave rebellions. Even Stowe moved from the heroic passivity of Uncle Tom to a story of slave revolt in *Dred* (1856). Significantly, virtually all these fictions adopt the slave's point of view.

Such examples might be expected as part of the dialogue between the oppressor and the oppressed, but it is more surprising that certain ostensibly antislavery novelists used and reinforced the same stereotypes that proslavery apologists employed to defend the peculiar institution. A number of self-described antislavery novels employed the Sambo stereotype—and could therefore be said to have done the slaves as much harm as good. For example, an explicitly antislavery novel like Sarah Hale's *Northwood* objectifies slaves in a manner most common to Southern plantation fiction.[35] Hale's slaves appear to enjoy their captivity greatly. Squire Romilly, the father of the main character, remarks at one point that slaves are "elevated" by their experience, and "the most miserable slave you can find in the South is an enlightened and civilized man compared to his heathen brothers in Africa" (167). Sydney Romilly, who plans at the novel's end to allow his slaves to buy their own freedom with their labor (they price themselves, with his help), justifies his plan to send them to Liberia because "two races, who do not intermarry, can never live together as equals. Frame laws as you will, the white race, being superior to the colored, in all that constitutes moral power, the Anglo-American will be master over the Negro, if the latter is near him" (405). Hale was the first American novelist to use slavery as a theme. Her religious mission, like Stowe's, was to dismantle slavery while Christianizing Africa.

After her revision of *Northwood* Hale wrote another novel, *Liberia; Or, Mr. Peyton's Experiments* (1853), that more explicitly describes her belief in Negro inferiority and her conviction that colonization was the only way to solve the problem of slavery. Mr. Peyton is a slaveowner who wants to free his slaves. He investigates and tries different methods, including setting them up as farmers on his own land and shipping them north to Philadelphia, but the former slaves consistently fail to prosper due to their own faults. That the blacks' own inferiority causes their failure is more than just Hale's implication; she has one former slave confess to Mr. Peyton that "a nigger can't be any thing but a nigger."[36] Mr. Peyton eventually comes to believe this himself, and settles on African colonization as the best alternative. As in *Northwood*, Hale here sets abolition as distinct from racial equality, and even from black personhood.

Though her antislavery sentiments are palpable, the slaves in her books become masses of dependent Sambos.

Another self-described abolitionist who falls under the Sambo spell is Frances Anne ("Fanny") Kemble, the British immigrant author of a popular narrative of a time she spent at her husband's Georgia plantation. Despite her earnest tone, Kemble's view of blacks is decidedly uneven. Though she deplores the peculiar institution, she exults in the contortions of "Jim Crow—the veritable James," a dancing slave whose "ludicrous display" strikes her as so funny that she can barely breathe for laughing.[37] Such oppositions make Kemble capable of striking mood swings. At one point she solemnly condemns slavery as a violation of God's law (154), but then a few pages later she reacts uproariously to a particularly abasing display of obsequiousness by a slave. Her explanation for her amusement at the slave's exaggerated bowing and scraping is particularly telling: "so sudden, grotesque, uncouth, and yet dexterous a gambado never came into the brain or out of the limbs of any thing but a 'niggar' " (161–62). With this offhand observation, Kemble unwittingly directs the reader to the tension that tugs at her view of slavery. Her view of the performing slave as "grotesque" and her connection of that grotesqueness to his race suggests that her condemnation of slavery is separate from her perception of its victims.

The examples of Hale and Kemble show that the Sambo stereotype receives nourishment in literature on both sides of the Mason-Dixon line. Told from the master's point of view, these narratives reinforce Fredrickson's findings on the more general subject of racialism.[38] Novels like *Northwood* and *Liberia*, and narratives like Kemble's *Journal*, show that political goals of abolitionists did not foreclose the possibility of their own racism—and the books illustrate how the benign nature of the Sambo stereotype eased the adoption of such attitudes. It took Stowe's *Uncle Tom's Cabin*, the best-known and by far the most successful antislavery novel, to make a persuasive issue of linking the politics of abolition to the humanistic values underlying the movement—though even Stowe believed in her own version of biological difference among races.

A significant part of the forensic success of *Uncle Tom's Cabin* can be traced to Stowe's unusual use of the contradictions that went into the Sambo stereotype. Specifically, Stowe understood the inherent unsoundness of the paternalism argument, how it rested on the central contradiction that the slave was both a piece of property and a family member at the same time. As Taylor shows, Stowe demolishes the argument for paternalism from within the context of the sentimental ideology that the South used so effectively for its own ends. Though Stowe points toward biological differences between white and black, she elides the inferiority question by resorting to "romantic racialism," asserting that blacks are better Christians than whites in a setting where Christianity is the highest virtue. (Stowe also avoids any inquiry into the question of black inferiority in *A Key to Uncle Tom's Cabin* [1853], in which she pointedly omits a section on "characteristics and development of the colored race" on the questionable grounds of lack of space.)[39] Stowe's own belief in racial difference is plain. She has George Harris, her mulatto hero and the mouthpiece for her social politics, describe blacks as "not a dominant and commanding race . . . [but] an affectionate, magnanimous, and forgiving one" (43:462).[40] George is himself a mulatto, having inherited from his white father "a set of fine European features and a high, indomitable spirit" (11:123). As a combination of "stern, inflexible, energetic" Anglo-Saxon and gentle, spiritual African, George stands at the biological apex of humanity in the novel, a natural leader for the Liberian colonization mission that he undertakes at the book's end.[41]

Eric Sundquist has asked whether Stowe's novel destroys paternalism or preserves it.[42] *Uncle Tom's Cabin* is an unusual book in that it does both: it attacks a stereotype whose origins it only partially dismantles. That is, Stowe undermines a certain kind of paternalism (the "positive good" argument), but she leaves in place the idea that blacks are different from whites and need help in white society because of the very gentle virtues that set them apart. Stowe thus takes a unique place in the debate: she accepts many of the assumptions behind the Sambo stereotype even as she attempts to refute many of its more insidious premises. *Uncle Tom's Cabin* stands out as a multilayered critique of the Sambo figure from the inside of the paternalist camp, a book that examines the character on many levels, going especially deeply into the hypocrisy behind the ideal of the happy slave.

Five months before he published *Clotel*, William Wells Brown wrote that Stowe's novel "has come down upon the dark abodes of slavery like a morning's sunlight, unfolding to view its enormities in a manner which has fastened all eyes on the 'peculiar institution.'"[43] The terms of Brown's praise suggest that Stowe answered—in advance—his call in *Clotel* for literature that would expose the naked objectification behind

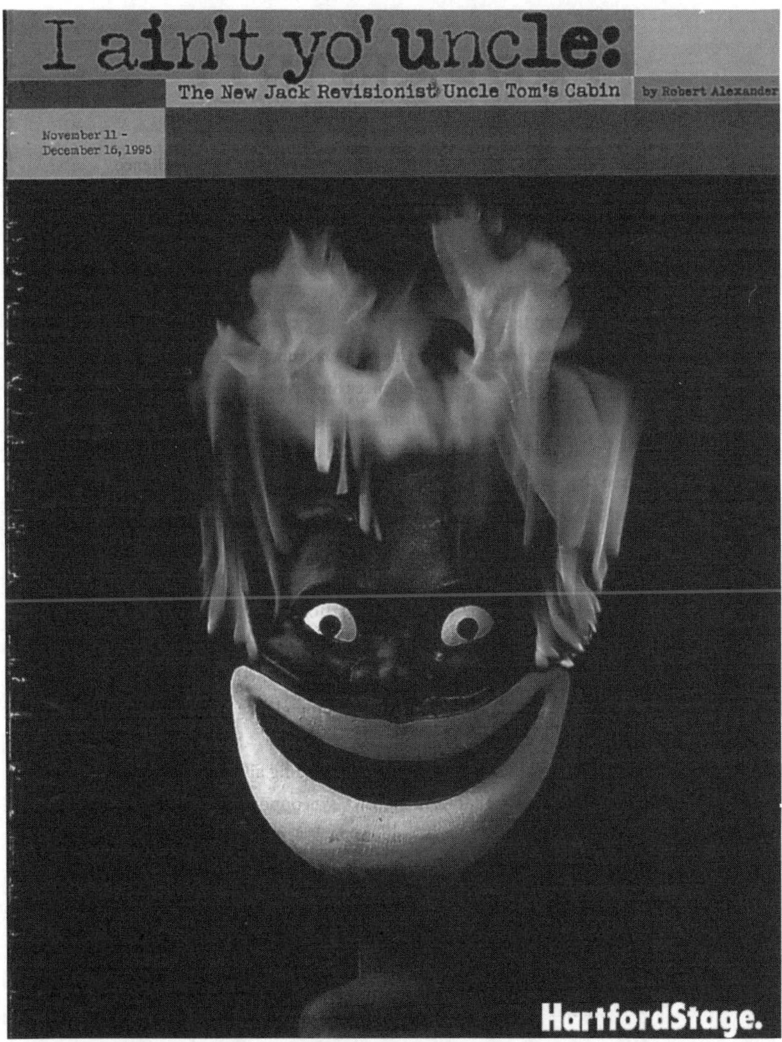

Fig. 4.1 Cover of a playbill for Robert Alexander's *I Ain't Yo Uncle: The New Jack Revisionist Uncle Tom's Cabin* (1995). The play revives the characters with special attention to the "calcified" stereotypes they have acquired over time.

Fig. 4.2 "A Dream Caused by the Perusal of Mrs. H. Beecher Stowe's Popular Work Uncle Tom's Cabin" (1855). This spectacular Southern nightmare vision of a hellish world where demonic blacks rule recalls the grotesquerie of Hieronymus Bosch. Stowe herself is pictured at the left, at the entrance to the subterranean "Underground Railway." (Reproduced by permission of the Photographs and Prints Division, Schomburg Center for Research in Black Culture, the New York Public Library; Astor, Lenox, and Tilden Foundations)

slavery. Stowe's awareness of the conflicts hidden by the Sambo figure was rarely matched in the fiction of her own time (an exception being the work of Herman Melville, the subject of the next chapter).

Uncle Tom himself stands out as the most obvious example of Stowe's rhetorical molding of the Sambo stereotype. As a hard-working and obedient slave who repeatedly spurns the chance to escape, Uncle Tom would appear to fit the stereotype snugly, but Stowe gradually makes it clear that he is motivated by his own desire for freedom, and that his obedience is primarily to a higher law. It is finally Tom's refusal to bend to the will of his master that results in his death. In addition to becoming a Christian martyr, he also turns into a kind of Sambo manqué.

In connection with Tom's martyrdom, it is of more than passing significance that one of the two slaves who beat him to death is named Sambo. Simon Legree trains Sambo and his partner Quimbo as slavedrivers, schooling them in "savageness and brutality as systematically as he had his bull-dogs" (32:370). As a result of this education, Sambo becomes a twisted burlesque of the stereotype whose name he bears: he is a most obedient slave, to be sure, but also a violent and cruel one who would hardly fit into a paternalistic plantation dreamscape. Of course he is right at home in Legree's antipaternalistic nightmare, a plantation whose owner does not even pretend to care for his slaves, and who is happy to explain that he finds it cheaper to work them to death and then buy more (31:364). In contrast to Tom's dedicated service to God, Legree's Sambo conveys Stowe's warning of the dangers of obedience to the slave master alone. Though Tom shows him the error of his ways before he dies, Sambo (along with Quimbo) turns out to be his killer.

Perhaps the most conceptually pointed of Stowe's attacks on Samboism is in her treatment of the character of Topsy. The author introduces Topsy as a mischievous Sambo figure, what Richard Yarborough calls a "stereotypical pickaninny."[44] Though essentially harmless, she is a seemingly incorrigible young scamp who clearly lacks good parenting. Significantly, she laughs at herself, such buffoonery being part of the self-deprecatory portrait of the "natural" slave. Augustine St. Clare's Northern cousin Ophelia, an armchair abolitionist, becomes Topsy's parental figure, but Stowe shows that in order for her to achieve that status, she has to accept Topsy as a fully human being. That is, Ophelia must acknowledge Topsy's humanity herself before she can teach Topsy to appreciate and nurture that humanity. Simply put, she must love her as a true parent and not as a master. Achieving this goal means raising Topsy from slavery, both morally and legally, and allowing her to mature from childhood to adulthood. By establishing the terms for Topsy's salvation in this way, Stowe renders the Sambo stereotype inoperable.

In accomplishing this reversal, the author carries the character of Ophelia a great emotional distance. When Ophelia says that she would "never let a child of mine play with Topsy" (20:269), she clearly places the slave in a separate category, supposedly because of her depravity, but really because of her race. Her cousin Augustine had already exposed Ophelia's feelings about blacks: "You loathe them as you would a snake or a toad, yet you are indignant at their wrongs" (16:195). Topsy knows this, and Stowe has her echo Augustine's words later on when she complains that Ophelia "can't bar me, 'cause I'm a nigger!—she'd 's soon have a toad touch her!" (25:304). Stowe (who closely identifies herself with her narrative persona) tells us that Ophelia "approached [Topsy] very much as a person might be supposed to approach a black spider" (20:260). Though a Northerner with abolitionist sentiments, Ophelia must fight her own habitual tendency to objectify.

This link to the objectification conflict is central to Stowe's attack on the paternalistic notion of the happy slave. Ophelia finds her desire to educate Topsy to be at odds with her own tendency to see the slave as nonhuman. She takes a self-contradictory stance that is best illustrated by her view of Topsy in performance:

> The black, glassy eyes glittered with a kind of wicked drollery, and the thing struck up, in a clear shrill voice, an odd Negro melody, to which she kept time with her hands and feet, spinning round, clapping her hands, knocking her knees together, in a wild, fantastic sort of time, and producing the native music of her race; and finally, turning a summerset or two, and giving a prolonged closing note, as odd and unearthly as that of a steam-whistle, she came suddenly down on the carpet, and stood with her hands folded, and a most sanctimonious expression of meekness and solemnity over her face, broken only by the cunning glances which she shot askance from the corners of her eyes.
>
> Miss Ophelia stood silent, perfectly paralyzed with amazement. (20:259)

This passage embodies Ophelia's struggle with Topsy, but its significance for Stowe goes far deeper, exemplifying her view of the slaveholder's dilemma of conflicted perceptions. Topsy appears first as a "thing" which emits "unearthly" sounds, but this impression shortly gives way to the human mien of a confidence trickster. The transformation from one to the other is grotesque; looking through Ophelia's eyes, we see a confusing and disturbing vision of Topsy as a person and a thing at the same time. In order for Ophelia to see Topsy as a fully human being, she must forcibly desensitize herself against her own views of blacks.

In highlighting the degree to which Ophelia's views had been shaped by her own misguided prejudices, Stowe points to a certain limited plasticity of human perception. Though the image of the human can never be fully denied, it can be thrown into doubt and liminal uncertainty—and this uncertainty is what causes one person to see another as grotesque. Prendick, the narrator of H. G. Wells's *Island of Dr. Moreau*, writes that after he had spent a while on Moreau's island laboratory he "became habituated" to the presence of the scientist's experimental animal mixtures, so "things that had seemed unnatural and repulsive speedily became natural and ordinary to me." This desensitizing process can also go the other way. American proslavery writers tried to shape the categories of perception to "sensitize" their audience to the deep differences they sought to create between black and white. Though proslavery forces found it impossible to deny the slave's humanity completely (witness Sambo), Stowe uses the character of Ophelia, a bigoted Northerner, to suggest the extent they succeeded in portraying the Negro as an unstable human/nonhuman mixture.[45]

Ophelia's change is no different from that experienced by the worker assigned to a hospital burn ward who gets used to seeing disfiguring injuries and soon ceases to fear them. The change is natural because the burn victims are human, not members of a different biological category. Stowe does not suggest that Ophelia will cease to divide, rank, and categorize what she sees in her life; she will, however, rethink the divisions and remake her hierarchy on different terms. Only after Ophelia establishes Topsy as a person in her own mind can she teach that person to be a Christian rather than a thief. Unless she makes the effort, her perceptions will continue to clash, and Topsy will remain grotesque to her. Stowe's goal for Ophelia mirrors that of abolitionist literature in general:

the writer seeks to expose and tear down the social barriers that partially impede the full recognition of blacks as human.

Stowe sets it up so that Ophelia has to make the first move. Only when she treats Topsy as a human being can Ophelia become Topsy's mother and loving guide. Ophelia first objects; she's not used to looking at blacks as love objects. She specifically recoils from kissing them (15:182). Little Eva teaches her cousin that the only way to be a parent is to show Christian love. She touches Topsy, and tells Ophelia of the need to "put our hands on them." Ophelia confesses her own prejudice and revulsion—and finally begins to overcome it (25:305). Before her death Eva professes her love for Topsy, and once again Ophelia follows her lead, thus establishing her parental credentials at last (27:321). The reformation is long and difficult for both Ophelia and Topsy, but the parent does a good job raising her adopted child after that, and Topsy becomes an educated success, eventually going off to do missionary work in Africa (43:463).

With the example of Topsy, Stowe takes the central Southern assumption behind the Sambo stereotype—that blacks are perpetual children in need of perpetual parental care—and explodes it from within by exposing the hypocrisy of the slaveowner's "love." Topsy's parental requirements include sincerity above all, and women do the best job of providing it. As many critics have shown, *Uncle Tom's Cabin* turns on female influence, with the women exhibiting the greatest capacity for virtue and the best possibility for social change from within. This logical extension of the sentimental model opposes the Southern paternalistic ideal of Father Knows Best.

Stowe's gallery of superior females set an example for writers about race during her own time and beyond. Brown, writing in the wake of *Uncle Tom's Cabin*, describes one of his heroines in *Clotel*, the white liberator Georgiana Peck, as the "superior" and "teacher" of her eventual husband Carlton, an impression he shares to the point where he is afraid to propose marriage to her (173, 196, 205). (She winds up informing him of her willingness to become his wife.) Frado, the autobiographical heroine of Harriet Wilson's *Our Nig*, begins as a lively Topsy-like character (as Carla Peterson has observed) and matures through suffering into a matron of gravity and sympathy. This line of strong women extends into Reconstruction, providing a continuing rebuttal to the degrading black portraits issued by Harris, Page, and their contemporaries.[46]

Stowe's corrective action in *Uncle Tom's Cabin* uses "sentimental power" to fuel a topical critique of slaveholders' arguments. Though she sees Negroes as biologically distinct from whites, Stowe pointedly denies the biological proslavery position that they are nonhuman (if they are, how could they be Christian?) and the social argument that slavery is good for them. St. Clare's parable of Quashy—which is, significantly, the West Indian name for Sambo—boils Stowe's position down to its essence: "because my brother Quashy is ignorant and weak, and I am intelligent and strong—because I know how, and *can* do it—therefore, I may steal all he has, keep it, and give him only such and so much as suits my fancy" (19:242). This attack hits directly at the rhetorical foundation of the Sambo stereotype. It is a measure of Stowe's success at doing so that Mary H. Eastman's *Aunt Phillis' Cabin*, an 1852 reply to *Uncle Tom's Cabin*, allows for a heaven in which the slave and master will be reunited with the difference between them erased—an implicit contradiction with the earthbound inequality that the book argues so strenuously for.

III

Humor and Fear

One of the defining features of Sambo is that he is funny, often unintentionally so. Boskin describes Sambo as a jester, but without the wisdom ascribed to that character in drama. Sambo humor is in fact the antithesis of wisdom, being rooted in a collectively imposed ignorance of the slave's human identity, an ignorance that gave further support to paternalism. If Stowe showed that Southern paternalism didn't work, she was only giving lucid expression to a set of unvoiced truths that follow from the unavoidable perception that the slave is human. This much was felt, if not known, by slaveowners all along. The problem was to avoid this awareness, and making Sambo a jokester offered a key opportunity to do this. Sambo humor had two main functions. In the first place, it deferred serious consideration of what the stereotype meant, for to laugh is—temporarily, at least—to avoid having to think. Second and perhaps more important, slave comedy was literally a command performance, one that reaffirmed the master's authority. Plantation fiction is filled with clownish darkies whose actions amuse their masters, and who seize the slightest excuse to play amongst themselves.

Sambo humor is mainly clownish buffoonery, a form of humor easily traceable to the feeling of superiority that Freud associates with the comic. The comic, says Freud, depends on comparison that results in a sense of mastery over the object of the joke. Constructing the slave as a fool makes him dependent on external circumstances, an easy target for comparison with those who control those circumstances. It also allows the slave to be easily caricatured, a process that, according to Freud, destroys the unity of a person's character through exaggeration of isolated qualities within it.[47] Despite Stowe's general assertion to the contrary in her preface to *Uncle Tom's Cabin* (vi), Sambo is most certainly a caricature.

The comedy of Sambo was, in Boskin's words, "a device of oppression," depriving its victim of "self-possession."[48] The slave receives such treatment from the slaveowner because the owner needs continually to experience mastery over the slave. This need stems partly from the need to exercise power, and partly from displaced anxiety over whether the slave will continue to accept this domination without resisting. For the white slaveowners, laughing at Sambo was an implicit assertion that he and his antics signified no harm.

Sambo humor thus participates in a collective form of repression by slaveowners, a delusion that they attempted—with some success—to extend to slaves, non-slaveholding Southern whites, and the Northern population generally. This repression covers more than the fear of violent rebellion (which I will consider next); it blankets the rationale for the Sambo stereotype itself, and with it the shaky assumptions of difference propping up the entire institution of slavery. Joseph Boskin shows how black playfulness "against circumstance" underwrites a whole theory of personality in which blacks were held "mirthful by nature." The point of this pseudoscience may be seen in the etymology of the name *Sambo*, which, says Boskin, probably arose from the Spanish word *zambo*, which describes a clumsy person whose bowlegged walk suggests a monkey's gait.[49]

Broadly speaking, slave humor fueled a shared white self-delusion that slavery was stable, rational, and sound. "For whites," says Boskin, "humor was the antithesis of rationality."[50] In this case, rationality would necessarily involve awareness of the contradictions and limitations embedded in the Sambo stereotype as well as the practical danger involved in the few exerting physical control over the many. The humor associated with Sambo hides the cracks in the image, becoming another barrier thrown up in a continuing effort to obscure the grotesqueness of the slave's condition.

Sambo's love of performance supports the illusion created by his humor. Boskin emphasizes the performing aspect of the stereotype in his study, an association underscored by the numerous stage portrayals of Sambo in the North and the South, both before and after the Civil War, in minstrel shows, melodramas, vaudeville, and on film. In the antebellum South, Sambo was less a stage performer than a born comic who achieved happiness through the child's pastime of play. Slaveowners made a place for slave performance within their convoluted vision of human objectification. Such behavior was acceptable to the master because if the "natural differences" between blacks and whites made the slaves into native performers, then it was possible to relate to them in that role since it underlined "their" difference from "us."

Eric Lott's analysis of Northern blackface minstrelsy sheds some indirect light on the slaveowner's complicated self-delusion. Lott sees minstrel shows as a staged effort to contain conflicting emotions about blackness and black culture within the medium of performance. He argues that blackface performance embodies a complex dialectic that condensed opposing emotions of fascination and dread, acceptance and rejection of blackness, within the performing black body. The blackface minstrel, a grotesque figure at the margins of humanity, stages a play of the white "racial unconscious," a show about the experience of white existence and the need to dramatize the combined fear and desire of blackness within the boundaries protecting that existence. But the psychological volatility of the blackface performance cannot be so contained. Of particular relevance is Lott's rediscovery of many minstrel song lyrics in which black people are turned into things, a common device that he persuasively ties to a white anxiety over slavery, the denial of which only increases its magnitude. Much of Lott's argument is geographically specific, but its basic oppositions can be used to understand the Southern slaveowner's construction of the performing slave. Though not literally white underneath, the master's image of the comical performing Sambo—a fictional character even when forced into corporeal existence—nonetheless reflected white concerns and white unconscious needs.[51]

Though the masters wanted to emphasize that the slaves sang and danced because it was part of their nature, it was the owners themselves who demanded such performance. In *Swallow Barn*, for example, Ned Hazard stages a race among slave children, a competition they enter with unrestrained "merriment" as he looks on with amusement (309–10).[52] On an earlier occasion in the book, the elderly slave Carey, a "minstrel of some repute," is called in to play the banjo for the narrator's benefit—and presumably also to satisfy his own "predominant passion" for music (101, 454). Similarly, Solomon Northup describes in his slave narrative how his talents as a fiddler were in great demand by slaveholding whites around the county (165). Although the performance component of the Sambo stereotype clearly functioned within the effort to permanently infantilize the Negro, examples like Kennedy's and Northup's suggest that this was not its key function. For one thing, slave performance took the slave's childlike nature practically as a given. I want instead to argue that its more distinct status was as a form of private show business in which the slave "voluntarily" gave the master pleasure on demand. Within this performance, slave and master interacted under a special set of expectations that were socially sanctioned under the rules of slavery.

Slaveholders actually coerced slaves to humor them, and this action had a distinct purpose, a purpose best understood within the context of Hegel's master-slave dialectic.[53] For whites, forcing blacks into the role of performer—and then witnessing the performance—conveys the desire for recognition. Because a performance normally centers on mutual recognition between performer and audience, the performing Sambo may be seen as an unconscious attempt by slaveowners to reconfigure the paradoxical dilemma of Hegel's master—that is, his dependence on the slave for human recognition, after he has already deemed the slave less than human. Not surprisingly, slaveowners had continual trouble getting slaves to play the part of industrious worker.[54] Setting up the slave instead as a "willing" performer creates a favorable illusion that is easier to maintain, for a presumably eager performing artist is of more value in conferring recognition than is an obviously unwilling slave.

Certain conceptual obstacles stood in the way of this "staged" recognition of the master by the slave. Frederick Douglass persuasively links the slaveowners' encouragement of slave performance to their continuing effort to control their slaves.[55] Indeed, masters carefully mediated slave performance. They controlled the surroundings, censored the humor, and created a joke cycle from slave behavior that ridiculed blacks, enabling the performance to be repeated over and over. This bid by the master for control of the slave through direction of his performance conflicts implicitly with the master's attempt to gain recognition through the same activity, because recognition (as Hegel defines it) must come from a human being acting freely. Since slaves did not perform voluntarily for the master, the question of recognition is theoretically moot—but not the possibility of the master's imagining its existence. The masters, says Fanon, "want to compel the acceptance of their fiction"[56]—but this compulsion extends to themselves as well as their slaves. The success of this act of self-persuasion (or delusion) hinged on the soundness of the Sambo stereotype itself—or more specifically, the illusion of the slave as a willing participant in this degrading activity. Accordingly, the *Swallow Barn* narrator describes the banjo picker Carey as requiring "but little encouragement to set him off" (101). For the master to feel recognized, he had to believe that the slave performed for his sake. A performer normally receives something in exchange for his performance. The slave received nothing, so the master had to imagine that the slave performed because he wanted to, because he liked singing and joking, and because he liked pleasing the master. This involved premise would have made the illusion of the happy slave easier to digest; it's easier, after all, to imagine a voluntary performer than a willing fieldhand.

Many former slaves have testified to the overseer's standing order that they sing while at work in the fields, and of the suspicion that fell on any who did not join in. Silence was frequently taken as a sign of a plot to escape or rebel. The comic Sambo amounts to a rhetorical step further away from the concrete reality of slavery, a movement from the happy laborer to the happy jester. For the master, the corresponding image shift was from cruel extractor of forced labor to grateful audience. Since the audience is normally passive and the performer active during a performance, the figure of the performing slave further obscures the image of the master as active agent of the slave's unhappiness.

In *Uncle Tom's Cabin* Stowe's use of slave performance consistently opposes the Southern image of that activity. She parodies the white view of performing slave, ripping away the fiction to expose the master's coercion that most fundamentally motivates the slave's public play. In *Uncle Tom's Cabin*, performance marks the slave's bondage, not the slave's pleasure. There is much hymn singing in the novel, for example, but the

Fig. 4.3 Nineteenth-century image of "happy" slaves enjoying a musical interlude. The artist has drawn them so that their grins make their faces appear misshapen and distorted. (Reproduced by permission of the Photographs and Prints Division, Schomburg Center for Research in Black Culture, The New York Public Library; Astor, Lenox, and Tilden Foundations)

songs are always about freedom, and their primary audience is the black characters in the book. When Stowe's slaves do perform for whites, their comedy opposes the master's goals. The best example of this subversion occurs early in the book. When the Shelbys' slave Eliza runs away to keep her son from being sold from her, the trader Haly enlists two other Shelby slaves, Sam and Andy, to help apprehend her. Sam and Andy embody Sambo at his most comic; they are, in Richard Yarborough's phrase, like minstrel darkies: seemingly "bumptious, giggling, outsized adolescents."[57] Predictably, these two jesters put on a performance, but in this case the performance undermines the master's purpose. Attending a series of deliberately contrived misadventures with "awful gravity" and "earnest and desperate simplicity" (7:69), Sam and Andy confuse Haly and delay the trader's pursuit for long enough to allow Eliza to escape across the Ohio River. Though the mock-pompous Sam reappears in several later scenes in a weak effort by Stowe at racial humor, her point remains clear: the performing slave is no fool.

In this scene and others, Stowe implicates the comic quality of the Sambo stereotype directly with the desire for freedom and the willingness to rebel that slaveowners used the stereotype to deny. She exposes the potential that lies in mimicry, a response whose power has been traced by Bhabha to its small departures from the original, "its slippage, its excess, its difference." By drawing mimicry in exaggerated comic terms, Stowe shows how this discourse "both against the rules and within them" becomes the basis for resistance.[58] For Sam and Andy, comic performance becomes a vehicle for rebellion. Haly knows this, but even so, he misjudges the effectiveness of the slaves' act and allows himself to be fooled. Stowe also draws on the Crafts' popular escape account in another version of role-playing in the novel; Eliza and George dress up as (male) master and servant for the last leg of their escape to the North. William Wells Brown also restages the Crafts' escape in *Clotel*, as the title character uses the color-and-gender-switching disguise ploy to escape with William, one of her fellow slaves. The Crafts' escape resonates within the novelists' art because of the implied reversal contained within it: the slaves use their skill at playing roles not to express their "joy" in slavery but rather to run from the institution itself.[59]

Stowe extends role-playing far beyond the comic in *Uncle Tom's Cabin*. She juxtaposes Eliza's and George's reenactment of the Crafts' successful escape in the novel with the plantation Gothic playlet that takes place during the last days of Uncle Tom's life. While Tom resists Simon Legree and dies from the consequent beating, Legree's slaves Cassy and Emmeline slowly frighten him literally to death by impersonating the ghost of his mother. Living in their master's attic by day and haunting his dreams by night, the two fugitives make their own escape possible by the success of their portrayal. By using slave performance—normally comic—as the vehicle for horror, Stowe links humor and fear, further suggesting a broad connection between masters' love of slave comedy and their deepest fears of slave resistance. This link between humor and fear touches the most fundamental meaning of the Sambo stereotype, the opposition between "the good Negro *in his place* and the vicious black *out of it*."[60]

By constructing Sambo as a comic figure, slaveowners associated the slave with the kind of broad humor that gave the comfort of mastery. As

I have said, this perception was both necessary for social control and crucial to the master's illusion of the slave's recognition of him. But the comic Sambo stereotype, with its accompanying sense of superiority, played another key role as well: to deflect the master's fear of slave rebellion. If the comic represents superiority that comes from the mastery of circumstances, then the uncanny (which Freud identified a few years later) is its dark opposite, the return of repressed material that has *not* been mastered, and which remains the source of the most fundamental fear.[61] Given this association, we might expect that Southern visions of racial harmony would conceal deep racial fear. And they do.

A brief comparison of three tales by Edgar Allan Poe, a native Southerner and confirmed foe of abolitionism, reveals the uncanny terror hiding behind Sambo's smile. "The Gold Bug" features the slave Jupiter, one of Poe's most infamous black characters. Jupiter is actually a former slave, but he refuses to leave his master even after being manumitted. A servant to William LeGrand, the treasure hunter in the story, Jupiter is a typical Sambo: a laughing and japing comic figure whose doglike devotion is matched only by his stupidity. Even with his limitations, Jupiter manages to aid his master, though his help comes thanks to the occasional good-natured death threat, and in spite of a lengthy and strenuous false start caused by the slave's failure to tell his right from his left. With Jupiter (and also the narrator) providing the brawn to complement LeGrand's brains, the group uncovers "a treasure of incalculable value" which all share.[62] The beatific vision of slavery in "The Gold Bug" thus enriches all involved. "Murders in the Rue Morgue," on the other hand, projects Poe's atavistic black nightmare. Inspired by separate Philadelphia newspaper accounts of a Negro murderer and an escaped orangutan, Poe conflates the two into a darkly colored ape who viciously kills white women. Detective Auguste Dupin eventually solves the case and sees the ape back into custody, but before the orangutan is identified as such, the killings ("a *grotesquerie* in horror absolutely alien from humanity") create a mood verging on panic, in which all black men are suspect.[63]

Taken as a matched pair, "The Gold Bug" and "Rue Morgue" offer a certain insight into the proslavery mind. Though neither tale is about slavery as such, the two stories suggest Poe's different moods as he contemplated the unstable social dynamic between white and black. *The Narrative of Arthur Gordon Pym* unites these two sides of Poe's Sambo diptych, even as the story reflects the extremes of Poe's oscillations on race between rational certainty and fearful anxiety. This opposition is clearest at the end of the story, when Pym and his shipmates go deep into the (polar) South and encounter a group of "savages" who act like Sambo at first, but soon transform into Nat. These natives bear a more than passing resemblance to the African stereotype: the men of the tribe are "muscular," while all have "jet black" skin and lips so "thick and clumsy. . . that, even when laughing, the teeth were never disclosed."[64] They eat raw meat, "recoil" from white skin, and display an irrational witlessness that recalls Jupiter of "The Gold Bug": they treat the ship as a living thing, avoid books (and other "very harmless objects" [850]), and the chief, Too-Wit, fears his own reflection in the mirror. Though the natives are initially very friendly to Pym and his mates, their amiability turns out to be the basis of a clever ruse so carefully plotted that the whites see "nothing in the manner of the natives calculated to raise suspicion" (856). A trading mission to the natives' "primitive" village, during which the whites hope to discover "what were the chief productions of the country, and whether any of these might be turned to profit" (855), results in an agreement to harvest the *biche de mer*, a native mollusk; the agreement brings with it a lowering of white suspicions. As the blacks' plot is being readied, they work industriously to set up the production, laboring "frequently without price, and never, in any instance, pilfering a single article" (859). They behave, in short, like contented slaves.

These accommodating Sambos conceal the spirit of Nat Turner. They ambush the whites as they prepare to leave the island, fabricating an earth slide that buries the whites alive, killing all but Pym and Dirk Peters, who barely escape. The blacks then attack the remainder aboard the ship with "brute rage" (866) and massacre them. The duplicity of the natives causes Pym to describe them in terms that recall the dark monster of "Rue Morgue." They are, he says, "among the most barbarous, subtle, and blood-thirsty wretches that ever contaminated the face of the globe" (859). Though Pym kills many of the murderous blacks as he eludes their clutches and goes on to explore further south, he obviously fails to extinguish the threat that they represent. Indeed, Poe appears uncertain about whether the threat can be reliably met at all. "The Gold Bug" masters the black, of course, projecting a comforting paternalistic vision of slavery. Though "Murders in the Rue Morgue" ends with the capture of the orangutan, this mastery is notably absent. Instead, the story gives free rein to the fear of the black man—especially his violence and supposedly unrestrained sexuality. Pym escapes the blacks without exterminating them, his trust in them obliterated. Taken together, these stories depict the deep concern and lingering insecurities that freight Poe's proslavery position. Behind the author's comic Sambo lurks the uncanny figure of the violent black, a true savage and literal nonhuman.

This dual view of slave character—comprising both Sambo and savage—emerged in the wake of insurrection panics after 1830.[65] It corresponded to the prime of the Sambo stereotype in antebellum Southern literature, and to the time of greatest fear of slave rebellion in the region, the years following Nat Turner's bloody 1831 revolt in Virginia. Turner's brief reign of terror left some sixty whites dead and the remainder badly shaken. It stimulated debate over the future of slavery, a surge in proslavery argument, a marked tightening of restrictions on slave behavior—and a fictional genre which held slavery a living fairy tale and rebellion a foolish fancy. Though rebellious American slaves faced "hopeless odds," especially compared to their more successful counterparts in the Caribbean and South America, white fear of black rebellion was very real in America. This fear of slave uprising was not new—it had been present from the beginning of New World slavery—but the Turner insurrection, preceded by a decade of rising slave unrest (including the Denmark Vesey conspiracy of 1823), brought tension and fear to a peak by demonstrating that public anxiety about slave uprising was not entirely without basis.[66]

What is the exact relationship between Sambo and Nat Turner in the mind of the slaveholder? Eugene Genovese says that every Sambo was also a potential rebel (a "Nat"), with circumstances dictating which type emerged at a given time.[67] John Blassingame argues further that the master saw, understood, and feared precisely that fact; every Sambo on the slavery stage called attention to the rebel "perennially in the wings." Blassingame concludes from the ever-tightening Southern controls over slave behavior that Sambo was an illusion in which slaveowners never really believed. Perhaps Blassingame overstates the case, but he makes a clear connection between the happy slave and his rebellious mirror image, the source of constant anxiety for whites. The greater their fear of rebellion, says Blassingame, the harder slaveowners tried to believe in Sambo, eventually pushing Nat back into their own collective unconscious—though after 1831 there was ever-increasing *conscious* fear of Nat as well.[68] As one Virginia delegate put it, the fear that every slave-owning household might harbor a Nat Turner was "eating into the very vitals of the South."[69] The memory of the Turner uprising consequently inspired numerous new laws in the slave states.

Sambo was never separate from the rebel, a shadowy figure in the back of the slaveowner's mind whose existence could never be fully denied. Though rebellion is hard to define precisely—dependent as it is on circumstances and surroundings—all slave resistance has its deepest roots in violence.[70] Slaveowners connected the fear of rebellion to the possibility of physical harm (as Frederick Douglass's resistance to Edward Covey demonstrates), but this fear of rebellion also extends to the institution itself. Rebellion tears the mask off the happy slave, exposing the angry face of a violent, frequently desperate captive. Admitting the rebel's existence as anything but an unnatural exception to the norm means not only the destruction of the Sambo stereotype but also the unraveling of the master's own self-construction as a benevolent father figure, an image whose coherence depends on the (imagined) happiness of the slave.

The degree of success of the Sambo stereotype in masking the masters' fear of slave uprising will remain debatable. Though the fear of the rebellious slave might never have been entirely banished by the image of the happy one, the slaveholders' involved Sambo fantasies must have had a considerable calming effect on them.[71] Nat Turner himself presented an intolerable enigma to Southern whites; his actions made him an anomaly in their eyes that had to be resolved as a rare and unnatural aberration. Thomas Gray, the white lawyer who inscribed Turner's "confession" a few days before his hanging, tried very hard to portray Turner as a "fanatic," an effort that surely reflected his own anxiety as well as that of the white society to which he belonged. To Sundquist, whose analysis of Turner's confession is the best yet, "the legal paradox embodied in the slave rebel or in any slave resisting his bondage—namely, that he was at once property and yet capable of volitional acts—was the central cause of Gray's ambivalence."[72] Such paradoxes are what make slavery a grotesque state of being in the eyes of both slave and master. Rather than scrutinize their own categories of being, the slaveowners instead located Turner in an artificially constructed liminal space as a "slave/nonslave" (for a slave would not rebel), resulting in his creation as a monster in their own eyes. Gray's mingled fear and fascination with Turner thus fits right into the world of Edgar Allan Poe.

Turner's rebellion generated immediate and voluminous response in the South because it forcibly tore away the master's soft Sambo fantasy and pressed the slaveowner against the conceptual bedrock of slavery beneath it: the attempt to objectify a person. Unlike Sambo, the rebellious slave was hard for slaveowners to categorize, for he violated all the carefully constructed boundaries of the master's Sambo-centered, convoluted world of slavery. Proslavery thinker Thomas Dew could hold Turner an aberration created by "poisonous" abolitionist influence, but neither he nor his allies could alter the fact that he had existed. The rebel, says Sundquist, "occupies the psychic territory, where slavery gives way to freedom, that slaveholders could not afford to recognize without jeopardizing more than their lives, but whose compelling logic they were nonetheless unable to deny."[73]

This language of in-betweenness points to the grotesque. When Sambo turns into Nat, he drops his pleasant exterior and reveals the twisted, grotesque logic of forced captivity that is at the heart of American slavery. The slave had resided in the liminal, grotesque space before Nat Turner came along, of course, but for many masters the shock of Turner's rebellion made this unwanted perception disturbingly clear. It is therefore significant that slaveowners saw Nat Turner as a "monster." (The etymology of *monster* is worth remarking on: it arises from either "to show" [*moneo*] or "to warn" [*monstro*].[74] Southern response to Nat Turner reflected a powerful desire to do both.) Whites had to view Turner as an anomalous, liminal creature because if they saw him any other way, his existence would have overturned the epistemological order of their world.[75] As a threat to that order, he was the worst kind of monster.

The proliferation of Sambos in plantation fiction likewise reflected the growing Southern fear of slave uprising during the decades leading up to the Civil War. Thomas Dew said that rebellious slaves like Turner should be considered "parricides," with the understanding that such an act destroys the extended plantation "family."[76] The literary response to this attempted murder was to rebuild the family fortress stronger than ever. The novelistic manufacture of bucolic Southern fantasies answered the violent statement made by Nat Turner, a statement verbally echoed by each of the dozens of fugitive slave narratives that proliferated during those years following his rebellion. William R. Taylor, for one, locates the entire plantation literary tradition in a fear of the rebel, a fear that requires a paternalistic ideology to house it, and a sentimental mode to express it.[77] This tradition is peopled with Sambos because only they can fit within its parameters.

Slave mischief, common enough in plantation romances and generally corrected by proper discipline, may be read as slaveowner culture's sanitized version of rebellion, an attempt to deny captive aggressiveness while maintaining a necessary link to reality.[78] Only rarely does actual violence erupt from behind the rhetorical veil of Samboism in plantation literature. William Gilmore Simms sets *The Yemassee*—really a historical romance and not a plantation novel—against the backdrop of an Indian revolt, but Simms carefully distinguishes between the Indian race (which he says cannot coexist with whites as an inferior caste) and the Negro race (which benefits from this low status). When slave rebellion does appear in proslavery fiction, as in Caroline Lee Hentz's *The Planter's Northern Bride* (1854), the rebellion is squelched and the social order unequivocally reaffirmed. Hentz's example notwithstanding, plantation fiction almost exclusively avoided the rebel slave, and for good reason: he was the declared enemy of the paternalistic order. The rebel overturned the master's vision of slavery as Christian charity, replacing it with a millennial vision of abolition that received its first full realization in *Uncle Tom's Cabin*. The rebel also represented an unacceptably inclusive egalitarian reading of the Declaration of Independence and the Constitution, a different interpretation of American revolutionary ideology than the stratified one favored by the slaveowner.[79]

Given the utter unpalatability of the rebel to proslavery ideologues, it certainly is not surprising that the character type appealed strongly to African-American writers. Martin Delany, for one, repudiated Uncle Tom and called for a charismatic black leader who would resist, not submit. He invented one in *Blake*, his serialized novel of a slave rebellion in Cuba.[80] Though he was an admirer of *Uncle Tom's Cabin*, with its pacifist hero, Frederick Douglass also created a rebellious hero in his only work of fiction, *The Heroic Slave*. Madison Washington, the title character of the novella, leads a mutiny aboard the brig *Creole*, liberates the slaves, and steers the ship into safe harbor at the British territory of Nassau. Douglass structures his account so that it turns precisely on the objectification idea: the British soldiers allow the slaves safe harbor because they do not see their instructions to "protect property" as extending to slaves.[81] Tom Grant, the *Creole* first mate who narrates the last part of the story, admits in the face of Washington's courage and bearing that he "was in the presence of a superior man" (68). Washington's stature prevents Grant from sustaining the slaveholder's view of human-as-thing, so he renounces it. Washington effectively forces Grant to see him as a person, thereby making an abolitionist out of a slave ship officer (65).

Stowe herself experimented with rebellious slaves, but was obviously uncomfortable with the type. In *Uncle Tom's Cabin* George Harris overflows with rebellious rhetoric, as does the title character of *Dred*, a swamp-dwelling fugitive who actually plans a slave uprising. For all their speeches, though, neither commits any serious act of violence. George actually shoots Tom Loker, one of the bounty hunters chasing after him, but the shot (which is clearly fired in self-defense) doesn't slow his pursuer; it is the Quaker Phineas Fletcher who throws Loker into a gorge, injuring him seriously. As for Dred, after numerous impassioned speeches he is shot and dies in the swamps before he can carry out his revolt. One wonders how Stowe could have brought it off, for the slaves in *Dred* prove much more resistant to education than those in *Uncle Tom's Cabin*.

The comic Sambo and the fearful Nat comprise two sides of a diptych in the slaveholder's mind. That the slaveowner should see the slave as comic and fearful at the same time is more than passing strange, for the combination of humor and fear is the source of the majority of definitions for *grotesque* from antiquity to the present.[82] The dynamic tension between Sambo and Nat further illustrates the slave's liminality, a quality linked to grotesqueness. This is a permanent state for the slave, because the very core of the identity assigned him by his master—as human/thing—is essentially unstable. Last chapter I argued that the American slave narrator was aware of his own grotesqueness in his master's eyes, and manipulated it to gain freedom. This chapter shows that the master is similarly aware of the slave's grotesqueness, and seeks relief from it by trying to imagine it away. But this attempt doesn't work. Even Sambo, the master's own vision of slave stability and contentment, constantly threatens to transform himself into his alter ego, Nat, before his owner's eyes.

The coexistence in the master's mind of the performing comic Sambo and the deadly serious rebel Nat shows, among other things, that Hegel's dialectical metaphor needs to be read more creatively against the panorama of the American slavery experience. Focusing last chapter on the mind of the slave, I suggested that violence should be considered a kind of "work" that contributes to the slave's progress within Hegel's scheme. Shifting to the master's mind in this chapter, it seems to me that more attention must be paid to the complications attached to the master's specific fear of the slave's violent rebellion. The American slaveowner surely fears loss of his identity as master (as Hegel suggests), but the complex construction in his mind of the layered Sambo stereotype, especially in partnership with Nat, Sambo's ever-present rebellious shadow, shows that the master fears much more than the slave's gradual independence through work.[83] The proliferation and function of Sambo within both pro- and antislavery literature shows that the master distinctly fears that the slave will rise violently against him, reversing the outcome of the original clash for recognition. The multiple roles that the master devised for Sambo—as culturally stunted child, biological throwback, happy worker, foolish jokester, willing performer—reflect a desperation on the part of the slaveholder. In effect, the master needs to escape the slave. He needs to escape because when all roles have been played and all makeup removed, the slave will show himself to be a prisoner, a prisoner who is very angry at the one who holds him captive and attempts to deny his human status. And the master knows it.

CHAPTER FIVE

THE RACIAL FREAK, THE HAPPY SLAVE, AND THE PROBLEMS OF MELVILLE'S UNIVERSAL MEN

> It is not unsurmised, that only when extraordinary stimulus is needed, only when an extra strain is to be got out of them, are these hapless 'Gees ennobled with the human name.
>
> —Herman Melville, *"The 'Gees"*

> Freaks are called freaks and are treated as they are treated—in the main, abominably—because they are human beings who cause to echo, deep within us, our most profound terrors and desires . . . .
>
> We are a part of each other. Many of my countrymen appear to find this fact exceedingly inconvenient and even unfair, and so, very often, do I. But none of us can do anything about it.
>
> —James Baldwin, *"Freaks and the Ideal of American Manhood"* *(later entitled "Here Be Dragons")*

Herman Melville was preoccupied with the problems of human objectification throughout his writing career and invented a gallery of characters who struggle with the issue in different fictional situations. This chapter focuses primarily on two texts, Typee *and* Benito Cereno, *with a brief discussion of* Moby-Dick *bridging the two. Together, these books illustrate the range of Melville's treatment of racial objectification, from the theoretical to the topical.*

Typee, *the autobiographically inspired story of an individual's encounter with a radically different culture and its customs, shows how difficult it is to rise above the beliefs of one's own group, and how elusive the ideal of open-minded human equality can be when those beliefs are challenged by experience. Though Melville's narrator consciously seeks to avoid objectifying the Typee natives, he recoils and panics when they offer to tattoo his face. Writing at the beginning of the American freak show's rapid rise to popularity—and during a time of heightened racial tension in the United States amid the rise of political abolitionism—Melville uses the practice of facial tattooing to link the black with the freak. The pairing of Ishmael and Queequeg in* Moby-Dick *offers a rosier version of a similar scenario, but* Benito Cereno, *a fictionalization of an actual 1799 slave ship revolt in the Caribbean, projects the laws and attitudes of slaveholding society into the center of a typically Melvillean moral muddle. Black rises up and enslaves white, and then black forces white to play the role of master before the outside audience of visiting Captain Amasa Delano. In a virtual omnibus of the themes of this study, Melville's drama of inversions temporarily turns on its head the freak show, the Sambo stereotype, and the Hegelian master-slave dialectic. Delano's objectifying gaze prevents him from seeing the reality of the scene aboard ship, and of slavery itself. As in* Typee, *the result is a pervasive loss of cultural balance and orientation.*

The Charter of the United Nations calls on all its members "to practice tolerance" and be "good neighbors." Written in 1945, this document emerged from the ashes of a war that defeated state-sponsored intolerance, but there has been good reason to wonder whether the world community remembers what it says—or whether tolerance may be a more elusive goal than the writers assumed. Following in the rutted groove of American individualism, the ongoing debate over race in the United States tends to treat tolerance as a simple individual decision. But learning it isn't always so simple—or so individual. Sometimes the beliefs of a whole culture are arrayed against the effort to be open-minded, as they were in pre-civil rights Mississippi, for example, against any white person who might have been inclined to treat African-Americans as friends or equals. Racist acculturation in the Jim Crow South put insidious pressure on well-meaning people to adopt local prejudices and follow public practices like, say, wiping one's hand after shaking hands with a black man. David Halberstam tells the story of how Tim McCarver, a white Southerner who thought he harbored no prejudice, came to realize as a young major league baseball player—on an integrated team—how he had unconsciously acquired racist beliefs and been drawn into such malignant practices without realizing it. Once enlightened, McCarver worked on shedding his beliefs and changing his behavior, soon demonstrating to his black teammates that he was no racist. But his early experience shows that when the beliefs and traditions of an entire society dictate against tolerance, even defending it becomes exceedingly difficult, let alone practicing it. In the end, talking the talk is usually easier than walking the walk.[1]

Herman Melville understood this difficulty before most others in his society ever confronted it, and he explored it throughout his career by creating characters less skilled at perceiving these problems, and then placing these characters into positions that expose their limitations in the face of racial and cultural difference. *Typee*, *Moby-Dick*, and *Benito Cereno* all illustrate the struggle with racial difference that originates in human limitation, and is marked by the racial grotesque.

I

Tattooing and the Racial Freak in *Typee*

Typee, Melville's autobiographically inspired 1846 novel of a Polynesian island sojourn, shows how fragile a person's beliefs can be when they are challenged by radically unfamiliar cultural practices. Based closely on Melville's own experience in the Marquesan Islands (and treated as non-fiction during its contemporary release), *Typee* features a narrator, Tommo, who jumps ship in the Marquesas, eventually finding himself amongst the Typee tribe.[2] Despite the notorious Typee reputation for cannibalism, Tommo brings the best of intentions to his relations with them. He consciously seeks to understand their customs and appreciate their lives from their perspective, not his own. In particular, he seeks to avoid the Western attitudes toward Polynesians that were prevalent during Melville's time. He pointedly rejects prevailing interpretations of them as subhuman barbarians, cannibals, and heathens. But this noble effort ultimately breaks down, and Tommo flees in a panic over the discovery of what he presumes is cannibalism. The result, Melville shows, is the loss of a moral and epistemological center of gravity for both the narrator and his audience.

Though the novel comments indirectly on racism and slavery—as I will show—it addresses something more basic than America's peculiar institution. Writing at a time when race had become the central issue in American political and social life, Melville seeks the roots of prejudice, the cause and effect of perceived difference among human beings. *Typee* dramatizes the encounter with racial difference through the adventures of a would-be anthropologist who at first appears to be a modern cultural relativist out of place and time, but who eventually shows his true colors—or rather his "true color." When he betrays a fear of blackness, Tommo shows himself to be more like his nineteenth-century American peers than he prefers to admit.

Melville uses several potent symbols to signal Tommo's position in the web of Western belief and practice, but the most important of these is the facial tattoo. Such Typee adornment—which Tommo dramatically refuses—becomes the literal marker in his mind between "normal" (linked to whiteness and American identity) and "freak," a figure who is foreign and black. My goal here is to assert a multiple connection expressed in *Typee* between the heyday of abolitionism (along with the glaring and newly exploitable weaknesses in slavery ideology that the movement reflected and fed off, and the heightened proslavery activity that rose to meet these Northern forces), and the rise of the freak show—all of which occurred in the United States at about the same time. The freak show entered American society when institutionalized racism became the subject of social scrutiny and public debate, when the socially constructed barriers separating black from white came under increasing attack. Tattooing in *Typee* visibly links racial otherness to freak status via the medium of the racial grotesque.

Simply put, I am arguing that it was no accident that the freak show was known in the circus trade as a "Nig Show," and that Melville crystallized the significance of that nickname in *Typee*.[3] The evidence for this link goes beyond the confluence of the rise of the freak show and the rise of abolitionism and proslavery activity, and the way that the decline of the freak show coincides with the rise of civil rights. Most important, I will suggest, is the way that the freak show—and especially its tattooed members, black and white—bring the physical anomaly, the racial other, and the racial freak together under the same tent. The existence and popularity of the racial freak suggests that the freak show drew most of its power from the psychic energy generated by a racially divided society in which whiteness was a construction that was coming under increasing attack. Tommo's fear of becoming a racial freak thus stands as an individual manifestation of an increasing tension that permeated American culture generally in 1846, a tension linked to the unraveling of the racial distinctions central to American social organization and the meaning of being "white."[4]

Resisting the Grotesque

Once he finds himself among the Typees, Tommo compares his own ways with theirs in an unusually fair-minded way for his time. Unlike the repressed missionaries to the Marquesan Islands described by T.

Walter Herbert, Tommo is consciously fascinated by the Typees' uninhibited nakedness, and intellectually curious about their unusual taboos.[5] He seeks to understand rather than dismiss the customs of the islanders. He learns to eat as they do (with their fingers) and dress like them (the latter gesture also in part to preserve his Western clothes and so maintain an escape hatch to his native culture). All the while, Tommo tries to learn as much as possible about the reasons for the islanders' behavior. Because of his unceasing curiosity coupled with a penchant for analytical description of the native customs, *Typee* reads in places like a twentieth-century anthropological ethnography from what Renato Rosaldo calls the "classic period" of cultural relativism.[6] Using a method strikingly similar to the modern anthropologist's, Tommo tries for most of the novel to understand his adopted culture from within.

But Tommo is decidedly not an anthropologist; that field of study did not exist at the time. Though the study of "exotic" cultures was catching on in the United States when Melville wrote *Typee* in the mid-1840s, anthropology did not enter the social sciences until the next century. Before it evolved a nineteenth-century science called ethnology which claimed the study of alien cultures as its province. By 1850 ethnology was firmly established; its methods were hierarchical, relying on a scale of humanity ranging from "primitive" to "civilized." (Not until the early twentieth century were the essentialist explanations of mid-nineteenth-century ethnology finally demolished, paving the way for cultural relativism to enter and make anthropology recognizable to the modern eye.)[7] Ethnology filled a social need for inequality that cultural anthropology does not. The social and legal institutions of the antebellum United States were racially and hierarchically organized, and the study of traditional culture naturally followed suit. The nineteenth-century study of "exotic" societies thus supported the assumptions of the Western culture that sponsored it.

Tommo's confrontation with the Marquesan islanders represents a challenge to his very idea of order. Though he does not realize it, he is putting his entire epistemology on the line. Recasting this conflict in terms of modern anthropological oppositions, the cultural difference of the Typee challenges Tommo's Western-based system of belief. As Mary Douglas shows, this situation—when the anomaly threatens a system of belief from without—is the most serious possible attack that can be mounted on a way of thinking. Though Tommo tries to suggest a different conclusion, Melville finally shows in *Typee* that even if one seeks to maintain an open mind, one can still feel challenged, even threatened, by a different culture—and this threat can result in a frightening encounter with the grotesque. All people divide up the world in order to understand it, not just dogmatists, and any encounter with a radically different culture, one outside the realm of expectation and understanding, will provoke a challenge to the realm of the familiar. When something challenges an individual's system of understanding, the system must accommodate or risk collapse.

In *Typee* the grotesque marks where the problem lies. Specifically, Tommo's capacity to meet his challenges may be measured by the way he perceives the grotesque. When he is doing well, he understands native practices in their own context. When such practices make him anxious or frighten him, they appear to him as grotesque. The grotesque thus emerges as the star player in *Typee*'s drama of cultural differences, not only representing the narrator's inability to assimilate into a different culture but also standing as a symptom and a symbol of his unwillingness to cross boundaries and join a different race.

Melville draws the lines separating American from Marquesan in *Typee* at the outset, and immediately underscores them with grotesque effects. The opening of the book cuts the narrator off from all that is known: "Six months at sea! Yes, reader, as I live, six months out of sight of land."[8] He implies the existence of strange climes where presumably anything can happen. When the ship arrives at the islands, Melville dramatically introduces the native men and women as grotesques. We see them first in a vision of transformation: as they swim toward the ship, they appear as something other than what they are. The men initially seem to be living coconuts:

> By some inexplicable means these coconuts were all steadily approaching towards the ship. As I leaned curiously over the side endeavoring to solve their mysterious movements, one mass far in advance of the rest attracted my attention. In its center was something I could take for nothing else other than a coconut, but which I certainly considered one of the most extraordinary specimens of the fruit I had ever seen. It kept twirling and dancing about among the rest in a most singular manner, and as it drew nearer I thought it bore a remarkable resemblance

> to the brown shaven skull of one of the savages. Presently it betrayed a pair of eyes, and soon I became aware that what I had supposed to have been one of the fruit was nothing else than the head of an islander. (2:13)

Melville has Tommo turn a fruit into a man here. This is certainly a grotesque transformation, albeit an unintimidating one. Still, the comparison carries some disturbing associations. The brief merger of the Typees with inanimate objects foreshadows the cultural confrontations to come, when Tommo again equates them with things.

We meet the women of the island in a similarly hallucinatory fashion, as a "shoal of fish" who turn out to be "*whinhenies*," or young girls (2:14). Tommo sees the women first as fish before he turns them into humans, but the comparison to mermaids, grotesque creatures by virtue of being neither human nor fish, indicates that he never really manages to see them as people. Yes, they are women, but not like the ones he knows. These particular grotesque effects mark Melville's method of comparing two different cultures from the perspective of one of them. The opening male and female transformations make comparisons that highlight cultural boundaries. These metaphors realize themselves as they are being described, and so become harbingers for the more emotionally fraught differences to be encountered later on.

Once ashore, Tommo examines some island taboos from his own perspective. He seeks to overturn the Typee religious prohibition against women in boats, for example, and eventually procures a dispensation for Fayaway, the special object of his affections. His description of his challenge shows that he knows exactly what he is doing: "Although the taboo was a ticklish thing to meddle with, I determined to test its capabilities of resisting an attack" (18:132). Later on, when he unwittingly violates an injunction against touching tappa cloth while it is being made, his reaction is to find out why the prohibition exists. "I subsequently found out that the fabric they were engaged in making was of a peculiar kind, destined to be worn on the heads of the females" (30:222). Though these taboos are illogical from Tommo's foreign perspective, he respects them because they matter to the Typees themselves. Tommo further understands that the native taboos can lead to grotesque effects that are perceived only by the islanders. His discoveries and comparisons furnish evidence of the cultural relativity of the grotesque.

This cross-cultural method exposes the grotesque at its subjective point of formation. We see through Tommo's eyes how island customs enter the Western category system and founder there. In some cases, the narrator keeps his bearings and makes adjustments, such as when he realizes that the Typees have their own eating etiquette even if they don't use silverware. He recognizes their nakedness not as amoral debauchery, but as "the easy unstudied grace of a child of nature" (11:86). He even keeps his composure when he sees men with green skin, remarking simply that they gain that strange cast when their tattoos start to age. Typee body tattoos, as Tommo explains, depict animal and vegetable growth. (And they do so very realistically: Tommo compares Kory-Kory's body to an illustrated nature textbook [11:83].) This kind of merging flora and fauna, and human and animal, is what the word *grotesque* was coined to describe.[9]

What is crucial here—and also remarkable—is that Tommo resists the urge to react to these phenomena as grotesque. He tries very hard to be tolerant. Instead of allowing visceral revulsion to take hold, he deliberately distances himself and examines things rationally. Sometimes he is shocked, but he always tries to recover. Green men are therefore described to us with nearly the same dispassion as the thatch of the native huts might be. Tommo's narration is so explicit (scaly skin, folded flesh, bald and puckered heads, and so on) that the reader can hardly fail to see the old men as grotesque, but the narrator himself seems unfazed.[10]

Melville's strategy is thus to incite the grotesque while showing Tommo's own seeming immunity to it. He describes bizarre native customs in such detail that we, his Western readers, might see them as grotesque, but he blithely demonstrates his own supposed lack of prejudice, remaining calm, intellectually curious, and apparently unaffected by what he sees. But Melville shows that for all his skill and balance, Tommo fails to master this technique. His unconscious mind occasionally reveals his suppressed alarm with seemingly offhand comments here and there. He refers to the green men at one point as "repulsive looking creatures" (12:93), for example, a description that betrays some buried Western value judgments. For all his considerable equanimity, then, Tommo offers clear hints that he is not without his prejudices. These suppressed values will eventually flare up and overwhelm his generous openness. Although he strives to transcend his Western bias, two Typee practices in particular combine to push him off his high perch.

As he falls, he betrays the judgments he thought he had been avoiding. These two disrupters of his seeming impartiality are tattooing and cannibalism. Tattooing will be my primary focus here.

Marking the Human

If the existence of cannibalism is the great mystery that Tommo tries to solve in *Typee*, tattooing stands out as his great preoccupation. His changing reaction to the practice eventually exposes his judgment of Typee society as a group that he is happy enough to visit as a tourist, but one that he would be terrified and horrified to join.

Initially, Tommo seems quite comfortable with the Typee practice of extensive tattooing, especially of males. He speaks of it as though it were removable decoration, a set of "simple and remarkable . . . ornaments" (11:78). He even calls the tattooing on one warrior "the best specimen of the Fine Arts I had yet seen on Typee" (18:136). Still, his language betrays a certain discomfort, as when he speaks rapturously of Fayaway's markings:

> Were I asked if the beauteous form of Fayaway was altogether free from the hideous blemish of tattooing, I should be constrained to answer that it was not. But the practitioners of the barbarous art, so remorseless in their inflictions upon the brawny limbs of the warriors of the tribe, seem to be conscious that it needs not the resources of their profession to augment the charms of the maidens of the vale. (11:86)

The narrator's conflicted diction ("Fine Arts" or "hideous blemish"?) shows that he is clearly of two minds about the native custom.[11] Tattooing is fine, he seems to be saying, except when it intrudes upon a beauty which he can appreciate according to his own standards.

This implicit distinction Tommo is trying to make receives a severe challenge when Karky, the local tattooist, seeks to adorn him in the local style. Before this crisis, Tommo remains his coolly analytical, fair-minded self about the custom. His detachment is apparent from his reaction to the tattooist at work on the face of a young man. He could choose to see this as a spectacle of grotesque mutilation, but instead he places the practice into the broad context of island culture as he understands it, analogizing the activity to one familiar to him: "Altogether, the sight of these strange instruments recalled to mind that display of cruel-looking mother-of-pearl handled things which one sees in their velvet-lined cases at the elbow of the dentist" (30:218). That Tommo views this practice in terms of his own ways (into which it does not exactly fit) is an ominous sign.[12] Even so, the dentist may actually come off the worse from this comparison. It is also worth noting that however disgusted the narrator may be by what he sees here (or later on), he never ceases to refer to Karky as an artist.

But everything changes for Tommo when Karky wants to tattoo *him*. The prospect makes Tommo almost hysterical in his opposition. When the tattooist examines the contours of his face, Tommo calls it an "attack." Fear takes over: "When his forefinger swept across my features, in laying out the borders of those parallel bands which were to encircle my countenance, the flesh fairly crawled along my bones. At last, half wild with terror and indignation, I succeeded in breaking away from the three savages" (30:219). From that point afterward, says Tommo, continuing demands to tattoo him made life a "burden." He even offers to have his arms done as an appeasement of sorts, but his great fear remains that of having his face marked.

What is behind Tommo's dread? Melville makes the answer quite clear: Tommo fears that his face will be "ruined for ever" (30:220). His reaction shows how alien to him the Typees remain. This judgment is much more than a matter of aesthetics. Tommo's diction suggests that if he were tattooed, his face would not be his own any longer. It would be a "ruined" representation of him; he would not look like himself anymore, not the way he is "supposed" to look.

Tommo still sees himself with Western eyes, as a Westerner. If he were tattooed, his adopted culture would then become his home, the place where his appearance would dictate he belonged. The tattooing would materially change his identity from "American" to "Typee." Tommo describes this in terms of religious affiliation—where he would become a Typee "convert" (30:220)—but his early description of Kory-Kory is more telling: he compares the native's striped facial tattoos to prison bars (11:83). This description implies that if Tommo were tattooed in this way, he would become a kind of prisoner himself, an American captive within Typee society with no choice but to join it. With his refusal to be tattooed, the narrator abandons his overarching pancultural perspective to reject this option.[13]

Nor does his fear end there. One remark of his is particularly telling, and will become the fulcrum for much of the argument that follows. It is a direct and highly revealing admission of what Tommo is really afraid of:

> What an object he [Karky] would have made of me! (30:219)

This retrospective observation—made after his escape and return to the United States—puts Tommo's alarm into sharp relief. He is concerned not simply with crossing the border separating American from Typee, but also with slipping over the one separating human being from thing. He feels that if he had been marked as a Typee, he would cease to be a person at all. Suppressed for much of his narrative, the grotesque here makes a clamorous appearance in Tommo's life.

Tommo's reaction to the threatened tattooing reveals that deep down, he has always seen the Typees as "objects." But he also sees them as people and interacts with them as fellow humans. By embedding this unarticulated, unconscious contradiction within Tommo's mind, Melville shows just how human objectification works—and fails. Tommo has divided Typees and Westerners into distinct categories and ranked the Typee category below his own, as a race of "objects." On the other hand, Tommo wants human company, and he readily embraces the society of the Typees. As he shows in his relationships with Kory-Kory, Fayaway, and others, the Typee are people whom he can respect, even love. (The true test of "belonging" to a culture may be the ability to fall in love with one of its members.) The Typee thus become grotesque in Tommo's eyes: now objects, now humans, in constant transit between the two categories.

Tommo's exclamation of fear is most obviously an expression of rage, but it is also an intimate confession. It's a loss of temper that is full of implications of identity: Tommo is declaring who he is by reviling against who—or what—he is not. His dramatic refusal to be tattooed is the most notable of a series of contextual links to the American culture of his day, marking a trail that leads to the entrance of one of nineteenth-century America's fastest-growing public attractions: the freak show.

Tommo fears becoming a freak. Part of his fear is of becoming a physical oddity, but there's more to it than that. He knows what happens to such anomalies: they are displayed before the eager eyes of others.[14] Indeed, the freak show was—and is, in the few that still exist—a carefully bounded form of human display that purported to spotlight the edge of humanity itself. These edges were populated by human anomalies including people with odd bodies, and also people from odd—that is, non-Western—cultures.

But Tommo is already an anomaly with an odd body who is displayed before the Typee populace. As an untattooed adult man, he appears as a kind of freak to the Typees. If facial tattoos would make him look like a freak in his own eyes, it's worth noting that they serve precisely the opposite function for the Typees themselves. To the Typees, Tommo would appear less like a foreign "object" if he wore tattoos than if he did not. Without tattoos, Tommo is a "non-Typee," an anomaly within Typee society and a freak of sorts in the eyes of the group. With the markings, he would embody normality—by their standards. Tommo's fear of losing his own membership in the American group of "normals" bears comparison with his fear of entering the Typee version of that category. One might say that the novel stages a version of what he fears would happen to him if he were tattooed and then left Typee—all based on the way that the Typee islanders respond to him while he is there. These multilayered Melvillean ironies inform the author's deeply nuanced evocation of the freak show and the complicated motivations behind its rapid growth.

Freaks and freak shows are the visible artifacts of an attempt to cast one group of humans outside the human category, but the fetishistic attention they receive serves alone as ample evidence of the failure of that attempt: if freaks were truly nonhuman, after all, they would have been held in zoos, not displayed on special stages that serve as liminal "freak spaces." And they would not have been displayed in ways that consciously evoked the reminder of the humanity that they possess all along ("armless wonders," for example, performed everyday human tasks like writing or sewing for their audiences).[15] As Leslie Fiedler eloquently puts it, "The true Freak . . . stirs both supernatural terror and human sympathy, since, unlike the fabulous monsters, he is one of us, the human child of human parents, however altered by forces we do not quite understand into something mythic and mysterious, as no mere cripple ever is."[16] The simultaneous attraction (or curiosity) and repulsion (or fear) of freaks results from the combination of both of these psychic vectors. Freaks are pushed out of the realm of humanity and held within it by the same exhibit.

This dynamic instability underlies the fascination of the freak show, even as the same tension between human and nonhuman was undermining the ideology of American slavery. Tommo's panic draws its force from all of these oppositions. In depicting his fear in these terms, I will be suggesting that in *Typee* Melville provides an indirect and typically prescient analysis of the racial tensions of 1840s America, in which he demonstrates that these tensions feed on the ambivalence of the racial grotesque, as embodied by the racial freak. To this end, I want first to offer some context, a brief examination of freak shows and the role of tattooed people in them, and the beliefs of their antebellum American audiences about such human anomalies.

The Tattooed Freak

Though human oddities have been exhibited for amusement and profit for untold centuries, the American freak show is generally considered to have coalesced as a distinct and recognizable institution beginning around 1835. Its rise to national prominence began at this time, with the 1840s and 1850s being the formative period when freak shows multiplied rapidly and evolved their distinctive format. The freak show arose roughly in tandem with the museum, which was originally a far less authoritative educational space than it is today. Early museums featured artifacts brought back by sailors and explorers. Human curiosities were included from the start. P. T. Barnum, the leading museum impresario of the day, opened his museum in New York in January 1842 and used such human oddities to make it a major attraction. Circuses—with freak sideshows—became popular around the middle of the nineteenth century.[17]

Melville wrote about freak displays in a short 1847 parody of P. T. Barnum contained in a series of sketches about Zachary Taylor, "Authentic Anecdotes of 'Old Zack.'"[18] The brief spoof shows a full awareness of the attraction of human curiosities and the consequent popularity of early museum culture. Tattooed sailors, as Melville certainly knew, were popular sidewalk exhibits before they became part of freak shows; their popularity can be dated back to the early nineteenth century.[19] When the freak show came to public prominence during the decades leading up to the Civil War, tattooed people quickly emerged as a popular exhibit that shortly became a freak show staple. Demand for them grew throughout the nineteenth century and into the twentieth (when the market for them became glutted after the Second World War). All freaks were elaborate social constructions, as Robert Bogdan has shown, and tattooed people were no exception. The typical exhibit featured the decorated person on display, with the tattoos serving as the basis for a wild story, usually concocted by the promoter and written up in a pamphlet offered for sale, containing a detailed account of how he became a marked man.

Tattooed men (tattooed women were not exhibited until after the Civil War) generally told fantastic tales of kidnap and captivity in which their tattoos were typically forced upon them as torture or punishment by barbaric savages. The English sailor John Rutherford was the first to ply his trade as a tattooed man. First displaying himself in 1828, he told an outlandish story of capture by primitives, six years of captivity, compulsory marriage to the chief's young daughter, and forcible tattooing of his body by tribespeople. Eventual exposure of the true story (a much more pedestrian affair) would ruin much of his appeal, but his invented tale gained long life in a different way: it became a narrative paradigm for those who followed him.[20] Such stories of tattooing branched from the broader category of "survival literature," which was itself a branch of travel writing. Survival literature first appeared during the eighteenth century; its dominant themes, as Mary Louise Pratt notes, were sex and slavery.[21] The tattoo narrative exploited the conventions of survival literature, with the actual tattoo acting as a symbolic conflation of these two main themes.

The first tattooed man exhibited in the United States was James O'Connell, who made his circus debut in the mid-1830s. O'Connell sold a book (written in 1836 by an amanuensis) and a pamphlet (later adapted from the book) that told a hair-raising story of adventures aboard ship and in exotic lands that featured—as Rutherford's story did—his forced tattooing. O'Connell claimed that he was made to submit to tattooing by Micronesian island maidens, with custom dictating that the final tattooist become his wife. O'Connell's story, and especially the pictures on his body that went with it, made him a financial success at the time of *Typee*.[22] His entrepreneurial acumen inspired many imitators, and the tattooed man became a freak show institution.

Neither Rutherford nor O'Connell were tattooed on their faces, unlike the Polynesian natives who were also on exhibit in freak shows at the time. By showing Tommo's dread of facial tattooing, Melville equates

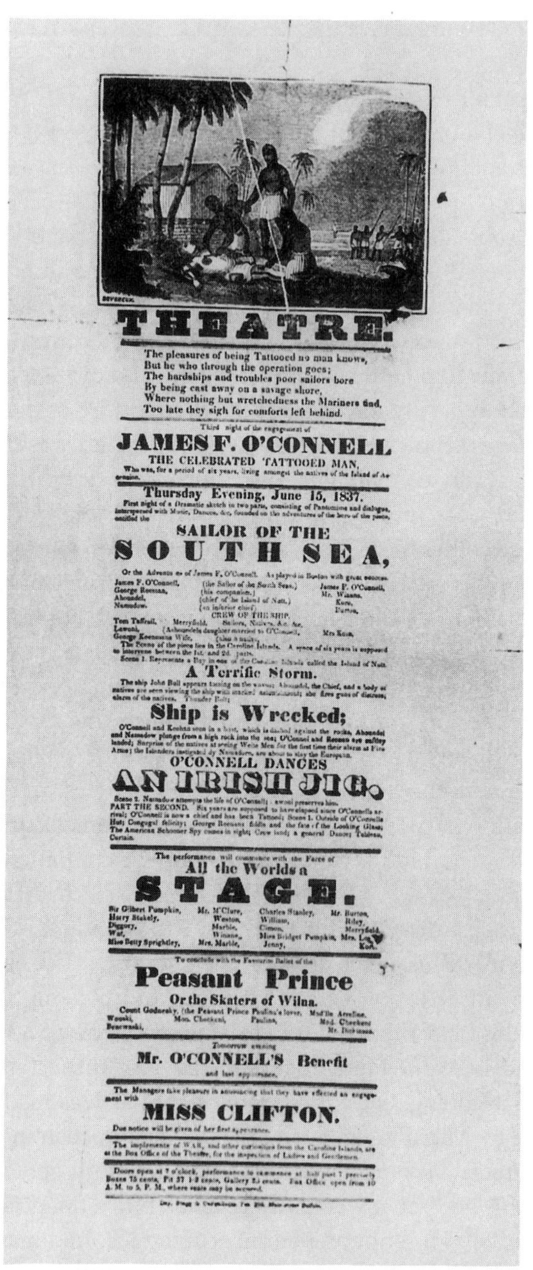

Fig. 5.1 Broadside advertising the appearance of James F. O'Connell, "The Celebrated Tattooed Man," 1837 (detail). The picture at the top illustrates O'Connell's account of his forced tattooing. (Reproduced courtesy of the Rare Book Room, Buffalo and Erie County Public Library)

Fig. 5.2 *Harper's Weekly* advertisement for Captain Costentenus (1877). This scene, in which he receives his tattoos, makes the racial and sexual tensions attached to the act especially clear. Note the "oriental" men who observe the spectacle from the background. (Reproduced courtesy of the Becker Collection, Syracuse University)

white tattooed freaks with such native exhibits, and so raises the stakes of the cultural game—even as he anticipates the evolution of the tattooed freak. The next famous tattooed exhibit after O'Connell was "Captain Costentenus," an attraction from the 1870s onwards whose face *was* tattooed (along with his entire body). Not surprisingly, Costentenus also told a fantastic, fabricated story of coercion, with his tattoos allegedly being a three-month torture and punishment at the hands of either Chinese or Burmese barbarians, depending on which version of the story one consults. Many more tattooed freak show acts followed the popular example of Costentenus, mostly telling variations on the standard story of capture and forced tattooing, until the popularity of the tattooed woman widened the story possibilities beginning in the 1880s.[23]

Typee appeared just at the time when the tattooed man was becoming a familiar freak show sight and his story a conventional tale of suspense, adventure, and unique torture. Melville imparts full awareness to Tommo of this subculture of commodified humbug, and with it a notable ironic ambivalence. Tommo's own account consciously feints toward coercion, effectively threatening to become the kind of account of forced tattooing that was told by countless tattooed freaks. In fact, Tommo's story—which unlike his face, he chooses to display publicly—can even be read as a tattooing narrative, minus the tattooing. So even though Tommo recoils from the tattooing itself, he embraces the stories and even the commercial ethos that surrounded the American display of the practice. In writing and selling his story of (near) tattooing, Tommo flirts with the role of tattooed freak, suggesting that part of him is attracted to the part, just as another part of him is clearly drawn to being a Typee.[24] But Tommo finally forbids himself such equivocation. In depicting Tommo's powerful fears of his own desires, Melville shows what tattooing puts at risk for him: national membership, class membership, racial membership, and, as a result, human membership as he understands it.

The generic story of captivity and forcible tattooing reflected on the teller in two important ways that would have terrified Tommo. First, it portrays the tattooed freak as someone without will, as one who had been unable to prevent his body—his most personal space—from becoming indelibly marked. Tattooing thus stands not only as a kind of torture that could not be prevented by force of will, but also as a reminder of that failure of will that is immediately visible to all. Ironically, tattooing was actually one of the few ways that an able-bodied person could voluntarily become a freak, yet the conventional exhibition of such people made this decision appear involuntary. Such paradox further suggests the crucial importance of volition to the construction of the tattooed freak. The role of women in the standard narrative also emphasizes this theme. Women are closely implicated with the coercive aspects of the standard tattooing narrative, with forced marriage frequently accompanying forced tattooing. (In O'Connell's case, the two are conflated, with the female tattooist literally marking him—against his will—as her husband.) This reversal of gendered power relations figures the tattooed man as a woman, and the bodily violation of tattooing as a figurative form of rape.[25] At a time when the gendered spheres of American society were growing further separate, the tattooed freak—and also the fear of becoming one that Tommo shows in *Typee*—tap into a deep well of anxiety over male power and sexual integrity.[26]

Second, the tattoos mark their bearer as someone without social mobility. Tattooed people are freaks, and because the tattoos are permanent, so must be the class status of the person who is marked with them. Once a tattooed man, always a tattooed man. Thus, if an unmarked man can normally live anywhere he likes, facial tattoos would turn him into a tattooed freak possessing a single vocation and a single location—with the freak show being the place where the two become one. Tattooing thereby knocks the rungs out of the American ladder to success, the climbing of which ostensibly translates hard work into personal improvement.

These unpleasant possibilities underlie Tommo's fear of being tattooed because they threaten to erase the primary coordinates that compose his sense of self. First, they violate his own expectations of himself as an American citizen, a free man who can, in theory, enact his own desires and rise as high as his initiative might take him.[27] As a tattooed man, Tommo's horizons would be necessarily limited. He sees this as a threatened loss of his nationality itself: "I should be disfigured in a manner as never more to have the *face* to return to my countrymen" (30:219). Second, the possible loss of will and social mobility threaten Tommo's self-image as quasi-modern anthropologist. If marked as a Typee, he would permanently become a Typee—no longer able to pass in and out of cultures the way that he does now. In effect, Tommo fears being imprisoned inside the narrative of a freak show exhibit pamphlet. Like the fugitive slave narrators who were his contemporaries in real life, he fears being catalogued and characterized by scientists of his day (whose judgments were prominently featured in such pamphlets), and he fears being permanently slotted in a space where he feels he does not, and cannot, belong.[28]

Tommo's fear of losing control points to the freak's passivity before the spiel of the carnival talker (they were not called "barkers"), who guides the spectator's gaze and therefore controls the terms of the display. It is the carnival talker who creates the human oddity as a grotesque freak by instructing the audience on how to look at the exhibit. Mercy Lavinia Warren Bump, the thirty-two-inch wife of the famous midget General Tom Thumb, declared, "I belong to the public"[29]—a thought that would be particularly upsetting to Tommo, who wants so badly to believe that he belongs to himself alone that he creates an illusion of himself as a pancultural man, a temporary member of whatever group suits his fancy. In the process, he represses his American cultural membership, his equivocal desire to be a Typee, and his nervous curiosity about what it might be like to be a tattooed man.

The spectacle of the tattooed freak clearly embodies great and disturbing fears for Tommo, but even this is not what frightens him most. His greatest fear arises from comparison with another group of tattooed people who were displayed at freak shows: the racial freaks. This group (which I introduced in chapter 3) was made up of people from non-Western cultures who became freak show exhibits simply because they lived differently, in a faraway place. The subjects of these outrageous exhibitions were always nonwhite, and were frequently tattooed according to their own custom. More than anything, Tommo fears becoming one of them.

Cannibalism and the Racial Freak

Virtually all freak shows displayed non-Westerners in full native regalia, with South Seas islanders as frequent subjects of this treatment, along with Africans. (The first Polynesian viewed in the United States was a tattooed man, whose 1774 exhibit antedated the freak show.) The continuing popularity of such displays reflected an American fascination with the other side of the world at a time when it could not be easily reached. It was standard practice to exhibit non-Westerners in freak shows as primitive humans or "missing links," with displays resembling crude living dioramas with rudimentary foreign or jungle backdrops.[30] Such racial freaks were among the most popular acts in the history of the institution.

Unlike the "Siamese twins," "pinheads," or "legless (and/or 'armless') wonders" who were also placed on display in museums and sideshows, racial freaks were not physically anomalous within the context of their own culture—that is, there was nothing "odd" about their bodies in the eyes of their own peers. Instead, it was their simple presence in the United States, among people who lived differently from them, that served as the basis for their being perceived as grotesque.

Allegations of cannibalism provided the rhetorical leverage to place them in this liminal space. Cannibalism was a hot issue in the nineteenth-century United States as it was in *Typee*, a source of national fear and fascination and one of the most potent American symbols of un-civilization. In connection with scientific discourses of the day, it was the key to turning "exotic" into "primitive" and "atavistic." Though some

South Seas islanders practiced cannibalism, the truth of the situation was less sensational than such labels would imply. Cannibalism has always and only been part of tribal ritual (as Peggy R. Sanday says, it is never "just about eating"), and only certain members of certain South Seas island societies practiced it.[31] But these facts mattered little to Americans unaccustomed to distinguishing among groups of dark-skinned people, and not at all to freak show promoters, who had no particular use for facts when a salacious story could be invented instead. As a result, all South Seas islanders were labeled as cannibals, and such loose allegations became the means of relegating such groups to a lower position on the chain of being. Not surprisingly, P. T. Barnum was the first to bring "cannibals" into the freak show mainstream.[32]

The stigma that United States society attached to cannibalism was hardly new. The idea of cannibalism has been used as Western rhetorical mortar to construct the "savage" since the early days of New World exploration. The method centers on what Sara Castro-Klaren describes (in language borrowed from Mary Douglas) as a series of "noxious, polluting, and poisonous contacts." These contacts center on a self-referential paradox that can be summed up this way: savages eat human flesh because they are uncivilized, and they are uncivilized because they eat human flesh. This closed system of belief then permits the colonizer to view the "cannibal" as an unalloyed, permanently different, not fully human other.[33] Such constructions of difference served a broad nationalistic use in America. A society accustomed to looking up to venerable European traditions seized upon cannibalism as the basis for positioning a group for themselves to look down on. The power of cannibalism to shock enabled it to support this hierarchical ordering of "civilized" and "savage" cultures. But this nonreasoning response (a literal "gut reaction") also helps to expose the self-interested "logic" of Tommo's "ethnologic" viewpoint, and of ethnology generally, even as curiosity about cannibalism fuels the forward movement of his narrative.

Though tattooing offers the most important window into Tommo's thought, cannibalism provides the central mystery of his story. Cannibalism also helps to conclude it, when his reaction to the sight of the remains of a human meal throws him into a panic that leads to his hurried escape from the island. The specter of cannibalism, with all of its associations, haunts Tommo from the beginning. "You may not blame me," the captain warns his shipmates before they put ashore, "if the islanders make a meal of you" (6:35). By this time, before so much as setting foot on land, Tommo has already learned that in the native tongue, the word "Typee . . . signifies a lover of human flesh" (4:24). Tommo appears to deviate from this common equation of cannibalism and savagery, but he nonetheless searches feverishly for cannibalism from the moment of his arrival, combining fear and curiosity, and apologizing all the while for what he knows he will find. When he does find apparent evidence of cannibalism, he rushes back to the safety of familiar values, followed by familiar places.

Melville undercuts the suspense of Tommo's search for cannibalism by having him answer the crucial question for his readers before he reaches the point of discovery in his own narrative. Of course there is cannibalism among the Typee, Tommo tells us. At two points he offers an apology for it before we even see that it goes on. First he seeks to preempt the reader's disgust by satirically comparing the practice ("a rather bad trait in their character it must be allowed" [17:125]) to some of the more gruesome Western penal rituals practiced upon men "found guilty of honesty, patriotism, and suchlike heinous crimes" (17:125). He saves his most passionate defense of the Typees for the point just before he encounters the physical evidence of the cannibals' meal:

> The reader will erelong have reason to suspect that the Typees are not free from the guilt of cannibalism; and he will then, perhaps, charge me with admiring a people against whom so odious a crime is chargeable. But this enormity in their character is not half so horrible as it is usually described. (27:205)

He goes on to describe the outlandishness of some accounts, which are so incredible as to lead many to doubt that cannibalism occurs at all. His answer speaks for the equivocal balance he tries to keep throughout the book:

> But here Truth, who loves to be centrally located, is again found between the two extremes; for cannibalism to a certain moderate extent is practiced among several of the primitive tribes in the Pacific, but it is upon the bodies of slain enemies alone; and horrible and fearful as the custom is, immeasurably as it is to be

> abhorred and condemned, still I assert that those who indulge in it are in other respects humane and virtuous. (27:205)

Here Tommo tries to put native practice into perspective from within as well as from without. To pull this off, he contorts himself rhetorically (how much cannibalism is "moderate"?) and conceptually (why is it somehow less awful to eat only one's enemies?).

If Tommo makes a strong case for the islanders, it speaks for his efforts to be fair. He wants his readers to follow his lead by viewing the cannibalistic ritual in the context of its own culture. This attitude remarkably presages that put forth by Sanday in her modern anthropological analysis of cannibalism, *Divine Hunger*. Sanday says that cannibalism "is not a unitary phenomenon but varies with respect to culture and meaning."[34] It is clear from *Typee* that cannibalism has a role to play in Melville's depiction of Marquesan culture; it is hardly unfettered savagery run amok. Through Tommo, Melville looks past the prejudices of his own culture in the same way Sanday does nearly 150 years later.

But Melville does not allow such a singular interpretation to stand alone, no matter how forward-looking Tommo's attitude appears. Tommo's retrospective defense of the Typee in spite of their cannibalism is actually a cover-up for a set of conventional nineteenth-century attitudes.[35] His rhetorical toleration of cannibalism stands in stark contrast to his first reaction to it and the events that immediately follow his discovery.

Like the rest of his narrative, Tommo's account of his detection of Typee cannibalism follows directly from a curiosity "which I could not repress" (32:238). He strongly suspects that cannibalism has occurred when he is barred from a certain festivity, and is actually looking for evidence when he looks under a covering in the sacred area:

> I raised one end of the cover; at the same moment the chiefs, perceiving my design, loudly ejaculated, "Taboo! Taboo!" But the slight glimpse sufficed; my eyes fell upon the disordered members of a human skeleton, the bones still fresh with moisture, and with particles of flesh still clinging to them here and there! (32:238)

The force of the sight keeps him up all night. The cannibalized human remains are a "horrid revelation" that brings him to a new awareness of his condition and causes him to hatch the plan that eventually leads to his escape. He takes great personal risk to put his plan into motion.

The impact of the cannibalism image on the narrator is evident from his description of it: the material turns grotesque in his hands. Like the other observers I have discussed throughout this book, Tommo cannot accept this transformation of person into thing (in this case, food). He sees human identity within the meat and bones. The tribes who practice cannibalism manage the volatile human image by openly acknowledging it in their ritual practice. By creating a special category for their act, they keep it out of their own realm of the grotesque.

Tommo sees things differently—for him, cannibalism most emphatically *is* grotesque. Because he does not share the Typees' religious convictions, he reacts to their cannibalism as an abhorrent attempt at human objectification. As a result, he recoils violently from the sight of the ritual meal, showing once more that the grotesque is culturally specific, and that he is not a Typee. Though Tommo tries to reverse himself later, his fear is palpable in his account of the flesh attached to the bones.[36] This fear is partly for his own safety, of course, but Tommo fears eating human flesh at least as much as he fears being eaten himself. Eating human flesh would make him Typee in his own eyes—and the eyes of others—just as submitting to facial tattoos would. Like the threat to tattoo him, the presence of cannibalism proves too much for Tommo's relativistic approach; he cannot free himself from his Western perceptions of such activity, nor his tendency to judge the Typee on that basis. His depiction of cannibalism as grotesque captures his uneasiness, which mixes together both his fear of and unfamiliarity with the ritual. Like the tattooing episode, cannibalism overpowers his rational faculty, which recovers only later. Only after he has achieved a safe distance, back in his own culture, can he defend the Typees and their rituals. Standing in front of the grisly remains of a human feast, he feels very differently.[37]

The contrast between Tommo's immediate reaction to Typee cannibalism and his later reflection upon it deserves close consideration. On one hand, he wants to view all Typee rituals as an inquiring and unprejudiced proto-anthropological observer. On the other hand, part of the reason he's fascinated by what he sees is because it violates the taboos he knows and fears deep inside himself. His response to these practices shows that in a time of personal crisis he returns to his old, secure frame of reference. Literally and figuratively, he dons his old clothes again.

Tattooing was the visible symbol of cannibalism and all the beliefs that went with it at that time. Tattooed tribes were considered to be cannibalistic tribes, and tattooing itself was seen as a sign of atavism, and a physical marker for the presence of cannibalism. Naturalists (the early equivalent of biologists) and ethnologists saw tattooing as the "ultimate sign of primitiveness," and the notorious Cesar Lombroso would cite tattoos—along with dark skin—as signs of criminality a few decades later.[38] Such beliefs helped to make tattooed islanders into the most marginal of all freaks—and the anticipation of being grouped with them is a major source of Tommo's terror at having his face marked.

For Tommo, this amounts to a fear of being "black." The possibility of labeling and displaying non-Westerners as barbaric, subhuman creatures—as freak show promoters did—lay in their color as well as their habits; their dark skin made it possible to exile them to the edges of the human category. The importance of color to the creation of racial freaks rests on the confluence of ethnological analysis of racial freaks with the various pseudoscientific results of nineteenth-century racial science. The ethnological scrutiny of native peoples took place in the larger context of the pseudoscientific debates over the species and origins of nonwhites (documented by Horsman and Gould) that I discussed in the last chapter in connection with the biological basis for alleged slave inferiority.[39]

Racial "science" and freak show pamphlets grow from the same root, with one emphasizing the narrative of pathology (a rational account of "how it got that way") and the other the narrative of wonder (an emotional response to compromised humanity).[40] The early study of the cultures of native peoples was part and parcel of the discourse of racial inferiority, and the goal of nineteenth-century science was the same as that of the freak show: to construct and scrutinize the edges of humanity. Thus, the discussion of tattooing and cannibalism in Tommo's time was part of a larger discussion about race—and Tommo's fear of being tattooed was essentially a fear of losing his membership in the white class that was doing the analyzing and setting the categories. The result would be his exile to the nonwhite class of "objects" being analyzed.

Tommo hints at this fear at different points in *Typee*. Consider, for example, his telling aversion to having "my white skin" marked (30:219). Such marking, as Samuel Otter points out, was at the subcuta-

Fig. 5.3 Racial Freaks: Promoter G. A. Farini with some of his "Earthmen," ca. 1884. These pygmies were among hundreds of Africans exhibited in American freak shows during the nineteenth century. The first recorded displays of pygmies were by P. T. Barnum in New York in 1860, where they were described as burrowing creatures who ate snakes, lizards, and bugs. The bows and arrows were props supplied by Farini. (Reproduced courtesy of the Becker Collection, Syracuse University)

neous skin layer that was thought during the nineteenth century to contain skin color—meaning that tattooing a white person would "color" him in more ways than one. Indeed, Western visitors to the Marquesas saw the tattoos of the natives as markers of a trip across the racial divide, with the marks literally turning them "black."[41]

Of course, being black in antebellum America presumed being a slave. Tommo relates his experience to slavery on a number of occasions. First, the lack of will inherent in the generic tattooing narrative—where the author has his tattoos "forced" upon him—implies an actual slavery which was indeed written into most of these narratives. Second, descriptions of Tommo as a kind of slave frame *Typee*: Tommo renders the sailor's lot as a kind of slavery and his own final escape from the Typees as the thwarted sale of a captive.[42]

Melville manipulates these descriptions to evoke the genre of the slave narrative. The allusions would have been topical; Melville wrote and published *Typee* during the height of popularity of fugitive slave narratives. Further, Melville incorporates many of the conventions of the fugitive slave's discourse both to underscore Tommo's portrait of himself as a slave, and to shorten the distance between the faraway Marquesan Islands and the United States of America. In the first case, Tommo recounts how he had "made up my mind to 'run away' " from a life in which his "tyrannical" captain/master neglects the sick and starves the healthy, meeting any protests with "the butt-end of a handspike" (4:20–21). This passage resembles the fugitive slave narrator's conventional description of his cruel treatment in slavery. In both cases, the account of mistreatment is meant to justify the decision to escape. When Tommo prepares to jump ship, he takes precautions to avoid being captured and brought back—the "ignominious" fate of a runaway slave (5:30). When he wants to escape again at the book's end, this time from the Typees, he witnesses a bargaining session for himself, in which his life is valued in terms of cotton cloth, gunpowder, and a musket, articles of "extravagant value" (34:249–50). This scene matches another conventionalized passage in the slave narrative, in which the slave describes his own sale, underscoring the incongruity of exchanging a human being for money.

Abolitionism and the Racial Freak

Freak shows also depended on such dealings in human flesh, but instead of selling differentiated bodies themselves, freak shows sold the privilege of gazing upon them. Broadly speaking, freak shows helped Americans establish the coordinates of who "we" were by showing what "they" were—thereby establishing what "we" were not. Many cultural tensions have been suggested as causes of the growth of the freak show, including urbanization, industrialization, immigration, and the early pressure to define national identity in postrevolutionary America.[43] But color was arguably the primary determinant of the dominant "we" of nineteenth-century America (as it may still be today). It follows that the American freak show rose in considerable response to racial tension, and that its most important purpose was the deflection of racial anxiety onto a class whose difference was (to the viewer) apparently undeniable and literally spectacular.

Racial difference was less reliable than bodily anomaly as a measure of such difference. The long (and ongoing) history of racial science—and its proliferation during the decades before the Civil War—reflects the fact that racial otherness is a construction that requires constant maintenance, remaining difficult and slippery. For proponents of such inequality, this was (and remains) a source of constant concern. I want to suggest that freak shows also reflect this anxiety in a reified form, on both sides of the Mason-Dixon Line.[44] Though they don't spotlight race directly, freak shows refract it through the prism of physical anomaly, supported by an underlying premise of human inequality. Little wonder, then, that the popularity of freak shows exploded immediately after the Civil War, when racial anxiety and ideologies of inequality persisted even though slavery did not. Freak shows did not truly dwindle in America until the 1940s. Though various reasons have been offered for the decline (increased communication; the popularity of socialistic thinking, which sought to minimize differences among people; the medicalization of human anomaly), it is, I think, no coincidence that the civil rights movement started to make itself felt around that time, with its social and legal successes making naked attempts at human objectification harder to sustain in mainstream society.[45]

Freaks were a more secure receptacle than race for American "not-me" for three main reasons. First, exposure to them was temporary, so that freaks (unlike blacks) always stayed unfamiliar. (The perils of familiarity to the objectifier's perspective are clear from the Puritan narratives of Indian captivity I discussed in chapter 2; recall, for example, the way that proximity helped make the Indians human to Rowlandson.) Second, the viewing of freaks was highly structured in a way that was possible precisely because it was temporary. This structured viewing experience could be manipulated to underscore the ideology of difference, while racial encounters (which could happen anytime) could not be so regulated. The freak show was consistently and primarily mediated by an enormous external show business emphasis on difference, an emphasis that, in the small performative doses in which it was presented, overwhelmed the truth of the situation: that these were simply people displaying themselves before other people.[46] Third, freaks, unlike blacks, represented no threat—sexual, economic, or otherwise—to dominant white culture. Their display took place at a socially marked physical distance from the audience as a safe spectacle, with the freak being a socially designated receptacle for the desire for dominance and recognition.

Tommo fears the distorting hyperexotic presentation of the exotic that is typified by the freak show, but his deeply felt fear of being tattooed similarly reflects the racial ideology that makes the freak show possible. Tommo's reaction to the Typee as "object[s]" shows Melville's awareness that ethno-logic thinking isn't underpinned by "logic" at all, but rather by deep fear, motivated in racialism, that "they" are the same as "us." Though he argues throughout his narrative that the Typees are essentially the same as Westerners, Tommo's panic proves that he never really believed it.

Tommo's fear causes his quasi-anthropological facade to collapse, revealing the nineteenth-century structures that it was built on. In charting Tommo's attempt at pancultural relativism, *Typee* thus predicts with startling accuracy the directions that anthropological thought would take, with Melville providing in his depiction of Tommo's frailties the sort of self-conscious scrutiny of ethnographic practice that prevails today.

Though current scholarship rightly questions the detachment of the cultural anthropologist and calls the practice of cultural relativism into question, the modern anthropologist has more self-awareness and clearly tries harder to examine native cultures on their own terms than her nineteenth-century counterpart did.[47] It is especially in these respects that Tommo's Typee travelogue anticipates the methods of modern anthropology. But Melville ultimately shows that his narrator is hobbled by the same ethnological assumptions that were current during his own time. It is yet another aspect of Melville's extraordinary prescience that *Typee* can be said to predict both the rise of cultural anthropology and its practitioners' subsequent analysis of their own practice. As an implicit critic of his ethnographer-narrator, Melville uses Tommo to examine the limitations of ethnology, but the critique easily extends to modern anthropology as well.

This argument owes much to T. Walter Herbert's pioneering reading of *Typee*, but it also marks an important distance from Herbert's analysis of the storytelling. By implicating Tommo's thoughts and feelings with the discourse of the spectacle of the racial freak and its contemporary background, I am pulling Tommo further into the American nineteenth century, even as I accord Melville a powerful forward vision that extends beyond that period.[48] Though I have followed Herbert's lead in reading *Typee* as a proto-anthropological text, I see Tommo as neither a true anthropologist nor a successful "beachcomber" whose view from the edges takes in the whole. Despite an exceptional desire to view the world nonhierarchically as he passes in and out of its cultures, Tommo cannot be considered a citizen of an imagined new world of tolerance toward native peoples. Instead, Melville makes him just like the rest of his antebellum American countrymen: a fascinated, repulsed, and finally ambivalent customer at the nationally sponsored freak show.

Freak shows filled a gap that they did not create. This space, between the desire for absolute racial difference and the fact that none exists, was wide and deep in a culture that relied on racial difference for so many of its very organizing principles. The gap was occupied by fetishizing practices like blackface minstrelsy, displacing strategies like plantation fiction and Sambo stereotyping, empirically driven attempts at denial like racial pseudoscience—and also by freak shows. The freak show thus stands as both a cultural symptom and a cultural tool. It was a symptom of a need (for hierarchy, for difference, for superiority), and a tool deployed—unsuccessfully—to meet that need. Like the performing slaves I discussed in the last chapter, Freak shows were a performance of one kind of imaginary difference in an effort to assert another.

Given that the United States has always been a racially obsessed society, why did freak shows arise precisely when they did? If, as I have suggested, their primary function was to deflect racial anxiety, then what was raising that anxiety to levels that would create a need for freak shows in the United States more than a decade before the Civil War? The answer, as Melville suggests in *Typee*, is that the 1840s was a key decade in the history of American race relations, a time when American society was heating to a boil that would, in less than a generation, become uncontrollable. With the 1822 slave conspiracy led by Denmark Vesey and the 1831 slave revolt by Nat Turner resonating in memory and fueling antislavery sentiment—thanks in part to the inflammatory rhetoric of the likes of William Lloyd Garrison and Frederick Douglass—abolitionism grew to become a visible, tangible force for change during the

1840s, even as the South furiously closed ranks against it. The decade witnessed the extension of the antislavery movement from the moral to the political arena, and the transformation of the United States into a society militantly divided over issues of race.[49]

Support swelled for abolition through American society generally during the 1830s and 1840s. Abolitionism was essentially a decentralized movement peopled mainly by middle-class workers, Northern men and women of modest means. The American Antislavery Society, formed in 1833 and dedicated to immediate emancipation, sprouted new shoots at an exponential rate; by 1840 it had over two thousand local auxiliaries, a number that continued to grow. Total membership has been variously estimated by historians at around 200,000 at the beginning of the decade.[50] The intractability of the South gave added impetus to the Northern movement, effectively pouring gasoline into the political fire. As early as 1835 a speaker at a Southern mass meeting declared that "freedom of speech does not imply a moral right to freely discuss the subject of slavery."[51] Meanwhile, the disingenuous genre of plantation fiction made its successful debut in 1831 and thrived during the following decades. On the Northern side, by contrast, discussion and debate flourished: between thirty and forty antislavery newspapers were published during the three decades leading up to the Civil War.[52] The best known and perhaps most influential of these was *The Liberator*, edited by Garrison. An admitted extremist and self-styled revolutionary, Garrison called for the "right of the free States to remonstrate against the continuance, and to assist in the overthrow of slavery." Though his advocacy of complete political and social equality for blacks made him more radical on the subject of race than most Americans at that time, Garrison was heard because people were willing to listen.[53] In just a decade or so, abolitionism had grown from a tiny group of agitators into a national social and political movement of transformative power. This antislavery force, aided by the recalcitrance of the Southern opposition, quickly matured into a juggernaut of popular opinion and political activity in the coming years, leading directly up to the Civil War.[54]

It was this racially divided American society of the 1840s that nurtured the freak show, which quickly took root and grew in its troubled soil. Like blackface minstrelsy, the freak show expressed "contradictory impulses" that made it an "index of racial feeling" in both the North and the South. In other words, the freak show expressed what Eric Lott calls

Fig. 5.4 This photograph incorporates many of the themes of this book. Olive Oatman was returned to white society in 1856 after living among the Mohave Indians, from whom she received her facial tattoos. Olive was sixteen when she and her eleven-year-old sister, Mary Ann, were taken into captivity after their parents died in a wagon attack. The fragile younger sister did not survive captivity, but Olive was found and brought back by her brother, Lorenzo, who also survived the attack, though both sisters had believed him dead. Olive eventually married, in 1865, and became a mother. Although she never wrote her own narrative, Oatman's story was first recounted in *Captivity of the Oatman Girls* (1857) by Rev. Royal B. Stratton. (Reproduced courtesy of the Arizona Historical Society, Tucson, Photograph #1927)

"the racial unconscious," implicating cross-cutting desires for difference and superiority—but it also expressed a desire for sameness by identifying freaks as fellow humans. These opposing desires feed the attraction/repulsion complex that the freak show evokes.[55]

By linking tattooing and blackness, and blackness and freak shows, Melville forges a signifying chain in *Typee* that leads revealingly back into the racial unconscious. Following it, we may understand the dark origins of the American freak show, and an important source of its powerful, inarticulate effect. When Melville published *Typee* in 1846, his book appeared before a reading public inflamed by racial conflict—and frequently amused by human oddities. In his first novel Melville shows that the two were deeply and intimately related for Northern and Southern readers alike.

II

Interlude, in the Shadow of the Whale

In *Typee*, Melville uses the tattoo as a code to bring together the black and the freak. In making this topical connection to race and slavery, he uses Tommo as an implicit comment on the pernicious social effects of racism, and the danger that results from one group's attempt to deny the humanity of another. Is this practice avoidable? Certainly. It follows from a tendency, not a deterministic biological demand. But Melville's references to his own country suggest that whether we like it or not, Americans are natural separators, driven to make hierarchies and divide ourselves into better and worse, into human and not human. From the Puritans onward, Americans struggle with the consequences of rigid and exclusive definitions of the "human."

Tommo is a divided soul, torn between a personal desire for flexibility and another that arises from the demands of a social matrix that he can't escape. He wants to see the Typees as equal to himself, but he also doesn't want them to reach that level. Through Tommo's narration, Melville tests the possibility of a more malleable system where "civilized" values are not absolute, and where anomalies don't pose such a dangerous threat. Tommo is remarkably tolerant, and by his tolerance he tries in effect to transcend the morals and mores of his own culture, reaching toward a more universal set of human values. Instead, he winds up falling back into his old ways of thinking just as he "fell" into the Typee valley in the first place.[56] Tommo essentially tries to embrace a new set of norms, and when he cannot fully do so, he retreats into the practice of racial objectification. His failure is the more disturbing for its accompanying good intentions, for it suggests that cultural differences transcend the human beings who create them.

Melville uses the racial grotesque to mark Tommo's doomed attempt to free himself from social fetters on his thinking. We see his effort to widen his perspective through his description of grotesques that do not appear to affect him. Later his failure is marked by the opposite reaction: when he becomes afraid, the grotesque, in the form of tattooing and cannibalism, is what he fears. How can human beings see clearly and understand fully when they can never free themselves from the limitations of their own perspective? Writing during troubled times in the United States, Melville is pessimistic. And he uses the grotesque to convey his pessimism.[57]

But the pessimism of *Typee* is only Melville's first word on difference, racial and otherwise.[58] Moby-Dick could be said to begin where *Typee* (and also *Omoo*) leave off, with a wide cultural gulf. The character of Queequeg personifies the *Typee* problem in *Moby-Dick*. Queequeg is a grotesque figure, a tribesman who bears considerable similarity to the Polynesians who give Tommo so much trouble. His head is shaved and his face and body are covered with tattoos. He celebrates bizarre religious rituals. He smokes through his weapon. He even has a string of shrunken heads, a sight in *Typee* that the narrator correctly links with cannibalism, his own ultimate taboo. Frightened by Queequeg's appearance and accoutrements, Ishmael draws the same conclusion. "Why didn't you tell me that infernal harpooneer was a cannibal?" (3:51) he complains to the landlord.[59] Queequeg is, in short, the very model for a racial freak—he needs only to be placed in an exhibit with the appropriate surroundings to make him into a spectacular commodity.

The beginning of *Moby-Dick* essentially presents an encapsulated version of the problems of *Typee*. Ishmael shows himself to be quite sensitive to racial difference even before he meets Queequeg.[60] The two go to sleep with bodies pressed on opposite sides of the bed, as if to emphasize the distance between their two cultures. This time, though, Melville resolves the problem quickly and explicitly: Ishmael and Queequeg wake up wrapped around each other. Remarks Ishmael, "You had almost thought

I was his wife" (4:52). Indeed, Queequeg's embrace is no imitation of affection; it's the real thing, as later events prove.[61]

For Ishmael, this somehow settles the problem of Queequeg. "I lay quietly eying him, having no serious misgivings now" (4:55). Indeed, he now comes to regard him as a civilized man, and says so. This change of Queequeg's status in Ishmael's eyes is accompanied by a corresponding change in the latter's behavior. He begins observing his roommate with the same welcoming air that Tommo exhibits during his more balanced moments in the Typee valley.

Ishmael's encounter with Queequeg assaults his civilized values, but they survive. Even cannibalism doesn't faze him (though it is true that the closest he comes to actually seeing it is when Queequeg devours barely cooked steak). Balanced and thoughtful after his earlier panic, Ishmael watches and reflects upon Queequeg's behavior. Unlike Tommo (who is first balanced and only later loses his cool), Ishmael does not preoccupy himself with Queequeg's differences, and in the end, he is able to look past the strange customs to the person underneath: the two men become friends. The ease with which Ishmael and Queequeg bridge the gap between their cultures contrasts remarkably with Tommo's difficulties in *Typee*.

The social treatment of Queequeg generally confirms this attitude. From the innkeeper onward, Queequeg is recognized for what he can contribute, rather than for any oddness of his native looks and ways. Queequeg does not join a freak show in either a literal or figurative sense. Instead, he becomes a respectable member of a laboring class aboard a whaling ship, signing on as a harpooneer who earns more than his white friend Ishmael. (It is worth noting that Queequeg achieves this rank in the same area—coastal Massachusetts—and in a similar business to the one in which Frederick Douglass is assaulted when he threatens to hold a "white" skilled job as a shipyard caulker.) Though he has the credentials to become one, Queequeg is no freak.

With this early series of strokes, Melville dismisses the differences that gave rise to the grotesque in his earlier novel. Melville seems to be saying that those old problems of *Typee* are just too simple this time around.[62] The grotesque in *Moby-Dick* leaves local differences behind to strive for the universal, centering on Ahab's quest to know the unknowable white whale (an animal that acts human). But we are not all capable of Ishmael's balancing act, as the creator of Tommo surely knows. The racial classification problems of *Typee* linger despite their quick treatment in *Moby-Dick*.

Typee is a notable book because of the way Melville addresses not just the effect of objectification (that is, racism), but also its origins in the human thought process. The objectification of human beings arises inevitably from culturally based classificatory systems. Open-mindedness is—at least in *Typee*—no defense against virtually reflexive prejudice.[63] But the relationship between Ishmael and Queequeg in *Moby-Dick* suggests the opposite conclusion. Melville emphasizes the bond between the two later in the book (in chapter 72) when Ishmael secures Queequeg by a monkey-rope while he works on a whale carcass. To Ishmael, this "Siamese ligature" means that they are "wedded." His diction is significant for more than its allusion to the "Siamese twins" of freak show fame: it also suggests that, in his eyes, the rope binds the two into one family, within which there are no separations, racial or otherwise.[64]

Melville wrestles with the idea of race in remote climes in *Typee* and *Moby-Dick*, exposing by analogy and implication the fragile boundaries and brittle assumptions housing knowledge and belief about race in his own culture. "The idea of civilization," says Herbert, "is, after all, an idea." But it's a pretty important idea—an ordering principle that people use to hold the world together. In *Typee*, the Marquesans and their ways represent a challenge to Tommo's Western vision of civilization. The challenge is serious, for the idea of the savage "is the polar construct that gives the qualities of civilization visibility and sharpness." The "savage," in other words, provides the contrast that defines the "civilized." When Tommo tries to elevate the islanders to civilized status, that means that he has nothing left to fill the category of "uncivilized" in his binary opposition. Unbalanced, his category system tips over, and the only way he can right it is by restoring the Typees to their former position on the "savage" side of the equation. Despite his exertions on their behalf, the natives finally fail to gain "civilized"—or unchallenged human—status in his eyes.[65]

Ishmael, on the other hand, solves this problem by appearing to abolish the categories altogether. Melville shows this most clearly by having Ishmael make a declaration that has been often quoted since:

> What's all this fuss I have been making about, thought I to myself—the man's a human being just as I am; he has just as

> much reason to fear me, as I have to be afraid of him. Better sleep with a sober cannibal than a drunken Christian. (3:51)

This flexible perspective resembles Tommo's in *Typee*, but the positive outcome emphatically opposes the pessimism of Melville's first novel: Ishmael's favorable judgment of Queequeg holds up—and as many critics have noted, his friendship with Queequeg is what indirectly saves him at the end of the book, providing him with the coffin-buoy that floats him to safety. This posthumous union with his friend offers a final testament to his remarkable conquest of his own perception of racial difference.

Is such deep and true tolerance possible? In *Benito Cereno* Melville flashes back to pessimism, as he meditates directly on slavery, explicitly targeting the divisive issue at length for the first time. The 1855 novella, written at a time of heightened racial tension in the United States, reconstructs the present through the manipulation of the past. Based on an actual 1805 slave revolt—which Melville moved back to 1799 as a way of invoking another revolt in San Domingo that year—*Benito Cereno* mixes quotations and extracts from legal sources and historical documents with Melville's own invention.[66] Melville offers no clear answers to the social questions provoked by the uprising. He instead asks whether violence and literally unspeakable cruelty result, perhaps inevitably, from the belief in race and the consequent attempt at human objectification that follows from it. *Benito Cereno* represents the potential energy of the racial grotesque to an American society about to crack along racial fault lines, and the novella does so with a comprehensiveness that makes it appropriate to conclude this study.

III

Benito Cereno: Form and Objectification

Benito Cereno suggests the complexity of human objectification through symbolic equivocation; the novella is set on the *San Dominick*, a slave ship that has been violently taken over by its cargo, who have in turn tortured and killed their former captors, enslaving the remainder, including the captain who gives the story its name. The drama in the story centers on the rebels' attempt to pretend enslavement under the few surviving whites for the benefit of Amasa Delano, the visiting captain from another ship. That they nearly pull off this spectacular inversion shows the blindness of white power as well as their own conspiratorial skill. But the power wielded by the blacks in the story results in large part from their monstrous viciousness. Their disturbingly potent presence is connected to their anomalous status in the story: they are quasi-human perpetrators of "inhuman" cruelty. Further complicating the situation, their viciousness is marked by their objectification of the whites—who had previously done the same thing to them. Melville renders Hegel's dialectic of autonomy and freedom almost unintelligible in this mixed-up context. At the same time, he deconstructs the Sambo stereotype, fusing the violent rebel and the docile and grateful worker together in a grotesque slavery masquerade that bears a more than passing resemblance to the freak show. Taken all together, this tense mix-up serves as a self-conscious and prescient commentary on the perils of the racial grotesque.

Images of human objectification frame *Benito Cereno*, symbolizing the nature of the conflict in the story. The black rebels mount the skeleton of Benito Cereno's friend Don Alexandro Aranda on the bow of the *San Dominick*. This event precedes the beginning of the story (though it is revealed later), while the head of the rebel leader Babo, severed by whites and mounted on a pole, ends the narrative. Both are attempts to reduce human bodies to dramatic statements. Both try to resolve the tension between blacks and whites by violent force. Both represent efforts to deny humanity, efforts made by opposing sides who see the world in different ways. Dana Nelson has observed that the authority behind such actions is arbitrary, but more important is that they simply don't work.[67] Just as the head of King Philip remains a person to the Puritans who mutilated his body, so do Babo and Aranda retain their humanity in the eyes of those who mutilate their bodies in special ways.[68] Babo and Aranda may or may not be fine human beings, but they are people all the same. This unavoidable fact touches all the characters in *Benito Cereno*; the opposing efforts to deny the humanity of either black or white shape the drama in which both participate.

Delano the Objectifier

As he does in *Typee* and *Moby-Dick*, Melville traces the difficulties in *Benito Cereno* to the conflicted and imperfect nature of human perception. Melville centers the story's narrative point of view on a character whose limitations become a significant part of the problem he faces: Captain Amasa Delano is an outside observer who for much of the story is duped by slaves-turned-masters who act out the role of slaves.[69] Delano's limited deductive ability not only prevents him from correctly interpreting the drama staged for him aboard ship, but more important, his view of blacks as simultaneously human and nonhuman exemplifies the slave-holding attitude that created the revolt in the first place. Locally and globally, Melville shows that the race problem in the story is merely the symptom of a larger perception problem.

The tension in *Benito Cereno* proceeds literally from Delano's objectifying gaze. Delano assumes that blacks are limited creatures, so he simply cannot imagine that they would revolt and take over a ship. (His fears center not on what actually happened but on the misguided suspicion that Cereno is somehow plotting his doom.) Delano interprets the world through a conventional objectifying process. He sees difference among people, then he divides them into categories, ranks these categories, and then selects only the top group for residence under the human banner. To Delano, whites are "the shrewder race," while blacks have "limited mind[s]."[70] He sees Babo, the shrewdest character in the story, as possessing the dumb devotion of "a shepherd's dog" (244). Indeed, the narrator tells us of Delano's "old weakness for negroes," that he "took to [them] . . . just as other men to Newfoundland dogs" (279).[71]

Delano cannot maintain the idea that blacks are not fully human. No one can. Unlike Tommo, Delano never sees the problem he has. But even without consciously realizing it, he struggles to resolve his competing views of blacks as property and people. His objectifying process breaks down before our eyes, like those before and after him in fact and fiction. To the slave Atufal, for example, Delano attributes "a royal spirit" (256). In the case of Babo, Delano sees the relationship between the slave and his "master" Benito Cereno as a beautiful friendship based on fidelity and confidence (250), a condescending view which nonetheless confers a certain humanity on the black as well as the white. He elsewhere comments on what "an uncommonly intelligent fellow" Babo is (285), but he also offers to buy the slave for fifty doubloons (265). The slaves swing back and forth between human and thing in Delano's mind. They become liminal: grotesque. (And their anomalousness persists even as the truth of the revolt aboard the *San Dominick* becomes known.)

Delano never notices these contradictions, but significantly, he *does* see the evidence of them. The following sentence, which Melville sets off as its own paragraph, follows a statement of trust in Babo by Benito Cereno. The point of view is Delano's:

> Here Babo, changing his previous grin of mere animal humor into an intelligent smile, not ungratefully eyed his master. (261)

Delano actually sees the difference between Babo as animal and Babo as person here, but what he sees is incompatible with his own racial hierarchy.[72] Unable to integrate the idea of Babo as fully human into his personal cosmology, Delano unconsciously constructs what for him is an oxymoron: a slave who is also a human being.

Captain Delano's problems can finally be traced to his own category-making and the inconsistency that is built into it. Delano sees race as a key to inner nature (e.g., 284), and he can't believe that Cereno ("the Spaniard") would betray his "own species" to league with the blacks.[73] Granted—as Edward Said suggests—that people are bound to divide things up in order to understand them, Delano makes the wrong divisions and consequently misunderstands the situation.

Melville shows Delano's internal contradictions at the most fundamental level, in the way that the captain organizes his sight and thought. He renders Delano's perception as a series of conflicting analogies; for example, one slave looks to him "like a begging friar of St. Francis" (251), while a nursing mother is "naked nature, now; pure tenderness and love" (268). Babo shaving Benito is alternately a tableau of execution (an "antic conceit" Delano dismisses [280]) and the scene of a conspiracy by Babo and Benito against himself, a thought likewise "banished" (282). With such tableaux, *Benito Cereno* confirms the power of Homi Bhabha's theory of mimicry, even as Melville inverts the positions of its actors. Mimicry, says Bhabha, threatens the "reforming, civilizing mission" of the colonizer through "the displacing gaze of the disciplinary double."[74] The concealed slave revolt in *Benito Cereno* literally realizes this displacement, bringing the threat into true existence. The special situation—freed rebels needing to act as slaves—requires the mimic to demonstrate obvious power (over the white captives) and obvious submission (to the white visitors) at the same time. This strange tension brings Bhabha's imperative to life. Bhabha labels the "desire to emerge as 'authentic' through mimicry" as the "final irony" attached to the act, but Melville adds another layer: by reversing the positions of slave and master, he makes both parties' desire for authenticity into an actual matter of life and death.

Delano, the figure at the top of this power relation, controls the interpretation of all that he sees. His metaphoric thinking proves him an inept reader of what lies before him. Delano's objectifying worldview is unsound, and it makes him a poor interpreter. The story shows that Delano—and other whites also—don't do well in the role of objectifier, and that objectification itself is an impossible stance to maintain. Dana Nelson has shown how Delano uses metaphors of race to understand the world. Whites, she says, must willfully blind themselves to part of their experience in order to maintain the rationale behind their own dominance.[75] To this I would add that the means of their dominance is metaphor put into social practice. The distorted, self-referential form of the white-dominant social structure results from the continuing attempt by whites to imagine blacks as nonhuman: they must maintain their position as objectifiers, as dictators of message and meaning, even if it leads them to conflict and contradiction.

Suppressing the conflict and papering over the contradiction means controlling metaphor itself. With Cereno's deposition at the end of the story, a retelling that follows the narrative from Delano's point of view, Melville represents the social attempt to do just that. In stark contrast to Delano's image-laden indirect discourse, the anonymous voice of the law speaks in a language utterly drained of metaphor. This arid discourse fixes the relationships that have already been decided upon by the dominant group. In effect, the comparisons between white (human) and black (nonhuman) have already been made, and the purpose of the law is to carry their results into practice; no confusing, destabilizing images—images that would inevitably allow the human to reassert itself—can be permitted once the hierarchy has been established. The purpose of the law thus becomes clear in the story: it is a social instrument to enforce perception. In *Benito Cereno*, the contradictions inherent in that perception require the full foreclosure of metaphor in legal discourse.

Delano is "a man of such native simplicity as to be incapable of satire or irony" (257), but his beliefs are also typical of his time. Sandra Zagarell argues that through Delano, Melville shows that "*all* meaning in his readers' world derives from convention, and that meaning itself is therefore unfixed."[76] Captain Delano, a creature of slaveholding convention, is surely ill-served by that convention in his dealings aboard the *San Dominick*. His assumptions are a natural extension of those widely shared by his society; one gets the sense that Delano could reject slavery as easily as he believes in it, so long as that were also the view of those around him. Melville thus shows that Delano is only a particularly obtuse variation on the prevailing view—with that view itself being the problem.

Sambo Through Rose-Colored Glasses

Delano's perception of the relationship between Benito Cereno and Babo reveals particularly clearly not only Delano's own objectifying eye but also Melville's understanding of the grotesque Sambo stereotype as an attempt to evade the reality of objectification. Delano witnesses a revolt, but as I will suggest, he sees a freak show.

Delano sees Babo and Benito as participants in a fairy tale of slavery: the happy, respectful, and talented slave supplies the master's every want or need before he articulates it. Most important here is the happiness of the slave—especially his delight in his captive state. Delano constructs a portrait that goes Sambo one better: it is an idealized version of a stereotype that was itself constructed as an ideal. Delano takes his own fairy tale as reality and literally tries to buy into it by offering to purchase Babo for himself.

The reality behind the scene is of course completely opposed to what Delano sees. Babo is in fact using Benito to enact what might be termed a malignant parody of the Sambo stereotype. Eric Sundquist has observed that Babo embodies the "Nat" personality type of the rebellious slave, but the more important point is the contrast of his rebellious character with his clever portrayal of Sambo. If, as historians have suggested, the Sambo stereotype conceals a fear of violent uprising, then Melville enacts this truth literally in *Benito Cereno*. Every slave in the book plays both Sambo and Nat Turner, with Babo the lead actor in what Sundquist calls "a farce of a minstrel show" where the master is the slave's captive audience and the slave's "natural" performing ability upends slavery instead of supporting it.[77]

Delano's stereotyping is so extreme that he sees Babo in a way that is almost beyond historical possibility: a smart, neat, fully domesticated, hard-working Sambo who has domesticated his playful urges, showing them only in indirect gestures like the use of the Spanish flag as a shaving bib for Cereno. This inaccurate view exemplifies the blurring effect of Delano's objectifying gaze. Delano sees Babo's choice of the flag as a bib as merely the expression of the love of color that he believes blacks possess; he sees the slave as too stupid and childlike to act on any other motive. Delano's perception of Babo's gesture as puckish rather than darkly humorous shows how his desire dictates what he sees. Similarly, because Delano can't give Babo credit for a subversive impulse, he misreads the slave's disapproval of his co-conspirator Francesco's excessive shuffling (284). Babo obviously thinks that Francesco is going too far and will expose the plot, but Delano approves so strenuously of this obsequious behavior that instead of questioning it, he uses it as the benchmark for his own mistaken reading of the scene.

Delano possesses all of the silly sentimentalism of the masters in antebellum plantation romances. Carolyn Karcher sees Cereno as the stereotype of effete Southern planter, but Delano may resemble that type even more closely under the skin, passively submerged as he is in fuzzy ideals of masterly benevolence and Negro turpitude.[78] His view of the world reflects the underlying ideology of that class, a benevolence based on a hypocritical vision of friendship within slavery. Recall that it is Delano who imputes friendship to the "spectacle of fidelity" he imagines to exist between Benito and Babo. In a later example of this ill-founded sentiment, Delano imagines a "love-quarrel" between Babo and Benito in the aftermath of the shaving scene (283).

Many critics have argued over whether Melville uses scenes like these to turn notions of white supremacy around. Michael P. Rogin argues that in playing master-slave relations as a charade, Melville shows the bond to be a pure social construct, not a family or even part of the natural order. Sandra Zagarell extends this insight, observing that Delano wants to see a ship as a "comfortable family" even though he admits (a bit earlier) that it is "a dictatorship beyond which, while at sea, there is no earthly appeal." In this and other instances, Delano has it both ways without realizing it.[79]

This ability of Delano's to conflate contradiction is central to his role in the novella. Specifically, these scenes show how the objectifying impulse guides and shapes Delano's perception, smoothing out contradiction and massaging the facts until everything conforms to the same smooth, bland worldview. Ultimately, Delano's desire to see domestic felicity between whites and blacks dictates the incorrect conclusions that he draws aboard the *San Dominick*. The picture of Babo as dumbly devoted and doglike clashes implicitly with Delano's earlier observation of the slave's intelligence; his idealized Sambo tableau arises from his own link between blacks and faithful pets, a link he preserves because of his exceptional ability to manufacture reality to fit the contours of his beliefs.[80] In other words, Delano's view of Babo as Sambo illustrates the assumptions that lie beneath the stereotype. Delano's wish to see happy slaves depends on the assumption that blacks are somehow not fully human.

In this respect, Delano brings to the ship the same set of expectations that he would if he were entering a freak show tent—and the show that he sees aboard the *San Dominick* actually *is* a kind of freak show. Delano believes that he is seeing performers who mimic humanity with skill, despite what he believes to be their obvious deficiencies—and that is just what a freak show offers. At the time that Melville wrote *Benito Cereno* in 1855, people were lining up in then-unprecedented numbers to pay money to see other people without legs "walk" on their hands or others without arms sew or draw with their feet. The desire to witness these spectacles came from the need to feel superiority, as did the urge to gawk at Africans and South Seas islanders in the same exhibit, with the latter group aggressively proclaimed by their managers to be the atavistic inferiors of their white audiences.

Like the freak show, the *San Dominick* appears to Delano as a performing space for quasi-humans, a group of showmen staging a scripted response to Delano's expectations, even as these expectations are being inverted by the blacks themselves (who have a different agenda, of course) and by Melville, who occupies the outermost of the concentric perspectives in the story. From the moment he steps aboard the *San Dominick*, Delano wants to see a structured display of carefully mediated performance by his quasi-human inferiors, a performance designed to reinforce his own sense of powerful whiteness—and thanks to Babo's understanding of his ilk, that is just what he gets. Given that freak shows experienced a continuously high demand for African "cannibals," "warriors," pygmies, and the like,[81] the *San Dominick* literally resembles a ship of freaks. It is one of the many ironies of the story that the resemblance is more than physical. Each slave appears to Delano to be a racial freak "imitating" a human being by performing human tasks. The truth of the situation exposes the freak show for what it is: a tawdry display of the desire of one group of people to assert that they are more human than another.

Hegel in a Fun-House Mirror

In *Benito Cereno* Melville also bears out Hegel's assertion that the black is not easily kept in the nonhuman space denominated by slavery or the freak show. It is not known whether Melville read Hegel's *Phenomenology*, but *Benito Cereno* reads as a sophisticated comment on the master-slave dialectic, if a very strange one. Delano wants to see a happy slave, so he does. In Hegel's terms, he is a master looking for recognition, and the kind of recognition he wants is expressed by obsequious deference. Delano is therefore willing to stay focused on the surface of a deception that gives him what he enjoys. The deception itself has at its center the picture of Babo and Benito, a slave and a master—and vice versa. The falseness of appearances is the idea that guides the novella; so it is with the slave, an objectified human who, like all of Melville's ambiguous symbols, constantly shifts in meaning and perception. *Benito Cereno* literally asks who belongs to whom. Hegel's dialectic raises the same question, illustrating how the master comes to need the slave for recognition more than the slave needs him, but because the master has taken away the slave's humanity, he cannot be satisfied with the recognition that the slave gives him. The slave, says Hegel, paradoxically winds up the master of the situation because of his self-sufficient sources of recognition in his own labor.

Benito Cereno parodies the master-slave relation in an unusual way, distorting its drama without questioning its meaning. Hegel inverts the positions of master and slave by showing that the master becomes the dependent one, but Melville reverses them again by having the slaves assume the role of master, and then again by having these new masters pretend to be slaves. Benito Cereno describes in his deposition how Babo enslaved him and gave him his orders (306). But if Benito needs to please Babo to live, it is also true that Babo needs Benito's cooperation in order to survive Delano's visit. Both of them become slaves, locked in dependent relation to each other. Little wonder that the recurring phrase "Follow your leader" means so many different things in *Benito Cereno*.

The balance of power between slave and master is a fight for the power to objectify. Before the narrative begins, the master (Cereno) had objectified the slave (Babo), and then in the rebellion the slave violently reversed their roles. Babo then objectifies the master, and is finally objectified himself at the end of the story when his head is mounted on a pole. Babo's defeat is actually foreordained, not only because his world is filled with people like Cereno and Delano but also because he himself is like them. If Babo's beheading is a kind of castration, it needs to be contrasted to Cereno's empty scabbard; the two are linked. (It is also worth noting Bhabha's argument that the colonizer's desire for mimicry arises from symbolic castration.) White ways of power are the only ones that Babo knows; the viciousness of his regime shows his dependence on the ways of his conquerors. His failure, like Delano's obtuseness, shows that objectification cannot be sustained.[82]

In this context, Babo's final silence makes consistent sense. I earlier used the structure of slave narratives to argue that through rebellion, the slave gains the consciousness of action, and then—as expressed by the narrative itself—a voice with which to speak freedom, to liberate himself from the grotesque space between human and nonhuman. Babo's rebellion fails. He consequently loses his voice: "His aspect seemed to say, since I cannot do deeds, I will not speak words" (315). Even so, the last word somehow belongs to Babo, as his lifeless gaze, still human, follows Benito Cereno to his death.

That Peculiar Tension

Given the prolonged state of ignorance that Melville depicts in *Benito Cereno*, it is not surprising that tension is the element most often spotlighted in analysis of the story. The tension in the novella—moral, dramatic, narrative—naturally corresponds to the tension generated by the slavery question in American society of Melville's time, but it is possible to draw an even more specific comparison to the tension brought on by the attempt to objectify human beings. These two forms of tension happen to be literally connected to each other in the novella: the objectification of blacks for money is what makes the whole story possible. Just as the objectified person flashes back and forth between human and thing in the mind of the objectifier, so the situation aboard the *San Dominick* shifts back and forth from one interpretation to another, not only in Delano's mind but also in the reader's. Melville makes this ambiguity pervasive in *Benito Cereno*—ontological, moral, even spatial, for the story takes place on the liminal world of a ship, a space between land and water. It seems that everything in the story is tensely suspended between categories.

Perhaps foremost among the critical explorations of tension in *Benito Cereno* is Eric Sundquist's close examination of the involuted narrative coil of the novella. Sundquist writes that *Benito Cereno* suspends and collapses fundamental distinctions, keeping the narrative perpetually "poised" but never leaping, with its key opposing elements fused in a way that both emphasizes difference and binds its elements together. The central such oppositions are between Delano and Benito, master and slave, black and white, right and wrong. Sundquist's careful reading has myriad implications for my own argument. He describes a Melvillean tension that is rich, complex, and ultimately tautological—a series of oppositions that cannot be divided, for different views are forcibly equated with each other, leaving in the end only silence.[83]

I want to link that narrative tension to the psychological tension I have been describing throughout this book—the tension that accompanies any attempt to deny people's humanity. Specifically, I want to argue that the tension of *Benito Cereno* is directly connected to the objectification conundrum that lies at the core of slavery, and that the narrative tension of *Benito Cereno* structurally represents the difficulty that accompanies human objectification, a difficulty that Sundquist shows to be embedded within the architecture of the narrative itself. The silence that culminates the story and follows Benito and Babo to their graves illustrates the unspoken, cruel logic of objectification, a logic that can be identified only from outside the tale.

Only the reader can see this logic—and that is an important part of Melville's point. The author invites the audience to interpret the action on their own terms. The deposition offers an apparent moral and legal resolution, but the ambiguity remains even after the official explanation is given for the strange events aboard ship. The critical history of *Benito Cereno* shows that "resolving" the situation in favor of black or white only invites more debate, an ongoing dispute similar to the one conducted by the competing objectifiers within the story itself. Sundquist demonstrates that the best way to read *Benito Cereno* is to work with the doubt and equivocation from the outside. The cruelties of Benito and Babo lie at opposite extremes of a spectrum of belief; neither character is capable of understanding the other because each labors under different assumptions about the natural order of humans and things—including which is which. Captain Delano, the story's point-of-view character and the real-life historical figure upon whose narrative the tale relies, remains oblivious of this spectrum of differences. Readers are offered a chance to inform themselves of it, but the opportunity is filled with critical pitfalls.

Melville thus shows that in order to appreciate what the slave system tries to do, one must stand outside the epistemological system that houses it. By setting *Benito Cereno* in 1799, he sidesteps the escalating, increasingly vituperative struggle between abolitionist and proslavery forces that was taking place in his own time (the armed fighting in "Bleeding Kansas" in 1854 being a particularly potent example of the then-current state of the slavery debate). Melville instead sends his readers back to a period before abolitionism, when American antislavery sentiments were only beginning to be publicly articulated. In effect, the author gives his contemporary audience the chance to establish a certain distance from the events. The distance may seem false to us because most of the essential realities of slavery were the same in 1855 as in 1799, but for Melville's readers those years offered space for a distanced perspective, a possible approach to the untenable logic of human commodities that underwrites the action in the tale.[84] In other words, Melville sees that it's impossible to turn a human being into a thing, but he also sees how difficult it can be to recognize this fact when one is laboring within a cultural system that takes the possibility of such a transformation for granted. *Benito Cereno* is a critique of the slave system that appears to originate within that set of beliefs, but Melville's critical perspective in fact points outside of it; he shows that the different kinds of cruelty ordered and endorsed by Benito and Babo result not from their corrupted individual natures, but rather from the corrupted logic of a social system that calls for the impossible: to take away the humanity of a human being. The peculiar tension of *Benito Cereno* remains to the end of the story because the peculiar institution remains likewise in place. Human objectification remains a convoluted legal and economic reality at the end of the story, leaving human beings to cope with the liminality and grotesqueness that it visits upon their own.

IV

Categories and Perspective

Reading *Benito Cereno* in these terms aligns it with the argument that I have made about the origins of the objectifying impulse in *Typee* and *Moby-Dick*. Tommo, Ishmael, and Delano may appear to have little in common, but they do share a goal: to bypass cultural boundaries in their efforts to arbitrate life's ambiguities. These variously flawed Melvillean versions of Universal Man have their problems escaping the limits that define their beliefs and capacities. Only Ishmael can claim any lasting success at rising above his cultural constraints, and even his conquest of prejudice is dubious: he winds up exactly where he began: alone in the world and afloat on his only possession, a coffin.

Melville's ability to limn the categories of perception has been getting a lot of attention lately. In a survey of recent Melville criticism, Andrew Delbanco locates the future of the industry—which he says will be bright—in Melville's striking ability to walk in and out of category systems. Delbanco concludes that if Melville is imprisoned at all by culturally imposed systems of belief, the prison is "minimum security." This capacity for mobility has been noticed before in Melville, and admired. Herbert calls it the freedom of the beachcomber, a position that, for Melville, "provided a narrative standpoint from which to look upon latent features of white activities in Polynesia, a perspective from which the question of perspective itself becomes visible." Toni Morrison cites what must be considered an example of this remarkable vision when she traces Melville's perceptiveness of the meaning of race to "his recognition of the moment in America when whiteness became ideology," and his consequent ability to examine it.[85]

Melville's treatment of race proceeds from his ideas about objectification because he saw that the concept of objectification underlies and precedes racial consciousness, and is what makes it possible. Objectification, marked by the grotesque, literally colors Melville's view of the world, from *Typee* onward. Melville depicts objectification in action from all different angles in his fiction, showing in explicit detail how the grotesque arises from the failure of the attempt to deny humanity. More important, he takes the process apart as he dramatizes it, showing *why* it works, why it endures, and—as he suggests in his darker moods—why it appears that humans cannot escape it.

From the beginning of his career onward, Melville sees and emphasizes the restrictiveness of perspective, and the danger created by its limits. He reveals the limitations of cultural orientation by creating characters less skilled at perceiving or coping with these limitations than himself. For these characters, the struggle with human objectification determines the nature and outcome of human relations. *Typee*, *Moby-Dick*, and *Benito Cereno* all show that the struggle with racial difference originates in human limitation: the desire to perceive sameness in other people and deny it at the same time.

EPILOGUE

This Way to the Egress

This book ends with a balloon.

Imagine someone holding a balloon underwater. Because air is lighter than water, it requires great effort to keep the balloon submerged, but as long as this effort is expended, the balloon is deformed by the water pressure, reduced in size and altered in shape. But once the force holding it down slackens, the balloon shoots to the surface and reexpands to its normal volume.

Those watching can see how brute force keeps the balloon from floating on top of the water, where it "wants" to be. It's obvious to anyone who knows balloons that the effort to keep one underwater can't permanently succeed, so it's worth asking why someone would want to put forth the effort to keep it there. For the one actually holding the balloon underwater, there is a certain urgency that accompanies the attempt, an urgency borne of the reality of physics: once the effort eases, the balloon will instantly pop above the water again. Meanwhile, the balloon takes unusual shapes underwater in response to the pressure being placed on it.

Objectifying a person is something like trying to hold a balloon underwater. It's an obvious literal spectacle, but it results from hard-to-articulate desires, and it causes strange shapes. Both the effort and the results repay close attention, in both the past and the present, in the United States and elsewhere.

NOTES

EXORDIUM

1. Toni Morrison, *Playing in the Dark: Whiteness and the Literary Imagination*, 52–53. Morrison elsewhere calls it "fruitful" to show "instances where early American literature identifies itself, risks itself, to assert its antithesis to blackness" ("Unspeakable Things Unspoken: The Afro-American Presence in American Literature," *Michigan Quarterly Review* 28 [1989]: 18–19).

2. Jean-Paul Sartre, preface to Frantz Fanon's *The Wretched of the Earth*, translated by Constance Farrington, 22.

3. Henry Louis Gates, Jr., "Critical Fanonism," *Critical Inquiry* 17 (1991): 462.

ONE: *Human Objectification and the Racial Grotesque*

1. Annie Dillard, *Pilgrim at Tinker Creek*, 5–6.

2. William R. Taylor, *Cavalier and Yankee: The Old South and American National Character*, 7.

3. There has been lively debate in recent years over whether the idea of race has any scientific basis, or whether it is a fiction or an empty metaphor. The battle has ranged from science (with Stephen Jay Gould being a famous critic of scientific conceptions of race) to social science (Ashley Montagu), and more recently

to literary theory (Henry Louis Gates, Houston Baker, Joyce A. Joyce, Eric Cheyfitz) and philosophy (Kwame Anthony Appiah).

My position is essentially tangential to this debate. I am suggesting that as long as people see racial difference (and they most certainly did see it before the Civil War, as well as after it), the grotesque process of racial objectification will take root at its conceptual base and grow from the idea of difference itself. Race may well be a fiction or metaphor, but it has a long and continuing history as an experiential reality. As Toni Morrison puts it: "For over three hundred years black Americans insisted that 'race' was no usefully distinguishing factor in human relationships. During those same three centuries every academic discipline, including theology, history, and natural science, insisted 'race' was *the* determining factor in human development" ("Unspeakable Things Unspoken," 3).

In a typical example of the white side of this reality, Dr. John Augustine Smith wrote in a medical journal in 1809 that the use of the term "race" was intended "merely to express the fact that differences do exist" (quoted by Winthrop Jordan, *White Over Black: American Attitudes Toward the Negro, 1550–1812*, 489). This book examines a concrete and pernicious result of the historical reality of race: human objectification, which leads to the racial grotesque.

Of course race is not the only cause of human objectification, nor are Americans its only victims. A survey of the attempts by anti-Semites to objectify Jews over the centuries would likely draw on similar ideas, for example, as might an analysis of the treatment of Chinese immigrants to the United States. Moving back in history, John Block Friedman's *The Monstrous Races in Medieval Art and Thought* documents efforts at racial objectification as they were bolstered by an early form of Orientalism. The book on objectification of women is already being collectively written; the topic is a powerful recurring theme of feminist writing, from mainstream reformist analysis of the disenfranchisement of women (see, for example, the ongoing debate on pornography [e.g., Andrea Dworkin, *Pornography: Men Possessing Women* (New York: Perigee Books, 1981)], postmodern psychoanalytic feminism (such as that of Helene Cixous and Luce Irigaray), and Marxist analysis (see n. 34 below).

Not surprisingly, human objectification also thrives in the presence of physical deformity, but that too is a discussion for another book; such a book has been written by Rosemarie Garland Thomson, *Extraordinary Bodies: Figuring Physical Disability in American Literature and Culture* (New York: Columbia University Press, 1996). Thomson's feminist-oriented analysis is, of all the works mentioned here, most compatible with my own.

4. In outlining this progression, I am drawing partially on Edward Said's general description of binary cultural comparison in *Orientalism*. Said says that polarization is a natural consequence of cultural differentiation (46).

5. Claude McKay, *Selected Poems of Claude McKay*, 37.

6. The grotesque has historically been seen most often as a combination of the humorous and the horrible, with these terms receiving different definition and emphasis. Though this definition probably begins with Victor Hugo (in the preface to *Cromwell*), it receives its first systematic treatment by John Ruskin in "Grotesque Renaissance," in *The Stones of Venice*. This fusion thesis has been updated variously over the years (see Philip Thomson's *The Grotesque* for a good

summary of most major attempts to define the term). Wolfgang Kayser's vast compendium of information and examples, *The Grotesque in Art and Literature*, is less satisfying in that regard, but the author's vast learnedness makes it an invaluable resource.

Of course not all treatments of the grotesque focus on the fear and laughter thesis. Two ambitious analyses of the grotesque, Geoffrey Galt Harpham's *On the Grotesque* and John Clark's *The Modern Satiric Grotesque and Its Traditions*, place little emphasis on definition. Both acknowledge the workings of the grotesque within the cultural sphere, but are mainly concerned with using it as an exegetical tool. Mikhail Bakhtin, in *Rabelais and His World*, to cite an important example, argues that the grotesque must be understood as a carnivalesque breach of the boundaries of the body. The only sustained treatment of the grotesque as a socially constructed phenomenon is Peter Stallybrass and Allon White's excellent book, *The Politics and Poetics of Transgression*, which has a strong Bakhtinian influence. For analysis and further application of my own view of the grotesque (elaboration of which follows in the text), see Leonard Cassuto, "Jack London's Class-Based Grotesque," in Michael Meyer, ed., *Literature and the Grotesque*, 113–28.

7. Clifford Geertz, *The Interpretation of Cultures*, 36.

8. Geertz, *Interpretation of Cultures*, 50.

9. Renato Rosaldo, *Culture and Truth: The Remaking of Social Analysis*, 63.

10. Victor Turner comes to a similar conclusion in his study of the Ndembu healing ritual known as *Isoma*, a ritual exorcism from a woman of the spirit of a deceased relative whose presence among the living was believed to be preventing her host from bearing children. The ceremony involves, among other things, the beheading of a red cock. Says Turner: "Isoma is not grotesque in the sense that its symbolism is ludicrous or incongruous [to the Ndembu]" (*The Ritual Process: Structure and Anti-Structure*, 43).

A more familiar example of the cultural specificity of the grotesque might be that of a Western guest at an Arab banquet who might recoil from eating the eyeball of a roasted goat. His host, on the other hand, would then be offended, for the eyeball is a delicacy reserved by Arab custom for the guest of honor. Vice President Albert Gore was nearly confronted by this gastronomic dilemma in a 1993 trip to Kazakhstan: "Even as he was advised to swallow the eye whole, the Vice President toyed with the idea of flinging it behind his shoulder and pretending that he had eaten it" (Richard L. Berke, "Gore Abroad: Capitalism, Hockey and a Goat's Eye," *New York Times*, December 18, 1993, A5). This typical example illustrates how social boundaries govern perception of what is grotesque.

11. See Alan Dundes's *Cracking Jokes* for an analysis of sick humor as a projection of cultural anxiety. Dundes argues that such jokes are a way of expressing unacceptable feelings, such as revulsion at the physically handicapped.

Sick jokes also release anxious tension. In an interview Melvin Konner recalled how a group of medical students "[gave] a cadaver the nickname of 'Shop' and end[ed] a dissection with the remark that it was time 'to close up Shop'" (*Chronicle of Higher Education*, June 2, 1993, A7). This joke expresses anxieties attached to dissection (an objectifying procedure), but it gets its humor not so much from the fact that the cadaver is a thing (in which case calling it "Shop" wouldn't carry much resonance), but rather from the fact that it *is* a person, and its identity as a person is what makes the nickname so incongruous. Whether one finds the joke funny or in poor taste (or perhaps both), the emotional reaction to it is fueled by the perception of the cadaver as a learning tool that remains a human being.

12. For more on the social construction of freaks, see Robert Bogdan, *Freak Show: Presenting Human Oddities for Amusement and Profit*. I will be examining Bogdan's argument in more detail in chapter 5.

13. Philip Thomson, for example, uses tension alone to define the term. He describes the grotesque as "the unresolved clash of incompatibles in work and response" (*The Grotesque*, 27).

14. Sigmund Freud, *Totem and Taboo*, trans. James Strachey, 95.

15. Geertz, *Interpretation of Cultures*, 140.

16. Wolfgang Iser notes that our strategy is much the same when we read a text: "If we try to break down the areas of indeterminacy in the text, the picture that we draw for ourselves will then be, to a large extent, illusory, precisely because it is so determinate. The illusion arises from a desire for harmony, and it is solely the product of the reader" ("Indeterminacy and the Reader's Response in Prose Fiction," in J. Hillis Miller, ed., *Aspects of Narrative*, 40).

17. See Rosaldo, *Culture and Truth*, 97ff.

18. Geertz, *Interpretation of Cultures*, 127, 131. Or as Claude Lévi-Strauss puts it: "Being in their place is what makes [objects] sacred for if they were taken out of their place, even in thought, the entire order of the universe would be destroyed. Sacred objects therefore contribute to the maintenance of order in the universe by occupying the places allotted to them" (*The Savage Mind*, trans. George Weidenfeld, 10).

19. Herman Melville, *Moby-Dick, or The Whale*, ch. 100, p. 564.

20. Sigmund Freud, "The Antithetical Sense of Primal Words" (1910), trans. Alan Tyson, in *Five Lectures*, SE 11:157.

21. For Bakhtin, of course, the human body is the only possible subject of the grotesque. I am outlining a more flexible interpretation of the term here. When Dan Ackroyd whirls a whole fish in a blender in a mock commercial for the "Bass-a-matic" on *Saturday Night Live*, for example, the moment is grotesque, but where is the human body? One could argue that it exists by analogy in the form of the fish, but this seems to stretch Bakhtin's definition somewhat. I share Bakhtin's belief that the grotesque originates in the human, but would suggest that its source is the human context (including the body) rather than the body alone. This "human context" results from the anthropomorphic quality of our perception, which I will be discussing later in this chapter.

22. See Jordan, *White Over Black*, 167–78 (quotation at 178), and Carl N. Degler, *Neither Black Nor White: Slavery and Race Relations in Brazil and the United States* (New York: Macmillan, 1971), 223–45. Jordan shows through a comparative study of colonial legal codes and other documents how "America afforded little opportunity for blacks to become whites through intermixture" (171). Degler attaches great significance to the classification of mulattoes in his comparative study of slavery in Brazil and the United States. He sees the response to mulattoes as a kind of cultural barometer: "when a society develops a place for the mulatto, as

occurred in Brazil, then certain other responses to the presence of black men in a white-dominated society, such as those that were worked out in the United States, for example, are foreclosed" (*Neither Black Nor White*, 225). Degler calls this "the mulatto escape hatch." For a discussion of mulatto-related white difficulties in the American nineteenth century, see George M. Fredrickson, *The Black Image in the White Mind: The Debate of Afro-American Character and Destiny, 1817–1914*, 121–24.

African-American fiction writers regularly spotlighted the mulatto woman in their indictments of slavery; literary critics speak today of the character of "the tragic mulatta," a subgenre that began with Lydia Maria Child's short story "The Quadroons" (1842), a central source for the very first African-American novel, William Wells Brown's *Clotel* (1853). Stories of tragic mulattas continued to appear long after the Civil War.

23. Timothy W. Ryback, "Evidence of Evil," *New Yorker* 69, no. 38 (November 15, 1993): 68.

24. Smrek and Zak are quoted in Ryback, "Evidence of Evil," 69.

25. Studs Terkel, *Race: How Whites and Blacks Think and Feel About the American Obsession* (New York: New Press, 1992), 369.

26. Examples from Swift and Terkel provide literal evidence for Toni Morrison's assertion that "the trauma of racism is, for the racist and the victim, the severe fragmentation of the self, and has always seemed to me a cause (not a symptom) of psychosis" ("Unspeakable Things Unspoken," 16).

The following passage from *Gulliver's Travels* is to the point: "I finished a sort of *Indian* canoo; but much larger, covering it with the skin of *Yahoos*, well stiched together, with hempen threads of my own making. My sail was likewise composed of the skins of the same animal; but I made use of the youngest I could get" (book 4, ch. 10, 246). Gulliver's apparent inability to see the humanity of the people whose skins he's using is the central element of Swift's satire; at this point in the story Gulliver identifies not with his fellow Yahoos but with the Houhynyms (a race of intelligent horses).

27. A 1787 recollection by James Arnold, a ship's surgeon (quoted in George Dow, ed., *Slave Ships and Slaving*, 295).

28. Henry Aaron, *I Had a Hammer*, 238.

29. Harris based Lecter partly on a number of actual serial killers, but the character's emotional independence (which allows him to view people as playthings, thereby enabling him to objectify them) is a fabrication. No serial murderer has ever displayed such inner security and self-containment; all known cases have in fact been abnormally deficient in this area.

One could argue, though, that not even Lecter escapes the complexities of human objectification. First, by ritually consuming his fellow humans, he admits the special importance of such an act; and second, in his emotional seduction of FBI agent Clarice Starling, Lecter forges a genuine personal relationship with a fellow human based on mutual need and gratification gained from human contact.

30. Fanon, *The Wretched of the Earth*, 41.

31. Julia Kristeva describes such presences on the borders as "abject"—a term that creates a useful connection to the condition of the enslaved or colonized other (see *Powers of Horror: An Essay on Abjection*, trans. Leon S. Roudiez). Homi K.

Bhabha also locates the place of otherness on the edges, as a "pressure . . . along the boundary of authorization" ("Signs Taken for Wonders: Questions of Ambivalence and Authority Under a Tree Outside Delhi, May 1817," in Henry Louis Gates, Jr., ed., *"Race," Writing, and Difference*, 171).

32. See Bhabha, "Signs Taken for Wonders." Bhabha describes the origins of hybridity this way: "Produced through the strategy of disavowal, the *reference* of discrimination is always to a process of splitting as the condition of subjection: a discrimination between the mother culture and its bastards, the self and its doubles, where the trace of what is disavowed is not repressed but repeated as something *different*—a mutation, a hybrid" (172).

33. I extend the idea of industry to the more general effects of industrial culture as well. Alienation has been the focus of a good deal of feminist writing on objectification, with the conceptual framework drawn in varying degrees from the Marxian model. See, for example, Ann Foreman, *Femininity as Alienation: Women and the Family in Marxism and Psychoanalysis*; Alison Jaggar, *Feminist Politics and Human Nature*; Sheila Rowbotham, *Woman's Consciousness, Man's World*; Nancy Hartsock, *Money, Sex, and Power*; and Juliet Mitchell, *Woman's Estate*.

34. Elaine Scarry, *The Body in Pain*, 246–47.

35. See Karl Marx, *Capital*, trans. Ben Fowkes, esp. 287–96, and also *Grundrisse*, the series of notebooks in which he collected ideas for the former volume. In her reading of these works, Elaine Scarry points to "the unity of sentience with the things it reaches" in the idealized state, before imperfect economic systems wreck things (*The Body in Pain*, 249). See also Isidor Wallimann, *Estrangement: Marx's Conception of Human Nature and the Division of Labor*, chs. 2 and 3. Marx actually says that "labor's realisation is its objectification" (*Economic and Philosophical Manuscripts of 1844*, in Karl Marx and Frederick Engels, *Collected Works* 3:272). Alienation is the sign that things have gone awry.

Marx defines the term "objectification" differently than I do here. To clarify the vocabulary: for Marx, a certain kind of "objectification" (involving the mutual metaphoric identification of the worker and the work) is desirable; the problem is when this exchange of identification is disrupted, causing "alienation," which roughly corresponds to what I have been calling "objectification."

36. Scarry cites Marx's "deep sympathy" with the imagination as part of her argument for the dynamism of his views (*The Body in Pain*, 244). Indeed, Marx's ideas form the deeply embedded conceptual foundation of the most challenging recent discussions of objectification and technology in American culture. Two of the most pertinent to my task are Cecelia Tichi's *Shifting Gears: Technology, Literature, and Culture in Modernist America* and Mark Seltzer's *Bodies and Machines*. Both of these books examine metaphors of objectification as embodying a dynamic tension between human and machine, but Seltzer alludes most directly to my own mission. His examination of turn-of-the-century naturalism spotlights "the miscegenation of nature and culture," which can be expressed, among other things, by what he calls "the racialized body," or the body set apart and abstracted because of race. Seltzer clearly appreciates the tension involved in objectification, as shown by his discussion of "conflation" of categories and "relative disembodiment"—relative, that is, to specific historical forces (cultural, social, natural) meeting and mixing at a specific time in America.

37. For a detailed discussion of the early debates over the place of Negroes in the taxonomic hierarchy of being (including the question of whether they were a different species), see Jordan, *White Over Black* (esp. 218–28, 483–510).

38. See Albert Memmi, *The Colonizer and the Colonized*, esp. xii–xiii.

39. Todorov refers to his investigation as the "problematics of the exterior and remote other" (*The Conquest of America*, trans. Richard Howard, 3). The subtitle of his book is "The Question of the Other."

40. James Baldwin, "Here Be Dragons," in *The Price of the Ticket: Collected Nonfiction, 1948–1985*, 678. Baldwin originally published this essay, one of his last, under the title "Freaks and the American Ideal of Manhood."

41. Stewart Guthrie, *Faces in the Clouds: Religion as Anthropomorphism*, 3. Guthrie argues that religion is a form of anthropomorphism, arising from our general tendency to look at the world in terms of ourselves. He brings together and analyzes centuries of disparate theories about anthropomorphism, along with scores of examples from different areas of human experience. He disputes each of the two broad categories of explanations that have been offered for anthropomorphic perception: what he calls the "confusion" and the "familiarity" theories. Confusion theories hold that we anthropomorphize because we see an illusion of what we want to see (people) and don't know any better than to accept it (Nietzsche defends this view). "Familiarity" theories assert that we use what we know and rely on (ourselves) to explain what we don't know and fear (Hume argues this position at length in *Dialogues Concerning Natural Religion*). Guthrie argues that our search for significance in the world is best served by an anthropomorphic way of looking at it: "we look first for what matters most" (90). He sees no clear line between religious and secular anthropomorphism (ch. 4).

One way to interpret the animal rights movement in light of Guthrie's argument would be to say that its most fervent activists try to deny any anthropocentrism in themselves; they consciously seek to view animals in the same special way that most people reserve only for humans. This would of course explain why animal experimentation (which naturally implies objectification) upsets them so much.

42. H. G. Wells, *The Island of Dr. Moreau*, 73.

43. Martin Luther King, Jr., "Letter from the Birmingham Jail," in David A. Hollinger and Charles Capper, eds., *The American Intellectual Tradition* 2:238.

44. For a survey of (pre-Darwinian) Enlightenment views, see Jordan, *White Over Black*, 218–28, 483–510. Continuing the chronology, Fredrickson analyzes scientific theories of race in America during the period leading up to and encompassing Darwin's historic overturning of old ideas about species division and the interrelation of all life (*Black Image*, 71–90).

Darwin himself recognized and deplored that human exceptionalism was used to buttress racial inequality and the accompanying effort to imagine human beings as things. In the 1830s, over twenty years before the *Origin*, he wrote in his notebooks that "the white man, who has debased his nature and violated every such instinctive feeling by making slave of his fellow Black, [has] often wished to consider him as another animal." Such behavior, Darwin suggests, "is the way of mankind" (quoted in Gillian Beer, "Problems of Description in the Language of Discovery," 40).

45. As one of Studs Terkel's interviewees, Frank Lumpkin, put it, "Race is only used when it's to somebody's advantage" (*Race*, 89).

46. Bogdan, *Freak Show*, 10. Geertz himself notes that the "right" to construct a savage can also be abused: "To demonstrate that such a constructed savage corresponds to Australian Aborigines, African Tribesmen, or Brazilian Indians is another matter altogether" (*Interpretation of Cultures*; all quotations at 347).

The designated "other" group supports the dominant group's definition of humanity by providing necessary contrast. My broad point is that when a group defines its humanity in direct, central opposition to certain other humans (as opposed to reliance on animal totems, for instance), maintaining the difference—and hence the definition—will be continually tense and difficult.

47. Rosaldo, *Culture and Truth*, 17, 19.

48. Werner Sollors, *Beyond Ethnicity*, 18. Tocqueville based his analysis on the Indians' refusal to give up their freedom in order to live with whites, and blacks' lack of such a choice, having been enslaved from their arrival on American shores (*Democracy in America*, ed. J. P. Mayer and trans. George Lawrence, 321–63). I am following Todorov's progression here, but the continuum between the treatment of Indians and slaves in America has been demonstrated explicitly by more recent critics. For example, Carolyn Porter says that the paternalism of Southern slaveowners originates in the similar justification that evolved for Indian removal (*Seeing and Being: The Plight of the Participant Observer in Emerson, James, Adams, and Faulkner*, 232–33). I will be discussing this issue further in chapter 4.

49. Morrison, "Unspeakable Things Unspoken," 16.

50. Richard Wright, "How Bigger Was Born," in *Native Son*, xxxiv.

TWO: *The Puritans and Their Indians*

1. Geertz, *Interpretation of Cultures*, 52; Sollors, *Beyond Ethnicity*, 26. Sollors treats racial difference as a specific case of ethnicity (38).

2. See Homi K. Bhabha, "Narrating the Nation," in Bhabha, ed., *Nation and Narration*, 1–7, and Benedict Anderson, *Imagined Communities*, 19. Timothy Brennan says that the ideology of nationalism "has always implied unequal development"; although he is analyzing modern times, Brennan's assertion is surely borne out by Puritan-Indian relations in colonial New England ("The National Longing for Form," in Bhabha, ed., *Nation and Narration*, 43–70; quotation at 59).

3. Bhabha, "The Other Question: Stereotype, Discrimination, and the Discourse of Colonialism," in *The Location of Culture*, 77.

4. I am aware that my rhetoric conflates the myriad of Puritan voices into a single chorus here. I do it temporarily, in the interest of felicity, and on the grounds that the broad statements that I make in the name of American Puritan society reflected the views of the great majority of American Puritans. As the chapter unfolds, however, I will more closely examine individual views and so expose the diversity of perceptions of Indians in colonial New England.

I am restricting my focus to the Puritan encounter with the Indians, but the cultural symptoms the Puritans exhibit are hardly limited to their own experience; a similar tendency to objectify the natives in the name of God can be observed in other settlements along the frontier during the seventeenth century and later, with similarly equivocal results. (One good example: in his analysis of Francis Parkman's *The Oregon Trail* [1849], Philip G. Terrie sees Parkman's perception flashing back and forth between the Indian as beast and image of the noble savage; Terrie, "The Other Within: Indianization on the Oregon Trail," *New England Quarterly* 64, no. 3 [1991]: 376–92.) My decision to concentrate on the Puritans arises primarily from the way that their writings (especially the captivity narratives) display the complex side effects of objectification in particularly high relief.

5. John Canup's *Out of the Wilderness: The Emergence of an American Identity in Colonial New England* demonstrates an important diversity of Puritan views on Indian policy, a shifting spectrum of opinion and debate that is colored by typology, politics, war, economics, and the state of the missionary movement, among other things.

6. Aristotle, *Politics*, trans. Benjamin Jowett, in *The Works of Aristotle*, vol. 10, ed. W. D. Ross (book 1, ch. 4, p. 1254).

7. The Puritans were serious enough about the equation of un-Christian behavior to bestiality to apply it to themselves on frequent occasion. For a good overview of this rhetorical tendency, see Canup, *Out of the Wilderness*, 29–33.

8. John Winthrop, *Winthrop's Journal: History of New England, 1630–1649*, ed. James Kendall Hosmer, vol. 2, p. 18.

9. William Bradford, *Of Plymouth Plantation*, ed. Samuel Eliot Morrison, 62. Bradford also sees the Indians as cannibalistic, describing them in lurid fashion early on as "not being content only to kill and take away life, but delight to torment men in the most bloody manner that may be; flaying some alive with the shells of fishes, cutting off the members and joints of others by piecemeal and broiling on the coals, eat the collops of their flesh in their sight whilst they live, with other cruelties too horrible to be related" (26).

Most of these tortures have been documented by historians, though it is worth noting that the Indian tribes of New England rarely engaged in ritual cannibalism of any sort.

10. In Alan Heimert and Andrew Delbanco, eds., *The Puritans in America: A Narrative Anthology*, 43.

11. Heimert and Delbanco, eds., *The Puritans in America*, 43–44.

12. John Winthrop, "General Observations for the Plantation of New England," in *The John Winthrop Papers* 2:120.

13. Mitchell Breitwieser, *American Puritanism and the Defense of Mourning: Religion, Grief, and Ethnology in Mary White Rowlandson's Captivity Narrative*, 132 (see also ch. 1, esp. 24–26). Breitwieser discusses the typological treatment of Indians in ch. 4.

14. Roy Harvey Pearce, *Savagism and Civilization*, 21.

15. See Alden T. Vaughan and Edward W. Clark, eds., *Puritans Among the Indians: Accounts of Captivity and Redemption 1676–1724*, 17; and Alden T. Vaughan and Daniel K. Richter, *Across the Cultural Divide: Indians and New Englanders, 1605–1763*, 83.

16. Cotton Mather, *Diary of Cotton Mather* 2:151 (January 1712). Soon afterward, Mather resolved that he "must make the poor Indians as well as the poor English, the Objects of my poor Dispensations" (2:240; September 1713).

Mather mentions his Indian ministry work numerous times in his diary. He cites "the horrid Evil of debauching the *Indians*, by selling *Drink* unto them; a crime committed by too many in the Countrey; a Crime fruitful in Wickedness and Confusion" (*Diary* 1:342; April 1700). The result of this sentiment was *A Monitory and Hortatory Letter, unto those English, who debauch the Indians, by selling strong Drink unto them*. Similar publications include *An Epistle unto the Christian Indians* (1700) and *A Letter About the Present State of Christianity, Among the Christianized Indians of New England* (1705). Earlier, in his 1689 election sermon "The Way to Prosperity," Mather had criticized those English who taught the Indians "our vice," lamenting also how the colonists themselves "Indianize" (A. W. Plumstead, *The Wall and the Garden: Selected Massachusetts Election Sermons, 1620–1715*, 133–34).

17. Cotton Mather, *Magnalia Christi Americana* 1:561–62. Further citations will be given parenthetically in the text.

18. Mather's Indian rhetoric was among the harshest of all Puritan writers, which is really saying something. His account in the *Magnalia* of King Philip's War describes the Indians as "rabid animals" (2:499). For an interesting complement to this discussion, see Dana Nelson's deconstructive reading of Mather's views on Negro slaves, in which she demonstrates that he is more concerned with their present economic value than their immortal souls (*The Word in Black and White*, 24–29). Mather's sensitivity to skin color may be further elucidated through his frequent references to Indians as "tawnies."

19. Mather, *Diary* 2:328–29.

20. This strategy for coping with an anomaly is not uncommon. Todorov shows how Columbus did the same thing in 1492, deciding that "those [Indians] who are not already Christians can only be slaves" (*Conquest of America*, 46).

21. See Noel Carroll, *The Philosophy of Horror*, ch. 1. Carroll makes a special point of insisting that the monster be supernatural as well as anomalous—that is, outside of what can be rationally and scientifically expected. I will be arguing implicitly against this requirement in the remainder of this chapter. Mary Douglas's classic study, *Purity and Danger: An Analysis of Concepts of Pollution and Taboo*, is a valuable source of Carroll's analysis, and also my own.

22. Throughout this paragraph I have drawn on the excellent survey of this material by Katherine Park and Lorraine J. Daston ("Unnatural Conceptions: The Study of Monsters in Sixteenth and Seventeenth Century France and England," *Past and Present* 92 (August 1981): 20–54, esp. 23–34). The authors document various public displays of prodigies (monstrous children and animals) in the sixteenth century ("Unnatural Conceptions," 34). Narratives of prodigies were popular entertainment as well as ostensibly didactic; along with broadsides, they were collected in what became a new genre: the prodigy book (ibid., 28–30). These exhibits and publications presaged the freak shows and freak show pamphlets of modern times.

Also see Lorraine Daston, "Marvelous Facts and Miraculous Evidence in Early Modern Europe," *Critical Inquiry* 18 (Autumn 1991): 93–124, esp. 95–100.

23. Johnson, *Wonder-Working Providence*, quoted by Peter N. Carroll, *Puritanism and the Wilderness: The Intellectual Significance of the New England Frontier, 1629–1700*, 205.

24. Winthrop, *Winthrop's Journal* 1:267.

25. Thomas Laqueur, *Making Sex: Bodies and Gender from the Greeks to Freud*, 122; Winthrop, *Winthrop's Journal* 1:267–68.

26. On the hospitability of Puritanism to the New Science, see Paul H. Kocher, *Science and Religion in Elizabethan England*, 17–19. Among the factors Kocher cites are Calvin's enthusiasm for the study of nature, the iconoclasm of Puritan doctrine, and the middle-class, mercantile membership of the movement. "Puritan worldliness," says Kocher, "was ultimately to aid science more than Puritan otherworldliness was to inhibit it" (19). Perry Miller's analysis of the Puritan relationship between faith and reason shows how "knowledge is not only useful, it is a part of theology" ("The Marrow of Puritan Divinity," in *Errand into the Wilderness*, 48–98; quotation at 77). For a useful discussion of the shift to the scientific interpretation of prodigies as natural events in England and New England, see Michael Winship, "Prodigies, Puritanism, and the Perils of Natural Philosophy: The Example of Cotton Mather," *William and Mary Quarterly*, 3d ser., 61 (January 1994): 92–105. For a feminist reading of the early interpretations of monstrosity and the eventual scientific control over such meaning, see Marie-Helene Huet, *Monstrous Imagination*.

27. For a detailed historical analysis (including various statistical breakdowns) of "Indianized" Puritans and "Friend-Indians" who crossed over to the Puritan side, see Vaughan and Richter, *Across the Cultural Divide*. I will examine the Puritans' attitude toward Praying Indians in more detail in the section on "Strategies for Managing the Monster."

28. Tara Fitzpatrick identifies a more wide-ranging ambivalence in Puritan captivity narratives. Her analysis ties this conflicted equivocation to the changing relations among church, community (and women's roles in it), and the land itself. Fitzpatrick, "The Figure of Captivity: The Cultural Work of the Puritan Captivity Narrative," *American Literary History* 3 (1991): 1–26.

29. The full title of Williams's account is *The Redeemed Captive, Returning to Zion: A Faithful History of Remarkable Occurences* [*sic*] *in the Captivity and the Deliverance of Mr. John Williams, Minister of the Gospel*, in Vaughan and Clark, eds., *Puritans Among the Indians* (quotation at 172). Future page references will appear parenthetically in the text. Williams wrote his narrative at the urging of Cotton Mather, and it proved very popular.

30. See John Demos's remarkable *The Unredeemed Captive: A Family Story from Early America* for a detailed and thoughtful retelling of the story of Eunice Williams.

31. See chapter 1, above. Interpreting a long tradition of anthropomorphic thought, Stewart Guthrie argues that humans employ a perceptive strategy which aims at uncovering the presence of other humans (*Faces in the Clouds*).

32. Another good example of a threat to the human-animal boundary is the veterinary surgery of H. G. Wells's Dr. Moreau. The narrator of the story describes Moreau's anomalous creations as "grotesque animalism" (*Island of Dr. Moreau*, 51). This epithet says much about where the grotesque comes from. Moreau's monsters are animals molded in the manner of humans, but they are decidedly not human. On the other hand, they aren't animals, either. They're in-between—and that's what makes them grotesque. The narrator's term for them reflects his awareness of the challenge to his own category system.

33. The full title of Rowlandson's work is *The Sovereignty and Goodness of God, together with the Faithfulness of His Promises Displayed; Being a Narrative of the Captivity and restoration of Mrs. Mary Rowlandson, Commended by her to all that Desire to Know the Lord's Doings to, and Dealings with Her. Especially to her Dear Children and Relations*. Her narrative appears in Vaughan and Clark, eds., *Puritans Among the Indians*. Future citations will be given parenthetically in the text.

34. Lévi-Strauss, *The Savage Mind*, 95.

35. Jane Tompkins, "'Indians': Textualism, Morality, and the Problem of History," 70.

36. Breitwieser, *American Puritanism*, 147. Rowlandson also exchanges with the Indians such few valuables as she has (e.g., a knife). Richard Slotkin and James K. Folsom briefly note Rowlandson's progression toward regarding the Indians as human (*So Dreadfull a Judgment: Puritan Responses to King Philip's War, 1676–1677*, 306–307), as does Breitwieser at greater length (see *American Puritanism*, ch. 4). Breitwieser ties this movement to his larger argument centering on mourning, but I think that it bears the wider application I have given it here.

37. Douglas, *Purity and Danger*, 162.

38. The Nuer example comes from E. E. Evans-Pritchard (*Nuer Religion*, 84), as quoted by Douglas (*Purity and Danger*, 39). Another telling example is the killing of twins at birth in certain West African cultures to avoid having to confront the uncanny phenomenon of doubling (ibid., 39).

39. Cited by Winship, "Prodigies, Puritanism, and Natural Philosophy," 92.

40. Winthrop, *Winthrop's Journal* 2:83.

41. The full title is *Memoirs of Odd Adventures, Strange Deliverances, etc. in the Captivity of John Gyles, Esq., Commander of the Garrison on St. George's River*. Connotations of adulthood notwithstanding, Gyles was taken by Indians while a child of ten in 1689. Gyles's narrative appears in Vaughan and Clark, *Puritans Among the Indians*. Future citations will be given parenthetically in the text.

42. For an analysis of ethnographic rhetorical strategy in Indian captivity narrative, see David R. Sewell, "So Unstable and Like Mad Men They Were: Language and Interpretation in Early American Captivity Narratives," in Frank Shuffelton, ed., *A Mixed Race: Ethnicity in Early America*, esp. 42–43. For a discussion of Gyles as "White Indian," see June Namias, *White Captives: Gender and Ethnicity on the American Frontier*, 71–72.

Gyles's tolerance recalls that of Roger Williams, another rare American Puritan capable of taking a wide-angled view. "I have strong convictions upon the consciences of many of [the Indians]," wrote Williams in 1643, in *A Key into the Language of America, Or, An Help to the Language of the Natives in that part of America, called New-England* (Perry Miller, ed., *Roger Williams: His Contribution to the American Tradition*, 59). With what Larzer Ziff calls a "remarkable ability to separate the secular from the spiritual" (*Puritanism in America*, 171), Williams saw the Indians as false worshipers but did not condemn them for it. Miller says that this ability to treat Indian culture respectfully made Williams unique in his generation (*Roger Williams*, 52). Further notable was Williams's understanding that the Indians played the role of the "other" in New England thought, and that every culture has its "Indians" to play that role (*Key*, as quoted by Robert F. Berkhofer, Jr., *The White Man's Indian: Images of the Indian from Columbus to the Present*, 15).

Of course, Williams hardly occupied the mainstream of Puritan thought. A pariah of sorts, much of his experience with Indians came from living with them during his ideologically motivated exile from the larger community.

43. Alden T. Vaughan and Daniel K. Richter offer statistics suggesting that captive children (especially girls) between the ages of seven and fifteen had the highest probability of remaining with the Indians (*Across the Cultural Divide*, 64). James Axtell illustrates how this bond of friendship can form in his detailed description of the ways that the Indians assimilated their captives into their society. In many cases (usually of children), this process was so successful that the New Englanders went on to live their lives as Indians. James Axtell shows also that long-term attachments such as that between Gyles and his Indian master were frequent, if not common (see *The Invasion Within: The Contest of Cultures in North America*, ch. 13, esp. 308–18).

44. The Puritans, for example, valued Indian wampum (which they used as currency since it was hard to counterfeit), food, skins, and copper, while the Indians sought Puritan tools, guns, and textiles, among other things. A good deal of documented commerce took place between the two groups. For a detailed look at Puritan commercial and legal dealings with the Indians, see Alden T. Vaughan's *The New England Frontier: Puritans and Indians* and James Axtell's *The European and the Indian*.

45. Said, *Orientalism*, 67, 237. See Axtell, "The Scholastic Philosophy of the Wilderness," in *The European and the Indian*.

46. Michael Zuckerman, "Identity in British America: Unease in Eden," in Nicholas Canny and Anthony Pagden, eds., *Colonial Identity in the Atlantic World, 1500–1800*, 153.

47. See Cotton, "God's Promise to His Plantations" (1630), and Shepard, "The Clear Sun-shine of the Gospel Breaking Forth upon the Indians in New-England" (1648; as quoted by Delbanco, *The Puritan Ordeal*, 105), and Morton, *The New English Canaan* (1632), written after the author's deportation back to England; William Wood, *New England's Prospect* (1634), ed. Alden T. Vaughan, 88; Berkhofer, *The White Man's Indian*, 19. For a fuller historical account of the proposed Indian-Jewish connection, see Canup, *Out of the Wilderness*, 64–73. Richard W. Cogley examines the question from Eliot's own evolving point of view in "John Eliot and the Origins of the American Indians," *Early American Literature* 21 (1986–87): 210–25.

48. The Puritans' stress on the experience of grace through personal experience of the divine word meant that the Bible had to be translated (or else read in English), and that the Indians had to be able to understand sermons, and so on. The Spanish emphasized ritual over words; perhaps because of this, they were more successful at conversion than the Puritans ever were.

49. Heimert and Delbanco, eds., *The Puritans in America*, 43, 80; Berkhofer, *The White Man's Indian*, 20. Delbanco also notes the dramatic failure of President Dunster of Harvard to raise money for an Indian college. His patrons didn't take the idea of educating Indians seriously; they thought he was using a false pretext to trick them into funding a new building (*The Puritan Ordeal*, 110–11).

50. Todorov elsewhere explains enslavement as an ideology "that reduces the other to the status of an object," a point he illustrates by citing Spanish atrocities committed against Indians: "Their flesh is used to feed the surviving Indians or

even the dogs; they are killed in order to be boiled down for grease, supposed to cure the wounds of the Spaniards; thereby they are identified with animals for the slaughterhouse" (*Conquest of America*, 175).

51. Ingles was writing to William Johnson, the British Superintendent for Indian Affairs (quoted by Axtell, *The Invasion Within*, 133).

52. Massachusetts Colonial Records, quoted in Axtell, *The Invasion Within*, 139.

53. The Puritans established a total of fourteen praying towns before King Philip's War interrupted their missionary efforts. Vaughan and Richter cite a 1674 tally by Daniel Gookin which shows that well under 10 percent of "Christian Indians" were admitted to full membership in the Puritan church (*Across the Cultural Divide*, 34). They argue that Puritan prejudice against Indians was always a barrier to their assimilation, but it became an almost insurmountable one after the beginning of the second great Indian war in 1675 (44).

Though Vaughan labors hard on the Puritans' behalf in his earlier history, he still admits that Indians who found themselves enmeshed in the Puritan justice system had "a special status" different from English miscreants. For example, there were laws in New England prohibiting the sale of liquor to Indians living in Puritan society; this prohibition (with its infantilizing implications) gives a sense of the low social position of such "Friend-Indians" (*The New England Frontier*, 190). James Axtell documents such treatment more frankly, detailing the special legislative treatment the Indians of the praying towns received in many matters, ranging from public behavior to personal hygiene (*The Invasion Within*, esp. 139–78). James Schramer and Timothy Sweet argue that the missionary effort represented a policy of control and containment of the Indian population, rather than assimilation ("Violence and the Body Politic in Seventeenth Century New England," *Arizona Quarterly* 48 (1992): 26–27). Jill Lepore links the liminality of "praying Indians" to the issue of literacy in her interesting analysis of the story of John Sassamon, a praying Indian whose 1674 murder touched off King Philip's War ("Dead Men Tell No Tales: John Sassamon and the Fatal Consequences of Literacy," *American Quarterly* 46 (1994): 479–512).

54. Homi K. Bhabha, "Of Mimicry," in *The Location of Culture*; quotations at 87, 91.

55. Breitwieser, *American Puritanism*, 186.

56. See Axtell, "The White Indians," in *The Invasion Within*. Axtell's study covers all of colonial North America, not just Puritan New England. He recounts the story of fourteen-year-old John McCullough of Pennsylvania, who, in order to be taken back to white society after over eight years among the Indians, had to be bound hand and foot to his horse. Even so, he escaped and returned to the Indians for a year before being recaptured and permanently removed (307).

57. Though it is admittedly dangerous to generalize across chronological and tribal boundaries, it is nevertheless worth noting that most Indians of the nineteenth-century South were quick to acknowledge and defend the humanity of Negro slaves. John Blassingame describes how wilderness-dwelling runaway slaves ("maroons") formed alliances with the Seminole Indians, and how the Indians refused to return these fugitives to their masters as a condition of any negotiated peace with whites. Their continuing refusal presented a forty-year stumbling block to negotiated peace that lasted until the end of the Civil War (*The Slave Community*, 121–24).

58. Axtell, *The Invasion Within*, 302. For discussion of John Williams's personal struggle, see Rosalie Murphy Baum, "John Williams's Captivity Narrative: A Consideration of Normative Ethnicity," in Shuffelton, ed., *A Mixed Race*, 63.

59. Delbanco, *The Puritan Ordeal*, 112.

60. Increase Mather actually went so far as to tie the failure of Puritan missionary work to a sign of God's disfavor (see *Ichabod . . . A Discourse Shewing What Cause There Is to Fear That the Glory of the Lord, Is Departing from New England*, as quoted by Delbanco, *The Puritan Ordeal*, 109). Mason's 1637 memoir was titled *A Brief History of the Pequot War* (quoted by Delbanco, ibid., 112). His fear that the Puritans were taking on Indian ways was later echoed by Increase Mather in the aftermath of King Philip's War: "How many that although they are *Christians* in name, are no better than *Heathens* in heart, and in Conversation? How many Families that live like *profane Indians* without any *Family prayer*?" (*An Earnest Exhortation* [1676], Mather's emphasis; reprinted in Slotkin and Folsom, *So Dreadfull a Judgment*, 174–75). This anxious rhetoric recalls the end of George Orwell's *Animal Farm*, when the animals witness the last step of a similar transformation: "The creatures outside looked from pig to man, and from man to pig, and from pig to man again; but already it was impossible to say which was which" (118).

61. Samuel Nowell, *Abraham in Arms*, an election sermon (Slotkin and Folsom, *So Dreadfull a Judgment*, 287).

62. This "paranoid discourse of the body politic" described by Schramer and Sweet ("Violence and the Body Politic," 23) builds on Slotkin and Folsom's argument that the Puritans were attracted to Indian ways, felt guilty about the attraction, and so felt obliged to destroy the Indians to cleanse themselves of the guilt (*So Dreadfull a Judgment*, 39). Timothy Brennan says that "the 'national idea' flourish[es] in the soil of foreign conquest" ("The National Longing for Form," in Bhabha, ed., *Nation and Narration*, 59).

63. Pearce, *Savagism and Civilization*, 31. Pearce provides a good capsule history of the Puritan missionary movement (see esp. 26–35). Alden Vaughan gives a more detailed account which is rather more charitable to the Puritans in *The New England Frontier* (chs. 9–11). Francis Jennings is more skeptical of New England motives in his history (*The Invasion of America: Indians, Colonialism, and the Cant of Conquest*, see esp. ch. 14). Vaughan and Jennings both call attention to the numerous rules and tests established by Puritan missionaries which made Indian conversion to Puritan religion a most difficult endeavor. The presence of such rules reflects the distance that the Puritans were eager to maintain between their own kind and the Indians.

64. The Puritan category of "Praying Indian" thus springs from the same creative root as Edward Said's description of the Western view of Near Easterners: "An Oriental man was first an Oriental and only second a man" (*Orientalism*, 231).

65. For an account of this expansion see Peter N. Carroll, *Puritanism and the Wilderness*, 217ff.

66. See Winship, "Prodigies, Puritans, and Natural Philosophy," 95–96. For a detailed account of the Anglican attack on Puritan providentialism, see Winship, *Seers of God: Puritan Providentialism in the Restoration and Early Enlightenment*, ch. 2, which is in press at this writing. I am grateful to Professor Winship for sharing part of the manuscript with me.

67. For various discussions about the relationship between captivity and providence narratives, I am grateful to my colleague Jim Hartman, whose recent dissertation, "The Indian Captivity Narrative as Providence Tale," asserts the connection. I will argue that the captivity narrative presents a generic story of a miracle—a providential tale of deliverance in which the captive is miraculously delivered by the grace of God—in a way that specifically sidesteps debate over whether the event is natural or supernatural.

68. I am relying in this paragraph on Winship's persuasive conclusions in "Prodigies, Puritanism, and Natural Philosophy," esp. 95–100. Winship argues that Mather's public and private relationship to prodigies and the New Science exemplifies some of the pressures that helped to transform seventeenth-century Puritanism (93). Winship elaborates his conclusions and extends them in chapter 5 of his book, *Seers of God*.

69. Daston, "Marvelous Facts," 117.

70. Kocher, *Science and Religion in Elizabethan England*, 114. Kocher does not specifically discuss prodigies, restricting himself to miracles, which he sees as the key contested space between religion and the New Science; the specific question was whether they were natural or supernatural. Though the English side of this conflict goes back to Elizabethan times, the forces of the New Science were clearly winning by the mid-seventeenth century, imposing the order of natural philosophy and devaluing the discourse of the supernatural (which was expressed through prodigies as well as miracles). Mather wanted to come down on the correct side of this divide (Winship, "Prodigies, Puritanism, and Natural Philosophy," 100); one might also say that he *needed* to, for the sake of his community's interests. See also Park and Daston, "Unnatural Conceptions," 40.

71. Miller, "The Marrow of Puritan Divinity," in *Errand into the Wilderness*, 94. For a more detailed explanation, see David D. Hall, *Worlds of Wonder, Days of Judgment: Popular Religious Belief in Early New England*, ch. 4, esp. pp. 90–94, and Winship, *Seers of God*, ch. 1.

72. Mather, *Magnalia* 2:560.

73. Winship calls Mather's debate with the Royal Society on monstrous births "discreet and defensive," offering it as evidence of Mather's continuing private belief in prodigies ("Prodigies, Puritanism, and Natural Philosophy" 100). His excellent analysis of Mather's *A Voice from Heaven* (1719)—his interpretation of the appearance of the aurora borealis that year—shows how Mather preserved the desire for and rhetoric of belief in prodigies, all beneath a layer of diverting, disguising rhetoric (ibid., 100–105). I am arguing that narratives of Indian captivity do the same thing, but are a smoother and more broadly applicable dodge of unpleasant scientific politics. (For a more widely focused account of Puritan defenses of their providentialism, see Winship, *Seers of God*, ch. 3.)

Indians became a field for scientific study in the early nineteenth century, as the U.S. frontier moved rapidly westward. Early scientists sought to prove that Negroes and Indians were separate races with separate lines of descent, their efforts forming part of the larger justification for slavery and western expansion. Reginald Horsman examines the frequently intertwined fates of Native Americans and African-Americans in science and politics in *Race and Manifest Destiny: The Origins of American Racial Anglo-Saxonism*; for an overview of nineteenth-century Indian policy, see 189–93.

74. Daniel Gookin, *Historical Account of the Doings and Sufferings of the Christian Indians in New England in the Years 1675, 1676, 1677* (completed 1677, published 1836). Winship describes Boyle as an "emblematic figure linking piety, experimental philosophy, and social respectability" (*Seers of God*, 64).

75. James Axtell's large body of work has been of definitive importance to understanding colonial-Indian relations in this light. Also, the arguments of John Canup and Michael Zuckerman bear special mention. Canup argues that close examination of Puritan views of the wilderness and its Indian inhabitants can be a key to some of the deeper recesses of the Puritan mind (*Out of the Wilderness*). Zuckerman sees the colonial struggle to define and manage the Indian as reflective of the problems accompanying the quest for identity in the New World. He sees the colonists' Indian difficulties as emblematic of the contradictions surrounding their attempt to forge an identity independent of England ("Identity in British America," 115–57).

76. Said's *Culture and Imperialism* is an extended account of how nation and narration inform each other within the context of the ideology of empire.

77. See Rosaldo, *Culture and Truth*, ch. 3. He describes a paradox where the destroyers grieve for what they have destroyed.

78. Charles Brockden Brown, *Edgar Huntly* (1798), in S. W. Reid, ed., *Novels and Related Works of Charles Brockden Brown* 4:194, 224. I have argued elsewhere that Edgar's conflicted views and actions stem from survivor guilt connected to his parents' death at the hands of Indians. Leonard Cassuto, "'[Un]consciousness Itself Is the Malady': *Edgar Huntly* and the Discourse of the Other," *Modern Language Studies* 23, no. 4 (Fall 1993): 118–30.

79. René Girard, *Violence and the Sacred*, trans. Patrick Gregory; Schramer and Sweet, "Violence and the Body Politic," 24. Because a worldview based on otherness and alterity underwrites so much history, cultural critics have long struggled to articulate an alternative to it. In a relevant recent analysis of the meeting of cultures, Paul B. Armstrong calls for "play" between them to understand and appreciate differences ("Play and Cultural Differences," *Kenyon Review* [1991]: 157–71).

80. Church's narrative, with the amusing and revealing title *Entertaining Passages Relating to Philip's War*, is collected in Slotkin and Folsom's *So Dreadfull a Judgment* with a useful headnote; for Slotkin's interesting reading of Church's account, see *Regeneration Through Violence: The Mythology of the American Frontier, 1600–1860*, esp. 161–73).

81. The head remained in place for many years. Philip's hands were also cut off, these being sent to Boston. This mutilation supports Ann Kibbey's argument that the Puritans "fetishized" the Indian body (*The Interpretation of Material Shapes in Puritanism: A Study of Rhetoric, Prejudice, and Violence*, 102). Kibbey is speaking of the Pequots, but Philip's treatment provides evidence to extend her argument to the later generations.

THREE: *A Different Power of Blackness*

1. See Olmstead's *A Journey in the Back Country* (1858), quoted in Kenneth M. Stampp, *The Peculiar Institution: Slavery in the Ante-Bellum South*, 193. Among histori-

ans of slavery, Stampp shows particular sensitivity to the conflict generated by objectification, reflected in the need to see the slave simultaneously as "chattel personal," a human being requiring food and clothing (and who is to be uplifted by exposure to "civilized" culture), and a simple piece of goods to be bought, sold, or bartered (*The Peculiar Institution*, ch. 5).

2. In teaching and assigning tasks, for example, the master acknowledged the slave's human intelligence. David Brion Davis calls attention to this paradox in *The Problem of Slavery in Western Culture*.

3. Tocqueville, *Democracy in America*, book 1, p. 361; epigraph quotation at 342.

4. Sidney Mintz and Richard Price, *The Birth of African-American Culture: An Anthropological Approach*, 25. Anthropologists Mintz and Price emphasize that "slaves were defined as property; but, being human, they were called upon to act in sentient, articulate, and human ways" (25). As will become clear, I do not see the American slaveholder admitting the humanity of his property so easily, at least not consciously. The master's reluctance to recognize the slave becomes the source of continued struggle.

5. Blacks were legally liminal and ambiguously human in America from the beginning. Slavery laws antedated the Constitution, a document that itself treated slaves as people and property at the same time. The Connecticut Compromise, a crucial agreement between North and South at the Constitutional Convention, dictated that each slave was worth three-fifths of a (white male) person for purposes of representation. David Brion Davis shows how the political compromises made for the sake of united rebellion against the Crown may have allowed the peculiar institution to endure much longer in the United States than it otherwise would have. Debate on interstate slave commerce, for example, centered in part on whether the word *slaves* would better serve in the text than *persons* ("The Constitution and the Slave Trade," in Allen Weinstein, Frank Otto Gatell, and David Sarasohn, eds., *American Negro Slavery*, 27).

James Codman Hurd's 1858 study documented a gradual accretion over time of statutes that acknowledged the slave's humanity, including laws against starving slaves, protecting slave life and limb, and the like (Willie Lee Rose, *Slavery and Freedom*, ed. William W. Freehling, 23–24). James Oakes discusses the masters' consequent legal quandaries in his later book of the same title (*Slavery and Freedom: An Interpretation of the Old South*, esp. 125–26).

6. For citations from the slave codes, see Willie Lee Rose, *A Documentary History of Slavery in North America*, 192, 177. Thomas R. R. Cobb, *An Inquiry into the Law of Negro Slavery in the United States of America* (1858), quoted in Rose, *A Documentary History*, 199.

7. See Helen T. Catterall, ed., *Judicial Cases Concerning American Slavery and the Negro* 1:318. Harriet Beecher Stowe also cites the murder case (*Souther v. The Commonwealth*, 1850) in the appendix to *Dred* 2:218–19. Kenneth Stampp gives a lively legal survey of the convoluted state slave codes (*The Peculiar Institution*, 206–31). He connects the inconsistency of the courts' treatment of the slave's status to a similar inconsistency on the parts of individual slaveholders (193).

8. Frederick Douglass, "What to a Slave Is the Fourth of July?" in John W. Blassingame et al., eds., *The Frederick Douglass Papers, Series One: Speeches, Debates, and Interviews* 2:371.

9. All these theories, informed by a historical view of the African as "savage," made appearances in proslavery literature at one time or another. I will be exploring these views in more detail in chapter 4.

10. Orlando Patterson, *Slavery and Social Death: A Comparative Study*, 322.

11. See *Slavery and Social Death*, ch. 2 (esp. 51–62). Patterson also cites shaving as a marginalizing practice, but argues that it was less important in America because the difference between Caucasian and Negro hair was a major identifying badge of slavery here (61). (It is nonetheless worth pointing out that the shaving of captives did take place on American slaveships.) For other historical evidence of mutilation of slaves, see Stampp, *The Peculiar Institution* (188–89), and Davis, *The Problem of Slavery in Western Culture* (48–49). Winthrop Jordan links the castration of slaves in early America to a fear of the "aggressive" and "uncivilized" sexuality of Negroes (*White Over Black*, 154–59). One is reminded in this case of the grisly castration scene at the end of Faulkner's *Light in August* in which the mulatto Joe Christmas is mutilated before he is killed.

A terrifying fictional example of how physical mutilation becomes a component of social death is Paul Bowles's "A Distant Episode," in which a linguist's tongue is cut out as a preliminary to his transformation into a mindless captive clown.

12. The following discussion of Hegel (whose tightly involuted style has fueled a large critical industry) is informed in part by the lucid analyses performed by Barry Cooper, Alexander Kojève, Judith Shklar, and Steven B. Smith. Of these, Kojève's reading is probably the most influential, having acquired a legendary status in many Hegelian circles that has given it an intellectual life of its own.

13. Judith N. Shklar, *Freedom and Independence: A Study of the Political Ideas of Hegel's Phenomenology of Mind*; quotations at 58–59.

14. Georg Wilhelm Friedrich Hegel, *The Encyclopedia Logic*, trans. T. F. Geraets, W. A. Suchtins, and H. S. Harris, 241.

15. Shklar, *Freedom and Independence*, 61.

16. Kenneth Stampp was the first to dissect the contradictory paternalism of the peculiar institution. Though Stampp was no Hegelian, his reasoning is similar to Hegel's when he says that the unarticulated goal of slave-breaking was to take the slave's identity away and instill in him not just obedience but absolute submission accompanied by a genuine desire to serve (*The Peculiar Institution*, 143–48). Predictably, the latter need for recognition was not met; it was either resisted by the slave (examples of which I examine here), or else the master found in the slave's obedience not love but fear (381). Hegel argues that the broken slave offers no useful recognition at all, creating an ultimately unsolvable problem for the master. Patterson accepts Hegel's version of the slave's dilemma up to a point, but he accords the slave a good deal more flexibility in response and awareness of the master's paradoxical dependence on him. Moreover, Patterson strongly disagrees with Hegel about the extent of the master's dependence, arguing that the slaveholder could and did receive recognition from other members of his community, such as other masters (*Slavery and Social Death*, 334–42, 99–100).

See also Stanley Elkins's controversial analysis (and the many debates that it occasioned) of the Sambo stereotype as a role-playing survival strategy of the slave in response to expectation of childlike behavior by the master, who believed that his slaves were enjoying their place as he enjoyed his own (*Slavery: A Problem in American Institutional and Intellectual Life*, 122–32). I will be addressing Sambo stereotyping in chapter 4.

17. Georg Wilhelm Friedrich Hegel, *Phenomenology of Spirit*, trans. A. V. Miller, 118–19.

18. Steven B. Smith, *Hegel's Critique of Liberalism*, 120.

19. This unhappy self-consciousness is for Hegel part of the historical process. As I am concerned primarily with Hegel's treatment of the objectification idea, my own summary stops here. But the disequilibrium between unfulfilled master and actualized—and now dissatisfied—slave moves forward into Stoicism, Skepticism, and beyond; thus, according to Hegel, slavery is a condition that is historically surpassed.

20. Aristotle, *Politics*, book 1, ch. 4, p. 1253; book 1, ch. 6, p. 1255.

21. Orlando Patterson reconfigures Hegel's dialectic in terms of parasitism, focusing on the master's paradoxical dependence on the slave (*Slavery and Social Death*, 334–42). I will be returning to this idea next chapter in an analysis of the master's view of his relationship with the slave; for now I am concerned with the slave's achievement of consciousness and the case of open rebellion (which is, as Patterson says, one possible outcome of that consciousness).

22. Georg Wilhelm Friedrich Hegel, *The Philosophy of History*, trans. J. Sibree, 93–99. Mrs. Henry R. Schoolcraft quotes Hegel at some length in *The Black Gauntlet: A Tale of Plantation Life in South Carolina*, her 1860 novel extolling and defending slavery (405); David Brion Davis, *The Problem of Slavery in the Age of Revolution, 1770–1823*, 558.

Most of the analysis of Hegel that I could find in African-American literary criticism—with two notable exceptions—centers on *The Philosophy of History*. The most challenging, least dismissive treatment of that work is by James A. Snead, who uses Hegel's progressively cyclical model of history as the basis for reading black culture in terms of performance. Snead sees Hegel's "simply negative" reading of black culture as only the beginning of a cycle of repetition that contributes to an "ongoing reconciliation" of European and black culture ("Repetition as a Figure of Black Culture," in Henry Louis Gates, Jr., ed., *Black Literature and Literary Theory*, 63, 75).

In the specific case of the slave narrative, Charles T. Davis and Henry Louis Gates, Jr., point to the Hegelian implications of the slave's act of autobiography, but only to rebuke Hegel's views on Africa (*The Slave's Narrative*, xxviii); see also Gates's separate indictment of Hegel in *Figures in Black: Words, Signs, and the "Racial" Self*, 105–106. Another rare mention of Hegel in the critical literature of the slave narrative is by Donald Wesling, who says that the historical specificity of narratives like Douglass's are "a reproach to Hegel," whose discussion is abstract and general ("Writing as Power in the Slave Narrative of the Early Republic," *Michigan Quarterly Review* 26 [1987]: 460). The following pages may be read in significant part as a disagreement with these blanket condemnations.

The two exceptions, both very recent, to this widespread literary neglect of the *Phenomenology* (and more specifically, the master-slave dialectic) are Eric Sundquist's and Paul Gilroy's books, in which they persuasively outline the applicability of Hegel's master-slave dialectic to Frederick Douglass's situation (Sundquist, *To Wake the Nations: Race in the Making of American Literature*, 123–24; Gilroy, *The Black Atlantic: Modernity and Double Consciousness*, 60–63). This chapter broadens their analysis and applies it to the work performed by the American slave.

Among historians, Eugene D. Genovese has long drawn on Hegel for insight into the slave's situation, even singling out Douglass as evidence on brief occasions. See *Roll, Jordan, Roll: The World the Slaves Made*, 88–89, 293, and his critique of Elkins's Sambo thesis (*In Red and Black: Marxian Explorations in Southern and Afro-American History*, 73–101), which is underwritten by Hegelian assumptions, and—with Elizabeth Fox-Genovese—the critique of Fogel and Engermann's economic thesis in *Fruits of Merchant Capital: Slavery and Bourgeois Property in the Rise and Expansion of Capitalism*, 151. Genovese generally frames his argument in terms of nation—that is, groups of people—rather than the individual. For another notable Hegel-inspired description of the master-slave relationship, see Willie Lee Rose, *A Documentary History* (11).

23. John G. Cawelti, *Adventure, Mystery, and Romance: Formula Stories as Art and Popular Culture*, 34–35.

24. Early slave narratives were mostly accounts of conversion; this spiritual tradition provides the foundation and point of departure for the evolution of the genre. The genre became more confrontational and violent during the mid-nineteenth century, as the tradition split into two strands: "providential and inexplicable" narratives and "historical and understandable" ones. Both strands draw on religious ideology and imagery, but the latter thread is the one that includes the popular fugitive slave narratives I am focusing on here (William L. Andrews, *To Tell a Free Story: The First Century of Afro-American Autobiography, 1760–1865*, chs. 2–4; quotation at 47).

Frances Smith Foster's religious overplot shows how later slave narratives draw on their religious roots. Foster describes the movement of the mature slave narrative as "a Judeo-Christian mythological structure on both the material and the spiritual levels" (*Witnessing Slavery: The Development of Antebellum Slave Narratives*, 84). The narrator begins in the Eden of her innocence, wanders in the wilderness, where she struggles for freedom and experiences providential intervention, and then finally enters the Promised Land of freedom. Loss of innocence corresponds to the slave's discovery of her enslaved state. This is followed by a resolve to be free and a consequent decision to escape. The success of the escape, aided by divine intervention, leads to freedom (85).

25. Andrews, *To Tell a Free Story*, 65. See Stephen Jay Gould, *The Mismeasure of Man*, Horsman, *Race and Manifest Destiny*, and Fredrickson, *The Black Image in the White Mind*. I will be looking more closely at these views in chapter 4.

26. Over 400,000 antislavery petitions were sent to Congress each year during the late 1830s and early 1840s. The 1837–38 drive, for example, resulted in 412,000 petitions to the House of Representatives and 270,000 to the Senate, with an average of fifty-nine signatures per petition. Henry B. Stanton reported in *The Liberator* that the drive produced around two million signatures, a figure that, given a certain amount of overlap, would be roughly consistent with the above (Edward Magdol, *The Antislavery Rank and File: A Profile of the Abolitionists' Constituency*, 55–56).

27. See Richard H. Sewell, *Ballots for Freedom: Antislavery Politics in the United States, 1837–1860*, 167–68. The two swing states were New York and Ohio. I will be discussing the rise of abolitionism further in chapter 5.

28. Cawelti, *Adventure, Mystery, and Romance*, 32.

29. See David Roediger, *The Wages of Whiteness: Race and the Making of the American Working Class*, and Eric Lott, *Love and Theft: Blackface Minstrelsy and the American Working Class*. Roediger argues that the construction of class was always implicated with race and slavery in the antebellum North. Lott (whose work I will examine in more detail next chapter) argues that blackface minstrelsy expressed the "racial unconscious" of the Northern working class. Also noteworthy is Alexander Saxton's *The Rise and Fall of the White Republic: Class Politics and Mass Culture in Nineteenth-Century America*, in which he examines—through its social supports and various cultural symptoms—the social construction of a segregated egalitarian reality for nineteenth-century American whites that was based on racism.

30. For a demographic profile of the abolitionist movement, see Edward Magdol, *The Antislavery Rank and File*.

31. Among the many literacy-centered readings of the *Narrative*, Houston Baker's argument that Douglass's future is determined by his discovery of "the power of the word" is possibly the most influential (see *The Journey Back: Issues in Black Literature and Criticism*, 32–46). Henry Louis Gates, Jr., builds on Baker's work when he says that it is Douglass's mastery of white language that makes him into an active historical agent rather than a passive object (*Figures in Black*, 116–25). Among more recent interesting examples, see Teresa A. Goddu and Craig V. Smith ("Scenes of Writing in Frederick Douglass's *Narrative*: Autobiography and the Creation of Self," *Southern Review* 25 (1989): 822–41), and John Burt ("Learning to Write: The Narrative of Frederick Douglass," *Western Humanities Review* 42 [1988]: 330–44), and especially Eric Sundquist's argument that Douglass uses language as a form of self-fathering ("Frederick Douglass: Literacy and Paternalism," *Raritan: A Quarterly Review* 6 [1986]: 108–24). Lucinda MacKethan extends these ideas perhaps the farthest in her reading, arguing that language (as opposed to force or violence) is both the medium and the message of the Covey scene ("From Fugitive Slave to Man of Letters: The Conversion of Frederick Douglass," *Journal of Narrative Technique* 16 [1986]: 65).

As might be expected, almost every reading of Douglass's *Narrative* cites Douglass's fight with Covey in one context or another. My argument for the formative importance of the actual violence of the episode amounts to a difference of emphasis with these critics rather than a notice of blatant omission. Among previous readers to dwell on the Covey incident in more detail, Ronald Takaki highlights the connection between violence and freedom in Douglass's life (*Violence and the Black Imagination: Essays and Documents*, 21–22), while David Leverenz focuses on the differences in the telling of the scene in Douglass's first two autobiographies, arguing that the first centers on freedom and drama, the second on manhood and power ("Frederick Douglass's Self-Refashioning," *Criticism* 29 (1987): 341–70). Waldo Martin also sees the fight as a "psychological declaration of independence" (*The Mind of Frederick Douglass*, 47), while Donald B. Gibson says that Douglass de-emphasizes his escape in order to make the fight with Covey into the climax of the *Narrative* ("Reconciling Public and Private in Frederick Douglass's *Narrative*," *American Literature* 57 [1985]: 549–69). In a kind of sequel to that essay, Gibson returns to the fight scene in "Christianity and Individualism: (Re-)Creation and Reality in Frederick Douglass's Representation of Self" (*African-American Review* 26 [1992]: 591–603), in which he argues that the struggle with Covey is the central event in Douglass's realization of his own individuality, and of individualism generally. Nancy Bentley has persuasively read the Covey scene as an example of the black body's ability to exert force as a measure of humanity. For Douglass, freedom becomes a "reclaiming of [the] physical powers" of the mortal flesh ("White Slaves: The Mulatto Hero in Antebellum Fiction," *American Literature* 65 [1993]: 519).

32. Baker, *The Journey Back*, 32.

33. Frederick Douglass, *Narrative of the Life of Frederick Douglass, an American Slave, Written by Himself*, ed. Benjamin Quarles, 23. Future citations to the *Narrative* refer to this edition and will be given parenthetically in the text.

34. Gates, *Figures in Black*, 89–90.

35. Douglass's erasure of his mother was partly rhetorical. He gives her a more prominent (though still small) role in his childhood when he recounts it again ten years later in *My Bondage and My Freedom* (see n. 39, below). For an interesting parallel interpretation of this passage, see Genovese's *Roll, Jordan, Roll*, in which he argues that Douglass is describing a "general education in the meaning of time" (294). Douglass describes his childhood in slavery in greater detail in the more ethnographically oriented *My Bondage and My Freedom*; the absence of such description in the *Narrative* thus underlines the slave's objectification.

36. This attitude corresponds to Hegel's description of Stoicism, which follows the slave's discovery of his own humanity. Douglass connects this discontent to the vistas afforded by his literacy, but this link is not essential. For the as-yet-illiterate William Wells Brown, kind treatment could be enough, as he describes in his own narrative: "Mr. Willi treated me better than Dr. Young ever had; but instead of making me contented and happy, it only rendered me the more miserable, for it enabled me better to appreciate liberty" (*Narrative of William Wells Brown, a Fugitive Slave*, in Paul Jefferson, ed., *The Travels of William Wells Brown*, 58).

Brown learns to read sometime during the period covered by his 1847 narrative but, interestingly, he does not even bother to note the event. (He says early on that he is unable to read a note, but by the time he reaches the threshold of Canada, he is reading books.)

37. According to Guthrie, this strategy involves a gamble. We bet that the thing is alive, and if it is, there is a payoff of added significance in our world. If the entity is human, the significance is all the greater (*Faces in the Clouds*).

38. It is possible that Douglass's description of his bestial mental condition is a rhetorical pose only. It certainly *is* part of a larger rhetorical strategy—as will presently become clear—but given Douglass's scrupulous accuracy and the mysterious source of his resistance (he confesses that he "[knew] not where" the impetus for it originated), he may have been telling the truth about his temporary loss of human consciousness.

39. Frederick Douglass, *My Bondage and My Freedom* (New York and Auburn:

Miller, Orton, and Milligan, 1855), 246–47. Future citations refer to this edition and will appear parenthetically in the text.

40. William L. Andrews emphasizes Douglass's later suggestion in *My Bondage and My Freedom* that it was "the devil" that inspires him to resist Covey (*To Tell a Free Story*, 227–30). Obviously, Douglass is being disingenuous here; he means that his "fall" from the "grace" of the slaveholders' religion is what opens his eyes to his fallen state. This interesting reading of the Covey scene and its aftermath nicely meshes with Douglass's rhetorical attack on slaveholders' Christianity throughout the *Narrative*.

41. Gilroy, *The Black Atlantic*, 61. Gilroy reads Douglass through Hegel in the service of a broad critique of post-Enlightenment debates between "Eurocentric rationalism" and "occidental anti-humanism" (54). He argues that "the time has come for the primal history of modernity to be reconstructed from the slaves' points of view" (55).

42. In reading this outcome as a victory for Douglass, I differ with Gilroy, who sees it as an "impasse" and the basis for "a vernacular variety of unhappy consciousness" (the step in Hegel's formulation that follows the master-slave dialectic), as witnessed in DuBois, Wright, and others (*The Black Atlantic*, 62, 56). Without opposing this latter conception, I would argue instead that the slave's achievement of a grudging acknowledgment of equality in combat from the master must be seen as a great advance; Douglass's violent achievement of personhood is what propels him into a condition that makes "unhappy consciousness" possible.

43. Foster, *Witnessing Slavery*, 96.

44. Though Douglass's later experience hiring himself out in Baltimore and bitterly giving the money to his master fits Hegel's paradigm more closely, I would argue that the Covey experience had already fundamentally shaped his beliefs about the value of a slave's work.

45. Nicholas K. Bromell's reading of Douglass's autobiographies makes a useful distinction between "working" and "slaving," concluding that "the slave sometimes finds within self-motivated work an effective escape from the master's control" (*By the Sweat of the Brow: Literature and Labor in Antebellum America*, 182). Hegel's ideas are clear in Bromell's argument that when "the slave seems to be taking possession of his work—as, for example, when he performs skilled labor—he affirms the existence of his mind and will and his possession of his body and his labor" (187).

46. Cobb, *An Inquiry into the Law of Slavery*, quoted by Oakes (*Slavery and Freedom*, 156).

47. Patterson, *Slavery and Social Death*, 99.

48. Frantz Fanon, *Black Skin, White Masks*, trans. Charles Lam Markmann, 220–21; Jean-Paul Sartre, preface to Frantz Fanon's *Wretched of the Earth* (18); Fanon, *Black Skin, White Masks*, 57. Fanon's general context is the colonial legacy of discrimination. His reading of Hegel goes further from the source than mine; Fanon says that the master wants only work from the slave, not recognition (220). In chapter 4 I will argue that the master shows that the slave's recognition is ultimately more important to him than the slave's work.

49. Samuel Ringgold Ward, *Autobiography of a Fugitive Negro*, 37, 42. Among slave

narrators, Ward is the most eloquent spokesman for the work ethic. His book is less slave narrative than hortatory polemic, partly because the author lived only a few years as a slave before escaping with his parents, and so had little to tell of his life in bondage. For a general discussion of the rhetorical use of work in slave narratives, see Stephen Butterfield, *Black Autobiography in America*, 17ff.

50. Frederick Douglass, *Life and Times of Frederick Douglass, Written by Himself* (2d ed., 1892), 266. Douglass notes that his underground railroad work was "not entirely free from danger," recalling Hegel's emphasis on the importance of risking one's life for recognition and freedom (*Life and Times*, 266). Douglass also privileges work in *The Heroic Slave* (1853), his only work of fiction. His hero, Madison Washington, combines escape, physical confrontation, and even trained labor (in this case, sailing) in an adventure that suggests that they're all related.

51. For example, Solomon Northup successfully sues for his freedom by proving that he had been a freeman kidnapped into slavery. This must be considered an act of resistance.

52. Martin Green, *The Great American Adventure*, 1; Cawelti, *Adventure, Mystery, and Romance*, 39.

53. For a survey of various slave strategies of mostly covert resistance, see Rose, *A Documentary History*, sec. 6. For a historical analysis of stealing by slaves, see Genovese, *Roll Jordan, Roll* (599–612).

54. Green, *The Great American Adventure*, 5–6. These generic criteria also describe the genre of "survival literature," a form of travel writing whose dominant themes were sex and slavery (see Mary Louise Pratt, *Imperial Eyes: Travel Writing and Transculturation*, 86). Survival literature first appeared in the eighteenth century and clearly influenced the development of the fugitive slave narrative during the next century.

55. Cawelti, *Adventure, Mystery, and Romance*, 18, 40. This idealized image, says Cawelti, arises from the different sort of identification that formulaic literature creates, compared to mimetic literature (18). One result of this idealized identification, according to Cawelti, is that the adventure hero can be either exceptional or one of us, a superhero or an ordinary hero (40). In the fugitive slave narrative, he is both. Though Cawelti's argument focuses on fiction, I think it can be reliably extended to adventure stories of all kinds.

56. William C. Spengemann, *The Adventurous Muse: The Poetics of American Fiction, 1789–1900*, 121, 126–27. Spengemann views fiction through the lens of American travel writing; his reading of Tyler's *The Algerine Captive* is consistent in many ways with my reading of the fugitive slave narrative genre.

Jay Fliegelman ties the popularity of the English *Robinson Crusoe* in the United States to the way that Defoe's novel "offered the American public a theologically and hence politically acceptable model for filial disobedience, a justifiable assertion of independence" (*Prodigals and Pilgrims: The American Revolution Against Patriarchal Authority, 1750–1800*, 76).

57. Cawelti, *Adventure, Mystery, and Romance*, 34; Green, *The Great American Adventure*, 221, 219.

In keeping with the masculinism of adventure stories, the slave narrator-hero is almost always male. So too with fugitive slave narrators—but it should be noted that most fugitive slaves were men. (Men escaped slavery more often because women were frequently tied to the responsibilities of childrearing.) Similarly, most American adventure tales—with notable exceptions (such as Catherine M. Sedgwick's *Hope Leslie* [1827] and E.D.E.N. Southworth's *The Hidden Hand* [serialized 1859])—were written by men for a male audience. Green describes the adventure experience as the "sacramental ceremony of the cult of manhood" (*The Great American Adventure*, 6). This association was particularly crucial for the fugitive slave narrator, whose manhood was feared by whites and denied in various ways ranging from literal castration (mainly an eighteenth-century practice) and other mutilations to the convoluted logic of the discourses of racial science and proslavery literature, which held the slave to be an eternal child. (I will discuss these positions more fully in chapter 4.)

58. Green, *The Great American Adventure*, 5.

59. The full title of Walker's 1829 pamphlet was *David Walker's Appeal to the Coloured Citizens of the World, but in particular, and very expressly, to those of the United States of America*.

60. Sterling Stuckey, *Slave Culture: Nationalist Theory and the Foundations of Black America*, 137.

61. Bruno Bettelheim, *The Informed Heart: Autonomy in a Mass Age*, 258–59. Bettelheim's source for this incident is Eugen Kogon's *Der SS-Staat* (Frankfurt, 1946).

62. I will be considering collective uprisings in more detail next chapter. For collated accounts of individual resistance see, for example, Eugene Genovese, *Roll, Jordan, Roll* (613–21), John Blassingame, *The Slave Community* (211–14), and, focusing on women, Deborah Gray White, "Female Slaves in the Plantation South," in Edward D. C. Campbell, Jr., and Kym S. Rice, eds. *Before Freedom Came*, 101–21 (esp. 110–11). The single richest source of such incidents is surely Helen T. Catterall's multivolume redaction of Southern court cases on slavery and the Negro.

63. Oakes, *Slavery and Freedom*, 151. Oakes sees each act of slave rebellion as an attack on the epistemological foundations of an unsound legal system, a system already in a state of tension between the rights of the master and the regulatory power of the state.

64. John Thompson, *The Life of John Thompson, a Fugitive Slave, Containing His History of Twenty-five Years in Bondage and His Providential Escape, Written by Himself*, 54; Solomon Northup, *Twelve Years a Slave*, ed. Sue Eakin and Joseph Logsdon, 80 (future citations will appear parenthetically in the text); William Wells Brown, *Clotel, or The President's Daughter*, in William L. Andrews, ed., *Three Classic African-American Novels*, 158–59 (future citations will appear parenthetically in the text).

In an example of a slaveowner's retaliation, Thompson tells of how his sister rejects her master's advances and is whipped "until the blood stood in puddles under her feet" (32). Charles Ball and J. D. Green also cite instances of severe retaliation to slaves' resistance (see Charles Nichols, *Many Thousands Gone: The Ex-Slaves' Account of Their Bondage and Freedom*, 36). For a useful account of female resistance, see Deborah Gray White, *Ar'n't I a Woman?*, ch. 2.

65. Hegel, *The Philosophy of History*, 99.

66. William Craft, *Running a Thousand Miles for Freedom*, in Arna Bontemps, *Great Slave Narratives: Selected and Introduced by Arna Bontemps*, 301.

Frederick Douglass complained that when slave narrators advertised their specific methods of escape, they deprived others of the chance to follow in their footsteps. This accusation may have been just, but it discounts the propaganda value of the narratives to the abolitionist cause. Though Douglass omitted all details of his own escape from his 1845 narrative, he supplied the missing information ten years later in *My Bondage and My Freedom*. Robert Stepto ties Douglass's refusal to discuss his escape in the *Narrative* to a strategy of narrative control that results in his self-creation as an orator at the end (*From Behind the Veil: A Study of Afro-American Narrative*, 25).

67. Harriet Beecher Stowe and William Wells Brown wrote lightly fictionalized accounts of the Crafts' well-known deception into their novels, *Uncle Tom's Cabin* and *Clotel*. Both books appeared more than five years before William Craft's slave narrative. Brown's account resembles Craft's especially closely, raising the possibility that in writing his autobiography Craft may have drawn on a fictional version of himself.

68. Brown, *Narrative*, 65. Future citations will appear parenthetically in the text.

69. Jacob Stroyer, *My Life in the South* (1885), quoted in Rose, *A Documentary History*, 401–405; quotation at 403. Stroyer's childhood memories are analyzed by Rose (*Slavery and Freedom*), Blassingame (*The Slave Community*), and Charles Joyner ("The World of Plantation Slaves," in Campbell and Rice, eds., *Before Freedom Came*), among others.

Also worth noting are George Tucker's early abolitionist writings, where he describes how a typical slave boy one day realizes that he's a slave and is whipped into accepting the fact (quoted in Jean Fagan Yellin, *The Intricate Knot: Black Figures in American Literature, 1776–1863*, 21–22). Tucker went on to become a strong advocate of slavery.

70. Rose, *Slavery and Freedom*, 38–39. John Blassingame says that slaves learned from their parents to conform and resist selectively, and to fight masters and overseers to protect relatives (*The Slave Community*, 98–102).

71. William Douglas O'Connor, *Harrington*, 9. Future citations will appear parenthetically in the text.

72. Albert Memmi argues that "in every dominated man, there is a certain degree of *self-rejection*, born mostly of his downcast condition and exclusion" (*Dominated Man: Notes Toward a Portrait*, 86). One might say that "internal objectification" is a result of these despairing feelings overpowering any sense of hope in the slave.

73. Another brief example of internal objectification is that of Henry Bibb, who, after he has run away and been apprehended, is prepared for the torture that will be his punishment: "My arms were bound with a cord, *my spirit broken*, and my little family standing by weeping" (*Narrative of the Life and Adventures of Henry Bibb, an American Slave, Written by Himself*, 131; emphasis added). Bibb is whipped and paddled, collared, and sent back to work in despair. Unlike Douglass, Bibb tells of no dramatic emotional rebound; after a while, he simply recovers his desire to escape and tries again.

Solomon Northup describes how he was "compelled" to whip a fellow slave named Patsey, part of a punishment that permanently changes her. "From that time forward," he says, "she was not what she had been" (*Twelve Years a Slave*, 199).

This example falls into a slightly different category, however, because Patsey is given no voice to describe her own state of mind.

74. Many historians have analyzed the unexpectedly cohesive power of the slave family. Herbert Gutman's study, *The Black Family in Slavery and Freedom, 1750–1925*, is the pioneering source that has shaped research in the field. See also, for example, Leslie Howard Owens, *This Species of Property: Slave Life and Culture in the Old South*, 182–213; Genovese, *Roll, Jordan Roll* (482–534); Blassingame, *The Slave Community* (77–103); and Oakes, *Slavery and Freedom* (145–51).

75. Bibb, *Narrative*, 38. Future citations will appear parenthetically in the text.

76. Stephen Symonds Foster, *The Brotherhood of Thieves, or A True Picture of the American Church and Clergy* (1843; quoted by Foster, *Witnessing Slavery*, 131).

77. Kenneth M. Stampp points to an additional tragic irony of this practice: that it generally worked. Stampp says that the slaves cooperated because of the rewards offered, coupled with the fact that "large families meant no increased responsibilities and, if anything, less toil rather than more" (*The Peculiar Institution*, 248).

78. Frances E. W. Harper, *Iola Leroy, or Shadows Uplifted*, 27.

79. Harriet Jacobs, *Incidents in the Life of a Slave Girl*, ed. Jean Fagan Yellin, 44.

80. Gates, *Figures in Black*, 92.

81. For an insightful discussion of the many conventions of the slave narrative genre, see James T. Olney, "'I Was Born': Slave Narratives, Their Status as Autobiography and as Literature," in Davis and Gates, eds., *The Slave's Narrative*, 148–75. My reading of Brown's opening lines is partially indebted to William Andrews's analysis (*To Tell a Free Story*, 27–28).

82. Andrews, *To Tell a Free Story*, 63.

83. See Abdul JanMohamed, "Humanism and Minority Literature: Towards a Definition of Counter-Hegemonic Discourse," *Boundary 2*, 12, no. 3–13, no. 1 (1984); and Abdul JanMohamed, *Manichean Aesthetics*.

84. Bhabha, "Signs Taken for Wonders," in Gates, ed., *"Race," Writing, and Difference*, 172.

85. Fanon, *Black Skin, White Masks*, 42.

86. The phrase is Benita Parry's ("Problems in Current Theories of Colonial Discourse," *Oxford Literary Review* 9, nos. 1–2 [1987]: 28).

87. Green, *The Great American Adventure*, 67.

88. Austin Steward, *Twenty-two Years a Slave, and Forty Years a Freeman; Embracing a Correspondence of Several Years While President of Wilberforce Colony, London, Canada West*, 86; Frederick Douglass, *The Heroic Slave*, in *Three Classic African-American Novels*, ed. William L. Andrews, 67; Harriet Wilson, *Our Nig; Or, Sketches from the Life of a Free Black*, 105.

In *Hard Facts: Setting and Form in the American Novel*, Philip Fisher argues persuasively that in the case of *Uncle Tom's Cabin*, the structure of the sentimental novel keys the extension of human status to the slaves (see ch. 2, "Making a Thing into a Man: The Sentimental Novel and Slavery," esp. 100–101).

89. The generic pattern of the freak show pamphlet that has been anatomized by Robert Bogdan: the history of the freak (including "capture" or in the case of American oddities, birth and development) is followed by a "scientific" or "medical" explanation of "its" condition, endorsements of authenticity, and in the case of exotics, a description of the native land (*Freak Show*, 19–20).

90. My summary here is informed by Bernth Lindfors, "Circus Africans," *Journal of American Culture* 6, no. 2 (1983): 9–14, and Bogdan, *Freak Show*, ch. 7. ("Racial freak" is my own term.)

91. The Chicago World's Fair of 1933–34 featured a "Darkest Africa" exhibit that was "Presented by Buck, Who Brings 'Em Back Alive" (quoted in Bogdan, *Freak Show*, 195).

92. The managers of freaks often posed for photographs with their exhibits (whom they often had legal title to), with the body language suggesting a sense of possession, and of Hegelian master-slave linkage, for the manager has nothing to manage without "his" freak (cf. Bogdan, *Freak Show*, 13, 198).

93. Bogdan, *Freak Show*, vii.

94. Green, *The Great American Adventure*, 4.

95. Brown quotes a fragment of a poem to this effect after seeing his mother for the last time:

> "— — the glory of my life,
> My blessing and my pride!
> I half forgot the name of slave,
> When she was by my side."
> —*Narrative* (56)

96. Andrews, *To Tell a Free Story*, 105. Gayatri Chakravorty Spivak maintains that "no perspective *critical* of imperialism can turn the Other into a self" ("Three Women's Texts and a Critique of Imperialism," in Gates, ed., *"Race," Writing, and Difference*, 272), but as the foregoing should make clear, I have a lot of trouble with this generalization. The outlines of the Hegelian master-slave relation militate against it, of course, but judging by the uneasiness of the encounter with the grotesque (brought into being by the attempt to objectify), it further seems to me that Spivak underestimates the difficulty experienced by the dominant side of managing its unruly creation. The slave narrator takes advantage of this difficulty to gain a voice and take rhetorical control of the encounter.

97. Ann Kibbey, "Language in Slavery: Frederick Douglass's *Narrative*," *Prospects* 8 (1983): 171, 169.

98. I am defining the term *resistance* politically (in terms of rejecting an ideology imposed from outside), rather than psychoanalytically (where it refers to the psychological forces opposing the conscious desire to change), though as various critics have shown, these two apparently opposing meanings actually do intersect. See Lennard Davis, *Resisting Novels: Ideology and Fiction*, 12–13.

99. Edward Said, *Culture and Imperialism*, 216. Said cites two other major themes of the literature of resistance: the reappropriation of history to restore a national language and culture, and the establishment of an integrative view of community (ibid., 215–16). The latter does not really emerge in American writing until the African-American literature of Reconstruction and beyond.

100. Said, *Culture and Imperialism*, 269. Spivak rejects the conflation of imperialism and racism (Spivak, "Strategies of Vigilance: An Interview with Gayatri Chakravorty Spivak," interview by Angela McRobbie, *Block* 10 [1985]: 7, quoted

by Parry, "Problems in Current Theories of Colonial Discourse," 52). There is obvious historical truth to Spivak's assertion of difference, but the philosophical—one might say epistemic—basis of both practices is the same: human objectification. It is on this basis that I consider them together.

101. See Angela McRobbie's interview with Spivak, in which she rejects binary oppositions as a way of representing the colonial relationship ("Strategies of Vigilance." 9, quoted by Parry, "Problems in Current Theories of Colonial Discourse," 28). This model also implicitly opposes Abdul JanMohamed's argument that the other can create from the colonial struggle a discourse that will be independent of the colonizer's original attempt to objectify.

The battle over Fanon's legacy (in which Spivak and JanMohamed are among the major contestants) centers on interpreting the highly complex, shifting relationship between the colonizer and the colonized in his work—in effect, to determine the nature of the otherness that exists in the relation between them. For a useful overview of the arguments, see Henry Louis Gates, Jr., "Critical Fanonism," and Parry, "Problems in Current Theories of Colonial Discourse."

102. Bhabha, "Signs Taken for Wonders," 169.

103. Carla L. Peterson points to a paradox of the slave narrator's liberation: the authors wind up reobjectifying themselves as commodities, selling their lives for titillation of the audience in exchange for money in the capitalist system ("Capitalism, Black (Under)development, and the Production of the African-American Novel in the 1850s," *American Literary History* 4 [1992]: 562). Fiction, Peterson says, was an option that partly insulated the black author from this commodification. One possible rebuttal to Peterson's argument is Andrews's insistence that slave narratives exist as a dialogic enterprise, always assuming a relationship with a reader that is more than pecuniary (*To Tell a Free Story*, 17–18).

104. The grotesque is foremost a visual effect; the pictures are a frank message in that medium. For more on the convention of including photographs in slave narratives, see Olney's article in Davis and Gates, eds., *The Slave's Narrative* (155).

105. Andrews, *To Tell a Free Story*, 9.

FOUR: *Sambo Agonistes*

1. *Uncle Tom's Cabin* stimulated plantation fiction's period of greatest concentrated activity, as apologists for slavery rushed to answer Stowe with their own versions of plantation life. Thomas F. Gossett counts twenty-seven novels between 1852 and 1861 that responded to Stowe's book to greater or lesser degree. Virtually all were proslavery, even the handful written by Northerners (*Uncle Tom's Cabin and American Culture*, 430). See, for example, Mary H. Eastman's *Aunt Phillis' Cabin* (1852), or John Page's *Uncle Robin in His Cabin in Virginia and Tom Without One in Boston* (1853).

Ironically, the success of Stowe's novel prompted William Gilmore Simms, himself a prolific proslavery novelist and Southern man of letters, to inveigh against using fiction as a means of social criticism (quoted in Gossett, *Uncle Tom*, 195).

2. Patterson, *Slavery and Social Death*, 96. In *Proslavery: A History of the Defense of Slavery in America*, Larry E. Tise convincingly qualifies the uniqueness of the "positive good" thesis (about which more below) to America, but it still must be allowed that American slaveholders expended more effort defending this position than their counterparts from other countries. For a persuasive argument in favor of this latter position, see Oakes, *Slavery and Freedom*, 29–31.

3. Bhabha, "Of Mimicry," in *The Location of Culture*, 90, 92. Also see Bhabha's "The Other Question: Stereotype, Discrimination, and the Discourse of Colonialism," in the same volume. In his poststructuralist psychoanalytic reading of the intermingling of "pleasure/unpleasure, mastery/defence, knowledge/disavowal" within the context of the colonial encounter, Bhabha sees racial stereotype as the result of a fetish (an "arrested, fixated form of representation" [75]). His reading bears clear relevance to the larger focus of this book on the complications attendant upon the creation of a person/thing. In particular, Bhabha's analysis of stereotyping as "an ambivalent text of projection and introjection, metaphoric and metonymic strategies, displacement, overdetermination, guilt, aggressivity, [and] the splitting of 'official' and phantasmatic knowledges" (82) reflects in broad terms the specific argument that I will elaborate on the masked complexities of Sambo.

4. Elkins, *Slavery: A Problem in American Institutional and Intellectual Life*, 82. The critical controversy over Elkins's work centers on just how deterministic is his historical conjecture that Sambo behavior is a consequence of the slave's situation. Most prominent historians of the period have entered this long-running debate. See, for example, Eugene Genovese, *In Red and Black*, 73–101; George Fredrickson, *The Arrogance of Race: Historical Perspectives on Slavery, Racism, and Social Inequality*, 206–15; and John Blassingame, *The Slave Community*, 184–216, to name three major disputants. This continuing argument aims at establishing the historical reality of slave behavior. I have a different project in mind, an analysis of Sambo as his master created him, a construct informed in no small part by the literary imagination. For a similar analysis of the female slave stereotype of Mammy, see White, *Ar'n't I a Woman?*, ch. 1.

5. Joseph Boskin, *Sambo: The Rise and Demise of an American Jester*, 13.

6. Boskin, *Sambo*, 13. Carla Peterson says that the characters in *Clotel* subvert the Sambo stereotype by appearing to conform to it while they make fun of the white characters ("Capitalism," 570). My analysis of Brown's novel throughout this chapter supports and expands this contention.

7. Boskin traces the earliest appearances of the happy slave stereotype, the Sambo name, and their gradual union during the late eighteenth and early nineteenth centuries (*Sambo*, 33–39, 97). The stereotype enjoyed a resurgence after the Civil War, with its popularity peaking during the period 1880–1920.

8. Porter, *Seeing and Being*, 232. Michael Paul Rogin, one of Porter's sources, analyzes the link between paternalism and Indian removal in *Fathers and Children: Andrew Jackson and the Subjugation of the American Indian*, showing how Jackson first portrayed the Indians as "children of nature," and then cast whites as their father figures, acting for their good (see chs. 4, 6, and 7, esp. pp. 113–25, 188–93, 206–12).

9. Genovese, *The World the Slaveholders Made*, 149. Oakes discusses slaveowners'

guilt in *The Ruling Race*, 105–22, esp. 117–20, and in *Slavery and Freedom*, 21–22. Other historians have explicitly connected Sambo to white guilt. See, for example, Ronald Takaki, *Iron Cages: Race and Culture in Nineteenth-Century America*, 120–21, and Boskin, *Sambo*, 63.

10. That Sambo could embody essentially contradictory qualities (docile/mischievous, loyal/lazy, etc.) is a consequence of the construction of the stereotype according to the logic of the master's needs, not the slave's reality (cf. Memmi, *The Colonizer and the Colonized*, 83).

Thomas P. Riggio argues that Southern Reconstruction fiction (by Joel Chandler Harris, Thomas Nelson Page, and others) marked a postwar attempt by Southern writers to justify the ways of the Old South to the Northern reader and so attempt reconciliation ("*Uncle Tom* Reconstructed: A Neglected Chapter in the History of the Book," *American Quarterly* 28 [1976]: 59). I am suggesting that antebellum proslavery fiction pretends to do the same thing.

11. Indeed, Caroline Lee Hentz, a prolific proslavery storyteller, has the heroine of *Robert Graham* (1855) describe the Southern scenery as "a second edition of the garden of Eden, only revised and improved" (quoted in Herbert Ross Brown, *The Sentimental Novel in America*, 251). For a useful survey of the plantation tradition and beyond, see Sterling Allen Brown's *The Negro in American Fiction*. Reconstruction fiction took a more nostalgic, folkloric approach, glorifying the lost slavery past and praising its agricultural remnants.

12. Davis, *The Problem of Slavery in Western Culture*, 213. Charles Nahl's 1867 painting, *Sacramento Indian with Dogs*, illustrates this kind of rhetorical co-optation perfectly. The Indian is a household servant; he is pictured dressed in his Sunday best in a group portrait of all of the household "pets."

13. See Oakes, *Slavery and Freedom*, 131.

14. See Jordan, *White Over Black*, 388–89, and Tise, *Proslavery*, 116. Tise argues broadly for the consistency of proslavery ideology over time in America, and also elsewhere. The shift to morally based justifications for slavery did not, says Tise, result in any new justifications for slavery, but rather in a difference in emphasis (*Proslavery*, 122).

15. A third set of arguments—outside my focus—centered on comparative political economy, based on the idea that slave society was the best possible social organization, given the demographic and geographic realities of the South. Proslavery forces also marshaled religious arguments (as did abolitionists), but these are hard to separate from other social arguments. For a quantitative survey of these and other proslavery positions, see Tise, *Proslavery*, ch. 5.

16. Taylor, *Cavalier and Yankee*, quotations at 299, 304. Frederickson, *Black Image*, quotation at 58. Fredrickson says that these assumptions derive in part from the widely held view of the Negro as a slave to emotion rather than the master of his reason (*Black Image*, 101)—a dichotomy that recalls the Puritans' similar view of Indians.

17. See, for example, Tise, *Proslavery*, 244–45. Arguments on the basis of positive good led logically to the incredible proposition that the British laborers should be enslaved for their own good. Such antidemocratic ideals occupy a central position in Eugene D. Genovese's argument that Southern culture was dom-

inated by an inherently undemocratic master class whose motivations may be understood in the context of their opposition to market capitalism. Fitzhugh's thought has paradigmatic importance in Genovese's scheme. See especially *The World the Slaveholders Made*.

18. Fitzhugh viewed slaves as infantiles whose enslavement was an essential part of his distinctive brand of socialism. Slavery, Fitzhugh argued, protected slaves from economic competition for which they were ill-suited. The cannibals of his title are not the slaves, in fact, but capitalists who consume without producing. For analysis of Fitzhugh's later racism, see Fredrickson, *Black Image*, 69–70, Genovese, *The World the Slaveholders Made*, 235–39, and Oakes, *Slavery and Freedom*, 132.

19. See Fredrickson, *Black Image*, ch. 2 (esp. pp. 47, 55, 60, 68). Fredrickson traces the beginning of the biological-social dichotomy to Thomas R. Dew's *Review of the Debate in the Virginia Legislature of 1831 and 1832*, an important essay widely regarded as having turned proslavery activity into a sustained movement in America. Though Tise has demonstrated that there was little that was new in Dew's thought (*Proslavery*, 70–73), the influence of his work is beyond dispute.

20. See Gould, *The Mismeasure of Man*, 70–71.

21. See Horsman, *Race and Manifest Destiny*, esp. chs. 7 and 8, and Gould, *The Mismeasure of Man*, ch. 2. Though Darwin did not publish *The Origin of Species* until 1859, evolutionary thought was familiar and popular during the decades before his dramatic introduction of his theory of natural selection, and these ideas, frequently intertwined with religious dogma, informed much early racial science. (Because natural selection, with its lack of teleology, did not meet with universal acceptance, racial science continued more or less unabated after Darwin, albeit with some new vocabulary.) Horsman focuses on phrenology and Gould on craniometry as roots of polygenesis.

22. Rose, *Slavery and Freedom*, 25.

23. Fredrickson, *The Arrogance of Race*, 212.

24. Schoolcraft, *The Black Gauntlet*, quotation at 218–19. Mrs. Schoolcraft uses her narrative in large part as a framework to support a huge mass of proslavery argument, satire, citation, and anecdotes. The undiscriminating and frequently contradictory quality of her views is evident throughout, especially the unacknowledged opposition between biological and social black inferiority arguments (e.g., vii, 52, 112, 213, 241, 408–11, 472, 503–504, 523–24). Mrs. Schoolcraft also has her say on Indians (e.g., 494–95).

25. The best-known expression of this specious sentiment in Southern fiction is William Gilmore Simms's oft-quoted depiction in *The Yemassee* of the slave Hector's long, impassioned refusal to accept manumission from his master: "You make Hector free, . . . he git drunk and lie in de ditch," etc. (391–92).

26. Taylor, *Cavalier and Yankee*, quotations at 302, 303, 304.

27. John Pendleton Kennedy, *Swallow Barn; Or, A Sojourn in the Old Dominion*, introduced by Lucinda H. MacKethan, 450. Future citations will appear parenthetically in the text.

28. Kennedy makes this observation in the preface to the original 1832 edition of *Swallow Barn* (xxxviii). Though his use of the word "grotesque" here (and also

elsewhere in the book) draws mainly on its early artistic connotations of strange ornamentation, those etymological roots also carry the disturbing sense of bizarreness and liminality that characterizes modern usage of the word.

29. Another ideologically charged description of an animal is Frank Meriwether's panegyric to the horse, whose self-sacrifice and loyalty to his master constitute "moral virtues" (*Swallow Barn*, 437–39).

30. Among the numerous references to monkeys, see, for example, 138, 308–309, 327, 446. Kennedy represents other animals in slave description as well. Carey, an elderly slave, is described in canine terms (37), while children are compared to ducks (309). The young slave Beelzebub receives the epithet of "goblin" (118). Jean Fagan Yellin offers a useful catalogue of such animal references in *The Intricate Knot* (56).

31. J. V. Ridgely draws the contradictory treatment of slavery in *Swallow Barn* into a larger web of oppositions in the book, between past and present, and provinciality and progress (*Nineteenth-Century Southern Literature*, 41–42).

32. Porter, *Seeing and Being*, 231–32.

33. For an overview of romantic racialism, see Fredrickson, *Black Image*, 102–103. Fredrickson attributes the rise of romantic racialism in the 1830s to a number of Northern intellectuals, including William Ellery Channing, Charles Stuart, and Alexander Kinmont (who Fredrickson suggests was Stowe's main intellectual source [110]; see also Gossett, *Uncle Tom's Cabin and American Culture* [83–84]). Fredrickson identifies the 1840s as when the notion of racial difference took hold in the North. See also James McPherson, who discusses abolitionist racism in *The Struggle for Equality: Abolitionists and the Negro in the Civil War and Reconstruction* (see esp. 143–53). Fredrickson disagrees with McPherson's conclusion that racial equality ultimately wins out against racialism in the abolitionist community (*Black Image*, 127). According to Ronald Takaki, the link between blacks and children (and beneath that benign image, the savage) was widespread within the North as well as the South because it buttressed the Northern market ideology (*Iron Cages*, 116).

34. Objectification certainly fueled the abolitionist lecture circuit. For example, Frederick Douglass writes of being introduced as "a '*chattel*'—a '*thing*'—a piece of southern '*property*'—the chairman assuring the audience that *it* could speak" (*My Bondage and My Freedom*, 360).

35. Sarah Josepha (Buell) Hale, *Northwood; Or, Life North and South*. Hale originally wrote *Northwood* in 1827, subtitling it *A Tale of New England*. She revised the novel in 1852, adding new material and giving it a new subtitle, *Life North and South*. My reading is based on this latter version. All page references are to this edition and are given parenthetically in the text.

36. Sarah Josepha (Buell) Hale, *Liberia; Or, Mr. Peyton's Experiments*, 67.

37. Frances Anne Kemble, *Journal of a Residence on a Georgian Plantation in 1838–1839*, 96–97. Future citations will appear parenthetically in the text.

38. Fredrickson and McPherson both note a similarly dialogic novel, Mary Lowell Putnam's anonymously published *Record of an Obscure Man* (1861), which (as Fredrickson observes) paternalistically argues for the "degradation" of the slaves even while calling for their freedom (see *Black Image*, 127–29; *The Struggle for Equality*, 140–41).

39. See Thomas Graham, "Harriet Beecher Stowe and the Question of Race," in Elizabeth Ammons, ed., *Critical Essays on Harriet Beecher Stowe*, 129. Though Graham generally defends Stowe against charges of racism, he does allow that her thinking was based on "the undefined but firmly held impression that each race had distinguishing 'peculiarities' which she attributed to differences in 'nervous constitution,'" but that this impression did not lead to any resolution: "the Negro remained an enigma to her" (129–130; quotations from Stowe's *A Key to Uncle Tom's Cabin*). A more thorough analysis along the same general lines may be found in Gossett's *Uncle Tom's Cabin and American Culture* (64–86). Gossett notes that Stowe consistently ascribed the most sinful, evil human traits to environmental factors; in this respect her racialism had a benign aspect, at least for her own time (70).

40. Harriet Beecher Stowe, *Uncle Tom's Cabin, or Life Among the Lowly*, ch. 43, p. 462. Future citations refer to the edition listed in the bibliography and will be given parenthetically in the text by chapter and page.

41. Stowe also has Harris describe the Haitian "race" in opposition to the African one as "worn-out" and "effeminate" (43:460). William Gilmore Simms attacked Stowe's conceptions of race and intelligence in his review of *Uncle Tom's Cabin*, arguing that if George's intelligence comes from whites, that hardly amounts to an argument for freeing him, or other slaves (*Southern Quarterly Review* 24 [1853], quoted by Richard Yarborough in Eric Sundquist, ed., *New Essays on "Uncle Tom's Cabin,"* 59). Even so, Stowe's convictions put her largely in step with her contemporaries. Even William Wells Brown was capable of making the statement that "the negro, constitutionally, is fond of dress and outward appearance" (*Clotel*, 194). (Though it should also be said that Brown argued seven years later for Negro superiority on the grounds of the descent of the race from ancient civilizations, as quoted in McPherson, *The Struggle for Equality*, 139.)

Stowe also wrote in her *Handbook* that the white European race is more beautiful than the black African one. "The Indians at St. Augustine," her newspaper account of her 1877 visit to Indian reservations in Florida, further confirms her beliefs about the differences among races. She wrote of her pleasure in seeing the way that the "uncivilized" Indians were being given the ways of whites.

42. Sundquist, ed., *New Essays*, 32.

43. Letter, *The Liberator*, June 3, 1853, p. 87, quoted in Richard Yarborough, "Strategies of Characterization in *Uncle Tom's Cabin* and the Early Afro-American Novel," in Sundquist, ed., *New Essays*, 68.

44. Yarborough, "Strategies of Characterization," 48.

45. Wells, *Island of Dr. Moreau*, 85. One also recalls Flannery O'Connor's story, "The Artificial Nigger," in which young Nelson, who had grown up in rural Southern isolation without ever seeing a Negro, passes right over his "first nigger" with no reaction (Flannery O'Connor, *The Complete Stories* [New York: Farrar Straus and Giroux, 1971], 255). He overlooks the man because, in looking for black creatures (as he had been taught to do by his uncle), all he had seen was a person with "tan" skin.

46. Peterson, "Capitalism," 573. For postwar black response to negative depictions of blacks, see, for example, Frances Harper's *Iola Leroy* (1892) and Pauline Hopkins's *Contending Forces* (1899), both recently reissued.

47. Sigmund Freud, *Jokes and Their Relation to the Unconscious*, trans. James Strachey, 196–201.

48. Boskin, *Sambo*, 14.

49. Boskin, *Sambo*, 54, 38. Boskin's first quotation is drawn from Thomas R. R. Cobb's 1858 defense of slavery (see ch. 3, n. 6, of the present volume).

50. Boskin, *Sambo*, 63.

51. Lott, *Love and Theft*; this redaction is mainly drawn from chs. 2, 5, and 6 (see esp. pp. 59–61).

52. Critics have compared this scene to the degrading "Battle Royal" in Ralph Ellison's *Invisible Man*. See, for example, Jean Fagan Yellin, *The Intricate Knot* (57), and Lucinda MacKethan (introduction to *Swallow Barn*, xxiv).

53. Boskin says that in addition to assuaging guilt, the Sambo stereotype "assumed a centripetal energy of its own," which resulted in slaveowners humoring their slaves (63). As the following pages make clear, I disagree with this interpretation and argue instead that it was no accident, that the image of the slave as performing comic enforced the master's authority in fundamental ways.

Boskin also notes that slave performance was not limited to singing and dancing, but extended to sport and other contests of all kinds, such as drinking (52), a practice reflected in the fiction, such as the race scene in *Swallow Barn*.

54. For a discussion of slave resistance to assuming the role of laborer in the master's interest, see Blassingame, *The Slave Community* (148, 150ff.).

55. Douglass, *Life and Times*, 147–48.

56. Fanon, *Black Skin, White Masks*, 212.

57. Yarborough, "Strategies of Characterization," 47.

58. Bhabha, "Of Mimicry," in *The Location of Culture*, quotations at 86, 89.

59. Also worth noting is Douglass's implicit critique of performance in *My Bondage and My Freedom*, where he contrasts the slavebreaker Covey's devious, serpentlike behavior (for example, pretending to leave and then circling back to make sure that his slaves continued to work [215]) with his own honest directness (when Covey asks Douglass whether he means to continue resisting, the slave looks his master in the eye and replies "a polite '*yes sir*'" [243]). Douglass's attack on performance is consistent with his factual analysis of slavery in his autobiography; Stowe's novelistic treatment of the issue is more ironic.

60. Fredrickson, *The Arrogance of Race*, 215.

61. According to Freud's essay on the subject, the uncanny—Freud's German word was "unheimlich," which translates more closely to "unfamiliar"—results from the return of repressed fear. The familiar ("heimlich," or "homelike") evolves toward the unheimlich through the injection of mystery, something hidden which creates ambivalence. See "The Uncanny," trans. Alix Strachey, in *An Infantile Neurosis and Other Works, SE* 17: 217–52.

62. Edgar Allan Poe, *The Complete Tales and Poems of Edgar Allan Poe*, 56.

63. Poe, *Complete Tales and Poems*, 161 (Poe's emphasis). For an account of Poe's newspaper sources for this tale, see Richard Kopley, *Edgar Allan Poe and the Philadelphia Saturday News*.

64. *The Narrative of Arthur Gordon Pym*, in Poe, *Complete Tales and Poems*, 849, 854. Future citations will appear parenthetically in the text.

65. Even abolitionists split the slave's nature in their arguments. See, for example, the epigraph quotation by James Freeman Clarke, published in 1846 (quoted in Foster, *Witnessing Slavery*, 67).

66. According to Willie Lee Rose, the size and reach of the Vesey conspiracy "imparted fears that were never entirely allayed in South Carolina" (*A Documentary History*, 116). For a thorough documentation of white fear of slave uprising, see Herbert Aptheker, *American Negro Slave Revolts*, 18–52. I omit specific numbers here because the definition of "revolt" is open to debate. Aptheker's definition is inclusive (it includes conspiracies, for example), so his tally is high. For a more restrained overview of the subject, see Genovese, *Roll, Jordan, Roll*, 587–97; quotation at 594.

67. Genovese, *In Red and Black*, 94–95. Writing some years before Genovese, Albert Memmi puts forth a more general version of this idea in *Dominated Man*, 7–15.

68. See Blassingame, *The Slave Community*, 139ff. Blassingame identifies three types of slave behavior—not only Sambo the willing slave but also Nat the rebel, and, in between them, Jack the sullen, pragmatic opportunist.

69. Remarks of James McDowell and Henry Berry in the Virginia House of Delegates, quoted in Russel B. Nye, *Fettered Freedom: Civil Liberties and the Slavery Controversy, 1830–1860*, 24. In an interesting echo of this phrase on the Northern side of the divide, William Lloyd Garrison described slavery in 1829 as "a gangrene preying upon our vitals" ("Address to the American Colonization Society," July 4, 1829, quoted in William Cain, ed., *William Lloyd Garrison and the Fight Against Slavery: Selections from "The Liberator,"* 62).

70. See Sundquist, *To Wake the Nations*, 42.

71. For historians' discussions of how the Sambo stereotype masks fear of slave rebellion, see Fredrickson, *Arrogance of Race*, 212–13, and Takaki, *Iron Cages*, 120–21.

72. Sundquist, *To Wake the Nations*, 50. Homi Bhabha locates this ambivalence in what he calls "hybridity," a difference achieved by the "strategic reversal of the process of domination through disavowal" ("Signs Taken for Wonders," 173). This definition fits Nat Turner's actions very well. Hybridity, says Bhabha, is based on doubleness (what he calls a "metonymy of presence"), an unconscious splitting of the colonial object during representation. On the other hand, the grotesque (as I have defined it) draws its disturbing power from a sense of incompleteness, the failure of an object to fit completely into a category defined by collective experience. Accordingly, the slaveowners' struggle to represent Nat Turner reflects an anxiety over his failure to conform to the category boundaries of a system whose unsoundness they naturally sensed but were unwilling to admit.

73. Thomas Dew, "Abolition of Negro Slavery" (1832); reprinted in Drew Gilpin Faust, ed., *The Ideology of Slavery: Proslavery Thought in the Antebellum South, 1830–1860*, quotation at 68; Sundquist, *To Wake the Nations*, 52. Russel B. Nye documents numerous instances where Southerners attributed real or imagined slave rebellions to "the vile emissaries of abolition, working like moles underground" (*Fettered Freedom*, 25).

74. Leslie Fiedler supplies this information in *Freaks: Myths and Images of the Secret Self*, 20.

75. Gray describes Turner's band in language that recalls Mary Rowlandson's encounter with the Indians: he calls them "monsters," "fiends," "ruthless sav-

ages," a "ferocious . . . diabolical . . . band of murderers" ("The Confessions of Nat Turner," reprinted in Herbert Aptheker, *Nat Turner's Slave Rebellion*, quotations at 148–49, 129–30). Thomas Dew warned that to allow the Negro to exercise his passion unimpeded by reason "would be to raise up a creature resembling the splendid fiction of a modern romance." As Aptheker points out, this is a portrait of a monster (2).

76. Dew, "Abolition of Negro Slavery," in Faust, ed., *The Ideology of Slavery*, 59. Sundquist makes this point in *To Wake the Nations*, 35.

77. Taylor, *Cavalier and Yankee*, 304. Willie Lee Rose makes a similar argument minus its literary component; she says that fear of slave rebellion stimulated the creation of the real-life version of the paternalistic system in the nineteenth century (*Slavery and Freedom*, esp. 26–27).

78. For a good example of the white stereotype of such "scamps," see Schoolcraft's *The Black Gauntlet* (41–42).

79. Eric Sundquist closely analyzes the figure of Nat Turner as rebel, arguing that he is an Africanized messiah figure whose rhetoric is infused with American revolutionary ideals (*To Wake the Nations*, 36–83). Brown's *Clotel* is the first of many African-American novels to cite the Constitution and the Declaration in support of abolition (168, 263).

80. For more detailed analysis of Delany's ideas, see Sundquist, *To Wake the Nations*, 192–95, and Robert S. Levine, "*Uncle Tom's Cabin* in *Frederick Douglass' Paper*: An Analysis of Reception," *American Literature* 64 (1992): 71–93.

81. Douglass, *The Heroic Slave*, 69. Future citations will appear parenthetically in the text.

82. See chapter 1, n. 6. Though I have concentrated on a cultural view of the grotesque in this book, I do not reject the fear and laughter thesis, but rather have sought to qualify it with the important caveat that humor and fear have strong cultural determinants.

83. Orlando Patterson's reconfiguration of the Hegelian metaphor as a one-sided parasitism (master depending on slave, but believing the opposite) is very valuable here as a means of understanding the master's anxiety over his own identity, as Eric Sundquist shows (see Patterson, *Slavery and Social Death*, 334–42; Sundquist, *To Wake the Nations*, 40–42). Sidney Mintz and Richard Price anticipated Patterson's model of dependence in their recently reprinted 1973 analysis of the formation of African-American culture (*Birth of African-American Culture*, 27). My own position—not history but a literary interpretation of writings about slavery by blacks and whites—falls closer to the master-slave interdependence originally put forward by Hegel and adapted to the American slave community by Genovese, but with the added emphasis on the threat of violence (both immediate and distant) as a motivation for both sides.

FIVE: *The Racial Freak, the Happy Slave, and the Problems of Melville's Universal Men*

1. Charter of the United Nations, preamble (June 1945); David Halberstam, *October 1964*, 221–22.

2. Charles R. Anderson was the first to compare Tommo's account in *Typee* with the known facts surrounding Melville's stay in the Marquesas. The many discrepancies "expose" *Typee* as a fiction and not a factual travel narrative, the latter being a label that Melville actually encouraged (Anderson, *Melville in the South Seas*). For a useful summary of the major differences between Melville's life and his fictional retelling of it, see George Woodcock's introduction to the Penguin edition of the novel (Herman Melville, *Typee*, 7–27).

3. Lindfors, "Circus Africans," 10. Bogdan argues that the presentation of racial freaks served to justify slavery (*Freak Show*, 187) and helped to sustain inequality after the war (197). This is true as far as it goes, but it also rather simplifies the cultural work of the freak show. The freak show, like the minstrel show, is a site of racial conflict, not of resolution. It represented fears and anxieties at a time when the ideology of inequality tried to sustain itself against powerful social and political forces that threatened to erode it.

4. This also provides a good example of the way that blackness acts as an invisible shaping force behind whiteness, a process noted by Toni Morrison in *Playing in the Dark*.

5. See T. Walter Herbert, *Marquesan Encounters: Melville and the Meaning of Civilization*, esp. ch. 3. In contrast to Tommo, Herbert shows how deeply the Christian missionaries to the Marquesan islands feared equating their own beliefs with those of the islanders. When one's view of the world is as unbending as theirs was, great stress can lead to a literal breakdown. Not surprisingly, the Marquesan missionaries suffered from their encounter with cultural difference much the way the Puritans did in their attempt to fight off the humanity of the Indians. Disunification of the missionaries' grand schemes of order undermined their whole world and created a real danger of madness for more than one of them.

6. This "classic period" extends, in Rosaldo's view, from 1921 to 1971 (*Culture and Truth*, 48). This period ends when anthropologists lose their faith in the "innocence of the detached observer" (67).

7. See Carl N. Degler, *In Search of Human Nature: The Decline and Revival of Darwinism in American Social Thought*, sec. 2.

8. Herman Melville, *Typee*, ed. Harrison Hayford, Hershel Parker, and G. Thomas Tanselle, ch. 1, p. 3. Future citations will be given parenthetically within the text, by chapter and page number.

9. A brief note en passant: the narrator uses the word *grotesque* five times in the text. A quick examination of these instances reveals that Melville does not appear to have assigned the word any specific meaning. Once the word is applied to the ornate style of a native's tattoos (11:78), though it is also used later on to indicate the horrifying appearance that these tattoos give Kory-Kory (18:134). On another occasion Tommo uses it as a synonym for *comical*, with bizarre overtones (12:96). Finally, he uses it twice to describe logs, one of which is carved into a human form and is now decaying (24:178), while the other is a naturally occurring tree limb which appears to have legs (15:115). This melange of old and new usage suggests that Melville treated the word *grotesque* unsystematically.

10. Mitchell Breitwieser describes Tommo's ultimately unsuccessful resistance as "imaginative imperialism," where his vacillation between seeing the

Typees as happy primitives and menacing savages marks his failure to control his cultural distance from them ("False Sympathy in Melville's *Typee*," *American Quarterly* 34 [1982]: 396–417; quotation at 398). As will become clear, I share Breitwieser's skepticism about Tommo's anthropological abilities.

11. Herbert does an excellent job of exposing the meaning hidden behind the narrator's rhetoric in *Typee*, but he is less convincing in his treatment of the narrator himself. Commenting upon Tommo's remark, "How often is the term 'savages' incorrectly applied" (*Typee*, 4:131), Herbert argues that, "Melville has not broken out of the conceptual framework whose validity he is implicitly challenging. He points out that the term 'savages' is *incorrectly applied*, suggesting that it may have some proper applications among primitive people (though none has been discovered)" (*Marquesan Encounters*, 173). The implied author of this statement, Herbert concludes, is someone who can himself pass judgment upon civilization (*Marquesan Encounters*, 154).

This is acute close reading, but it also reveals a weakness in Herbert's approach that shows up frequently in his analysis of *Typee*: he treats Melville and his narrator as though they were the same person. Though the novel is highly autobiographical, Melville and Tommo are emphatically different. Melville always maintains a distance from his narrators, creating an additional perspective from which we may view them and the world they describe. *Typee* is no exception.

12. Edgar Dryden has noted Tommo's tendency to do this (*Melville's Thematics of Form: The Great Art of Telling the Truth*, 45); the outcome of his Typee encounter exposes this perceptive practice for what it is: an example of what Tzevetan Todorov calls "the experience of alterity . . . grounded in egocentrism" (*Conquest of America*, 42).

13. Other critics have noted Tommo's refusal to be tattooed. Milton R. Stern links the issue to the opposition between "mind and mindlessness" in the book, noting that the facial tattoos hide the eyes and mouth, the "agents of communication and understanding" (*The Fine Hammered Steel of Herman Melville*, 59). Bryan C. Short says that Tommo must remain tattoo-free in order to preserve "the unspecified nature of his identity," a key to Short's reading of the novel (*Cast by Means of Figures: Herman Melville's Rhetorical Development*, 32).

14. John Evelev precedes me to this point in his interesting biographical reading of *Typee*. His focus on Tommo's threatened tattooing and potential freak status centers on the "conflict between Melville's romantic rejection of an objectifying mode of literary representation"—represented in the novel by Tommo's refusal to be written on by Karky—and Melville's "desire to find a place and succeed within that same system," as illustrated by his real-life willingness to make various changes necessary to sell his book and make a name for himself ("'Made in the Marquesas': *Typee*, Tattooing, and Melville's Critique of the Literary Marketplace," *Arizona Quarterly* 48, no. 4 [1992]: 21).

15. Racial freaks (whom I will be discussing below) were exhibited the same way, but what was "normal" for them (clothing, food, cultural practices) was not seen that way by their audience—which was, of course, the point.

16. Fiedler, *Freaks*, 24.

17. Bogdan, *Freak Show*, 29, 32, 40, 288*n*12. Much of the following historical summary is drawn from this excellent book.

18. Herman Melville, "Authentic Anecdotes of 'Old Zack,'" *The Piazza Tales and Other Prose Pieces, 1839–1860*, ed. Harrison Hayford, Alma A. MacDougall, G. Thomas Tanselle et al., 215, 218–219, 225. Melville mocks Taylor's heroic reputation by imagining Barnum making entreaties to display in his museum a tack from the general's saddle, his pants, and finally Taylor himself. Barnum promises that Taylor would enjoy treatment commensurate with that accorded Tom Thumb.

19. Bogdan, *Freak Show*, 241. Evelev draws a more specific parallel between Melville's time in New York and the museum appearances there by James O'Connell, the first tattooed white man to display himself in the United States ("'Made in the Marquesas,'" 29–30). O'Connell's career is briefly summarized below.

20. Bogdan, *Freak Show*, 242.

21. Pratt, *Imperial Eyes*, 86–88. As I noted in chapter 3, fugitive slave narratives are of course a form of survival literature as well.

22. O'Connell exhibited himself at circuses and museums (including Barnum's) from at least the mid-1830s until his death (probably in the mid-1850s). Saul H. Riesenberg carefully documents O'Connell's life in "The Tattooed Irishman" (*Smithsonian Journal of History* 3 [1968]: 1–17), an examination that exposes many inconsistencies in O'Connell's own account, and from which my own summary is largely drawn. For a brief overview of O'Connell's career, see Bogdan, *Freak Show*, 242–43.

23. Bogdan, *Freak Show*, 243–46, 250–51.

24. In noting this ambivalence, Evelev places it within the context of Melville's conflicted view of fame, financial success, and the capitalist market system that defined and housed these goals ("'Made in the Marquesas,'" 26, 35).

25. This implication becomes explicitly clear in *Tattoo* (Joseph E. Levine, 1980; written by Joyce Bunuel; directed by Bob Brooks), a kinky film thriller in which Bruce Dern plays a sexually obsessed tattoo artist who kidnaps and tattoos the woman he is fixated on.

26. The popularity of tattooed women effectively drove tattooed men out of the freak show business (Bogdan, *Freak Show*, 251–52), and Carol J. Clover's gender-based analysis of horror movies offers a clue as to why. Clover argues that the protagonist of slasher horror films is invariably female—Clover calls her the "Final Girl"—because her gender enables the (predominantly male) audience for such movies to identify with her fear and anxiety through a socially acceptable (i.e., female) receptacle for those emotions (see *Men, Women, and Chain Saws: Gender and the Modern Horror Film*, ch. 2). In other words, the Final Girl refracts male fear through a female character because it's considered "acceptable" for women to scream and cry. It's possible that the tattooed woman deflected male fears (and desires?) in the same way.

27. I am indebted to Rosemarie Garland Thomson's description from her *Extraordinary Bodies* of the way that the freak generally embodies a lack of will. Breitwieser suggests that tattooing creates powerlessness because one is written on rather than writing ("False Sympathy," 412).

28. For a description of the narrative conventions of a freak show pamphlet, see Bogdan, *Freak Show*, 19.

29. Bogdan, *Freak Show*, 161.

30. Ibid., 178, 106. The scenery backing the displays of racial freaks got more involved as the practice became more popular over time.

31. Peggy Reeves Sanday, *Divine Hunger: Cannibalism as a Cultural System*, 3. Ritual cannibalism has been reliably documented in nineteenth-century Fiji, a South Seas island society that neighbored Typee. See Sanday, *Divine Hunger*, 151–68; and Marshall Sahlins, "Raw Women, Cooked Men, and Other 'Great Things' of the Fiji Islands," in Paula Brown and Donald Tuzin, eds., *The Ethnography of Cannibalism*, 72–93.

32. For a discussion of the sensational aspects of South Seas cannibalism in nineteenth-century America, see Gavan Daws, *A Dream of Islands: Voyages of Self-Discovery in the South Seas*, 18–19. For a brief account of Barnum's exploitation of "cannibals," see Bogdan, *Freak Show*, 178–79.

33. Sara Castro-Klaren, "What Does Cannibalism Speak? Jean de Lery and the Tupinamba Lesson," in Pamela Bacarisse, ed., *Carnal Knowledge: Essays on the Flesh, Sex and Sexuality in Hispanic Letters and Film*, 28. As a way of showing how the categorization of cannibalism so often becomes self-referential, Castro-Klaren facetiously describes French explorer Jean de Lery's view of the Brazilian natives: "The Tupi are ferocious warriors because they eat human flesh and they eat human flesh because (despite appearances) they are ferocious warriors who wage war in order to eat human flesh rather than conquer other people's lands or possessions" ("What Does Cannibalism Speak," 32).

For further examples and discussion of the way that European explorers equate difference with cannibalism and savagery in order to construct a rationale for the imperialistic practice, see Stephen Greenblatt, *Marvelous Possessions: The Wonder of the New World*, 71–72, 134–36.

34. Sanday, *Divine Hunger*, xi.

35. Breitwieser argues this point very effectively. He says that Tommo's romantic rebellion comes "from the same root" as imperialism; in this way, he is "both anti-American and typically American" ("False Sympathy," 398, 401). While Breitwieser focuses on the way that Tommo uses the Typees as a foil against which to define his own relationship to America, my emphasis—a more psychological one—is on the construction of race as the basis for the narrator's national identity. I would therefore suggest that this retroactive nostalgia is a defense against the disorientation caused by the grotesque that Tommo felt while in Typee society.

36. John R. Clark identifies cannibalism as a major locus of the grotesque, tying our discomfort at the ritual to "our unconscious sense of our own roots, our own origins" (*The Modern Satiric Grotesque and Its Traditions*, 132). However, this analysis does not account for the differing American and Typee reactions to the practice. Richard V. Chase offers a Freudian reading of Melville's text, tying Tommo's anxiety to a fear of castration (*Herman Melville: A Critical Study*, 12).

37. W. Arens argues that recorded documentation of cannibalism is entirely based on "rumors, suspicions, fears and accusations," and ought to be approached very skeptically for this reason (*The Man-Eating Myth: Anthropology and*

Anthropophagy, 21). Though Sanday may be correct in her assessment that Arens overstates his case (*Divine Hunger*, 9–10), his argument has the merit of spotlighting the irrational response that cannibalism generates in the Western mind, and the power that the idea has displayed over the years to allure and unbalance even the most judicious anthropologists.

38. Bogdan, *Freak Show*, 241–43, and Gould, *The Mismeasure of Man*, 123–43, esp. 129.

39. See Horsman, *Race and Manifest Destiny*, esp. chs. 7 and 8; and Gould, *The Mismeasure of Man*, ch. 2. The early "sciences" of phrenology and craniometry overlapped conceptually with "teratology," or the study of monsters, an early approach to the taxonomy of freaks whose American use is documented by Bogdan. Bogdan observes that while nineteenth-century science supported and justified the freak show, twentieth-century science has undermined it by medicalizing its "human monsters" (*Freak Show*, 27, 67, and passim). For more on nineteenth-century racial science, see chapter 4 of this study.

40. Stephen Greenblatt compares this experience of wonder to "ravishment, ... an overpowering intensity of response [to] ... something amazing" (*Marvelous Possessions*, 16). He calls it "a primary or radical passion ... that precedes, even escapes, moral categories" (17, 20). "When we wonder," says Greenblatt, "we do not yet know if we should love or hate the object at which we are marveling; we do not know if we should embrace it or flee from it" (20). The idea that freak narratives pair pathology and wonder is drawn from Rosemarie Garland Thomson's *Extraordinary Bodies*.

41. See Samuel Otter, *Melville's Anatomies* (forthcoming, University of California Press). Otter's emphasis on the Marquesan context for tattooing and race in *Typee* usefully complements my own focus on the American scene.

42. Robert S. Levine has noted the analogy that Melville makes between the sailor and the slave. See *Conspiracy and Romance: Studies in Brockden Brown, Cooper, Hawthorne, and Melville*, ch. 4.

43. For a brief discussion of some of these possible causes, see Bogdan, *Freak Show*, 10; I am mainly drawing on a more sustained discussion in Rosemarie Garland Thomson's *Extraordinary Bodies*.

44. Eric Lott has shown in *Love and Theft* how blackface minstrelsy reflects the racial anxieties of the Northern working class before the Civil War; my thesis is similar, focusing on a different cultural practice.

45. For speculation on the decline of freak shows, see Bogdan, *Freak Show*, 62–68 and passim, and Fiedler, *Freaks*, 16. Dolores Mitchell has shown how white women became the subjects of iconographic slavery fantasies after slavery was abolished, with some of the more popular themes centering on Orientalist imagery and Circassian beauties, the latter a freak show staple ("Images of Exotic Women in Turn-of-the-Century Tobacco Art," *Feminist Studies* 18, no. 2 [Summer 1992]: 327–50). Given the nexus I suggested earlier linking tattooing, rape, and freak status—and the link I am also making between tattooing and "blackness"—it is no surprise to see women standing in for blacks in this postemancipation cultural equation.

46. Susan Stewart calls this "the pornography of distance," founded upon a triangular relationship among viewer, the object being viewed, and the mediator

guiding the encounter (*On Longing: Narratives of the Miniature, the Gigantic, the Souvenir, the Collection*, 110).

47. For analysis of the anthropological practice, see, for example, the work of James Clifford, Michael M. J. Fischer, Renato Rosaldo, and Clifford Geertz.

48. Herbert, *Marquesan Encounters*, esp. 149–91. See discussion of Herbert's treatment of the narrator in *Typee* at n. 11, above.

49. Most historians of abolitionism share Louis Filler's view that the shift from reform to politics was "inevitable" (*Crusade Against Slavery: Friends, Foes, and Reforms, 1820–1860* [Algonac, Mich.: Reference Publications, 1986], 172; revised reprint of *The Crusade Against Slavery* [New York: Harper and Row, 1960]). Dwight Lowell Dumond argues that direct political action rechanneled much of the abolitionist energy previously devoted to moral reform, but the parallel growth of both political and social abolitionism from the late 1830s onward would suggest that new blood was infusing both sides of the movement (Dumond, *Antislavery Origins of the Civil War in the United States*, 87–88). Richard H. Sewell provides the most sustained analysis of this aspect of the antislavery movement in *Ballots for Freedom*, arguing that reform and politics were contiguous parts of an ideological whole, informing each other from the beginning; the rise of politics thus stands as a visible manifestation of an interest that had existed all along.

50. For a demographic profile of the abolitionist movement, see Edward Magdol, *The Antislavery Rank and File*. By the 1840s the auxiliaries of the American Antislavery Society were the collective repository of the movement's power, with this decentralization serving to avoid policy differences at the national level (Russel B. Nye, *William Lloyd Garrison and the Humanitarian Reformers*, 129–31). Louis Filler estimates that by 1835 the American Antislavery Society had 328 auxiliary societies. By 1838 the number had gone up to about 1,350 with an estimated 250,000 members (Filler, *Crusade Against Slavery*, 87). These and other estimates were drawn in part from tallies from within the movement, with these originating with James Birney, the Liberty Party presidential candidate; Birney's estimate of total membership at that time—which was never officially added up—was on the low end of the scale at 120,000. William Lloyd Garrison estimated that 1,200 antislavery societies were in existence by 1837; New York alone had 274 of them. See Herbert Aptheker, *Abolitionism: A Revolutionary Movement*, 56.

51. Nye, *William Lloyd Garrison and the Humanitarian Reformers*, 100.

52. Nye, *Fettered Freedom*, 94. Plantation fiction entered its most fecund period in the wake of the popularity of *Uncle Tom's Cabin*, when dozens of proslavery writers moved to "refute" Stowe. This reaction illustrates the way that the opposing sides in the slavery debate fed off each other.

53. Garrison, "Address to the American Colonization Society," July 4, 1829, quoted in Cain, ed., *William Lloyd Garrison and the Fight Against Slavery*, 65. Garrison called from the beginning for equal privileges for blacks, including immediate enfranchisement. This prospect horrified not only Southerners but also many from the North—for not everyone who opposed slavery believed in black equality (see *The Liberator*, December 14, 1833, quoted in Cain, ed., ibid., 92).

54. See McPherson, *The Struggle for Equality*, 81–90. Though early Union defeats set back the cause somewhat from 1861 to 1863, it revived during the last two years of the war (127).

55. Lott, *Love and Theft*, 4, 5. Not surprisingly, minstrelsy enjoyed its greatest popularity during the period 1846–1854 (9), coeval with the heyday of abolitionism and Southern plantation fiction—and with *Typee*. "For a time in the late 1840s," says Lott, "minstrelsy came to seem the most representative national art" (8).

56. Melville's persistent and ironic comparison of the Typee valley to Eden (e.g., Tommo and Toby "fall" into it and straightaway devour a rotted piece of fruit) has been taken up by numerous critics. Reading *Typee* in terms of the deviance from the biblical fall hinted at in the allusive narration has in fact generated the bulk of the critical literature on the book. The idea of Typee as Eden originates with D. H. Lawrence in his *Studies in Classic American Literature*, 134–40; for some representative modern examples, see Lawrance Thompson, "Eden Revisited," and Richard Ruland, "Melville and the Fortunate Fall: *Typee* as Eden," both reprinted in Milton Stern, ed., *Critical Essays on Herman Melville's "Typee."* Also, Toni H. Oliviero ties the Edenic imagery to the book's central paradox: that Tommo and Toby are trapped in paradise ("Ambiguous Utopia: Savagery and Civilization in *Typee* and *Omoo*," *Modern Language Studies* 13 [1983]: 39–46). In the present context, such comparisons show Melville commenting on the large amount of cultural baggage that the narrator brings with him to this new culture.

57. Among recent critics of *Typee*, John Samson comes to the similar conclusion that Melville's cultural criticism reaches "to the roots" of ideology, undermining the "lies" that white culture uses to justify its behavior, and subversively rewriting original historical sources in a way that shows the "absurdity," "lack of meaning," and "racism" in the white encounter with the Marquesans (*White Lies: Melville's Narratives of Facts*, 11–12, 53, 56).

58. In *Mardi*, for example, Melville treats slavery directly in a brief allegorical scene (ch. 162, "They visit the extreme South of Vivenza"). Though Melville acknowledges here that the politics of the situation are complicated, the tone of the passage is strongly antislavery. "The 'Gees," a short piece written just before *Benito Cereno*, treats the question satirically. In *Shadow Over the Promised Land: Slavery, Race, and Violence in Melville's America*, Carolyn Karcher argues that the piece is a stylistic parody of the scientific arguments for black inferiority (see ch. 6, "A Stranger Need Have a Sharp Eye to Know a 'Gee: A Riposte to Scientific Racism").

Melville's continually broadening scope of inquiry culminates in the cosmic sweep of *Moby-Dick*. If *Typee* seeks to go beyond the limits of culture, then *Moby-Dick* extends the attempt even further to try to grasp the widest possible perspective: he creates a character who wants to transcend everything.

59. Herman Melville, *Moby-Dick, or The Whale* (Indianapolis: Bobbs-Merrill, 1964), ch. 3, p. 51. All subsequent references are to this edition and will be given parenthetically, by chapter and page, in the text.

There has been some critical debate over the years about whether Queequeg is an American Negro or not. Carolyn Karcher says that the character is a "composite . . . created to undermine racial categories" (*Shadow Over the Promised Land*, 64–65). (Interestingly, John Huston has a white actor portray him in his film of Melville's novel.)

Much of the following discussion of *Moby-Dick* is informed by Karcher's analysis in *Shadow Over the Promised Land* (65–75), a book that provides a useful overview of race in Melville generally. One point of argument especially needs noting, however: Karcher says that Queequeg teaches "lessons in racial tolerance," as in *Typee*. As is clear from the foregoing, I read *Typee* very differently.

60. Walking the streets of New Bedford in search of an inn, for example, Ishmael enters a black church by mistake and compares it to a vision of hell (2:33).

61. When Queequeg rescues Tashtego from drowning inside the whale's head later on, Ishmael proudly calls him "my brave Queequeg" (78:331).

62. Another allusion to conquest of the problems faced in *Typee* comes in "A Bower in the Arsacides" (ch. 102), when Ishmael gets a tattoo (though on his arm and not his face). This time the effect is comic, a sign that the problem is mastered, at least in this case.

63. *Alien Nation*, the 1988 movie and subsequent television series, offers an interesting current treatment of this theme. The alien "newcomers" to earth receive the same kind of racist treatment formerly reserved for human minorities. The strange appearance of the aliens outweighs their exceptional intelligence and ability—and thereby highlights the grotesque roots of the material.

64. The suggestion that Ishmael and Queequeg are married actually comes up earlier. When the two swear a pact of friendship while in New Bedford, Queequeg says that "henceforth we were married, meaning, in his country's phrase, that we were bosom friends" (10:84). When they go to bed later, Ishmael describes them as "a cosy, loving pair" on "our hearts' honeymoon" (10:86).

65. Herbert, *Marquesan Encounters*, 15, 125.

66. See Levine, *Conspiracy and Romance*, 203.

67. Nelson, *The Word in Black and White*, 129.

68. Decapitation of conspirators followed by public display of their heads was a fairly common warning to would-be slave rebels. Many of Nat Turner's slave allies, for example, had their severed heads displayed on pikes by their white executioners. Orinooko, leader of a seventeenth-century slave revolt in Suriname, experienced a more extreme fate than Babo's; he was tied to a stake and dismembered alive by the order of a Governors' Council that wanted to make an example of him. Fittingly and predictably, this attempted objectification serves only to enhance the humanity of the victim as a heroic martyr, as he is glorified in Aphra Behn's 1688 novel, *Orinooko; Or, The History of the Royal Slave* (for a pertinent commentary on the novel, see Davis, *The Problem of Slavery in Western Culture*, 472–79).

69. For an excellent discussion of Melville's implicating narrative account of Delano's shifting perceptions, see Levine, *Conspiracy and Romance*, 198–223.

70. Herman Melville, *Benito Cereno*, in Warner Berthoff, ed., *Great Short Works of Herman Melville*, 270, 279. All subsequent page references are to this edition and will be given parenthetically in the text.

71. It is of more than passing significance, I think, that Delano consistently assesses the color of those who pass before him as white, black, or mulatto. The category of color is prominent in his perceptive matrix.

72. Harold Beaver uses this passage as evidence of Delano's own limited intelligence, observing that he is unable to draw a conclusion from what he sees (introduction to Herman Melville, *Billy Budd, Sailor and Other Stories*, 30).

73. Beaver extends this blindsight to the blacks as well as the whites: "A 'creature' each 'species' remains, to the other an 'it'" (introduction to *Billy Budd, Sailor*, 35). Sandra Zagarell elaborates persuasively on the way that Delano's expectations of people are based on race and, in the case of Cereno, ethnicity ("Reenvisioning America: Melville's 'Benito Cereno,'" *ESQ* 30 (1984): 247).

74. Bhabha, "Of Mimicry," in *The Location of Culture*, 86.

75. Nelson, *The Word in Black and White*, 113–14. Nelson's reading builds on Marvin Fisher's observation that the abundant metaphors that mark Delano's view of the world point to Melville's overall suspicion of perception, and his belief that the process is fraught with uncertainty (*Going Under: Melville's Short Fiction and the American 1850s*, 104–17).

76. Zagarell, "Reenvisioning America," 251.

77. Eric J. Sundquist, "*Benito Cereno* and New World Slavery," in Sacvan Bercovitch, ed., *Reconstructing American Literary History*, 110; Sundquist, *To Wake the Nations*, 153.

78. See Karcher, *Shadow Over the Promised Land*, 136, 133. Karcher sees a suppressed sexual aspect to Delano's paternalism (134).

79. Michael Paul Rogin, *Subversive Genealogy: The Politics and Art of Herman Melville*, 231–35; Zagarell, "Reenvisioning America," 247, 246. Numerous critics have weighed in on this question, with most recent entrants arguing that Melville uses *Benito Cereno* as a vehicle for antislavery sentiments. Karcher makes a strong case for this position in *Shadow Over the Promised Land*. The most influential voice on the other side is probably Sidney Kaplan's "Herman Melville and the American National Sin: The Meaning of 'Benito Cereno,'" *Journal of Negro History* 41 (1957): 11–37, an essay that gained many adherents during the last generation.

80. This follows from Sandra Zagarell's point: "Because they filter out information which could challenge his ideology, Delano's modes of perception keep his faith in the social order intact" (248).

81. Bogdan, *Freak Show*, 187.

82. Bhabha argues that the colonizer's desire for mimicry, for a "difference that is almost the same, but not quite," results from castration (the "subject's lack of priority"), and leads to "a historical crisis in the conceptuality of colonial man . . . as the subject of racial, cultural, national representation" ("Of Mimicry," in *The Location of Culture*, 86, 90). Zagarell notes that because Babo has no basis for independent authority, he can only perpetuate the white way of doing things: "He is completely circumscribed by the slave system." It is thus appropriate that Senegal—where Babo wants to go—is a country where blacks enslave blacks (253).

83. Eric J. Sundquist, "Suspense and Tautology in *Benito Cereno*," *Glyph* 8 (Johns Hopkins Textual Studies; Baltimore: Johns Hopkins University Press, 1981): 124.

84. There has been much insightful commentary linking the events in Melville's story to the American national mission and slavery's complication of it. Lucy Maddox argues that Melville's frequent references to Delano as "the American" show that he wants the character to be understood as a representative figure (*Removals: Nineteenth-Century American Literature and the Politics of Indian Affairs*, 79). Sandra Zagarell earlier links *Benito Cereno* to the emergent doctrine of manifest destiny. This connection builds on Allan Moore Emery's reading of Delano as

cavalier and profiteering ("The Topicality of Depravity in *Benito Cereno*," *American Literature* 55 [1983]: 316–31). Eric Sundquist sees the shipboard masquerade as testing "the limits of America's innocence" in the context of a volatile business conducted in a rapidly changing world ("*Benito Cereno* and New World Slavery," 93).

85. Andrew Delbanco, "Melville in the '80s," *American Literary History* 4 (1992): 723; Herbert, *Marquesan Encounters*, 147; Morrison, "Unspeakable Things Unspoken," 15. Also worthy of note is Lucy Maddox's statement that Melville is able to rise above the Indian politics of his day, that he is the only one to critique the "civilization-or-extinction" argument, even if he can offer only silence in its place (*Removals*, 11–12).

WORKS CITED

Aaron, Henry. *I Had a Hammer*. New York: Harper and Row, 1992.

Anderson, Benedict. *Imagined Communities*. London: Verso and New Left Books, 1983.

Anderson, Charles R. *Melville in the South Seas*. New York: Dover, 1966.

Ammons, Elizabeth, ed. *Critical Essays on Harriet Beecher Stowe*. Boston: G. K. Hall, 1980.

Andrews, William L. *To Tell a Free Story: The First Century of Afro-American Autobiography, 1760–1865*. Urbana: University of Illinois Press, 1986.

Aptheker, Herbert. *Abolitionism: A Revolutionary Movement*. Boston: G. K. Hall, 1989.

——. *American Negro Slave Revolts*. New York: Columbia University Press, 1943.

——. *Nat Turner's Slave Rebellion*. New York: Humanities Press, 1966.

Arens, W. *The Man-Eating Myth: Anthropology and Anthropophagy*. New York: Oxford University Press, 1979.

Aristotle. *Politics*. Translated by Benjamin Jowett. In *The Works of Aristotle*, vol. 10, edited by W. D. Ross. Oxford: Clarendon Press, 1921.

Armstrong, Paul B. "Play and Cultural Differences." *Kenyon Review* 13 (1991): 157–71.

Axtell, James. *The European and the Indian*. New York: Oxford University Press, 1981.

——. *The Invasion Within: The Contest of Cultures in North America*. New York: Oxford University Press, 1985.

Baines, Barbara J. "Ritualized Cannibalism in "Benito Cereno': Melville's 'Black-Letter' Texts." *ESQ* 30 (1894): 163–69.
Baker, Houston. *The Journey Back: Issues in Black Literature and Criticism*. Chicago: University of Chicago Press, 1980.
Bakhtin, Mikhail. *Rabelais and His World*. Translated by Helen Iswolsky. Cambridge, Mass.: MIT Press, 1968.
Baldwin, James. *The Price of the Ticket: Collected Nonfiction, 1948–1985*. New York: St. Martin's/Marek, 1985.
Beaver, Harold. "Introduction." In Herman Melville, *Billy Budd, Sailor and Other Stories*, 9–50. New York: Penguin, 1970.
Beer, Gillian. "Problems of Description in the Language of Discovery." In George Levine, with the assistance of Alan Rauch, *One Culture: Essays in Science and Literature*, 35–58. Madison: University of Wisconsin Press, 1987.
Bentley, Nancy. "White Slaves: The Mulatto Hero in Antebellum Fiction." *American Literature* 65 (1993): 501–22.
Berkhofer, Jr., Robert F. *The White Man's Indian: Images of the Indian from Columbus to the Present*. New York: Knopf, 1978.
Bettelheim, Bruno. *The Informed Heart: Autonomy in a Mass Age*. New York: Free Press, 1960.
Bhabha, Homi K. *The Location of Culture*. New York: Routledge: 1994.
——. "Signs Taken for Wonders: Questions of Ambivalence and Authority Under a Tree Outside Delhi, May 1817." In Henry Louis Gates, Jr., ed., *"Race," Writing, and Difference*, 163–84. Chicago: University of Chicago Press, 1986.
Bhabha, Homi K., ed. *Nation and Narration*. London and New York: Routledge, 1990.
Bibb, Henry. *Narrative of the Life and Adventures of Henry Bibb, an American Slave, Written by Himself* (1849). Rpt., Miami: Mnemosyne, 1969.
Blassingame, John. *The Slave Community*. New York: Oxford University Press, 1972.
Bogdan, Robert. *Freak Show: Presenting Human Oddities for Amusement and Profit*. Chicago: University of Chicago Press, 1988.
Bontemps, Arna. *Great Slave Narratives: Selected and Introduced by Arna Bontemps*. Boston: Beacon Press, 1969.
Boskin, Joseph. *Sambo: The Rise and Demise of an American Jester*. New York: Oxford University Press, 1986.
Bowles, Paul. *Collected Stories, 1939–1976*. Santa Rosa: Black Sparrow Press, 1986.
Bradford, William. *Of Plymouth Plantation*. Edited by Samuel Eliot Morrison. New York: Knopf, 1953.
Breitwieser, Mitchell. *American Puritanism and the Defense of Mourning: Religion, Grief, and Ethnology in Mary White Rowlandson's Captivity Narrative*. Madison: University of Wisconsin Press, 1990.
——. "False Sympathy in Melville's *Typee*." *American Quarterly* 34 (1982): 396–417.
Bromell, Nicholas K. *By the Sweat of the Brow: Literature and Labor in Antebellum America*. Chicago: University of Chicago Press, 1993.
Brown, Charles Brockden. *Edgar Huntly* (1799). In S. W. Reid, ed., *Novels and Related Works of Charles Brockden Brown*. Series editor, Sydney J. Krause. Vol. 4. Kent, Ohio: Kent State University Press, 1984.

Brown, Henry Box. *Narrative of the Life of Henry Box Brown, written by himself.* Manchester, Eng.: Lee and Glynn, 1851.

Brown, Herbert Ross. *The Sentimental Novel in America*. Durham, N.C.: Duke University Press, 1940.

Brown, Sterling Allen. *The Negro in American Fiction*. Port Washington, N.Y.: Kennikat Press, 1968.

Brown, William Wells. *Clotel, or The President's Daughter* (1853). In William L. Andrews, ed., *Three Classic African-American Novels*, 71–283. New York: New American Library, 1990 (Mentor paperback).

——. *Narrative of William Wells Brown, a Fugitive Slave* (1847). In Paul Jefferson, ed., *The Travels of William Wells Brown*, 21–70. New York: Markus Wiener, 1991.

Burt, John. "Learning to Write: The Narrative of Frederick Douglass." *Western Humanities Review* 42 (1988): 330–44.

Butterfield, Stephen. *Black Autobiography in America*. Amherst: University of Massachusetts Press, 1974.

Cain, William, ed. *William Lloyd Garrison and the Fight Against Slavery: Selections from "The Liberator."* Boston: St. Martin's, 1995.

Canup, John. *Out of the Wilderness: The Emergence of an American Identity in Colonial New England*. Middletown, Conn.: Wesleyan University Press, 1990.

Carroll, Noel. *The Philosophy of Horror*. New York: Routledge, Chapman, and Hall, 1990.

Carroll, Peter N. *Puritanism and the Wilderness: The Intellectual Significance of the New England Frontier, 1629–1700*. New York: Columbia University Press, 1969.

Cassuto, Leonard. "Jack London's Class-Based Grotesque." In Michael Meyer, ed., *Literature and the Grotesque*, 113–28. Amsterdam and Atlanta: Rodopi, 1995.

——. " '[Un]consciousness Itself Is the Malady': *Edgar Huntly* and the Discourse of the Other." *Modern Language Studies* 23, no. 4 (Fall 1993): 118–30.

Castro-Klaren, Sara. "What Does Cannibalism Speak? Jean de Lery and the Tupinamba Lesson." In Pamela Bacarisse, ed., *Carnal Knowledge: Essays on the Flesh, Sex, and Sexuality in Hispanic Letters and Film*, 23–41. Pittsburgh: Ediciones Tres Rios, 1993.

Catterall, Helen T., ed. *Judicial Cases Concerning American Slavery and the Negro*. Washington, D.C.: Carnegie Institute of Washington, 1929.

Cawelti, John G. *Adventure, Mystery, and Romance: Formula Stories as Art and Popular Culture*. Chicago: University of Chicago Press, 1976.

Chase, Richard V. *Herman Melville: A Critical Study*. New York: Macmillan, 1949.

Clark, John. *The Modern Satiric Grotesque and Its Traditions*. Lexington: University Press of Kentucky, 1991.

Clover, Carol J. *Men, Women, and Chain Saws: Gender and the Modern Horror Film*. Princeton: Princeton University Press, 1992.

Cogley, Richard W. "John Eliot and the Origins of the American Indians." *Early American Literature* 21 (1986–87): 210–25.

Cooper, Barry. *The End of History: An Essay on Modern Hegelianism*. Toronto: University of Toronto Press, 1984.

Daston, Lorraine. "Marvelous Facts and Miraculous Evidence in Early Modern Europe." *Critical Inquiry* 18 (Autumn 1991): 93–124.

Davis, Charles T. and Henry Louis Gates, Jr., eds. *The Slave's Narrative*. New York: Oxford University Press, 1985.

Davis, David Brion. "The Constitution and the Slave Trade." In Allen Weinstein, Frank Otto Gatell, and David Sarasohn, eds., *American Negro Slavery*, 21–32. 3d ed. New York: Oxford University Press, 1979.

——. *The Problem of Slavery in the Age of Revolution, 1770–1823*. Ithaca, N.Y.: Cornell University Press, 1975.

——. *The Problem of Slavery in Western Culture*. Ithaca, N.Y.: Cornell University Press, 1966.

Davis, Lennard. *Resisting Novels: Ideology and Fiction*. New York: Methuen, 1987.

Daws, Gavan. *A Dream of Islands: Voyages of Self-Discovery in the South Seas*. New York: Norton, 1980.

Degler, Carl N. *In Search of Human Nature: The Decline and Revival of Darwinism in American Social Thought*. New York: Oxford University Press, 1991.

——. *Neither Black Nor White: Slavery and Race Relations in Brazil and the United States*. New York: Macmillan, 1971.

Delbanco, Andrew. "Melville in the '80s." *American Literary History* 4 (1992): 709–25.

——. *The Puritan Ordeal*. Cambridge: Harvard University Press, 1989.

Demos, John. *The Unredeemed Captive: A Family Story from Early America*. New York: Knopf, 1994.

Dillard, Annie. *Pilgrim at Tinker Creek*. New York: Harper's Magazine Press, in association with Harper and Row, 1974.

Douglas, Mary. *Purity and Danger: An Analysis of Concepts of Pollution and Taboo*. New York: Praeger, 1966.

Douglass, Frederick. *The Heroic Slave* (1853). In *Three Classic African-American Novels*, 23–69. Edited by William L. Andrews. New York: New American Library, 1990 (Mentor paperback).

——. *Life and Times of Frederick Douglass, Written by Himself* (2d ed., 1892). Rpt., New York: Collier Books, 1962.

——. *My Bondage and My Freedom*. New York and Auburn: Miller, Orton, and Milligan, 1855.

——. *Narrative of the Life of Frederick Douglass, an American Slave, Written by Himself* (1845). Edited by Benjamin Quarles. Cambridge: Harvard University Press, 1960.

——. "What to a Slave Is the Fourth of July?" In John W. Blassingame et al., eds., *The Frederick Douglass Papers, Series One: Speeches, Debates, and Interviews* 2:359–88. New Haven: Yale University Press, 1982.

Dow, George, ed. *Slave Ships and Slaving*. Port Washington, N.Y.: Kennikat Press, 1969.

Dryden, Edgar. *Melville's Thematics of Form: The Great Art of Telling the Truth*. Baltimore: Johns Hopkins University Press, 1968.

Dumond, Dwight Lowell. *Antislavery Origins of the Civil War in the United States*. Ann Arbor: University of Michigan Press, 1959.

Dundes, Alan. *Cracking Jokes*. Berkeley, Calif.: Ten Speed Press, 1987.

Dworkin, Andrea. *Pornography: Men Possessing Women*. New York: Perigee, 1981.

Eastman, Mary H. *Aunt Phillis' Cabin; Or, Southern Life as It Is*. Philadelphia: Lippincott, Grambo, 1852.

Elkins, Stanley M. *Slavery: A Problem in American Institutional and Intellectual Life*. Chicago: University of Chicago Press, 1968.

Emery, Allan Moore. "The Topicality of Depravity in *Benito Cereno*." *American Literature* 55 (1983): 316–31.

Evans-Pritchard, E. E. *Nuer Religion*. New York: Oxford University Press, 1956.

Evelev, John. "'Made in the Marquesas': *Typee*, Tattooing, and Melville's Critique of the Literary Marketplace." *Arizona Quarterly* 48, no. 4 (1992): 19–45.

Fanon, Frantz. *Black Skin, White Masks*. Translated by Charles Lam Markmann. New York: Grove Press, 1967.

——. *The Wretched of the Earth*. Translated by Constance Farrington. Preface by Jean-Paul Sartre. New York: Grove Press, 1968.

Faulkner, William. *Light in August* (1932). New York: Vintage, 1972.

Faust, Drew Gilpin, ed. *The Ideology of Slavery: Proslavery Thought in the Antebellum South, 1830–1860*. Baton Rouge: Louisiana State University Press, 1981.

Fiedler, Leslie. *Freaks: Myths and Images of the Secret Self*. New York: Simon and Schuster, 1978.

Filler, Louis. *Crusade Against Slavery: Friends, Foes, and Reforms, 1820–1860*. Algonac, Mich.: Reference Publications, 1986; rev. reprint of *The Crusade Against Slavery*. New York: Harper and Row, 1960.

Fisher, Marvin. *Going Under: Melville's Short Fiction and the American 1850s*. Baton Rouge: Louisiana State University Press, 1977.

Fisher, Philip. *Hard Facts: Setting and Form in the American Novel*. New York: Oxford University Press, 1985.

Fitzhugh, George. *Cannibals All! or, Slaves Without Masters* (1857). Edited by C. Vann Woodward. Cambridge: Harvard University Press, 1960.

Fitzpatrick, Tara. "The Figure of Captivity: The Cultural Work of the Puritan Captivity Narrative." *American Literary History* 3 (1991): 1–26.

Fliegelman, Jay. *Prodigals and Pilgrims: The American Revolution Against Patriarchal Authority, 1750–1800*. Cambridge: Cambridge University Press, 1982.

Foreman, Ann. *Femininity as Alienation: Women and the Family in Marxism and Psychoanalysis*. London: Pluto Press, 1977.

Foster, Frances Smith. *Witnessing Slavery: The Development of Antebellum Slave Narratives*. Westport, Conn.: Greenwood Press, 1979.

Fox-Genovese, Elizabeth and Eugene D. Genovese. *Fruits of Merchant Capital: Slavery and Bourgeois Property in the Rise and Expansion of Capitalism*. New York: Oxford University Press, 1983.

Fredrickson, George M. *The Arrogance of Race: Historical Perspectives on Slavery, Racism, and Social Inequality*. Middletown, Conn.: Wesleyan University Press, 1988.

——. *The Black Image in the White Mind: The Debate of Afro-American Character and Destiny, 1817–1914*. New York: Harper and Row, 1971.

Freud, Sigmund. "The Antithetical Sense of Primal Words" (1910). Translated by Alan Tyson. In *Five Lectures on Psycho-Analysis, Leonardo da Vinci, and Other Works*, 153-61. Vol. 11 in the *Standard Edition of the Complete Psychological Works* (hereafter, *SE*), translated and edited by James Strachey (except as noted). 23 vols.

(London: Hogarth Press and the Institute of Psycho-Analysis, 1953–1966).
——. *The Future of an Illusion* (1927). Translated by James Strachey. *SE*, vol. 21. New York: Norton, 1961.
——. *Jokes and Their Relation to the Unconscious* (1905). Translated by James Strachey. *SE*, vol. 8. New York: Norton, 1960.
——. *Totem and Taboo*. Translated by James Strachey. New York: Norton, 1955.
——. "The Uncanny" (1919). Translated by Alix Strachey. In *An Infantile Neurosis and Other Works*. *SE* 17:217-52.
Friedman, John Block. *The Monstrous Races in Medieval Art and Thought*. Cambridge: Harvard University Press, 1981.
Gates, Jr., Henry Louis. "Critical Fanonism." *Critical Inquiry* 17 (1991): 457–70.
——. *Figures in Black: Words, Signs, and the "Racial" Self*. New York: Oxford University Press, 1987.
Geertz, Clifford. *The Interpretation of Cultures*. New York: Basic Books, 1973.
Genovese, Eugene D. *In Red and Black: Marxian Explorations in Southern and Afro-American History*. New York: Vantage, 1972.
——. *Roll, Jordan, Roll: The World the Slaves Made*. New York: Pantheon, 1974.
——. *The World the Slaveholders Made: Two Essays in Interpretation*. New York: Pantheon, 1969.
Gibson, Donald B. "Christianity and Individualism: (Re-)Creation and Reality in Frederick Douglass's Representation of Self." *African-American Review* 26 (1992): 591–603.
——. "Reconciling Public and Private in Frederick Douglass's *Narrative*." *American Literature* 57 (1985): 549–69.
Gilroy, Paul. *The Black Atlantic: Modernity and Double Consciousness*. Cambridge: Harvard University Press, 1993.
Girard, René. *Violence and the Sacred*. Translated by Patrick Gregory. Baltimore: Johns Hopkins University Press, 1977.
Goddu, Teresa A. and Craig V. Smith. "Scenes of Writing in Frederick Douglass's *Narrative*: Autobiography and the Creation of Self." *Southern Review* 25 (1989): 822–41.
Gombrich, Ernest. *Art and Illusion: A Study in the Psychology of Pictorial Representation*. 2d ed. Princeton: Princeton University Press, 1969.
Gookin, Daniel. *Historical Account of the Doings and Sufferings of the Christian Indians in New England in the Years 1675, 1676, 1677* (completed 1677, published 1836). Rpt., New York: Arno Press, 1972.
Gossett, Thomas F. *Uncle Tom's Cabin and American Culture*. Dallas: Southern Methodist University Press, 1985.
Gould, Stephen Jay. *The Mismeasure of Man*. New York: Norton, 1981.
Green, Martin. *The Great American Adventure*. Boston: Beacon Press, 1984.
Greenblatt, Stephen. *Marvelous Possessions: The Wonder of the New World*. Chicago: University of Chicago Press, 1991.
Guthrie, Stewart. *Faces in the Clouds: Religion as Anthropomorphism*. New York: Oxford University Press, 1993.
Gutman, Herbert. *The Black Family in Slavery and Freedom, 1750–1925*. New York: Pantheon, 1976.

Halberstam, David. *October 1964*. New York: Random House, 1994.

Hale, Sarah Josepha (Buell). *Liberia; Or, Mr. Peyton's Experiments*. New York: Harper and Bros., 1853.

——. *Northwood; Or, Life North and South* (1827; rev. ed., 1852). Rpt., New York and London: Johnson Reprint, 1970.

Hall, David D. *Worlds of Wonder, Days of Judgment: Popular Religious Belief in Early New England*. New York: Knopf, 1989.

Harper, Frances E. W. *Iola Leroy, or Shadows Uplifted* (1892). Rpt., New York: Oxford University Press, 1988.

Harpham, Geoffrey Galt. *On the Grotesque*. Princeton: Princeton University Press, 1982.

Harris, Thomas. *The Silence of the Lambs*. New York: St. Martin's, 1988.

Hartsock, Nancy. *Money, Sex, and Power*. Boston: Northeastern University Press, 1985.

Hegel, Georg Wilhelm Friedrich. *The Encyclopedia Logic*. Translated by T. F. Geraets, W. A. Suchtins, and H. S. Harris. Indianapolis, Ind.: Hackett, 1991.

——. *Phenomenology of Spirit*. Translated by A. V. Miller. Oxford: Clarendon Press, 1977.

——. *The Philosophy of History*. Translated by J. Sibree. New York: Dover, 1956.

Heimert, Alan and Andrew Delbanco, eds. *The Puritans in America: A Narrative Anthology*. Cambridge: Harvard University Press, 1985.

Hentz, Caroline Lee. *The Planter's Northern Bride*. Philadelphia: A. Hart, 1854.

Herbert, T. Walter. *Marquesan Encounters: Melville and the Meaning of Civilization*. Cambridge: Harvard University Press, 1980.

Horsman, Reginald. *Race and Manifest Destiny: The Origins of American Racial Anglo-Saxonism*. Cambridge: Harvard University Press, 1981.

Huet, Marie-Helene. *Monstrous Imagination*. Cambridge: Harvard University Press, 1993.

Iser, Wolfgang. "Indeterminacy and the Reader's Response in Prose Fiction." In J. Hillis Miller, ed., *Aspects of Narrative*. New York: Columbia University Press, 1971.

Jacobs, Harriet. *Incidents in the Life of a Slave Girl* (1861). Edited by Jean Fagan Yellin. Cambridge: Harvard University Press, 1987.

Jaggar, Alison M. *Feminist Politics and Human Nature*. Totowa, N.J.: Rowman and Allanheld, 1983.

JanMohamed, Abdul. "Humanism and Minority Literature: Towards a Definition of Counter-Hegemonic Discourse." *Boundary 2*, vol. 12, no. 3–vol. 13, no. 1 (1984).

——. *Manichean Aesthetics*. Amherst: University of Massachusetts Press, 1983.

Jennings, Francis. *The Invasion of America: Indians, Colonialism, and the Cant of Conquest*. Chapel Hill: University of North Carolina Press, 1975.

Jordan, Winthrop. *White Over Black: American Attitudes Toward the Negro, 1550–1812*. Chapel Hill: University of North Carolina Press, 1968.

Joyner, Charles. "The World of Plantation Slaves." In Edward D. C. Campbell, Jr., and Kym S. Rice, eds. *Before Freedom Came*, 51–100. Richmond: Museum of the Confederacy and the University Press of Virginia, 1991.

Kaplan, Sidney. "Herman Melville and the American National Sin: The Meaning of 'Benito Cereno.'" *Journal of Negro History* 41 (1957): 11–37.

Karcher, Carolyn L. *Shadow Over the Promised Land: Slavery, Race, and Violence in Melville's America*. Baton Rouge: Louisiana State University Press, 1980.

Kayser, Wolfgang. *The Grotesque in Art and Literature*. Translated by Ulrich Weisstein. Bloomington: Indiana University Press, 1963.

Kemble, Frances Anne. *Journal of a Residence on a Georgian Plantation in 1838–1839* (1864). Rpt., Chicago: Afro-Am Press, 1969.

Kennedy, John Pendleton. *Swallow Barn; Or, A Sojourn in the Old Dominion* (1832; 2d rev. ed., 1851). Introduction by Lucinda H. MacKethan. Baton Rouge: Louisiana State University Press, 1986.

Kibbey, Ann. *The Interpretation of Material Shapes in Puritanism: A Study of Rhetoric, Prejudice, and Violence*. Cambridge: Cambridge University Press, 1986.

——. "Language in Slavery: Frederick Douglass's *Narrative*." *Prospects* 8 (1983): 163–82.

King, Jr., Martin Luther. "Letter from the Birmingham Jail." In David A. Hollinger and Charles Capper, eds., *The American Intellectual Tradition*, vol. 2, *1865 to the Present*, 238–47. New York: Oxford University Press, 1989.

Kocher, Paul H. *Science and Religion in Elizabethan England*. San Marino, Calif.: Huntington Library, 1953.

Kojève, Alexander. *Introduction to the Reading of Hegel: Lectures on "The Phenomenology of the Spirit."* Edited by Allan Bloom. Translated by James Nichols, Jr. Ithaca, N.Y.: Cornell University Press, 1980.

Kopley, Richard. *Edgar Allan Poe and the Philadelphia Saturday News*. Baltimore: Enoch Pratt Free Library, the Edgar Allan Poe Society, and the Library of the University of Baltimore, 1991.

Kristeva, Julia. *Powers of Horror: An Essay on Abjection*. Translated by Leon S. Roudiez. New York: Columbia University Press, 1982.

Laqueur, Thomas. *Making Sex: Bodies and Gender from the Greeks to Freud*. Cambridge: Harvard University Press, 1990.

Lawrence, D. H. *Studies in Classic American Literature* (1923). Rpt., New York: Viking, 1961.

Lepore, Jill. "Dead Men Tell No Tales: John Sassamon and the Fatal Consequences of Literacy." *American Quarterly* 46 (1994): 479–512.

Leverenz, David. "Frederick Douglass's Self-Refashioning." *Criticism* 29 (1987): 341–70.

Levine, Robert S. *Conspiracy and Romance: Studies in Brockden Brown, Cooper, Hawthorne, and Melville*. Cambridge: Cambridge University Press, 1989.

——. "*Uncle Tom's Cabin* in *Frederick Douglass' Paper*: An Analysis of Reception." *American Literature* 64 (1992): 71–93.

Lévi-Strauss, Claude. *The Savage Mind*. Translated by George Weidenfeld. Chicago: University of Chicago Press, 1966.

Lindfors, Bernth. "Circus Africans." *Journal of American Culture* 6, no. 2 (1983): 9–14.

Lott, Eric. *Love and Theft: Blackface Minstrelsy and the American Working Class*. New York: Oxford University Press, 1995.

MacKethan, Lucinda. "From Fugitive Slave to Man of Letters: The Conversion of Frederick Douglass." *Journal of Narrative Technique* 16 (1986): 55–71.

Maddox, Lucy. *Removals: Nineteenth-Century American Literature and the Politics of Indian Affairs*. New York: Oxford University Press, 1991.

Magdol, Edward. *The Antislavery Rank and File: A Profile of the Abolitionists' Constituency*. New York and Westport, Conn.: Greenwood Press, 1986.
Martin, Waldo. *The Mind of Frederick Douglass*. Chapel Hill: University of North Carolina Press, 1984.
Marx, Karl. *Capital*. Translated by Ben Fowkes. New York: Random House, 1977 (Vintage paperback).
——. *Economic and Philosophical Manuscripts of 1844*. In Karl Marx and Frederick Engels, *Collected Works*. Vol. 3. New York: International Publishers, 1965.
Mather, Cotton. *Diary of Cotton Mather*. New York: Frederick Ungar, 1911.
——. *Magnalia Christi Americana* (1702). 2 vols. Rpt., New York: Russell and Russell, 1967.
McKay, Claude. *Selected Poems of Claude McKay*. With a biographical note by Max Eastman. New York: Harcourt, Brace, and World, 1953.
McPherson, James. *The Struggle for Equality: Abolitionists and the Negro in the Civil War and Reconstruction*. Princeton: Princeton University Press, 1964.
McRobbie, Angela. "Strategies of Vigilance: An Interview with Gayatri Chakravorty Spivak." *Block* 10 (1985).
Melville, Herman. "Authentic Anecdotes of 'Old Zack' " (1847). In *The Piazza Tales and Other Prose Pieces, 1839–1860*. Edited by Harrison Hayford, Alma A. MacDougall, G. Thomas Tanselle et al. Evanston and Chicago: Northwestern University Press and the Newberry Library, 1987.
——. *Benito Cereno* (1855). In Warner Berthoff, ed., *Great Short Works of Herman Melville*, 238–315. New York: Harper and Row, 1969.
——. *Moby-Dick, or The Whale* (1851). Indianapolis: Bobbs-Merrill, 1964.
——. *Typee* (1846). Edited by Harrison Hayford, Hershel Parker, and G. Thomas Tanselle. Evanston, Ill.: Northwestern University Press and the Newberry Library, 1968.
Memmi, Albert. *The Colonizer and the Colonized*. New York: Orion Press, 1965.
——. *Dominated Man: Notes Toward a Portrait*. New York: Orion Press, 1968.
Miller, Perry. *Errand into the Wilderness*. Cambridge: Harvard University Press, 1956.
Miller, Perry, ed. *Roger Williams: His Contribution to the American Tradition*. New York: Atheneum, 1962.
Mintz, Sidney and Richard Price. *The Birth of African-American Culture: An Anthropological Approach*. Boston: Beacon Press, 1992.
Mitchell, Dolores. "Images of Exotic Women in Turn-of-the-Century Tobacco Art." *Feminist Studies* 18, no. 2 (Summer 1992): 327–50.
Mitchell, Juliet. *Woman's Estate*. New York: Pantheon, 1971.
Morrison, Toni. *Playing in the Dark: Whiteness and the Literary Imagination*. Cambridge: Harvard University Press, 1992.
——. "Unspeakable Things Unspoken: The Afro-American Presence in American Literature." *Michigan Quarterly Review* 28 (1989): 1–34.
Namias, June. *White Captives: Gender and Ethnicity on the American Frontier*. Chapel Hill: University of North Carolina Press, 1993.
Nelson, Dana. *The Word in Black and White*. New York: Oxford University Press, 1992.
Nichols, Charles. *Many Thousands Gone: The Ex-Slaves' Account of Their Bondage and Freedom*. Leiden, Netherlands: E. J. Brill, 1963.

Northup, Solomon. *Twelve Years a Slave* (1853). Edited by Sue Eakin and Joseph Logsdon. Baton Rouge: Louisiana State University Press, 1968.

Nye, Russel B. *Fettered Freedom: Civil Liberties and the Slavery Controversy, 1830–1860*. East Lansing: Michigan State College Press, 1949.

——. *William Lloyd Garrison and the Humanitarian Reformers*. Boston: Little, Brown, 1955.

Oakes, James. *The Ruling Race*. New York: Knopf, 1982.

——. *Slavery and Freedom: An Interpretation of the Old South*. New York: Knopf, 1990.

O'Connor, William Douglas. *Harrington* (1860). Rpt., New York and London: Johnson Reprint, 1970.

Oliviero, Toni H. "Ambiguous Utopia: Savagery and Civilization in *Typee* and *Omoo*." *Modern Language Studies* 13 (1983): 39–46.

Orwell, George. *Animal Farm*. New York: Harcourt Brace, 1946.

Owens, Leslie Howard. *This Species of Property: Slave Life and Culture in the Old South*. New York: Oxford University Press, 1976.

Park, Katherine and Lorraine J. Daston. "Unnatural Conceptions: The Study of Monsters in Sixteenth- and Seventeenth-Century France and England." *Past and Present* 92 (August 1981): 20–54.

Parry, Benita. "Problems in Current Theories of Colonial Discourse." *Oxford Literary Review* 9, nos. 1–2 (1987): 27–58.

Patterson, Orlando. *Slavery and Social Death: A Comparative Study*. Cambridge: Harvard University Press, 1982.

Peterson, Carla L. "Capitalism, Black (Under)development, and the Production of the African-American Novel in the 1850s." *American Literary History* 4 (1992): 559–83.

Pearce, Roy Harvey. *Savagism and Civilization* (1953). Rpt., Berkeley: University of California Press, 1988.

Piaget, Jean. *The Child's Conception of the World*. London: Routledge and Kegan Paul, 1929.

Plumstead, A. W. *The Wall and the Garden: Selected Massachusetts Election Sermons, 1620–1715*. Minneapolis: University of Minnesota Press, 1968.

Poe, Edgar Allan. *The Complete Tales and Poems of Edgar Allan Poe*. New York: Vintage, 1975.

Porter, Carolyn. *Seeing and Being: The Plight of the Participant Observer in Emerson, James, Adams, and Faulkner*. Middletown, Conn.: Wesleyan University Press, 1981.

Pratt, Mary Louise. *Imperial Eyes: Travel Writing and Transculturation*. London and New York: Routledge, 1992.

Ridgely, J. V. *Nineteenth-Century Southern Literature*. Lexington: University Press of Kentucky, 1980.

Riesenberg, Saul. "The Tattooed Irishman." *Smithsonian Journal of History* 3 (1968): 1–17.

Riggio, Thomas P. "*Uncle Tom* Reconstructed: A Neglected Chapter in the History of the Book." *American Quarterly* 28 (1976): 57–70.

Roediger, David. *The Wages of Whiteness: Race and the Making of the American Working Class*. London and New York: Verso, 1991.

Rogin, Michael Paul. *Fathers and Children: Andrew Jackson and the Subjugation of the American Indian*. New York: Knopf, 1975.

——. *Subversive Genealogy: The Politics and Art of Herman Melville*. New York: Knopf, 1983.
Roper, Moses. *A Narrative of the Adventures and Escape of Moses Roper, from American Slavery* (1838). New York: Negro Universities Press of Greenwood Press, 1970.
Rosaldo, Renato. *Culture and Truth: The Remaking of Social Analysis*. Boston: Beacon Press, 1993.
Rose, Willie Lee. *A Documentary History of Slavery in North America*. New York: Oxford University Press, 1976.
——. *Slavery and Freedom*. Edited by William W. Freehling. New York: Oxford University Press, 1982.
Rowbotham, Sheila. *Woman's Consciousness, Man's World*. Baltimore: Penguin, 1973.
Ruskin, John. "Grotesque Renaissance." In *The Stones of Venice*, 112–65. London: Smith and Elder, 1853.
Ryback, Timothy W. "Evidence of Evil." *New Yorker* 69, no. 38 (November 15, 1993): 68–81.
Sahlins, Marshall. "Raw Women, Cooked Men, and Other 'Great Things' of the Fiji Islands." In Paula Brown and Donald Tuzin, eds., *The Ethnography of Cannibalism*, 72–93. Washington, D.C.: Society for Psychological Anthropology, 1983.
Said, Edward. *Culture and Imperialism*. New York: Knopf, 1993.
——. *Orientalism*. New York: Pantheon, 1978.
Samson, John. *White Lies: Melville's Narratives of Facts*. Ithaca, N.Y.: Cornell University Press, 1989.
Sanday, Peggy R. *Divine Hunger: Cannibalism as a Cultural System*. New York: Cambridge University Press, 1986.
Saxton, Alexander. *The Rise and Fall of the White Republic: Class Politics and Mass Culture in Nineteenth-Century America*. London: Verso, 1990.
Scarry, Elaine. *The Body in Pain*. New York: Oxford University Press, 1985.
Schoolcraft, (Mrs.) Henry R. *The Black Gauntlet: A Tale of Plantation Life in South Carolina* (1860). Rpt., New York: Negro Universities Press, 1969.
Schramer, James and Timothy Sweet. "Violence and the Body Politic in Seventeenth-Century New England." *Arizona Quarterly* 48, no. 2 (1992): 1–32.
Seltzer, Mark. *Bodies and Machines*. New York: Routledge, Chapman, and Hall, 1992.
Sewell, Richard H. *Ballots for Freedom: Antislavery Politics in the United States, 1837–1860*. New York: Oxford University Press, 1976.
Shklar, Judith N. *Freedom and Independence: A Study of the Political Ideas of Hegel's Phenomenology of Mind*. Cambridge and New York: Cambridge University Press, 1976.
Short, Bryan C. *Cast by Means of Figures: Herman Melville's Rhetorical Development*. Amherst: University of Massachusetts Press, 1992.
Shuffelton, Frank T., ed. *A Mixed Race: Ethnicity in Early America*. New York: Oxford University Press, 1993.
Simms, William Gilmore. *The Yemassee* (1835). Rpt., New York and London: Hafner, 1962.
Sinclair, Upton. *The Jungle* (1906). Rpt., Urbana: University of Illinois Press, 1988.
Slotkin, Richard. *Regeneration Through Violence: The Mythology of the American Frontier, 1600–1860*. Middletown, Conn.: Wesleyan University Press, 1973.

Slotkin, Richard and James K. Folsom, eds. *So Dreadfull a Judgment: Puritan Responses to King Philip's War, 1676–1677*. Middletown, Conn.: Wesleyan University Press, 1978.

Smith, Steven B. *Hegel's Critique of Liberalism*. Chicago: University of Chicago Press, 1989.

Snead, James A. "Repetition as a Figure of Black Culture." In Henry Louis Gates, Jr., ed., *Black Literature and Literary Theory*, 58–75. New York: Methuen, 1984.

Sollors, Werner. *Beyond Ethnicity*. New York: Oxford University Press, 1986.

Spengemann, William C. *The Adventurous Muse: The Poetics of American Fiction, 1789–1900*. New Haven: Yale University Press, 1977.

Spivak, Gayatri Chakravorty. "Three Women's Texts and a Critique of Imperialism." In Henry Louis Gates, Jr., ed., *"Race," Writing, and Difference*, 262–80. Chicago: University of Chicago Press, 1986.

Stallybrass, Peter and Allon White. *The Politics and Poetics of Transgression*. Ithaca, N.Y.: Cornell University Press, 1986.

Stampp, Kenneth M. *The Peculiar Institution: Slavery in the Ante-Bellum South*. New York: Knopf, 1956.

Stepto, Robert. *From Behind the Veil: A Study of Afro-American Narrative*. Urbana: University of Illinois Press, 1979.

Stern, Milton R. *The Fine Hammered Steel of Herman Melville*. Urbana: University of Illinois Press, 1968.

Stern, Milton R., ed. *Critical Essays on Herman Melville's "Typee."* Boston: G. K. Hall, 1982.

Steward, Austin. *Twenty-two Years a Slave, and Forty Years a Freeman; Embracing a Correspondence of Several Years While President of Wilberforce Colony, London, Canada West* (1856). Rpt., New York: Negro Universities Press, 1968.

Stewart, Susan. *On Longing: Narratives of the Miniature, the Gigantic, the Souvenir, the Collection*. Baltimore: Johns Hopkins University Press, 1984.

Stowe, Harriet Beecher. *Dred, A Tale of the Great Dismal Swamp, Together with Anti-Slavery Tales and Papers, and Life in Florida After the War* (1856). 2 vols. Rpt., New York: AMS Press, 1967.

——. "The Indians at St. Augustine." *Christian Union*, April 18 and 25, 1877 (part 1 at 345; part 2 at 372).

——. *Uncle Tom's Cabin, or Life Among the Lowly* (1852). Rpt., New York: New American Library, 1981 (Signet paperback).

Stuckey, Sterling. *Slave Culture: Nationalist Theory and the Foundations of Black America*. New York: Oxford University Press, 1987.

Sundquist, Eric. "*Benito Cereno* and New World Slavery." In Sacvan Bercovitch, ed., *Reconstructing American Literary History*, 93–122. Harvard English Studies. Cambridge: Harvard University Press, 1986.

——. "Frederick Douglass: Literacy and Paternalism." *Raritan: A Quarterly Review* 6 (1986): 108–24.

——. "Suspense and Tautology in *Benito Cereno*." *Glyph* 8 (Johns Hopkins Textual Studies; Baltimore: Johns Hopkins University Press, 1981): 103–26.

——. *To Wake the Nations: Race in the Making of American Literature*. Cambridge: Harvard University Press, 1993.

Sundquist, Eric, ed. *New Essays on "Uncle Tom's Cabin."* New York: Cambridge University Press, 1986.

Swift, Jonathan. *Gulliver's Travels* (1726). Rpt., New York: Norton, 1970.

Takaki, Ronald. *Iron Cages: Race and Culture in Nineteenth-Century America*. Seattle: University of Washington Press, 1979.

——. *Violence and the Black Imagination: Essays and Documents*. New York: Putnam, 1972.

Taylor, William R. *Cavalier and Yankee: The Old South and American National Character* (1961). Rpt., Cambridge: Harvard University Press, 1979.

Terkel, Studs. *Race: How Whites and Blacks Think and Feel About the American Obsession*. New York: New Press, 1992.

Thompson, John. *The Life of John Thompson, a Fugitive Slave, Containing His History of Twenty-five Years in Bondage and His Providential Escape, Written by Himself* (1856). Rpt., New York: Negro Universities Press, 1968.

Thomson, Philip. *The Grotesque*. London: Methuen, 1972.

Thomson, Rosemarie Garland. *Extraordinary Bodies: Figuring Physical Disability in American Literature and Culture*. New York: Columbia University Press, 1996.

Tichi, Cecelia. *Shifting Gears: Technology, Literature, and Culture in Modernist America*. Chapel Hill: University of North Carolina Press, 1987.

Tise, Larry E. *Proslavery: A History of the Defense of Slavery in America*. Athens: University of Georgia Press, 1987.

Tocqueville, Alexis de. *Democracy in America*. Edited by J. P. Mayer. Translated by George Lawrence. New York: Doubleday Anchor, 1969.

Todorov, Tzevetan. *The Conquest of America: The Question of the Other*. Translated by Richard Howard. New York: Harper and Row, 1982.

Tompkins, Jane. "'Indians': Textualism, Morality, and the Problem of History." In Henry Louis Gates, Jr., ed., *"Race," Writing, and Difference*, 59–77. Chicago: University of Chicago Press, 1986.

Turner, Victor. *The Ritual Process: Structure and Anti-Structure* (1969). Symbol, Myth, and Ritual Series. Rpt., Ithaca, N.Y.: Cornell University Press, 1977 (paperback).

Vaughan, Alden T. *The New England Frontier: Puritans and Indians*. Boston: Little, Brown, 1965.

Vaughan, Alden T. and Edward W. Clark, eds. *Puritans Among the Indians: Accounts of Captivity and Redemption, 1676–1724*. Cambridge: Belknap Press of Harvard University Press, 1981.

Vaughan, Alden T. and Daniel K. Richter. *Across the Cultural Divide: Indians and New Englanders, 1605–1763*. Worcester: Proceedings of the American Antiquarian Society (no. 90), 1980.

Ward, Samuel Ringgold. *Autobiography of a Fugitive Negro*. New York: Arno Press and the New York Times, 1968.

Wallimann, Isidor. *Estrangement: Marx's Conception of Human Nature and the Division of Labor*. Westport, Conn.: Greenwood Press, 1981.

Wells, H. G. *The Island of Dr. Moreau* (1896). Rpt., New York: New American Library, 1988 (Signet paperback).

Wesling, Donald. "Writing as Power in the Slave Narrative of the Early Republic." *Michigan Quarterly Review* 26 (1987): 459–72.

White, Deborah Gray. *Ar'n't I a Woman? Female Slaves in the Plantation South*. New York: Norton, 1985.

——."Female Slaves in the Plantation South." In Edward D. C. Campbell, Jr., and Kym S. Rice, eds., *Before Freedom Came*. Richmond: Museum of the Confederacy and the University Press of Virginia, 1991.

Wilson, Harriet. *Our Nig; Or, Sketches from the Life of a Free Black* (1859). Rpt., New York: Vintage, 1983.

Winship, Michael. "Prodigies, Puritanism, and the Perils of Natural Philosophy: The Example of Cotton Mather." *William and Mary Quarterly*, 3d ser., 61 (January 1994): 92–105.

——. *Seers of God: Puritan Providentialism in the Restoration and Early Enlightenment*. Baltimore: Johns Hopkins University Press, 1995.

Winthrop, John. *The John Winthrop Papers*. Vol. 2. New York: Russell and Russell, 1931.

——. *Winthrop's Journal: History of New England, 1630–1649*. Edited by James Kendall Hosmer. New York: Scribner's, 1908; rpt., New York: Barnes and Noble, 1966.

Wood, William. *New England's Prospect* (1634). Edited by Alden T. Vaughan. Amherst: University of Massachusetts Press, 1977.

Woodcock, George. "Introduction." In Herman Melville, *Typee*, 7–27. New York: Penguin, 1972.

Wright, Richard. *Native Son*. New York: Harper and Row, 1940.

Yellin, Jean Fagan. *The Intricate Knot: Black Figures in American Literature, 1776–1863*. New York: New York University Press, 1972.

Zagarell, Sandra. "Reenvisioning America: Melville's 'Benito Cereno.'" *ESQ* 30 (1984): 245–59.

Ziff, Larzer. *Puritanism in America*. New York: Viking, 1973.

Zuckerman, Michael. "Identity in British America: Unease in Eden." In Nicholas Canny and Anthony Pagden, eds., *Colonial Identity in the Atlantic World, 1500–1800*, 115–57. Princeton: Princeton University Press, 1987.

INDEX

Critical Praise for

Dr. Mercola's Total Health Program

"Dr. Joseph Mercola is widely considered to be the world's top natural health physician practicing today, and his dietary program—presented in its entirety in *Dr. Mercola's Total Health Cookbook & Program*—has deservedly become the leading plan among those truly committed to losing weight permanently, preventing disease, looking and feel younger, and living longer. If you seek another fad diet, look elsewhere. If you seek a proven and permanent solution, do yourself a big favor and read Dr. Mercola's Total Health book as soon as possible."

—John Gray, Ph.D., author of the blockbuster bestselling *Men Are From Mars, Women are From Venus* series of books

"Dr. Joseph Mercola is at the forefront of a health revolution that will change the face of our nation . . . This book, his most important written work yet, uses the wisdom gleaned from thousands of studies; more importantly, however, is that his program has actually succeeded in helping thousands of patients overcome seemingly "incurable" ailments . . . *Dr. Mercola's Total Health Cookbook & Program* is not a book to read once and put on your shelf to collect dust; instead, certainly for the recipes but also for the health and dietary insight in Part One and throughout, you'll find yourself referring back to it often as your trusted guide on the road to optimal health."

—Jordan S. Rubin, N.M.D., Ph.D., Founder & Chairman of Garden of Life, author of the mega-bestseller, *The Maker's Diet*